THE COUNTRY READER

D1417443

THE COUNTRY READER

Twenty-five Years of the *Journal of Country Music*

Edited by Paul Kingsbury

Foreword by Chet Flippo

THE COUNTRY MUSIC FOUNDATION PRESS
& VANDERBILT UNIVERSITY PRESS
NASHVILLE & LONDON

Copyright © 1996 by Country Music Foundation Press

All Rights Reserved under International and Pan-American Copyright Conventions

Published in cooperation with Vanderbilt University Press

First edition 1996

96 97 98 99 00   5 4 3 2 1

This publication is made from recycled paper and meets the minimum requirements of American National Standard for Information Sciences—Permanence of Paper for Printed Library Materials ∞

Frontis: Hank Williams, Minnie Pearl, Big Bill Lister, and Hank's Drifting Cowboys band, ca. 1951

LIBRARY OF CONGRESS CATALOGING-IN-PUBLICATION DATA

The country reader : twenty-five years of the Journal of country music
/ edited by Paul Kingsbury.

   p.   cm.

  Includes bibliographical references and index.

  ISBN 0-8265-1278-X

  1. Country music--History and criticism.   I. Kingsbury, Paul.

II. Journal of country music.

ML3524.C78   1996

781.642'09—dc20   96-13998

                                           CIP

                                         MN

Manufactured in the United States of America

CONTENTS

FOREWORD
CHET FLIPPO

▌ As country music enters its seventh decade of commercial existence, its performers and their comings and goings and successes and failures are daily chronicled in newspapers, on radio, on network and local and cable TV, on computer networks and the WorldWideWeb, in slick magazines and crude supermarket tabloids—and even in scholarly publications.

It wasn't always thus. Not so long ago, country music was considered beneath official notice. Rather than the legitimate folk art that it is, country was regarded as a loud and uncouth noise—rather like aural graffiti. Such snobbery especially prevailed in the conventional media. Until recently, it seemed like the only time a country artist's name appeared in a daily newspaper, for example, was in an obituary or an arrest report. A pivotal event in Hank Williams's career was a concert review that ran in the Richmond, Virginia *Times-Dispatch*. Williams was so outraged by the truthful account of his drunken performance that he sobered up long enough to berate the reviewer from the stage the next night.

Not to put too fine a point on it, country artists have always paid close attention to whatever media attention they received. As another example from more than twenty years ago, Waylon Jennings once summoned me to a meeting with him after I had run a very critical review of his *Ladies Love Outlaws* album in *Rolling Stone*. At the time, country music coverage in the popular press mostly consisted of boosterism and puffery in Southern dailies. The notion of actual critiques of the music was completely alien, and my articles on country music in the "hippie" journal *Rolling Stone* earned me a lengthy attack in the *Nashville Banner*. (Carpet-bagger coming down here and telling us how to do our music and all that.)

Knowing Jennings's reputation as a no-nonsense, straight-ahead man, I was a tad apprehensive about our conference. But he put me at ease, shook my hand, got me a beer, and said, "Hoss, you were right about that album. The things you said were right on target and I appreciate that. We need that."

We need that. I would later hear that same message, if phrased differently, from Willie Nelson and Dolly Parton and Kris Kristofferson, and from any number of country artists who cared deeply about the music and were becoming concerned about the chronicling of their music and their culture.

And that leads me to explain why I love the *Journal of Country Music* and its role in the world scheme. It's not just about history and not just about music. It's about chronicling and interpreting a unique folk art and the culture it represents and embodies. It's as much a social and cultural history as a musical one, and for that the *JCM* fulfills a mission unlike any other publication in the world.

When I got out of the Navy in 1969, I was already caught up in rock & roll's counterculture. I started writing for *Rolling Stone*, and I thought I knew it all. Then, on a visit home to Fort Worth, I ran across Bill Malone's epochal book *Country Music U.S.A.* in the downtown public library. It took my breath away. All of a sudden, I *understood* the birthright of Texas music that I had spurned as a child and teenager. The opportunity to see Bob Wills & the Texas Playboys hadn't registered to a rebellious child. Now it all fit into place and I couldn't wait to go buy every George and Tammy and Willie and Webb album in sight. I suddenly realized what it all meant.

Malone himself had overcome some obstacles. His book began as a doctoral dissertation at the University of Texas at Austin when country music was not in academic fashion. Fortunately, Dr. Joe B. Frantz at UT championed Malone's project. UT did have a tradition of folklore research, with such folklorists as J. Frank Dobie, whose studies of the West and its cowboys prefigure some of the *JCM*'s chronicles of country music and its attendant culture. Malone had much in common with Dobie and such precursor chroniclers of the West as the cowboy/writer Charlie Siringo, who referred to his own early coverage of the West as entering "an untrodden field."

Fortunately for me, the University of Texas remained receptive to graduate studies in music culture, and I was able to complete a master's thesis there on the magazine *Rolling Stone* and the culture that surrounds the music it covers. This again is what the *JCM* has succeeded so well in doing for country music.

You want a country record review, you want celebrity gossip, go somewhere else. You want to know what's happening within the culture and why, read the *JCM*. It's a forum unlike any other in this world, the only place where a Nick Tosches will intersect with a Roy Blount Jr.

This collection, *The Country Reader*, offers a great opportunity for those who have never encountered the *JCM* to get a taste of what they've been missing in country music coverage. As for those of us who already know and love the magazine, we now have a chance to reacquaint ourselves with this choice selection of the many groundbreaking articles, outstanding writers, and priceless photos that have appeared in the *JCM* over the years. Those words and pictures have captured and illuminated matters of fundamental and lasting importance. So read on, reflect, and listen. This is your country. Love it.

PREFACE
PAUL KINGSBURY
Editor, Journal of Country Music

▌ As Chet Flippo reminds us in his foreword to this book, not so many years ago a serious magazine about country music would have been unthinkable. As recently as 1960, there was virtually no serious writing about country music available anywhere: no books on the subject, no articles in academic journals, nothing. On those rare occasions when a general interest magazine deigned to report on country, the coverage often received a condescending slant. Typical was a 1952 *Newsweek* cover photo of Roy Acuff bearing the headline "The Corn Is Golden in Tennessee," suggesting that no matter how popular country music might be, it was still just so much corny, low-brow silliness. That was how the cognoscenti chose to define this truly native American music. They saw country music as the expression of poor, rural, working-class white people and pronounced it not worth taking seriously.

Imagine the hosannas among country fans when, on rare occasions, someone managed to publish an article that spoke admiringly of country musicians—as folklorist Alan Lomax did in 1959 with his justly famous *Esquire* profile on the "folk music with overdrive" of Flatt & Scruggs. That was the exception. As a rule, those who cared about country music could read about it only in fan magazines (such as *Country Song Roundup*), entertainment trade magazines (*Billboard*), or privately printed newsletters shared among small cadres of record collectors (*Disc Collector* and *Country Directory*). Even in these publications, discussions of artists and their work tended to be limited to mere description, with little analysis.

The long awaited watershed came in the late 1960s, more than forty years after the first commercial country music recordings of the 1920s. Within the space of a few years there came a flurry of groundbreaking publications. In the summer of 1965, the venerable *Journal of American Folklore* (founded 1888) published its "Hillbilly Issue," devoting an entire issue of a learned journal to the subject of country music for the first time. Almost concurrently (October 1965), UCLA's John Edwards Memorial Foundation, a country music archive founded on the bequest of an Australian record collector, issued the first *John Edwards Memorial Foundation Quarterly*, a journal devoted solely to the study of folk and country music. Shortly thereafter came the first two books to survey the entire landscape of commercial country music and define its boundaries: Robert Shelton and Burt Goldblatt's *Country Music Story* (1966) and Bill C. Malone's *Country Music U.S.A.* (1968).

Initially, the study of country music had been widely viewed as worthwhile only when it proceeded from the folklorist's need to find the traditional roots underpinning this music. But by the early 1970s, the study of commercial country music was finally being perceived as worthwhile in and of itself. Country, it appeared, was finally worth reading about. Such was the state of affairs when, in December of 1971, the Country Music Foundation, the largest archive and research center in the world devoted to a single form of popular music, published the first issue of the *Journal of Country Music* (numbered as Volume II, Number 4 because it was an outgrowth of a two-year-old *Country Music Foundation Newsletter*). According to an introductory note in that premier issue, the revamped publication would focus "on interpretive articles treating Country Music subjects. The *Journal of Country Music* will consider articles of any reasonable length on the following topics: Country Music, Old Timey Music, Bluegrass, Western Swing, Gospel Music, Anglo-American Folksong, Recording Studio Operation, The Business of Music."

During its first six years of publication, under editors Bill Ivey (now Director of the Country Music Foundation) and Doug Green (now better known as Ranger Doug of the singing group Riders in the Sky), *JCM* maintained that fairly strict academic focus and broke new ground in country music scholarship. Among the seminal articles published in those years were important analyses of the bluegrass community by John Rumble and of the Grand Ole Opry's beginnings by Professors Richard Peterson and Charles Wolfe, as well as detailed session discographies of the Delmore Brothers and Waylon Jennings.

In 1978, when Kyle Young (now Deputy Director of CMF) became editor, the *Journal of Country Music* underwent sweeping changes in appearance and editorial focus. New departments for book reviews, letters, and photo essays (the *JCM* Gallery) widened the audience for the magazine and broadened its editorial palette. Although academic articles would still be a regular feature of the *Journal*'s contents, journalists and other popular writers like Bob Allen, Roy Blount Jr., Wayne Daniel, Peter Guralnick, Bill C. Malone, Greil Marcus, Robert K. Oermann and Mary

A. Bufwack, Nolan Porterfield, Ronnie Pugh, and Nick Tosches increasingly appeared as regular contributors.

When I became editor of *JCM* in 1985, we began to feature occasional "Special Reports" on key issues like the contributions of African-Americans and the predicament of women artists in country music and to serialize articles too long to include in a single issue, such as the previously unpublished memoirs of country comedians Homer & Jethro. During the past decade, we have continued to add outstanding writers to our list of contributors, among them Rob Bowman, Bob Bradley, Barbara Ching, Kevin Coffey, Al Cunniff, Eddie Dean, Chris Dickinson, Colin Escott, Thomas Goldsmith, Jimmy Guterman, Mark Humphrey, James Hunter, Ross Johnson, Otto Kitsinger, Pete Loesch, Guy Logsdon, Michael McCall, Edward Morris, John Morthland, Jay Orr, Mark Schone, Chris Skinker, Lee Smith, Ken Tucker, David Whisnant, Jonny Whiteside, and Joe Wilson. Last but surely not least on this list is Daniel Cooper, writer of some of the most freshly thought articles to have appeared in the magazine over the past five years, who joined the *JCM* staff as associate editor in the summer of 1994.

This brings us up to the present and the book at hand. Twenty-five years seems a good time to stop and take stock of where we have been. A look back over the past two and a half decades in country music serves to remind us how unpredictable and dizzying the course of popular culture has become—and perhaps always was.

No form of popular music remains more conscious of its roots than country music. Indeed, without its ties to tradition, country music would quickly lose its identity. Back in 1971, country music was a generation closer to the rural soil from which it sprang. Hank Williams had been dead less than twenty years. Rock & roll, too, if we date it back to Elvis Presley's first recordings, was less than twenty years old. Pioneers like Maybelle Carter, Bob Wills, and record producer Art Satherley were still very much with us. Likewise, Johnny Cash, Dolly Parton, Charley Pride, and Merle Haggard were not only still on the record charts, they were topping those charts with #1 hits.

Who could have predicted the changes that would be rung since then? A country music singer has become the best-selling recording artist (bar none) over the past five years. Country line-dancing is now a national phenomenon. A bluegrass singer (a woman yet) has sold more than a million records and has won four CMA Awards. Merle Haggard *and* the Eagles are lauded with tribute albums from young country stars. The triumphant return of cowboy hats, fiddles, and honky-tonk country; the increasing presence of distorted guitars and thunderous drums in country; the creation of a national cable television channel owned by the company that runs the Grand Ole Opry; the increasing importance of music videos in marketing country artists, placing a profound emphasis on a singer's physical appearance (sometimes over singing ability)—the list could go on and on.

Not surprisingly, given what has come to pass and what the *JCM* has covered in the past twenty-five years, this anthology functions as a kind of country primer. Though every article in *The Country Reader* was chosen discretely and on its own merits, taken together they offer a rough outline of country music history, stretching from its earliest manifestations on up to the recent careers of Garth Brooks and Alan Jackson. The opening essay section mostly offers career retrospectives and profiles of monumental figures (like Bill Monroe and Elvis Presley) and important subgenres within country music (such as western swing and bluegrass), organized in roughly chronological order by subject. But this section begins with two broad and groundbreaking research articles: Charles Wolfe's in-depth examination of the Bristol Sessions of 1927 and Douglas B. Green's comprehensive overview of Hollywood's singing cowboy phenomenon.

The photographs in *The Country Reader*, culled from the *JCM* Gallery department, tell their own stories. In this section, selections from ten photographic collections appear, organized chronologically by date of publication in *JCM* and grouped by photographer to maximize their distinctive points of view.

The review section that follows offers additional background and context, focusing on major works and concepts in the literature of country music. For example, reviews of Bill C. Malone's revised version of *Country Music U.S.A.* (reviewed by Bill Ivey) and a trio of recent star autobiographies (reviewed by Bob Allen) help provide an overarching framework for the various figures discussed herein. All of the essays and reviews appear here in their originally published, unabridged form; we have only corrected errors where necessary.

Finally, we append two comprehensive indexes, arranged by title and by author, that we believe will be useful to all JCM subscribers, new and old, as well as to libraries, scholars, and readers wishing to find particular articles appearing in the first twenty-five years of this journal.

Although it remains tethered to tradition, country music continues to evolve and reinvent itself in ever-surprising ways. If country music has mirrored America's frustrations, fears, hopes, and dreams for itself over the past seventy-odd years—and I believe it has—then the *Journal of Country Music* helps us make sense of what we have seen. And along the way it has told some terrific stories. Some of the best are here in *The Country Reader*, and they are worth savoring.

❚ Many people and organizations, representing an enormous variety of skills, talents, and treasures, have made this book possible. Thanks go especially to the writers and photographers who have graciously allowed us to reprint their work here; to the University of Louisville's Photographic Archives for making their Caufield & Shook fiddle contest photographs available for reprint; to Chet Flippo for contributing a heartfelt foreword; to the director and staff of Vanderbilt University Press for their considerable editorial and other contributions to this volume; to Joyce Kachergis, who designed the book's interior, and to Jim Sherraden, who manages Hatch Show Print for the Country Music Foundation and who designed the cover; to the Board of Trustees and the hard-working staff of the Country Music Foundation, not only for aiding the production of this volume in innumerable ways but also for making the ongoing publication of the *Journal of Country Music* possible; to the CMF's Daniel Cooper, Ashley E. LaRoche, and Kelley Sallee Snead for advice and assistance in producing this collection; to CMF director Bill Ivey and deputy director for program development Kyle Young for far-sighted guidance and invaluable input in the *Journal of Country Music* and this book; and finally to the vast network of country music fans and musicians to whom all this work ultimately is dedicated.

PART ONE
ESSAYS

THE CARTER FAMILY

THE LEGEND THAT PEER BUILT
Reappraising the Bristol Sessions

CHARLES WOLFE

▮ Author Nolan Porterfield has called the Bristol Sessions the "Big Bang" of country music for good reason. Two of the most influential acts in the music's history, the Carter Family and Jimmie Rodgers, made their first recordings during those sessions. Though commercial country music did not begin with the field recording sessions that Ralph Peer supervised for the Victor label in the Appalachian town of Bristol in 1927, everything important in country music seems to have proceeded from that point. No one has added more to our knowledge of these seminal recording sessions than Charles Wolfe. A contributor to the *Journal of Country Music* from its earliest days, Wolfe has continued to supply the *JCM* with groundbreaking historical articles on a wide range of subjects. In the following essay, published in 1989, Wolfe looks at the Bristol Sessions from Peer's perspective and shows us that even though Peer may have been a little lucky in discovering both the Carter Family and Jimmie Rodgers in Bristol, his good fortune came in large part because of careful planning and a sure sense of what he was looking for.—Ed.

▮ In the late summer of 1927 RCA Victor Records—then known as the Victor Talking Machine Company—set up a temporary recording studio in Bristol, Tennessee. In the space of two weeks, they recorded seventy-six performances by nineteen different groups, including country music pioneers like Ernest "Pop" Stoneman and his family, guitarist-singer-harmonica player Henry Whitter, and topical-protest singer Blind Alfred Reed. The most dramatic of the recordings, however, were those made by two heretofore unknown acts: a singer then living in Asheville, North Carolina, named Jimmie Rodgers, and a family trio from nearby Maces Springs that called themselves "the Carter Family." All this has imbued the Bristol sessions with a legendary quality and has won for them mention in virtually every history, pop and serious, about country music. Bill Malone, in his definitive *Country Music USA*, has referred to the session as "one of country music's most seminal events"; Johnny Cash, whose wife's mother was one of the original Carter Family members, has said, "These recordings in Bristol in 1927 are the single most important event in the history of country music." Sixteen years ago, I published the first attempt to document the entire session (in the pages of *Old Time Music* magazine), and since then numerous other scholars and collectors have gathered still more pieces of the puzzle. With fresh research generated by the recent CMF Records reissue album *The Bristol Sessions*, by newly discovered discographical data, and by previously unavailable interviews, it seems an appropriate time to take a fresh look at the event, and to try once again to understand just what went on during that hot, distant summer that was to have such an impact on country music.

Almost from the start, the Bristol sessions have been surrounded by stereotype and romanticism. Some of this came from Victor itself, or from its session supervisor, Ralph S. Peer. In 1928, barely a year after the session, Peer gave an interview in which he recalled that Jimmie Rodgers had been "running around in the mountains" before the session, and that when he tried out "he was laughed at." In the 1930 Victor Records catalogue, the biographical sketch of Rodgers describes the session as "a Victor recording expedition into the mountains of Tennessee." Peer later recalled that when the Carter Family first appeared at his studio, they looked like they'd "come through a lot of mud" either by "horse and buggy or an old car. . . . He [A.P.] was dressed in overalls and the women are country women from way back there—calico clothes on. . . . They looked like hillbillies." Local tales in Bristol would even have the Carters never wearing shoes, never having been in town before, and even climbing in the studio via the fire escape because they were so embarrassed to be seen.

None of these images is accurate, and many of them are simply wrong. Jimmie Rodgers had been working on the radio in the city of Asheville before the session, and no one laughed at him when he tried out; indeed, Peer spent more time than usual with him. The Victor recording expedition (with the connotations of a jungle safari) was a fairly routine thing by 1927, and Bristol, a good-sized city, was hardly a mountain camp. The Carters routinely came into Bristol, and while they were simply dressed, none of them remembered recording barefoot, and in fact stayed with a cousin in town after they arrived. Why did Peer (and Victor) distort the picture so much? One possible reason was that they perceived that the commercial appeal of this newly-discovered "old time" music lay in its rustic, mountain quality. It was Peer, after all, who had first recorded Fiddlin' John Carson in 1923, thus setting off the boom for such music, and it was Peer who coined the name "Hill Billies" to describe a popular Virginia string band that became the first great string band in country music in 1925. Record jackets and catalogues featured rural or mountain scenes: fiddlers at old time dances, mules coming down mountain trails, singers sitting on cabin porches amidst Blue Ridge pines. Just as radio program directors like George D. Hay and John Lair would later create a hayseed image for their artists and music, Peer and other early record company publicists in the 1920s sought to authenticate their product by emphasizing its rural origins.

Another reason for a distorted image of the Bristol sessions has to do with our modern age's naiveté about the early recording industry, especially as it applied to country music. Doubtless the recording industry as represented in Bristol that summer was a lot simpler than the industry of today; still, it was by no means a case of Peer coming into town, making some primitive wax masters, paying everyone a flat rate, and going back to New York. As we will see, the trip was rather carefully planned—Victor had in fact appropriated some $60,000 for Peer's trip to Bristol, Charlotte, and Savannah. Peer knew pretty much what he wanted; Victor, though the world's largest record company, was lagging far behind its arch-rivals Okeh and Columbia in capitalizing on the country music boom, and had, in fact, hired Peer to build up its catalogue. "I had what they wanted," Peer later recalled. "They couldn't get into the hillbilly business and I knew how to do it." Peer actively sought "cover" versions of songs that were hits on other labels, and signed most of his artists to three separate contracts: a recording contract with Victor that generally paid them $50.00 a side up front, as well as a modest royalty on each record sold; a song publishing contract with Peer's newly formed Southern Music publishing company; and a personal management contract with Peer himself. The recordings themselves were not all that primitive, either; the old Victor session sheets show that Peer and his two engineers, Eckhart and Lynch, would often spend hours on a recording, doing three or even four takes, trying to get the best possible balance with their new Western Electric microphones. Recalling the equipment used in the Bristol session in a 1958 interview, Peer said that it "was very much like that used today." Though the studio was makeshift, the equipment was state of the art, and the commercial recording industry in general was already sophisticated, complex, and responsive to its market.

This, in part, was one of the reasons Bristol was selected for this field trip. Years later, when pressed on this question, Peer would admit: "I can't tell you why I picked Bristol, Tennessee—it just seemed to be a likely spot." In fact, there were good reasons for choosing Bristol. Flanked on the south by Johnson City, and on the west by the new "planned" city of Kingsport, Bristol was part of an early urban area called Tri-Cities, which in the 1920s boasted a collective population of over 32,000. This made it the largest urban area in Appalachia, bigger even than Asheville. It was on the Tennessee-Virginia border and within easy driving distance from three other states: Kentucky, North Carolina, and West Virginia. Peer told the Bristol newspapers, on his arrival there for the session: "In no section of the South have the pre-war melodies and old mountaineer songs been better preserved than in the mountains of east Tennessee and Southwest Virginia, experts declare, and it was primarily for this reason that the Victor Company chose Bristol as its operating base." It would be tempting to conclude that Peer's "experts" were in fact the pioneer folksong collectors like Cecil Sharp and John Harrington Cox, whose published collections of mountain songs had appeared in 1917 and 1925, respectively. There is only slim evidence that he knew of them, however. One of his singers, Ernest Stoneman, knew of and learned songs from Cox's *Folk Songs of the South*, and during one of Cecil Sharp's visits to America, the Victor company had engaged him to supervise a well-publicized series of recordings of English country dances which were, as the Victor catalogue put it, "gathered from the peasantry through years of search by Mr. Sharp himself." This was well before Peer's coming to Victor, but it is possible that someone in the Victor front office maintained contact with Sharp's work.

Peer's experts were probably the talent scouts from the other commercial record companies, men who had been going into the field since 1924 to collect these old songs on fragile wax masters. No one had actually gone into the Appalachians before, however, except for Peer himself: he had supervised a field session for Okeh in Asheville, North Carolina, in the summer of 1925. He also knew, in the small but hotly competitive world of early country records, that the area around Bristol was becoming known in the record trade as a hotbed for such music. By the middle of 1927, at least eleven acts from the area had already recorded: Fiddlin' Cowan Powers and Family (Victor, Edison), Henry Whitter (Okeh), Ernest Stoneman (Okeh, Victor), Dedrick Harris (Broadway), the Roe Brothers (Columbia), Charlie Bowman with the Hill Billies (Okeh, Vocalion), the Avocoa Quartet (Okeh), George Reneau (Vocalion), the Johnson Brothers (Victor), Am Stuart (Vocalion), and John Dykes (Brunswick).

The Bristol newspapers, far from being embarrassed over the hillbilly image their town was acquiring, saw the recording activity in the spirit of boosterism and covered events fully and sympathetically. Two months after Peer's sessions, for instance, an article summing up the year's record-making appeared in the Bristol *Herald-Courier* (September 25, 1927):

MANY PHONOGRAPH RECORDS MADE OF LOCAL TALENT DURING PAST SUMMER

Musical talent from this section is rapidly winning favor with the leading phonograph record producing companies. Three times since the first of January companies who are recognized as leaders in the recording field have utilized talent from this section in the production of their records. The latest company to secure the services of talent from this section is the Okay [*sic*] Record Company of New York City, recognized along with Columbia and Victor as the biggest record producer in the world.

Tobe S. McNeil, local dealer for the Okay company, induced F. B. Brockman . . . to come here early in August to hear local talent in a tryout arranged at the McNeil Furniture Company. Approximately 30 persons tried out before Mr. Brockman and after hearing them he finally selected the male quartet of Avoca Tennessee Methodist Church. Composed of O. M. Hunt, K. T. Hunt, W. R. Stidman, and W. H. Bowers, the quartet went to Asheville, North Carolina on September 12 and made six records for world distribution and probably 100,000 of them will be made.

Columbia was first to utilize local talent, H. W. Dolton coming here early in the year to hear talent recommended by Miss Margaret Owen, in charge of the Music Dept. at Boggs-Rice Company. Among those heard were Fred and Henry Roe, with Lewis Morrell. Dutton sent this trio to Atlanta in April, where they made three records, with Morrell doing the vocals.

Following this, Peer, Eckhart, and Lynch of Victor came here in July and set up a regular recording station on State Street in the building at one time occupied by the Buchanan Furniture Company. The record station was kept open for approximately two weeks, during which time talent from all parts of these sections had try-outs.

Among the talent was: The Tennessee Mountaineers, Tenneva Ramblers, West Virginia Coon Hunters, Blue Ridge Corn Shuckers, Ernest Phipps, Ernest Stoneman, B. F. Shelton, Mr. and Mrs. Baker, and Mr. and Mrs. Carter of Gate City, Virginia.

All three companies are planning tryouts in the near future, and Brunswick plans one as well.

The article was prophetic: Peer would return to Bristol to record again in the summer of 1928, while rival Columbia Records would set up shop in nearby Johnson City in 1928 and 1929. Brunswick, a latecomer, had to settle for field sessions in Knoxville in 1929 and 1930.

Just as Peer had good reasons for choosing Bristol, so did he lay his plans carefully. Part of the Bristol legend implies that Peer just wandered into town, improvising and relying on serendipity for his discoveries. Yet even this early, Peer was in the habit of making a preliminary trip to scout for talent. "I made two trips," he said in discussing his field techniques in general. "I had learned all of this at Okeh. The preliminary trip is to stir up local interest and find out if there actually is anything." His planning trip to Bristol took place in late June, though Cecil McLister, his local Victor dealer and contact, recalled that he had been there "two or three times before he made any recordings." McLister put him in touch with a local group who had recently auditioned for Brunswick, the Carter Family, and Peer corresponded with A. P., setting up a date. Another recommendation was Blind Alfred Reed, from Princeton, West Virginia, who had recently written a popular topical ballad called "The Wreck of the Virginian," about a train wreck. Locally, Peer contacted Charles and Paul Johnson, duet singers who worked with a Hawaiian guitar, and who had already recorded for him in New York. He also contacted Ernest Stoneman, over the mountains in Galax, and asked his help in setting up the session. Stoneman recalled:

I remember when Mr. Peer wrote me a letter, and wanted me to find a place in town, in Galax, rent an empty room, so he could hold auditions. And he asked me to go around over the country and find some string bands and singers that could come for an audition, and he could find which ones he wanted to record for Victor. I rented some rooms and went upon the mountain to the Lowes and Hankses, and I don't know how many places I did go, and I'd listen at them, and let them rehearse, so I could kind of tell whether he'd want to hear them or not. I took ever so many of them down there, but he didn't care about any except old Uncle Eck Dunford and Iver Edwards, a young boy from Ward's Mill who played harmonica and ukelele.

Through such efforts, Peer probably had over 60 percent of his time already blocked out when he arrived in Bristol. He knew in many cases who he was going to record, and in a few instances *what* he was going to record. In other cases, he knew of bands but not individual numbers. For instance, a Victor dealer named Walter Howlette in Hillsville, Virginia, auditioned groups much like Stoneman did. He found for Peer the Shelor Family–Dad Blackard band, as well as the band led by J.P. Nestor.

All of which creates a problem when we consider the next element of the Bristol legend: Peer's efforts to publicize his work so as to attract new talent. From diverse sources, it now seems apparent that only nine of the nineteen groups recorded had not really planned to record to start with, and of these, only Jimmie Rodgers, the Tenneva Ramblers (Rodgers's former band), gospel singer Alfred Karnes, and banjoist B. F. Shelton were to have any significant success. Yet Peer did work hard to spread the word about the sessions. For years, scholars looked in vain for the "newspaper advertisement" Sara Carter thought she remembered seeing, but the only advertisement that really appeared was a small box in a routine Victrola ad for Clark-Jones-Sheeler Company, the local dealer. It ran in the Bristol *Herald Courier* on Sunday, July 24, the day before the sessions began, and stated:

The Victor Co. will have a recording machine in Bristol for 10 days beginning Monday to record records—Inquire at our store.

This is hardly an invitation to make records and become a recording star; it seems designed to appeal to the curiosity of Victrola customers, or perhaps even to solicit custom recordings by parents who wanted to preserve their baby's talk.

The newspaper piece that attracted so much attention was not a paid ad, but a cleverly planted story which appeared on Wednesday, the third day of the sessions. Peer recalled years later in a *Billboard* article:

In Bristol, the problem [of finding talent and repertoire] was not easy because of the relatively small population in that area. The local broadcasting stations, music stores, record dealers, etc., helped me as much as possible, but few candidates appeared.

I then appealed to the editor of a local paper, explaining to him the great advantages to the community of my enterprise. He thought that I had a good idea and ran a half a column on his front page.

Peer's memory serves him wrong in one respect: the Bristol radio station, WOPI, did not go on the air until 1929. But his account of the newspaper story is indeed accurate. It described in detail the recording of "Skip to Ma Lou," with Eck Dunford and the Stoneman band, that took place that morning. The ringer, though, was the last paragraph:

The quartette costs the Victor company close to $200 per day—Stoneman receiving $100, and each of his assistants $25. Stoneman is regarded as one of the finest banjoists in the country, his numbers selling rapidly. He is a carpenter and song leader at Galax. He received from the company $3,600 last year as his share of the proceeds on his records.

The mention of this much money to be made from records had a more powerful effect on the poverty-stricken Appalachian community than any advertisement. In Peer's own words, "the story worked like dynamite and the very next day I was deluged with long-distance telephone calls from the surrounding mountain region. Groups of singers who had not visited Bristol during their entire lifetime arrived by bus, horse and buggy, trains or on foot." Peer wrote these words in 1953, long after he was being hailed as the discoverer of modern country music (i.e., the Carters and Jimmie Rodgers), and he understandably might have dramatized events. Nevertheless, there were a few acts who were almost certainly drawn in by this news story: the Bull Mountain Moonshiners, led by fiddler Charles McReynolds, from Coeburn, Virginia; the Alcoa Quartet, a gospel group from a town near Knoxville; Mr. and Mrs. J. W. Baker, cousins of the Carters, from a hamlet called Falls Branch near Bristol; the West Virginia Coon Hunters, a string band from up at Bluefield, West Virginia; and the Tenneva Ramblers, from Bristol. And, to be sure, the story did draw in Jimmie Rodgers, the session's dominant star. We cannot be sure how many singers and bands Peer auditioned and turned down, but he was apparently so busy during the second week that he had to resort to scheduling night sessions. In sum, though, Peer's "advertising" seems not to have played as great a role in the session as has been generally thought.

This fact, in turn, is related to yet another aspect of the Bristol legend: the extent to which it reflected traditional mountain music. One barometer of this is the extent to which the musicians saw themselves as professional—either on the vaudeville circuit, the theatrical venue, or through regular performances at dances, clubs, resorts, circuses, and the like. While we do not have detailed biographical information on all of the acts, we know that at least some of the artists considered themselves professional entertainers: Jimmie Rodgers, the Grant Brothers' band called the Tenneva Ramblers, Ernest Stoneman, Henry Whitter, the Johnson Brothers (who had perhaps the strongest vaudeville repertoire), and Red Snodgrass, a jazz band leader who worked at a Bristol hotel. Another group of the artists would have to be classified as gospel performers: Alfred Karnes, Blind Alfred Reed, the Alcoa Quartet, the Tennessee Mountaineers, Ernest Phipps and his Holiness Quartet, and the Dixie Mountaineers (a Stoneman group). All in all, thirty-one songs out of the seventy-six were gospel songs—about 40 percent, testifying to Ralph Peer's interest in gospel music, and confidence that it formed a significant part of the repertoire of old-time music as he saw it. About thirty-five of the songs were traditional by most folkloric definitions, even those done by professionals like Ernest Stoneman and the Tenneva Ramblers. These included some first or influential recordings of songs that would become traditional favorites: Eck Dunford's "Skip to Ma Lou," the first Southern recording of this song known to every school child; B. F. Shelton's haunting "Pretty Polly," the famed murder ballad, issued on a rare 12-inch format which gave the song over four minutes of playing time; Henry Whitter's harmonica showcase, "Henry Whitter's Fox Chase," which remained in the Victor catalogue until World War II; Mr. and Mrs. Baker's driving rendition of "The Newmarket Wreck," a train wreck ballad that influenced a generation of folksingers; the Tenneva Ramblers' "The Longest Train I Ever Saw," the most popular early recorded version of the song that would later be known as "In the Pines"; J. P. Nestor's "Train on the Island," with Norman Edmunds's rich fiddling, which found new favor during the folk revival of the 1960s and even generated a band by the same name; and the Carters' "Bury Me Under the Weeping Willow" and "The Storms Are on the Ocean," both to become country and bluegrass standards with roots deep in tradition.

Peer did not just take whatever his performers had worked up for him; he left no doubt that he was after a specific type of music. His famous comment about Jimmie Rodgers—"we ran into a snag almost immediately because, in order to earn a living in Asheville, he was singing mostly songs originated by the New York publishers"—testifies to his interest in old songs, both because his market demanded it, and because he wanted them for his publishing company. By the same token, he also wanted songs—vocal performances—as opposed to instrumentals, and wasn't above pushing his artists in this direction. Clarice Shelor, who recorded with the group known as the Shelor Family or Dad Blackard's Moonshiners, recalled the process her band went through:

They had Pa name over some old pieces and they'd say, "We got that, we've got that, we've got that," and Pa said, "Well I'm about named out." And he knew a lot of old pieces. But he finally mentioned some pieces they didn't have. They had all the tunes they already had in a big book. And they had more instrumental than singing records and said that singing helped sell the records. . . . I had to sit down over there and write out the words to that "Big Bend Gal." Lots of times I would sing just a verse here there but I never had tried to sing it all. They wanted it all sung. . . .

Ernest Stoneman told a similar story about Peer's reluctance to record some of the Galax area string bands that he had scouted up for the pre-session audition in Galax.

He turned down some pretty good music. But they didn't seem to be interested—they were bands. The trouble of it is, they couldn't none of them sing, and he [Peer] wanted songs. And Uncle Eck Dunford had a whole bunch of old songs, and that's what he was interested in.

Of the seventy-six recordings finally made, only seven (or about 9 percent) could really be called instrumentals, and four of these were harmonica novelty items. Four other recordings (two by the Shelors and two by J. P. Nestor) were string band sides with only incidental singing—possibly inserted at Peer's insistence.

The fact that veteran and respected mountain musicians like Clarice Shelor and Ernest Stoneman were surprised at the kind of music Peer was wanting casts some doubt on just how accurately he was judging the actual nature of Appalachian music. Fiddlers and string bands were certainly stock components of mountain music in the 1920s, and in fact had been featured on most of the earlier recordings of mountain music by Victor's rivals like Okeh, Columbia, and Vocalion. Yet Peer hesitated about recording them for his new series on Victor, or tried to convert them into singing groups with instrumental accompaniment. One reason was that Peer sensed he was developing a new commercial art form—it would later be called simply country music—and that this art form was to be derived from, though not fully reflective of, traditional mountain music. In spite of all his public relations posturing about "pre-war melodies" and "old mountaineer tunes," he didn't hesitate to tinker with his artists' style and their repertoire. Songs, of course, had more profit potential than instrumental tunes, and if Peer could land these for his new publishing company, they would most likely be recorded by others, and were more likely to be recognized as unique, as opposed to traditional—or what Peer called "legendary" songs. "My policy was always to try to expand each artist by adding accompaniment or adding a vocalist," Peer recalled in 1958. An added incentive to do this was a technological advantage Peer enjoyed over his earlier counterparts: he had the new electrical recording equipment recently designed by Western Electric. "I had all my experience, of course, from handling the Okeh situation," he remembered, "but now I had electronic equipment and two engineers instead of one." In spite of certain limitations with the new microphones—certain vowel sounds for instance, did not "take" through the new mikes—the equipment was far more sensitive than the old acoustic process, and this made possible the kind of balance needed to hear a singer in front of a string band. Songs, in sum, were now easy to record, were more copyrightable, had more profit potential, and had an audience appeal far beyond the confines of the southern Appalachians. The Bristol sessions thus became the first major field recording sessions to really emphasize vocal music—which, in the end, was possibly the most important *first* of all.

Peer's success with his new recording style was not immediate. In spite of popular legends about sudden, spectacular success with the Rodgers and Carter Family records, neither produced instant smashes. Neither had records issued in the first batch of releases from the session; Rodgers's was buried in the middle of the second bunch of releases, ranking number 8 or 9 in the releases, while the Carter Family debut was held up until the third batch, and then only released at the request of Bristol's Victor dealer. The Rodgers coupling ("Sleep, Baby, Sleep" and "The Soldier's Sweetheart") apparently sold adequately, but not so much that Peer scrambled to get Rodgers back into the studio, as he did with the Carter Family. The Rodgers's second series of recordings were, on the contrary, done when Rodgers presented himself at Peer's office in New York, where he had gone at his own expense.

What did Peer think would sell? As early as September 23, barely a month after Peer had returned to New York from the field trip to Bristol, Charlotte, and Savannah, he released the first two records from the Bristol session. Their "electrical" qualities were hailed by the Bristol *Herald Courier* in a story announcing the event:

More than fifty mountain singers and entertainers were brought to Bristol in July and August by the Victor company for the making of phonograph records. The recording was made by the microphone method and was in charge of Ralph S. Peer. Those who heard the actual recording and the new records that are out say that the reproduction is actually better than the original rendition.

The first two records were Victor 20834, two songs by Ernest Phipps's "holy roller" gospel group, and Victor 20835, a skit by Ernest Stoneman's group (The Blue Ridge Corn Shuckers) called "Old Time Corn Shuckin'," parts 1 and 2. The latter Peer probably rushed out because arch-rival Columbia had just struck paydirt a few months earlier with a similar sketch of rural comedy about a Georgia fiddling contest (by the Skillet Lickers). The former simply reflected Peer's confidence in gospel music as a strong seller: of the first six records issued from Bristol, five were gospel records. Advertised as "New Orthophonic Victor Southern Series Records," sixteen of the Bristol records—thirty-two songs—were issued by the end of 1927. Eventually all but seven of the Bristol sides would be issued, and would sell well enough that most of the performers would be asked back into the studios to record again. Indeed, only six of the groups did not return to the studios for later efforts.

In sum, then, what does a sixty-year perspective on the Bristol sessions show us? First, nothing has happened or has been revealed that diminishes the impact and importance of those recordings; if anything, they loom larger in the annals of American cultural history. But several aspects of the "Bristol legend" can be challenged. For one, the sessions were much better planned out ahead of time than previously thought, and the famous "advertising" Peer used was less effective than popular myth would indicate. The event was by no means a passive capturing of pure Appalachian folk music at a remote mountain hamlet full of barefoot hillbillies, but a calculated documentation of an emerging commercial art form in a bustling Southern city. Victor was not blindly thrashing around trying to understand a new music, but was making a sophisticated response to a perceived market demand. Gospel music played a large and significant role in the music of the sessions, and while many of the performers were bona fide traditional mountain musicians, others were fully experienced professionals from vaudeville or stage traditions. On the other hand, the sessions were among the first to be held in the Southeastern mountains, and the first to really use to advantage the new electric recording technology. They were the first sessions to emphasize vocal music and songs, and the first to generate an in-depth cross-section of Southern music for a major company. They yielded, finally, key debut performances by two of the most influential acts in country music history, as well as initial recordings of numerous individual songs that would become important standards.

All in all, the Bristol sessions formed an almost perfect representation of early country music: fiddle and banjo tunes, old traditional ballads, gospel music, old popular and vaudeville songs, rustic comedy, and instrumental showcases. The performers and their music also had an impact on later, modern country music. Jimmie Rodgers and the Carter Family are two obvious examples, but Ernest Stoneman, one of the greatest of the unsung pioneers, whose family dynasty was to reach down to the present day Nashville music, did some of his best work at the session. The Bull Mountain Moonshiners were led by Charles McReynolds, the grandfather of modern bluegrass greats Jim & Jesse. The Alcoa Quartet later performed on Knoxville radio with a young singer named Roy Acuff. Jack Pierce, of the Tenneva Ramblers, would later form a western swing band, the Oklahoma Cowboys, which would record for Bluebird. Blind Alfred Reed's songs would be popularized in the folk revival of the 1960s by the New Lost City Ramblers, and later be picked up by luminaries like Ry Cooder and Linda Ronstadt. Henry Whitter would a year later team up with famed fiddler and singer G. B. Grayson and become the first to record classics like "Train 45" and "Tom Dooley." Like a rock thrown into a still pool, the Bristol sessions would reverberate far beyond their time: they would send echoes down through the years, touching all kinds of people and their musics, and would emerge finally as the legend they deserve to be. The Bristol Sessions may not have ushered in a new type of music, but they did usher in a new era of music, and a new way of perceiving and merchandising that music.

A NOTE ON SOURCES

▌ My earlier study of the Bristol sessions is "Ralph Peer at Work: the Victor 1927 Bristol Session," in *Old Time Music* No. 5 (Summer 1972), pp. 10–15, supplemented by "The Discovery of Jimmie Rodgers: A Further Note" (which contains the 1928 newspaper interview with Peer) in *Old Time Music* No. 9 (Summer 1973), p. 24. The definitive account of Rodgers's role in the session is in Nolan Porterfield's *Jimmie Rodgers* (Urbana: University of Illinois Press, 1979). Peer's statements are taken from an unpublished interview with Lillian Borgeson, January and May 1958, Hollywood, in the files of the John Edwards Memorial Foundation, and in the author's files; other comments about the session are taken from Peer's article "Discovery of the 1st Hillbilly Great" in *Billboard*, LXV: 20 (May 16, 1953). Material on Cecil Sharp's relation with Victor is drawn from a company supplement, *New Victor Records*, dated November 1915. Material on the Peer-Asheville sessions and early Bristol recording artists taken from the author's files and unpublished research. Comments by Cecil McLister from an unpublished interview in the author's files, done in November 23, 1973, by Elizabeth Justus. Ernest Stoneman quotes are taken from an unpublished interview done May 24, 1962, by Mike Seeger, while material involving the Shelor Family comes from Tom Carter's "The Blackard-Shelor Story" in *Old Time Music* No. 24 (Spring 1977) 4–7 *et al.* I am also indebted to Richard Blaustein, who shared with me his memories of talks he had with Claude Grant; to Ed Kahn, the premier student of the Carter Family; to Bob Pinson, for sharing discographical and copyright research; to Carl Wells, for information about his father's Alcoa Quartet; to Edd Ward and Donald Lee Nelson for their information about Karnes and Phipps; to Ivan Tribe, for his continuing research on Ernest Stoneman; to Mrs. J. B. Hatcher for her help in Bristol; to L. S. Freeze; to Steve Davis; and to Richard Weize.

THE BRISTOL SESSIONS: A CHRONOLOGY

(NOTE: The following is derived from the original Victor sessions sheets, as well as the author's research)

Friday, July 22, 1927

Peer with his two engineers, Eckhart and Lynch, and his wife, arrives in Bristol and starts setting up studio at 408 State Street, 2nd and 3rd floors.

Saturday, July 23

Peer gives interview to reporter from Bristol *Herald-Courier* about purpose of his visit.

Sunday, July 24

Herald-Courier publishes initial story in its morning edition, as well as the small box advertsisement in the local Victrola ad.

Monday, July 25

8:30–10:00
Ernest Stoneman, Kahle Brewer, Ralph Mooney.

Dying Girl's Farewell (2 takes)	Victor 21129
Tell Mother I Will Meet Her (3)	Victor 21129

10:00–11:00
Ernest Stoneman, Irma Frost, Eck Dunford

The Mountaineer's Courtship (2)	Victor 20880

11:00–12:00
Ernest Stoneman, and Irma Frost,

Midnight on the Stormy Deep (3)	Unissued*
(*issued in 1987 on CMF-011)	

1:30–5:00
Stoneman's Dixie Mountaineers

Sweeping through the Gates (3)	Victor 20844

I Know My Name Is There (2)	Victor 21186
Are You Washed in theBlood (3)	Victor 20844
No More Goodbyes (2)	Victor 21186
The Resurrection (2)	Victor 21071
I Am Resolved (2)	Victor 21071

Tuesday, July 26

9:00–12:00 and 1:30–3:50

Ernest Phipps and His Holiness Quartet (Gray, KY)

I Want to Go Where Jesus Is (2)	Victor 20834
	Bluebird 5273
Do, Lord, Remember Me (3)	Victor 20927
Old Ship of Zion (2)	Victor 21186
Jesus Is Getting Us Ready for That Great Day (3)	Victor 21192
Happy in Prison (2)	Victor 21192
Don't You Grieve after Me (2)	Victor 20834

Wednesday, July 27

Editor from local newspaper, Bristol *News Bulletin*, attends the morning session, and later that afternoon publishes a long description in the evening paper.

9:00–10:00
Uncle Eck Dunford and Mrs. Hattie Stoneman

What Will I Do, For My Money's All Gone (3)	Victor 21578

10:00–11:00
Uncle Eck Dunford

The Whip-Poor-Will's Song (2)	Victor 20880
Skip to Ma Lou, My Darling (3)	Victor 20938

11:00–12:00
Uncle Eck Dunford and Ernest Stoneman
Barney McCoy (2)   Victor 20938

1:30–4:00
Blue Ridge Corn Shuckers
Old-Time Corn Shuckin'
Parts 1 & 2 (2/4)   Victor 20835

Thursday, July 28

According to Peer, phone calls and inquiries start pouring in. Nonetheless, he completes a very full schedule.

9:00–12:00
The Johnson Brothers, Charles and Paul
The Jealous Sweetheart (2)   Victor 21243
A Passing Policeman (2)   Unissued*
Just a Message from Carolina (2) Victor 20891
(*issued in 1987 on CMF-011)

12:00–1:00
Peer takes Johnson Brothers, and his two engineers, to a noon luncheon at the local Kiwanis Club; he talks about making records and the Johnsons play "My Carolina Home," "Alacazander," "Turkey in the Straw," "New River Train," "Old Happy Valley," and a Hawaiian march.

1:30–4:00
Blind Alfred Reed
Wreck of the Virginian
(Train No. 3) (2)   Victor 20836
I Mean to Live for Jesus (2)   Victor 20939
You Must Unload (2)   Victor 20939
Walking in the Way with Jesus (2) Victor 20836

4:00–5:30
Johnson Brothers, Charles and Paul
Two Brothers Are We
(From East Tennessee) (3)   Victor 21243
The Soldier's Poor Little Boy (3) Victor 20891
I Want to See My Mother (2)   Victor 20940

5:30–6:40
El Watson, harmonica soloist
Pot Licker Blues (2)   Victor 20951
Narrow Gauge Blues (2)   Victor 20951

Friday, July 29

Two artists appear from Corbin, Kentucky, traveling together, lured by the newspaper stories. Shelton performs solo with banjo, while Karnes accompanies himself on a guitar; on some selections, it sounds as if Shelton plays a second guitar behind Karnes.

9:00–12:30
B. F. Shelton
Cold Penitentiary Blues (2)   Victor 40107

O Molly Dear (2)   Victor 40107
*Pretty Polly** (2)   Victor 35838
*Darling Cora** (2)   Victor 35838
(*These represent 12-inch masters, running four minutes each.)

1:30–5:10
Alfred Karnes
Called to the Foreign Field (2) Victor 40327
I Am Bound for
the Promised Land (2)   Victor 20840
Where We'll Never Grow Old (2) Victor 20840
When I See the Blood (2)   Unissued
When They Ring the Golden Bells (2) Victor 20933
To the Work (2)   Victor 20933

Saturday, July 30—Sunday, July 31

Peer spent part of the weekend auditioning new acts, and part driving into the mountains with his wife. No recording was done.

Monday, August 1

Logs show no recording activity in morning, and we assume this was devoted to auditions.

9:00–11:00
Auditions

12:00–2:30
J. P. Nestor and Norman Edmunds, Hillsville, VA
Train on the Island (3)   Victor 21070
Georgia (1)   Unissued
John My Lover (1)   Unissued
Black-Eyed Susie (1)   Victor 21070

2:30–4:45
Bull Mountain Moonshiners, Coeburn, VA
Sweet Marie (2)   Unissued
Johnny Goodwin (2)   Victor 21141

6:30–9:30
Carter Family, Maces Springs, VA
Bury Me under
the Weeping Willow (2)   Victor 21074
Little Log Cabin by the Sea (2) Victor 21074
The Poor Orphan Child (2)   Victor 20877
The Storms Are on the Ocean (2) Victor 20937

Tuesday, August 2

9:00–10:45
Carter Family (minus A.P. Carter)
Single Girl, Married Girl (2)   Victor 20937
The Wandering Boy (2)   Victor 20877

11:00–12:30
Alcoa Quartet, Alcoa, TN
Remember Me, O Mighty One (2)   Victor 20879
I'm Redeemed (2)   Victor 20879

1:30–4:30
Henry Whitter, Fries, VA (harmonica solos)
    Henry Whitter's Fox Chase (3)   Victor 20878
    Rain Crow Bill (2)   Victor 20878

Wednesday, August 3

9:00–12:00
Auditions

1:30–5:00
The Shelor Family, Meadows of Dan, VA
    Big Bend Gal (3)   Victor 20865
    Suzanna Gal (3)   Victor 21130*
    Sandy River Belle (2)   Victor 21130*
    Billy Grimes, the Rover (2)   Victor 20865
    (*These sides released under name Dad
Blackard's Moonshiners.)

6:30–8:30
Mr. and Mrs. J. W. Baker, Falls Branch, TN
    The Newmarket Wreck (2)   Victor 20863
    *On the Banks of
    the Sunny Tennessee* (2)   Victor 20863

Thursday, August 4

8:00–11:00
The Tenneva Ramblers
(Jack Pierce and Grant Brothers), Bristol, TN
    The Longest Train I Ever Saw (2)   Victor 20861
    Sweet Heaven, When I Die (2)   Victor 20861
    Miss Liza, Poor Gal (2)   Victor 21141

11:00–12:00
Red Snodgrass and his Alabamians, local jazz band
    Weary Blues (3)   Unissued

2:00–4:20
Jimmie Rodgers
    The Soldier's Sweetheart (4)   Victor 20864
    Sleep, Baby, Sleep (3)   Victor 20864

Friday, August 5

10:00–1:00
West Virginia Coon Hunters, Bluefield, West VA
    Greasy String (2)   Victor 20862
    Your Blue Eyes Run Me Crazy (2)   Victor 20862

3:00–3:30
Tennessee Mountaineers (local church group)
    Standing on the Promises (3)   Victor 20860
    Beautiful River (2)   Victor 20860

1927–28 RELEASES FROM THE BRISTOL SESSIONS

Release Date, September 16

Victor #	Artist	Title
20834	Ernest Phipps and His Holiness Quartet	*Don't Grieve after Me* *I Want to Go Where Jesus Is*
20835	Blue Ridge Corn Shuckers	*Old Time Corn Shuckin'—Part I* *Old Time Corn Shuckin'—Part II*
20836	Blind Alfred Reed	*Walking in the Way with Jesus* *The Wreck of the Virginian*
20840	Alfred G. Karnes	*I Am Bound for the Promised Land* *Where We'll Never Grow Old*
20844	Ernest V. Stoneman and His Dixie Mountaineers	*Are You Washed in the Blood* *Sweeping through the Gates*
35838	B. F. Shelton	*Pretty Polly* *Darling Cora*

Release Date, October 7

Victor #	Artist	Title
20860	Tennessee Mountainers	*Standing on the Promises* *At the River (Beautiful River)*

Victor #	Artist	Title
20861	Tenneva Ramblers	*The Longest Train I Ever Saw* *Sweet Heaven When I Die*
20862	West Virginia Coon Hunters	*Greasy String* *Your Blue Eyes Run Me Crazy*
20863	Mr. & Mrs. J. W. Baker	*The Newmarket Wreck* *on the Banks of the Sunny Tennessee*
20864	Jimmie Rodgers	*Sleep Baby Sleep* *The Soldier's Sweetheart*
20865	Shelor Family	*Billy Grimes, the Rover* *Big Bend Gal*

Release Date, November 4

Victor #	Artist	Title
20877	The Carter Family	*The Poor Orphan Child* *The Wandering Boy*
20878	Henry Whitter	*Henry Whitter's Fox Chase* *Rain Crow Bill*
20879	Alcoa Quartet	*Remember Me, O Mighty One* *I'm Redeemed*

20880	E. Stoneman, Miss	*Mountaineer's Courtship*
	I. Frost, E. Dunford	*The Whip-Poor-Will's Song*
20891	Johnson Brothers	*The Soldier's Poor Little Boy*
		Just a Message from Carolina

Release Date, November 18

20927	Ernest Phipps and	*Do, Lord, Remember Me*
	His Holiness Quartet	*Old Ship of Zion*
20951	El Watson	*Pot Licker Blues*
		Narrow Gauge Blues

Release Date, December 2

20933	Alfred G. Karnes	*When They Ring the Golden Bells*
		To the Work
20937	The Carter Family	*The Storms Are on the Ocean*
		Single Girl, Married Girl

Release Date, December 16

20938	Uncle Eck Dunford	*Skip to Ma Lou, My Darling*
		Barney McCoy
20939	Blind Alfred Reed	*I Mean to Live for Jesus*
		You Must Unload

Release Date, January 20

21070	J. P. Nestor	*Train on the Island*
		Black-Eyed Suzie
21071	Stoneman's Dixie	*The Resurrection*
	Mountaineers	*I Am Resoved*
21074	The Carter Family	*Bury Me under the Weeping Willow*
		Little Log Cabin by the Sea

Release Date, February 17

21129	E. Stoneman, E. K.	*Dying Girl's Farewell*
	Brewer, M. Mooney	*Tell Mother I Will Meet Her*
21130	Dad Blackard's	*Suzanna Gal*
	Moonshiners	*Sandy River Belle*

Release Date, c. February 28

21141	Bull Mountain	*Johnny Goodwin*
	Moonshiners,	*Miss Liza, Poor Gal*
	Tenneva Ramblers	

Release Date, March 2

21192	Ernest Phipps and	*Jesus Is Getting Us*
	His Holiness Quar-	*Ready For*
	tet	*That Great Day*
		Happy in Prison

Release Date, March 16

21186	Stoneman's Dixie	*I Know My*
	Mountaineers	*Name Is There*
		No More Good-Byes

Release Date, April 6

21243	Johnson Brothers	*The Jealous Sweetheart*
		Two Brothers Are We

Release Date, October 5

21578	Uncle Eck Dunford	*What Will I Do, For My Money's All Gone*

Remaining issues were 40107—B. F. Shelton, released on 9-6-29, and 40327—Alfred Karnes, released on 12-5-30. Some of the 21000 series were out of print as early as March 1928, months before Peer's return visit to Bristol.

JIMMIE RODGERS (WEARING THE GLASSES) WITH THE TENNEVA RAMBLERS, A COUPLE OF MONTHS BEFORE THE 1927 BRISTOL SESSIONS.

GENE AUTRY

THE SINGING COWBOY
An American Dream
DOUGLAS B. GREEN

■ Editor of the *Journal of Country Music* from 1974 to 1977, Douglas B. Green is also the author of a fine survey of country music history called *Country Roots*, published in 1975. Today he is better known as Ranger Doug of the western group Riders in the Sky, whose weekly radio program is widely heard over National Public Radio. Who better, then, to expound on the colorful history of Hollywood's singing cowboys? The following encyclopedic study was originally published in 1978, shortly before Green formed Riders in the Sky. This is one of the most frequently cited articles that the *Journal of Country Music* has ever published.—Ed.

■ The American dream has always had the remarkably protean ability to become whatever the dreamer desired. No single goal—not fame, nor money, nor contentment—stands out as a common denominator; there are, in fact, no common denominators except for the assumption that it is right and proper for us to entertain the notion of such dreams, whatever form they may take.

The singing cowboy of films of the 1930s and 1940s, both the characters and the actors themselves, have long embodied a confluence of many of the aspects of the American dream, representing a sense of glamour and of adventure, a sense of the rugged individuality Americans have long prized; the fame and prestige of film stardom, the attainment of vast sums of money, the achievement of a kind of art, though an art long underrated, long appreciated by too few.

The America of today is a far different place from the nation that flocked to see the singing cowboy westerns of forty or more years ago. Yet far from rejecting these values in this enlightened age, we seem to be increasingly attracted to them, adding the warm patina of nostalgia to the inherent appeal of the embodiment of the American dreams they represent. In fact, as the 1970s become increasingly characterized by directionlessness, by a trend, if anything, to a lack of trends, the romance of the celluloid West becomes more and more attractive. This is nowhere more apparent than in the world of music, where the airwaves are filled with songs of tough but sensitive outlaws and their ladies, songs of today's cowboys written in Music Row song factories, songs listened to avidly by booted, jeaned, and hatted products of the baby-boom suburbs.

BEGINNINGS

▌ The singing cowboy was born of three parents: the romantic West of novels like Owen Wister's *The Virginian* (1902) and Zane Gray's *Riders of the Purple Sage* (1912), the cinematic West of *The Great Train Robbery* (1903) and a thousand subsequent films, and the musical West reaching out to America via radio and records, beginning with Carl T. Sprague's 1925 recording "When the Work's All Done This Fall." Interest in cowboy song predated records, of course. N. Howard Thorpe's *Songs of the Cowboys*, based on thirty years of research,[1] first appeared in 1908, followed closely by John Avery Lomax's *Cowboy Songs and Other Frontier Ballads* (1910). Then again, "made up" cowboy songs were nothing new: not only was some of the classic material of the genre being written while these works were being compiled, even Thorpe himself admitted in a later (1921) printing of his work that he had written one of the songs he had supposedly collected—the now-classic "Little Joe the Wrangler."[2] And, indeed, an 1891 potboiler by William Levi-Taylor called *The Cowboy Clan: or, Tigress of Texas* contains a remarkably synthetic cowboy song which might have been quite at home in the worst of the 1940s musical westerns:

> Lie down now cattle, don't heed any rattle
>   But quietly rest until morn.
> For if you skeedaddle, we'll jump in the saddle
>   And head you off, sure as you are born.[3]

These were the sources which existed in the years after World War I; they were galvanized by two new factors: the emergence of the "talking" film—with Al Jolson in *The Jazz Singer* in 1927—and the sudden development of the romantic cowboy song which transcended in poetry and vision the stock-in-trade tales of cowboy courage ("Utah Carrol"), cowboy pathos ("When the Work's All Done This Fall"), or cowboy humor ("Zebra Dun").

All these elements flowed together around 1930, ingredients in search of a catalyst, although the singing cowboy of fact and image did not emerge until a few years later. The emergence of this creation was hinted at, however, and it was Ken Maynard who proved to be the harbinger of all that followed, as he sang, hummed, and occasionally played the ban-jo, guitar, and fiddle in several of his films in the 1930–1934 era. Howev-er, Maynard was to remain only a precursor; according to film historians George Fenin and William K. Everson, "perhaps due to Maynard's own limitations as a singer, and the fact that he still adhered to the traditional Western, the idea for musical Westerns did not catch on at that time."[4]

Not only did Ken Maynard introduce songs and music to the western film, he also became the first of the celluloid cowboys to sing[5] on record. In September of 1930 he cut eight songs for the soon-to-be-bankrupt Columbia Graphophone Company: "Fannie Moore," "Betsy From Pike," "Prisoner for Life," "Jesse James," "Roundup's Done," "Home on the Range," and, the only two sides ever released, "Cowboy's Lament" and "Lone Star Trail" (Columbia 2310-D).[6]

Maynard's voice was indeed a coarse one, though appealing in a rough way. He himself said, "I had this kinda high, nasal-soundin' Texas voice, but it sounded real enough, I reckon, for me to get into talkies."[7] Not only did Ken play and sing, he also displayed some flair as a songwriter, composing "The Trail Drive" and "Wheels of Destiny" for films of the same name.[8] In addition he claimed the distinction of starring in the first film named for a popular western song, Universal's *The Strawberry Roan* in 1933, the Curly Fletcher song then popular in the Nat Vincent–Fred Howard expanded version,[9] and recorded by the Beverly Hillbillies, Bill Boyd's Cowboy Ramblers, and a host of other string bands. Within the film Maynard not only sang the theme (twice!), but fiddled a bit in the old-fashioned style, fiddle tucked in the crook of his arm.

Though his studio press did their best to make him a Texan (Mission, Texas, was the birthplace invented for him), Ken Maynard was actually born in Vevay, Indiana,[10] on July 21, 1895, and as early as the age of twelve he had run off and joined the circus. He became an expert horse-man, a legendary stunt man, and a competent enough actor to star in hundreds of films over the years, beginning with a bit part in *The Man Who Won* in 1923 and ending with *Harmony Trail* in 1944. By 1929 he was one of the top, if not the top, western star when he filmed *In Old Ari-zona*, which according to film historian Jon Tuska "was an experiment in an all-talking outdoor drama, a feat [Universal Pictures' head Carl] Laemmle's sound engineers said was impossible. . . . 'My Tonia' was the principal song, and the musical setting was charming."[11] Universal pro-ceeded to hire Maynard, and the musical content of his westerns contin-ued to play a minor role in all his films for that firm.

Maynard's major contribution to the singing cowboy genre was, in fact, neither his own singing nor his pioneering role as a singer: it was the introduction of Gene Autry to the world—in a 1934 Maynard feature called *In Old Santa Fe*—as a singer of modern cowboy songs. According to Jon Tuska, whose *The Filming of the West* stands as the most definitive work on western film,[12] Maynard could have been the film star that Autry was to become, for Maynard himself was apparently the object of the initial effort at the creation of a singing cowboy. Tuska relates that producer Nat Levine was impressed with what Ken had been doing at Universal.

When Junior Laemmle ousted Maynard from his contract, Ken took . . . a second European voyage. Nat reached Ken via long-distance telephone in London. It was Nat's intention to produce a series of musical Westerns in both serial and feature form. He commented that he agreed with Maynard that action by itself was no longer sufficient to keep audiences interested. The proposed Mascot contract would provide Ken with $10,000 a week for each week that he worked, and Nat wanted Ken for an undetermined number of pictures. Since both feature and serial production were on four-week shooting schedules by this time, Ken would be getting about the same as he had at Universal. "When I signed Ken Maynard for a serial at forty thousand dollars," Nat Levine remarked to me, "his name value justified the investment." No other screen cowboy was making as much in 1933–34.[13]

For whatever reasons—his unappealing voice probably the main one[14]—Ken Maynard never "happened" as a singing cowboy. When Gene Autry appeared, fresh and free of the expectations of the past, then and there a new genre, both in music and in film, was born.

Before turning to Gene Autry's career, his influence, and his complex relationships with differing and sometimes conflicting versions of the American dream, it is important to recognize a musical trend alluded to earlier which may in itself have been largely responsible for preparing the American public to accept the emergence of the singing cowboy. This was the sudden popularity of the romantic western song. Earlier cowboy songs—"authentic," if you will—had been written before the turn of the century; extremely romantic in very specific ways, they concentrated on the rough, lonely, difficult, sometimes wryly humorous life of the cowboy. From long work songs like "The Old Chisholm Trail" to humorous dialect pieces like Gail Gardner's "The Sierry Petes" ("Tying Knots in the Devil's Tail")[15] and reworked minstrel tunes like "The Little Old Sod Shanty on the Claim,"[16] these songs dealt in terms real or fanciful with such tangibles as housing, the art of branding, bronc riding, or a hundred other such specifics.

Few songs indeed concentrated on the beauty of the West, the romance of a generalized and dreamily appealing western life. The most notable was "Home on the Range." John I. White reports that "Lomax had published it, with piano accompaniment, in his anthology *Cowboy*

Songs and Other Frontier Ballads in 1910. . . . The earliest 'Home on the Range' recording of which I have any knowledge is that made by Vernon Dalhart and released by Brunswick in 1927. In 1928 Jules Verne Allen recorded it for Victor."[17] He adds, more importantly, that "thanks largely to the sudden growth of radio broadcasting, in the early 1930s America discovered and took to its heart what it thought was a genuine folksong. As the haunting, comforting strains 'Where seldom is heard a discouraging word/And the skies are not cloudy all day' miraculously came out of the air the country somehow felt that it had a good thing going, stock market crashes and depressions notwithstanding."[18]

"Home on the Range" was not the only song causing this reaction. A rash of "new" western songs fundamentally different from their predecessors were appearing, largely from the pens of Bob Nolan and Billy Hill; these songs were concerned not with the life of the cowboy, but with the romance of the West as an entity in and of itself. Entirely apart from the life or even the existence of the cowboy except by implication, they dealt with the beauty of its haunting scenery, and in spiritual rather than earthy terms.

Billy Hill was born in Boston on July 14, 1899, the same city in which he died on Christmas Eve, 1940. As a youth he had been struck by the natural beauty of the West while living in Utah, and began writing western songs—as well as a great deal of pop material—in New York in the early 1930s, often in collaboration with Peter DeRose. Beginning in 1933 a string of his classic western songs reached America's ears via hit shows on Broadway, radio, record, and film, beginning with "The Last Roundup" and "The Old Spinning Wheel" and followed by "Wagon Wheels" (1934), "Empty Saddles" (1936), and a great many others, including "Call of the Canyon," "Night on the Desert," and "The Oregon Trail."[19]

As successful over a longer period of time, and artistically more effective, was Bob Nolan, a founder with Tim Spencer and Leonard Slye (later known as Roy Rogers) of the Sons of Pioneers.[20] Nolan was born Robert Clarence Nobles on April 1, 1908, in New Brunswick, although a good deal of his youth was spent in Boston. At the age of fourteen the young student—even then a devotee of the English and Scottish poets Keats, Wordsworth, Byron, Shelley, and Burns—moved with his father to Arizona, a relocation which had a profound effect on the young man: "I came to Tucson, Arizona, right from the tall timber, out to the desert. It was awe-inspiring, to say the least, to wake up in the morning to see the desert beauty, with the sun shining through millions of drops of dew. It was just outstanding."[21] Nolan eventually followed his father to California in 1929, and, after a period of several years of roaming and occasional music-making, helped form the Sons of the Pioneers in 1933. By 1934 his song "Tumbling Tumbleweeds" had become a best-selling record for Gene Autry (as "The Last Roundup" had been the year before), and Bob Nolan had established a reputation as country music's most poetic songwriter, with romantic songs like "Way Out There," "Blue Prairie," "Song of the Bandit," "Love Song of the Waterfall," and "Song of the Prairie," which both shaped and established this new image of western music. Talking about the creation of perhaps his most famous song, "Cool Water," Nolan explains this new, more romantic approach to songwriting:

I don't think there's any philosophy behind it; I was strictly trying to paint a picture of the desert, and I missed miserably, because I picked up the wrong thing to write about—a mirage because you can't use the word mirage in a song: it just don't sing, and you can't rhyme it, and you're just up a tree, see? So I just left it out and everything was nebulous, but after I was through with it you couldn't help but know that I was talking about a mirage. You'd be surprised how many people never saw a mirage in the desert.[22]

This set of circumstances, plus the growing national interest in a romantic West, made the time ripe for something new. Though but a handful suspected it, that something was the singing cowboy.

GENE AUTRY, THE SINGING COWBOY

▌Into this vacuum stepped Gene Autry, the man who was ultimately to blend these disparate elements into the phenomenon of the singing cowboy, and whose career—regardless of one's sentimental favorites—is the single most important within the style.

Yet Autry's career is charged with paradox. It is a career which, like the man himself, is often nebulous, vague, and inexplicable. Gene Autry's career is surely one of the half dozen most important in country music, yet we really know little about it—just some names, dates, and facts, a bit of filmography here, a touch of discography there. We know virtually nothing of the inspiration that first fired his interest in music, the music which directed his talent (other than during his Jimmie Rodgers–influenced period) or the forces which shaped his music.

More often than not his legend and status have gotten in the way, obscuring many of the facts the country music scholar and fan seeks. For one thing, much of his legend was created in Hollywood, that land of illusion, and legends in Hollywood when written about are usually treated with reverent awe or with speculative gossip, neither of which is of much help, or interest. Writers and followers of Hollywood legends usually do not have a strong enough musical tradition on which to base their conclusions, and therefore end up concentrating endlessly on the ephemeral, the spurious, and the obvious.

A second reason Autry's influential career has been kept in an unfocused state is simply that he is a multimillionaire: nothing seems to obsess Autry historians like this most obvious manifestation of the American dream. That the compilation of his vast wealth has been his main concern since returning to civilian life after World War II is obvious. Autry is proud to recount for reporters his rapid rise from poverty to great wealth at the expense of discussing his musical origins. What about Autry's musical and film greatness?

Bill Malone spent a remarkable amount of time, given the restrictions of space, to the effects of Gene Autry's career in *Country Music USA: A Fifty Year History*, pointing out that "at the onset of the war Gene Autry was the most financially successful and possibly the most popular country performer."[23] My own essay in *Stars of Country Music: From Uncle Dave Macon to Johnny Rodriguez*[24] was the first serious look of any length at Gene Autry's music and its considerable effects on the development of country music. Most film critics have written off his career—with a tone either of condescension or bewilderment—as a bizarre and unhealthy fluke. Only Tuska has taken the time to examine what he calls "The Autry Phenomenon" in depth, and his conclusions are remarkable and enlightening. Yet Mr. Tuska does not know country music, and his great illumination only sheds light on half a career.

Autry's own long-awaited autobiography, *Back in the Saddle Again*, hardly touches upon these musical origins. As there is in Autry's estimation equal interest in his activities as a singer, an actor, a financier ("corporate cowboy" is his term), and owner of a major league baseball team, space is equally divided among these interests. He corroborates some stories, dispels others, but at the end of it all we are left with precious little more knowledge of the music that inspired him than we know now. Many musical figures of paramount importance in his career are scarcely touched upon: Johnny Marvin is mentioned a few times, as are Fred Rose and Johnny Bond; Art Satherley (his name consistently misspelled) only three times, Ray Whitley but once, and Jimmie Rodgers not at all. As one would expect, in reviewing his own life Autry sees music as but one of several careers to be touched on, and he does not devote lavish attention to any of them.[25]

Of course, the most prominent contributor to this enigma has not been the journalist unwilling to dig deep into a musical past but Mr. Autry himself. While certainly not in the Howard Hughes class, still Gene Autry is reclusive and leery of interviews, as James Horowitz's extremely amusing account in *Rolling Stone* (October 25, 1973) called "In Search of the Original Singing Cowboy" proved. If journalists are even seen at all when they come to talk with him, they come away with a few familiar stories of Will Rogers, Autry's years at Republic Studios, and his gold records; they hear about his deft combination of luck and skill in business (calculated, no doubt, to prove both his humility and business acumen), and his conservative politics. Or Autry tells of how his wife Ina persuaded him to record "Rudolph the Red Nosed Reindeer," a song he personally disliked, or how the California Angels will fare in the upcoming year's pennant race. Although some film critics have gotten to him, apparently no music scholar ever has, for the really important musical questions remain unanswered. And with the toll age takes, it is highly unlikely now that they ever will be. Gene Autry has been singularly unreflective concerning both the origins of his inspiration and his view of the effects of his music and film careers. Whether he ever ponders these and a hundred other questions we do not know, and likely will never know. It seems that Gene Autry is destined to remain both legend and enigma.

The basics of Gene Autry's early career are well-documented. Born to a rancher in Tioga, Texas, on September 29, 1907, Orvon Gene Autry learned the basics of the guitar from his mother. The family moved to Ravia, Oklahoma, when Gene was in his teens, and there he showed enough interest in music and show business to spend part of a summer with the Fields Brothers Marvelous Medicine Show, where he sang, acted, did blackface comedy, and even played the saxophone.

In his own words, "When the Fields Brothers Marvelous Medicine Show came to town one summer, looking for a local boy to sing with them, I was recommended to Professor Fields. I traveled with them for three months, softening up audiences with mournful ballads before the professor began pitching his wares: liniment and pills, and his own product, a patent medicine called Fields' Pain Annihilator. . . . I earned fifteen dollars a week. For a teen-aged boy, in the 1920s, this was more than money: it was the riches of Arabia."[26]

After graduation from high school in 1925 he was hired by the St. Louis & Frisco Railroad; he worked in a variety of positions before rising to the rank of relief telegrapher. Sometime in 1928 he fell under the influence of Jimmie Rodgers and became slavishly addicted to that sound. That year also saw the famed meeting with Will Rogers in Chelsea, Oklahoma. Rogers, in the railroad office to send a telegram, heard Autry singing and playing, whiling away the empty hours. His words of encouragement—surely they could have not been much more than a simple offhand compliment—stoked the fires of Autry's naive ambition, and taking advantage of the free railway pass available to all Frisco employees, and personal vacation time, he headed for New York, the entertainment capital of the world, where he knew absolutely no one.

Inexperienced but optimistic, he immediately set about looking up Johnny and Frankie Marvin, two of the most popular entertainers in the city. Johnny, in fact, was a toast of the town, a performer on record, on Broadway, in vaudeville (where he toured with Nat Shilkret's orchestra), and on radio as "The Lonesome Singer of the Air." Frank, seven years John's junior, was not only a comedian and musician in his brother's act, but recorded on his own as well.

If he had nothing else, Autry did have innocent confidence. He walked up to the Marvins and introduced himself with a big smile, saying that he was Gene Autry, a fellow Oklahoman, and that he, too, wanted to make records. Legends are made of this kind of youthful optimism, this blissful naiveté, and a legend was, indeed, in the making, though it was hardly overnight. As Frank Marvin remembers it:

He was out in Butler where my folks had a little hotel and a cafe and saw Johnny's picture on the wall and my picture on the wall. I was single at the time, staying at the old Manger Hotel, and he asked Mama where I was, so he came to New York and looked me up. I was making records, so I took him down to the old Edison Company and one of the sound men there played the piano, and he tried to make a test record of "Sonny Boy." He couldn't sing "Sonny Boy" yet! I told him, when we got back to the hotel, that if I was him I'd try to do some of those western-type songs.

I asked him if he could yodel, and he said, "I don't know; I never did try." So he tried to yodel and he had just a very little falsetto voice, so I told him, "Go back home and practice your singing and yodeling and come back here and I'll get you another test record."

So next time he come back, oh, three or four months later, I was going over to the old Gennett Company in Flushing, Long Island, and he made a test record and they liked him. Then we went to Victor and Johnny and I played guitars for him. He couldn't yodel yet, but I did some yodels for him.

So we kind of helped, and Johnny even brought him out on stage at the Palace, and they liked old Gene there, by golly![27]

This is a story Autry corroborates:

I had met the mother of Johnny Marvin, then a recording artist of some popularity at Victor. I stopped off one day in Butler, Oklahoma, where the family owned a cafe. Mrs. Marvin told me to look up Johnny if I ever got to New York, and I took the precaution of getting his address and phone number.

When I reached Johnny, he told me his younger brother, Frankie, had just gotten into town and we had a lot in common. Like me, Frankie was broke and trying to get started. I moved into his room at the Manger Hotel, which later became the Taft.

As the weather grew colder, we took turns wearing Frankie's topcoat. It was the only coat we had between us.

The days turned into weeks as I lugged my guitar up and down Broadway, to the rhythm of the record company doors slamming in my face. At the time, there were only a handful of companies—Victor, Columbia, Brunswick, Edison—and I tried them all, day after day, hoping for an audition. My first problem was to get past the reception desk.

I had been waiting for hours in the anteroom at Victor one day, guitar across my lap, when the thought must have struck the receptionist that I might not ever leave. She glanced up, smiled nervously, and asked what kind of songs I did.

"Cowboy stuff, mostly," I said, "and some hillbilly. When I can get anyone to listen."

"I'll listen," she said. "Go ahead, play something."

That was all the encouragement I needed. An audience of one. I was halfway through "Jeannine, I Dream of Lilac Time," when Nat Shilkret, the man who wrote it, by then working for Victor, strolled into the room. He stopped for a moment, then ducked into another office and reappeared with a fellow named Leonard Joy. I now had an audience of three. Joy turned out to be the Number Two man at the company, in charge of promoting new artists and their records.

Joy asked me to come back the next morning. "We're recording a band," he said, "and if you'll be here then we'll cut a test and see what you sound like."

When they opened the offices the next morning I was waiting on the doorstep like a bottle of milk. I sang "The Prisoner's Song," a weepy tune, and a Jolson hit, "Climb Upon My Knee, Sonny Boy," probably not the smartest choice on my part, and we cut the test record. After everyone listened to the playback, Nat Shilkret asked me to step into his office.

"You got a nice voice for records," he said, "but you need experience. My advice is go home. Take six months, a year. Get a job on a radio station. Learn to work in front of a microphone."

When I said good-by to the Marvin boys, Frankie offered a piece of advice. "Forget that Jolson stuff," he said. "Learn to sing some yodel songs. That's more to your style."

With that I rode my railroad pass back home to Oklahoma. Shilkret had given me a to-whom-it-may-concern letter, saying I had potential, and I used it to wangle a radio show over KVOO in Tulsa. I was billed as the Oklahoma Yodeling Cowboy, backed up by Jimmy Wilson's Catfish String Band. Meanwhile, I had gone back to my job as a relief operator working up and down the Frisco Line. The idea of paying for radio talent had not yet caught on in the Southwest.

For the next six months I traveled more back roads than a bootlegger, singing at Kiwanis clubs and high schools and private parties all over the state. I was ready to try New York again. I had gained experience and exposure and the next step, I thought, was a record contract.

Backed up by the guitars of Frankie and Johnny Marvin, I cut my first record for Victor. Johnny had written one of the sides, "My Dreaming of You." Jimmy Long had composed the other, "My Alabama Home."[28]

The date of those Victor sessions was October 9, 1929, just twenty days before the wildly careening jazz age would collide head on with the Depression.

It was to be a full sixteen months before the promising young singer would again return to the Victor microphones, for the Depression cut quickly and deeply into the booming recording business. Undaunted by the despair about him, however, Autry took advantage of another free pass and took a sixty-day leave of absence from the St. Louis & Frisco Railroad—to which he never returned—and ventured once again to New York. He soon was recording for a host of labels, exclusive contracts being rare then, including the American Record Company and its affiliate labels (Banner, Melotone, Oriole, Perfect, and Romeo), and Columbia, Grey Gull, and Gennett as well.

By the later sessions his shaky guitar playing had improved noticeably, and his voice, particularly his yodeling, had more authority. In the interim he had also come further under the spell of Jimmie Rodgers, whom he idolized and imitated, his voice at times virtually indistinguishable from Rodgers's. He began to develop his talents as a songwriter as well, although the early efforts were basically Rodgers-style blue yodels which would have fit unobtrusively into the repertoire of the Singing Brakeman. So far did this tribute go, in fact, that Autry recorded two of Rodgers's most intensely personal songs, "Jimmie the Kid" and "T. B. Blues," on Victor's budget label Timely Tunes, in the spring of 1931.

By the end of 1931, however, his records indicate that he was becoming a seasoned professional who was well aware that his own personal identity must be forged. While the Rodgers influence is quite evident, there are songs other than blue yodels, sung in a voice recognizable as a young version of the singing cowboy who would fill thousands of movie screens for three decades.

It was during this same time—October 1931—that Autry and Jimmy Long (a guitarist and singer who not only had been his boss on the St. Louis & Frisco, but was his uncle-in-law as well) recorded a sentimental mountain tune for the American Record Company called "That Silver Haired Daddy of Mine." It was to be the first of many Autry hit records, and it radically changed his life and his recording style. It turned him into an up and coming national star, and initiated a whole series of sentimental mountain ballads firmly in the tradition of "That Silver Haired Daddy of Mine."

Somewhere along the line came yet another change in the musical emphasis of his career, which in its early years displayed a remarkably chameleon-like ability to shift styles. From the Jimmie Rodgers blue yodels he moved smoothly to mountain ballads, and from mountain ballads shifted once again, this time to western songs and ultimately to the development of a sound and style quite his own. When and where the singing cowboy image was originally developed is still uncertain, but as early as 1930 he was appearing on KVOO in Tulsa, and despite the dire effects of the Depression he joined the National Barn Dance in Chicago in 1931 as "Oklahoma's Singing Cowboy."[29]

In addition, he obtained a radio show of his own, "Conqueror Record Time," in which he was portrayed as a cowboy fresh off the range, ready to sing a few western songs for the folks. This format, by Autry's own admission, was the brainchild of his producer, Art Satherley, and Ann Williams of the WLS production staff. Years later, Autry recollected the sequence of these events:

> Arthur Satherley made me a proposition, and told me that if I'd do exactly as he said, I'd never be sorry—an arrangement which I accepted and kept to this day.
>
> That sort of stuff didn't sound very glamorous to me, as my recollections of ranch life included aching muscles and endless days in the sun and dust. I wanted to be a dreamy-eyed singer of love songs like Rudy Vallee, but there was my promise to Arthur, and there was Ann Williams bringing the West back East with bright talk of the wind-swept plains, of coyote howls in the moonlight, and cowboys on galloping horses.
>
> Arthur's guidance brought me eventually to a $35-a-week job doing a daily broadcast in Chicago. There I met Ann Williams, the third influence [Johnny Marvin and Arthur Satherley were the first two] in the creation of the singing cowboy. Ann was the announcer for my broadcasts, which plugged the sale of my phonograph records. I sang cowboy songs, not because I felt the listeners liked 'em better, but because Arthur insisted upon it. Ann began to build-up my Oklahoma-Texas background and sprinkled the program with talk of sagebrush and tumbleweed.
>
> So between the three of them, Marvin, Satherley, and Ann Williams, they finally got it through my ornery skull that instead of doing poor imitations of all the popular singers of the day, I should stay in my own backyard and sing the songs I knew best.[30]

Soon Sears-Roebuck was boosting this cowboy singer's image and popularity with a host of songbooks[31] (one of which shows Autry doing a series of rope tricks) and through mail order sales of their Gene Autry Roundup guitar at $9.95. Yet it is important to note, as Malone has pointed out about this abrupt change of musical emphasis from country to western themes, that though "the subject matter was different . . . the style of presentation and instrumentation was substantially the same as those of most hillbilly bands of the time."[32]

Interestingly enough, as late as September 8, 1933, he wrote songwriter

Raymond E. Hall ("enroute" from Marquette, in Michigan's Upper Peninsula) asking not for western songs but for "a good old southern ballad":

I received your letter a few days ago, also the songs and wish to thank you for them. I have looked them over pretty well and think they are very good. However, I am returning them all to you with the exception of "Sweetheart of the Cimarron" and I want to hold it a few days as I think I can use it and as soon as I find out about it I will let you know just what the outcome of it will be.

Clayton told me about you saying something about a song "Life's Weary Ways." I am just wondering what you ever did with it and if you would send it to me as it seems to be a very good title and might be my type of song. Also I wish you would write me some stuff such as "Mississippi River Blues" or something of a good old southern ballad. I'm sure you know what I want.[33]

There is considerably more confusion concerning the how of Autry's career than the when. As always seems to happen in the case of unexpected success, there are quite a few who step forward to take credit for it. Of many accounts, the two involving Art Satherley and Nat Levine are particularly interesting. Satherley was, of course, Autry's producer on Conqueror Records, while Levine was a film producer associated with Mascot films. Two other figures loom as large in the story: Autry himself, who has remained characteristically vague about the sequence of events involved, and Herbert G. Yates, who not only was the head of the American Record Company—the outfit which controlled Conqueror as well as its complex of dime-store labels—but also was going about the business of consolidating a number of smaller film companies to form Republic Studios not long after Autry's first film. Yates, who died in 1966, may have given his account of these events, but if so it has not surfaced.

Satherley firmly asserts that he was due the credit for the remarkable creation of the singing cowboy on film, bringing Gene Autry to the attention of Yates, his boss:

Herbert Yates said to me one day, "Who is this cowboy guy that you've got selling records?" I said, "Gene Autry." He said, "Let me hear some of his records." And Yates [had gotten] . . . amalgamated I think with someone else by the name of Nat Levine on the West Coast here, who was associated in the development of films.

So he said to me one day, "Let me hear this fellow's records." So I took them upstairs to his fabulous office, he played them, and the next day he pressed the button for Art, he said, "Art, come on up here." I won't mention the words that he said, but he looked at me and he said, "Is *that* what you're talking about?" I said, "Yeah. Don't you like it?" He said, "What is it?" I said, "That's America! Country America! That's what we're selling, and this man is a star!" And I said, "This man is going into pictures."

"How do you know he's going into pictures?"

"Because they'll be after him very shortly—he has the looks, he has every-thing. Therefore, you have your own picture company called Republic Studios!"

. . . Then he said, "Well, I can't use the stuff." I said, "Well if you can't, let me have him!" I said, "I'll still remain with you if you like, but I could sell him tomorrow to another picture company that's already established!" "Well," he said, "How can you do that?" "Well," I said, "you just turned the guy down!" I said, "Think it over," and walked out.

About two days later he called me again and said, "Say, Art, come on up here." I won't use the words, of course, but he said, "The guy's fabulous. I don't know what the hell he's singing about, but there it is. Where is he?" I said, "He's in Chicago. He's on the air every day and he's getting fantastic publicity! Money can't *buy* the publicity that Sears-Roebuck has given to us for the thirty bucks a week we're paying him!"

"Well," he said, "I've got a fellow at the Blackstone Hotel's just come in from Hollywood. His name is Nat Levine. Could you have Gene clean himself up a lit-tle bit and go and see him and sing a little bit of 'That Silver Haired Daddy?' " And, of course, I said sure.

I got on to the phone to Gene and said, "Gene, meet this man at the Black-stone Hotel at this time. Get yourself ready, get your hair done nicely, get your pants pressed, go in there as a spic and span cowboy from the West." So he did. So Nat Levine signed him for the usual contract—I think it was $175 a week, which was the average in those days—and Gene signed. So that was the begin-ning of Gene going to the West.[34]

Levine, however, tells the same story from a rather different perspec-tive, as related by Jon Tuska:

Nat had a reputation for giving young, inexperienced talent a chance with his company. "I received a dozen letters from Autry during 1933," he wrote to me, "asking for an opportunity to work for me in anything I would suggest in pic-tures. Autry's name value at the time was limited to . . . a radio station in Chica-go, practically an unknown with questionable ability. On one of my trips East, I stopped off in Chicago, not to meet Autry, but for business I had with my distrib-utor. But I did get to meet Autry and he virtually begged me for an opportunity to come to Hollywood and work in pictures. While he was nice looking, it seemed to me he lacked the commodity necessary to become a Western star: virility! I wasn't impressed and tried to give him a nice brush-off, telling him I would think about it. For a period of six months he wrote to me continually, con-veying that he would do anything for the opportunity."

Yates was enlisted by Autry to put in a good word with Levine. Yates told Nat that Gene was selling a lot of records. When Ken Maynard signed with Mascot, Levine went ahead and put Autry on salary with a five year option. He also signed Lester "Smiley" Burnette, who had worked two years with Autry, and Frank Marvin, one of Gene's backup men. Autry was hired at a hundred dollars a week, Burnette and Marvin at somewhat less. It was Levine's notion to use Autry, who could sing, to support Maynard, who really could not. "Gene was completely raw material," Levine continued, "knew nothing about acting, lacked poise, and was awkward. A couple of days after his arrival I had him at my home and invited my production staff to meet him. The next day all of my associates questioned my judgment in putting him under contract. They thought I was slipping. But I persisted, and for the first four months he went through a learning period. We had at that time, in our employ, a professional dramatic and voice teacher, and Autry became one of her pupils. He wasn't much of a horseman either, so I had Tracy Layne and Yakima Canutt teach him how to ride."

"I don't believe he ever acknowledged my contribution to his career," Nat added, "nor did I ever receive thanks."[35]

Autry's recollection of these same events—as time-hazed and self-serving as Satherley's and Levine's—is substantially the same, yet from a significantly different viewpoint:

It seemed clear to Herb Yates that the Western movie needed a shot in the arm. He discussed it with Moe Siegel, then the president of American Records, and they agreed that the straight, action Western was a thing of the past. So they met again with Levine, and Yates said, "Nat, I'll give you the money, but on one condition. We have a fellow who sells a helluva lot of records for us. He's on radio in Chicago, on a national hookup, does the 'Barn Dance.' Nat, it would be worth your while to take a look at Gene Autry."

To get the financing for his picture, Nat Levine would have looked at a singing kangaroo. A day later I received a call from Yates and Siegel, telling me Levine was on his way to Chicago and wanted to meet with me. I had finished my show at WLS when he arrived . . . blew in, is the phrase I meant to use.

"They tell me you sell a lot of records," he said.

"Oh, I reckon so."

"I'm going to make this picture with Ken Maynard. Cowboy picture. Low budget. Usually, we try out a new actor, we give you a screen test, read lines, things like that. No need to bother. If you'd like to come out and appear in it, we've written in a barn dance scene. You can call the square dance, do a few songs. That can be your screen test. We'll see what kind of reaction we get when the movie plays."

I didn't know if it was my turn to talk or not.

"Well, Autry, how do you like it?"

"Sounds okay to me."

"Good. Call me before you come." He paused at the door. "You're a nice boy. You may call me collect."[36]

Regardless, Autry stole his first picture—*In Old Santa Fe* (1934)—from Ken Maynard, and an astonishing career began to mushroom seemingly out of the blue. With records aiding the success of his films and vice versa, Autry suddenly became one of the most popular film stars of the era, his films always landing near the top of box office lists; at the same time he was selling a remarkable number of records.

His overwhelming success has puzzled film historians for generations; few have been able to approach it with anything more than bewilderment. According to Autry's critics, his West was so totally devoid of any shreds of reality it was ridiculous. Though he is revered in the country music field as a singer, one cannot honestly say he was the best vocalist of his day, nor even the best country singer. Although his singing has always been affecting, this is not reason enough to explain a success so overwhelming. His success could not have been based merely on the novelty of the singing cowboy, for we have seen that Gene Autry was not the first singing cowboy on film, Maynard was. In fact, he was not even the second. John Wayne, of all people, made a short series of Singing Sandy westerns for Monogram in his early days as a B player, though his singing was dubbed in by big band leader and vocalist Smith Ballew.[37] Indeed, Bob Steele also appears to have made a singing western, *The Oklahoma Cyclone*, for Tiffany as early as 1930.

If historians agree on anything, however, it is that this deliberate lack of realism was as much a cause for his success as any other factor or set of factors. William K. Everson, for example, writes:

To offset expected criticisms that this new brand of musical Western was a travesty of tradition, Republic set them in their own never-never land, placing them quite apart from other Westerns. The earlier "historical" Cavalry-vs.-Indian Westerns that Autry had made—*Ride, Ranger, Ride* and *The Singing Vagabond*—were abandoned in favor of entirely modern Westerns. Autry frequently played a rodeo or radio star (and always under his own name); the props included high-powered cars, army tanks, airplanes, and radio stations; and the plots touched on contemporary politics, big business, social problems (the dust bowl), dairy farming as opposed to cattle ranching, problems of soil erosion and crop destruction by weeds. Against this thoroughly modern background, the traditional action ingredients—runaway stagecoaches and bar-room brawls, to say nothing of cowboys toting guns and engaging in full-scale range wars—were incongruous indeed, but here the musical elements came to the rescue. . . . All of this obviously artificial glamor and song put the Autry films into a deliberate kind of horse-operetta framework which disarmed any criticism.[38]

Jon Tuska, writing with even more insight, tackles the central question:

. . . the Fantasy inspiring the screenplays and, above all, Autry himself is so fervent that it seems instead to be a demonstration of an immutable law governing human behavior. I do not doubt for an instant that Autry believed totally in the Fantasy; I think for a time that audiences believed in it too.

I sincerely feel that Autry's massive appeal as a modest cowboy troubadour leading a uniquely charmed life, a musical magician who could turn darkness into light, sorrow into happiness, tarnish into splendor, a Pied Piper able to control men and alter the course of world events by means of a song, is the most tremendous single occurrence in the history of the American Western cinema. Gene Autry in his magnificent outfits, yodeling a pop tune, is an image so remote from the actual man of the frontier as to rival any fairy tale. If you compare Autry to Tom Mix, or even William S. Hart, of the previous generation, he appears hopelessly inept. But once you accept him on his own terms and find yourself enthralled by the Autry Fantasy, the others begin to look clumsy, plebian, vulgar. . . .

Gene Autry on screen met every reversal of fortune, every threat of villainy, with the honest reassurance of a song. Critics of the film mock Autry or dismiss him; they try to ignore him, term him an anomaly, discredit him as a temporary lapse into lunacy, reject him bitterly, sneer at him, or are silent; but Gene Autry made more money and was more consistently popular during his time in the movies than any of his Western peers. His career was without the rise and fall of nearly every other cowboy player. The Autry Fantasy like the Mix Legend only reinforces the fact that the Western is basically an imaginative myth. Yet Autry ruined the programmer Western at the same time because, as he moved further and further into the golden reaches of the Autry Fantasy, he only intensified the grand lie about the true nature of man which World War II began to shatter with its agony of genocide, concentration camps, and total destruction. Gene Autry, although he outlived it by a few years, belongs very much to that generation of Depression-weary gentlefolk who tried to hide from the truth until it mushroomed before their startled eyes at Hiroshima.[39]

A stirring and convincing answer to the question, to be sure, but likely not the only answer. The mystery of Autry's explosive and remarkably long-lived success has yet to be answered satisfactorily. Surely it is more than the fantasy he and his producers created on screen (though Shirley Temple's simultaneous if shorter-lived career seems to have been a result of just that); it is more than his engaging singing; it is more than an idea whose time had come; it is more than Depression-era escapism; it is more than the first nationwide demonstration of the absolutely national appeal of country music, an overwhelming referendum proving country music was a major musical form and force, the ballots being 78 rpm records and theater ticket stubs. Certainly, it was all of these, and much more.

MORE SINGING COWBOYS

▌Within months of Autry's first films hoards of singers and actors adopted singing cowboy roles. This is scarcely surprising, for if imitation is the sincerest form of flattery, Hollywood has always gone out of its way to flatter the hell out of surprise success. What is genuinely remarkable—saying much for the idea-whose-time-has-come-theory—is that singing cowboy imitations were not just extremely quick to appear on screen, they were virtually simultaneous:

Autry was catapulted to stardom, and practically overnight renown, by Nat Levine with *Tumbling Tumbleweeds*, released in September 1935. Immediately following in his footsteps . . . came Dick Foran, whose debut as a movie cowboy came for Warner Brothers two months later, in November 1935. Granted that the Warner boys were quick to perceive the impact of Autry's success with what amounted to a new form, it's dubious that they could have unearthed their own Western songbird, had the initial script on the studio floor and solidified plans to exploit this new property all in the space of a few months. The prospect must have arrived near-simultaneously in both camps. Also, Foran did not resemble Autry in the least, nor did he work like the Republic cowboy. Foran and his later compatriots Fred Scott and Jack Randall, if they could be likened to anybody, could be said to follow the trail of MGM's blonde thrush, Nelson Eddy. . . . Like Eddy, Foran, Scott and Randall possessed vocal equipment within the operatic sphere. Indeed, they would be entirely at ease with a robust rendition of "Stout-Hearted Men," but the simple bucolic pleasures of "Ridin' Down the Canyon" would be beyond them. . . . However, the booming baritones didn't last much beyond 1940, while Autry, and Tex Ritter, two of the more comfortable and idiomatic vocalizers, pursued lengthy careers in the field.

It is interesting that Warner Brothers should have been the company to follow the musical Western, since their production had been dormant after the John Wayne [Singing Sandy] series was halted in 1933. A new executive lineup at the studio paved the way for the move. . . . Songs written for Foran were pleasant and hummable, most of them by studio tunesmiths M.K. Jerome and Jack Scholl; but even here, the sound was closer to Tin Pan Alley than The Great Divide.[40]

It was indeed clearly an idea whose time had come. John Wayne and especially Maynard were the harbingers, Autry the realization. Would Dick Foran have obtained Autry's success had his series come out two months earlier than Gene's instead of two months later?

Foran was born in Flemington, New Jersey, on June 18, 1910, and was the son of Senator Arthur F. Foran. He graduated from Princeton University, and made his screen debut in *Stand Up and Cheer* in 1934;[41] in the following year, he became singing cowboy number five with the appearance of *Moonlight on the Prairie*. His film was not, however, terribly successful, particularly compared to the rocketing success of the Gene Autry westerns. Dick Foran went on to considerable success as a singer and actor in some eighty films, many of which were major productions. By no means were all the films westerns: among his best roles was in a sophisticated comedy called *Guest Wife* (1945) with Don Ameche and Claudette Colbert. Foran also appeared on Broadway and on television in his long career, and did limited recording for Decca and Universal in both studio-western and pop styles. He currently lives in the Los Angeles area.[42]

After Foran they came like a stampeding herd.[43] Of the thundering posse of singing cowboys which galloped across the screen in pursuit of Gene Autry in ensuing years, it is remarkable how few understood Mr. Autry's most basic gift: he was a country singer who was not only ingenuous but also believable, the qualities which not only make for great country music but also virtually define it. All too often, the prevailing feeling was that if Autry was all that popular with his country voice, then surely a "real" singer would be even more popular. It was tried again and again, never very successfully.

In 1935 western music began to abound in films, not only Autry's *Tumbling Tumbleweeds* and Foran's *Moonlight on the Prairie*, but in other places as well. The Sons of the Pioneers appeared in a Liberty film called *The Old Homestead*, released October 8,[44] a further indication of this trend. In addition, they had composed the title song for Foran's film, establishing the group as actors, singers, musicians, and songwriters all at the same time. The Sons of the Pioneers in particular, and later groups like the Jimmy Wakely Trio, Foy Willing & The Riders of the Purple Sage, the Cass County Boys, Andy Parker & the Plainsmen, even Bob Wills & his Texas Playboys, and Spade Cooley's Orchestra, all figure heavily in the sound and style of the musical western film; yet, except for certain individual members of any given band who stepped into starring roles or major support roles, they lie just a bit outside the scope of this essay, though they remain an intriguing topic for a study.

At any rate, helped by his earlier Conqueror recording of the Bob Nolan classic, Autry's *Tumbling Tumbleweeds* was a great success. This was followed by *Melody Trail*, a title which distinguished this new brand of singing western from just another cowboy film. This he followed with *Sagebrush Troubadour*. Autry stayed as busy the following year, cranking out nearly twenty singing westerns, his seventh entitled *The Singing Cowboy*, a description he not only deserved, but which in a way solidified his claim to the title, as 1936 proved to be the year when other studios, realizing his early success was not just a fluke, began scrambling to discover, develop, film, and present their own singing cowboys.

Charging close behind Foran was Fred Scott, who was billed as "The Silvery Voiced Baritone." His brief appearance as a singing cowboy in RKO's *The Last Outlaw* (1936) led to his feature performance in *Romance Rides the Range*, a Spectrum Production. Thus, Scott became the first singing cowboy to be developed by an independent studio. Fred Leedom Scott, born in Fresno, California, on February 14, 1902, had had considerable experience on stage as well as in film by the time he became a singing cowboy, having appeared in silents for Pathe in the 1920s. In the early 1930s he performed with the San Francisco Grand Opera, returning to films with the beginning of his singing cowboy series.

Scott was a capable actor, rider, and a fine singer, but in no way was he a country singer. A cowboy with a pleasant voice like Autry's (or a rough one like Tex Ritter's) seemed somehow fitting on screen, and did not endanger his credibility. A silvery-voiced baritone did, however, and Scott never found the popularity he and his producers hoped for. He drifted out of films after 1942, though he continued singing for a while before going into real estate.[45] Interviewed some years ago, he commented that "I enjoyed making *Songs and Bullets* about the most of all. It had enjoyable songs written by Don Swander and his wife, June. The Swanders also wrote 'Deep in the Heart of Texas'. . . . I don't ride anymore. I have a deal with the horses—I don't get on them and they don't sell any real estate."[46]

Hard on Scott's heels was Bob Allen, sometimes known as Tex, who began a series for Columbia which came to be called the Ranger series with *Unknown Ranger* (1936), followed by *Reckless Ranger, Rangers Step In, Rio Grande Ranger,* etc.[47] Allen had some vocal experience, but in no way, shape, or form could he be construed a country singer. Born Irving E. Theodore Baehr in Mt. Vernon, New York, he graduated from Dartmouth in 1929, and became one of the nation's most popular photographer's models. He moved to Hollywood, made the Ranger series after a run of society and other dramas, including a juicy part in *Crime and Punishment;* however, his vocal inauthenticity as a cowboy far overwhelmed his vaunted good looks, and his contract was not renewed. He made another series of non-western films for 20th Century-Fox in 1938–39, and finding little prospect of further work moved back to New York, where he had a long career as a model and actor on Broadway, in television, in industrial films, and in commercials.

Interestingly, Allen was one of many to vie for the new opening for a singing cowboy at Republic in 1937; he said of the experience, "When they found out I could not play the guitar they signed Roy Rogers."[48] Columbia's attempt at building a singing cowboy out of Tex Allen seems to have been a somewhat desperate and slapdash attempt to cash in on Autry's popularity. Not an outstanding singer and without a shred of authenticity in his voice, his lack of appeal as a singing cowboy seems obvious from the start.

It was also in 1936 that the co-hosts of the WHN Barn Dance in New York City headed west—independent of each other—to seek greener pastures in Hollywood. One was Ray Whitley, whose first speaking role was in *Hopalong Cassidy Returns* (1936), and who began a series of musical shorts for RKO the following year, all firmly in the singing cowboy genre. Always a bridesmaid and never a bride was to be Whitley's lot in the film industry.

Due to the success of his shorts, he was moved to singing sidekick roles with RKO through 1942, first with George O'Brien and then Tim Holt, always with the prospect of a full-length series of his own in sight. Whitley says of the era: "RKO seemed like they were ashamed of their western program. They didn't release them—they just let them escape."[49] He continued in the same kind of role with Rod Cameron at Universal before drifting out of films with a small role in *Giant* (1956), the bulk of his time spent touring[50] with bands of various sizes which included such country music figures as Merle Travis and Jesse Ashlock from time to time. Born near Atlanta in 1901, he had a pleasant country voice and was an adept yodeler as well. He made a number of records for Decca, ARC, Okeh, and many smaller labels. He will doubtless be best remembered for having written "Back in the Saddle Again" and co-written (with Fred Rose) several other Autry hits—"Lonely River," "Ages and Ages Ago," "I Hang My Head and Cry." Why the studios he worked for never gave him his own series is mysterious, for he was as good a singing cowboy as any.[51]

Whitley's co-host on the WHN Barn Dance was Woodward Maurice "Tex" Ritter, born in Murvaul, Texas, on January 12, 1905.[52] A dedicated student of western history at the University of Texas under J. Frank Dobie, Woodward showed up in New York in 1929, intent upon a career on the Broadway stage. There he appeared in some five productions (*Green Grow the Lilacs* the best known), did his first recording (October 31, 1932, for ARC), appeared on two radio shows (the other was "Cowboy Tom's Roundup"), and obtained the nickname "Tex."

Ritter was chosen by an independent producer by the name of Edward Finney to star in his own projected singing cowboy features, which he ultimately produced for Grand National. Finney said simply, "I wanted to make a series that would be really western with a personality who sang a good song. . . . I listened to some of the records he [Tex Ritter] had made for Decca, which were exactly what I had in mind."[53] He could not have made a better choice. Although Ritter was not a genuine cowboy as such, he was a Texan with a great love of genuine cowboy song and lore, and his rough-hewn voice suggested authority and authenticity unmatched among singing cowboys. Though he was not a great singer, he was an extraordinarily effective one, and this quality not only helped make him a film star, but made him one of country music's most popular and most recorded performers, especially after he signed with the brand new Capitol label in 1942. As Don Miller accurately states: "Ritter had what Autry had, and what Foran and Scott missed. He looked like a cowboy of the range, and not the drugstore variety . . . and his singing, while an acquired taste, did have the echo of the plains in its timbre."[54]

Ritter's first film for Finney and Grand National was *Song of the Gringo*, released on November 22, 1936, quickly followed by *Headin' for the Rio Grande*, released on December 20. He was to make fifty-seven more for Grand National, Monogram, Columbia (where he co-starred with Bill Elliott and later Johnny Mack Brown), Universal, and PRC before closing out his B western singing cowboy career with *Flaming Bullets* in 1945. Having signed with Capitol in 1942, after several fruitless years with Decca (1935–1939), he produced a long string of hits for this label, including "Jingle, Jangle, Jingle," "There's a New Moon Over My Shoulder," "You Two Timed Me One Time Too Often," "Jealous Heart," and many others, including the Academy Award-winning "High Noon" in the 1950s and "Hillbilly Heaven" in the 1960s. Ritter remained an active performer until the day of his death, January 2, 1974.[55]

Tex was a colorful man and a kind one; his singing was far from silvery-voiced, but it was appealing, and most important of all there was a genuineness about him that was unmistakable. He was more than an actor putting on odd clothes and singing songs of roundups and ramblings: he embodied much of what the audience thought a cowboy should be, while never placing too much distance between himself and them. He was a country singer and unashamed of it; like Autry, he was a singer whose voice seemed a natural extension of his personality, rather than an obtrusive and flashy bit of business thrown in to keep apace of other studios or stars. As an actor and a singer he had the sincerity which typifies the best of country music, and this accounted for his appeal on record which even exceeded his attraction on film. A simple thing, hardly worth explaining to those who know and love country music, yet many Hollywood heads were scratched in bewilderment over the success of singers like Autry and Ritter while "finer" singers in cowboy clothes did not draw patrons to the theaters and often were even unable to scare up record contracts at all.

THE SINGING COWBOYS: 1937

■ This was the situation as 1937 dawned, then, probably the most eventful year in the history of the singing cowboy: Autry, two years previously a regional star unknown in films, was now firmly ensconced among the top western stars in Hollywood, and with a long string of hit records already behind him: "Silver Haired Daddy of Mine" (1932), "Yellow Rose of Texas" (1933), "The Death of Jimmie Rodgers" (1933), "There's an Empty Cot in the Bunkhouse Tonight" (1933), "The Last Roundup" (1934), "Tumbling Tumbleweeds" (1934), "Nobody's Darling" (1935), and "Mexicali Rose" (1936). It found him free of his $175 a week contract, making large sums of money and pursued by a number of other singers who would eventually make a musical style out of the Autry approach to the western film. It also found him increasingly irritated with Republic Studios. Some attribute it to a swelled head, others to the legendary stinginess of Herbert Yates. Johnny Bond claims[56] it was Autry's righteous indignation at finding that exhibitors were forced to buy blocks of unprofitable Republic films in order to get the money-making Autry features.[57] Whatever the cause, Autry was to ask for a great deal more money and not get it, after which he simply refused to report for the filming of his next picture. The walkout lasted some months, resulting in both one of the most amusing and tawdry set of events in singing cowboy history, culminating in the signing of Roy Rogers in October.

As the pressure built within this pressure cooker, however, a great deal was also happening all over Hollywood concerning Gene Autry and the singing cowboys. Competing studios had begun full-scale attempts aimed at entering the fray, mounting their own singing cowboy stars and series in earnest, and, consequently, a wide variety of new performers found their way to the screen.

Early among them was a tall, lanky big band leader named Smith Ballew. No stranger to westerns, it was his voice which had been dubbed in for John Wayne's in the Singing Sandy series; he even had dubbed in Bob Nolan's voice in several of the Sons of the Pioneers' early ventures with Charles Starrett at Columbia. Ballew was born in Palestine, Texas, on January 21, 1902, but his background was far from country. He led his own big band at college and later in Chicago, and played and recorded with such swing bands as Joe Venuti's, Ben Pollack's, Red Nichols's, the Dorsey Brothers', Benny Goodman's, Glenn Miller's, and with his own orchestra on Okeh and Columbia. His first feature film was *Palm Springs* (1936), and 20th Century-Fox signed him on as their singing cowboy the following year with *Western Gold* (1937), the first of a short-lived series. As a singing cowboy he lasted but two seasons, his films more memorable for their own intrinsic appeal than his own. *Hawaiian Buckaroo*, for example, took place on an Hawaiian cattle ranch and pineapple plantation, while *Rawhide* found him co-starred with New York Yankee first basemen Lou Gehrig. His final singing cowboy film was *Panamint's Bad Man* (1938) after which he returned to the business of vocalizing with and leading big bands. At last account (1976) he was retired and living in the Dallas-Fort Worth area.[58]

A fellow by the name of Bob Baker was the next to enter the picture. When Universal announced in 1936 that it was auditioning for a singing cowboy, Stanley Leland Weed's mother sent a letter and photo of her son, who was a singer known as Tumble Weed on the National Barn Dance. Film historian Kalton Lahue writes "to everyone's great surprise (except Mrs. Weed's), a letter came back inviting him to make a screen test."[59] Not only did Weed take the test, but he landed the job over the expected host of competitors including Dick Weston, formerly known as Leonard Slye, soon to be known as Roy Rogers. As Tuska relates:

When Buck Jones decided to leave Universal . . . a frantic search was mounted for a suitable replacement. Two finalists emerged from all the screen tests, Dick Weston, a member of the Sons of the Pioneers, and Bob Baker. Baker was born Stanley Leland Weed at Forest City, Iowa, on November 8, 1914.[60] He first came to prominence on the National Barn Dance. Max Terhune persuaded him to try pictures and instructed him in how to act before a camera. Baker was finally chosen over Weston on the basis of physical maturity. Universal gave him the screen name of Bob Baker, with Baker opting to retain his stage name Tumble Weed, and starred him in a series of singing Westerns commencing with *Courage of the West* (Universal, 1937). Baker, no matter the reasoning behind his selection over Weston, projected rather an undernourished screen image. He could sing but was untrained. Universal discovered to their dismay, as did the others, that singing Westerns weren't the answer to Autry. Baker, like most of his peers, ignored the Autry Fantasy, and his writers weren't even conscious that there was such a thing.[61]

Baker, who had grown up in Colorado and New Mexico, began his musical career over KTSM in El Paso while in the Army. He joined the WLS National Barn Dance in 1935, and was featured on a program of his own as well. A good singer with a smooth, middle-of-the-road country flavor, it is a wonder to many film historians that he did not become extremely successful. Lahue says: "One would not think that a major studio like Universal would have so badly botched the new star's build-up, but they did and before long, Bob surfaced in the Johnny Mack Brown westerns. . . . When his contract expired in 1943 he simply left the screen."[62] To this Tuska adds the pungent coda, "However embittered he may have been at the time, Roy Rogers was most fortunate that he lost out to Baker and was signed at Republic instead."[63] After a small role in *Wild Horse Stampede* (1943) with Ken Maynard and Hoot Gibson—both by then rather long in the tooth—Baker left the screen for good, apparently, in the words of film historian Gerald F. Vaughn, "disenchanted with show business."[64]

Also strange is Baker's failure to have ever recorded, even for Universal's labels which released a series of records by some of its screen vocalizers in the 1940s. To the best of anyone's knowledge there were no records cut by Bob Baker or Tumble Weed or any other pseudonym. Baker moved to Arizona after his final fling in films and became a policeman, saddle shop owner, and operator of a dude ranch among other things before his death of a heart attack in 1975.[65] Was his lack of success due to Universal's poor handling of his career, his lack of screen presence, or his inability to secure a recording contract? Whatever the reason or combination of reasons, Baker's failure to emerge as a performer of considerable dimensions is a major unanswered mystery in the curious history of the singing cowboy.

Jack Randall was yet another who met with less than smashing success in much the same way. Though his background was not terribly authentic for westerns, he was a singer of note, and began a series of some twenty-two westerns for Monogram with *Riders in the Dawn* late in 1937. Born Addison Randall on May 12, 1906, the son of West Coast Associated Press editor Edgar Randall in San Fernando, California, he was also the brother of non-singing cowboy star Bob Livingston, who encouraged brother Jack to enter films. Stepping from the vaudeville and Broadway stage to the sound stage in 1934, his first feature film was *His Family Tree* in 1935, and he played romantic leads in a number of RKO films over the next couple of years.

Monogram, like all companies at this time, realized that singing cowboys were saleable products, and apparently had high hopes that Jack Randall would rocket to the top. Once again, they assumed that a better singer was a better singing cowboy, which as previously noted, ignores both the audience and the appeal of country music. Fenin and Everson write that Randall "had a fine voice, superior to those of most of his rivals,[66] but the market was flooded with musical Westerns, and when Monogram presented Randall as one more singing cowboy, there were audible protests from exhibitor groups [and] as a result, songs were deleted from completed Randall Westerns and the bulk of the series made as normal action Westerns. This was a pity, for Randall could outsing most of the others, and had he been introduced a year earlier he might well have become one of the top singing cowboys."[67]

Jack Randall went to war in the early 1940s, and upon his return he began filming another western called *The Royal Mounted Rides Again*. While on location at Iverson's Ranch in Chatsworth, he was killed while filming a chase scene on horseback on July 16, 1945, just two months past his thirty-ninth birthday.[68]

Donald Grayson, a non-country crooner, was also in the process of being developed into a singing cowboy by Columbia, playing second lead and providing songs in several Charles Starrett westerns, beginning with *The Old Wyoming Trail* in 1937. His intrusion into the otherwise fine back-up work of the Sons of the Pioneers was doubtless due to the dislike of some Columbia executives of Bob Nolan's voice. Grayson did not last beyond a few films, and before long Nolan was acting as second lead, as well as singing his own songs at last.[69]

Surely the most bizarre entry into the singing cowboy field trekked west in 1937: Herb Jeffries, a deep-voiced ballad singer from Detroit who had sung with Earl Hines's orchestra in Chicago and recorded several Brunswick sides for them. In 1937, he moved to Los Angeles seeking bigger things than the Midwest had to offer, appearing as a singer and emcee at the Club Alabam. He was contacted by Jed Buell of the newly-formed Associated Features in the same year, and his first film was premiered at the Paramount Theater in Hollywood and at the Rialto Theater on Broadway in New York City, where it opened for its first run.

Just another singing cowboy story, except that Jeffries was black, and his first film, *Harlem on the Prairie*, was widely touted as "the first 'all-colored' western musical!"[70] The following year Jeffries ground out three more all-black singing cowboy films: *Bronze Buckaroo*, *Harlem Rides the Range*, and *Two-Gun Man from Harlem* for Hollywood Productions. Several of the films contained the musical group The Four Tones—one is tempted to think of a combination of the Sons of the Pioneers and the Ink Spots—composed of Lucius Brooks, bass, Ira Hardin, guitar and baritone, Rudolph Hunter, and Leon Buck, tenor. They also accompanied Jeffries on a promotional tour of the South in 1939 to promote his films.

Unfortunately, the standards for Jeffries's films were even shoddier than for the standard singing cowboy films:

The producers took their small units out to excellent locations, and then lacked the knowhow to follow through. . . . The plots were the standard western themes, with stock dialogue amplified and exaggerated until, unwittingly, it reached near-burlesque proportions. Interestingly enough, there was no inverted racism in these films. The stories took place in a totally black West; there were no whites in them at all, even as villains! Yet the prolonged and padded comedy relief invariably consisted of the kind of material (the comic pal scared of ghosts, the chicken-stealing cook, the crap-shooting, lazy roustabouts) which the Negroes understandably objected to in regular Hollywood films. Apart from the "personality" stars like Herb Jeffries, the acting level was low. . . . The musical element was not stressed, and Jeffries was really the only singing cowboy that this small group produced.[71]

After the southern tour with the Four Tones, Jeffries resumed his singing career, recording a good bit of material for Victor with Duke Ellington in 1940 and thereafter, and on his own on Columbia, Mercury, and other small labels.[72]

However, the big story of 1937 was the departure of Gene Autry from beneath the wings of the Republic eagle. As mentioned, there are conflicting stories for the walkout, but when it occurred in the fall of 1937 it was a major upheaval, probably the major upheaval in this history. Art Satherley recalls the events in this way:

Gene Autry had found himself a manager on the Coast here, after he'd been here a year or so, so Yates said to me, "Art, you'd better go and get your boy Autry and get him off his damned pony and kick that damn manager in the ass and get him out of here. He's signing up and now wants double the money per picture! And I'm not going to pay it."

So Gene, he called me and said, "I'm walking off the lot and Mr. Yates can go to hell," or something like that, and he sent me a four page telegram addressed to Art Satherley of American Records, which was owned by Yates, so it got to Yates and came down to me opened. And in there he wanted me to go down to the dock and find out how much it would cost to pack up all his show and take it to South America! And they figured about 150 animals all told, and all the trappings and everything for a boat to there. So I called Gene with the figures and said, "When do you want this done?" And he said, "Well, as soon as you possibly can!" But nevertheless I don't think he had quite that much money at the time, so I stalled it, you know, and I said, "Gene, think this over."

So I went out to the Coast, went to Gene's home, we played golf, and he said, "I'm not going to work for him anymore—why the hell should I? I want double the amount!" So I said, "Gene, so far as I know you're still from Sapulpa, Oklahoma. You're not that big yet to have to force up on a guy." I tried to break that thing, but I found that he was so tightly in that I called Yates after six weeks and I said, "Herb, this guy is so tightly up I can't do anything with him. He's going to stick by that guy win or lose."

So in the meantime this guy Seigel, Sol, was out on the lot working on these pictures and he said, "Well, get somebody else." So they had been employing the Sons of the Pioneers, and in the Sons of the Pioneers was Roy Rogers, so Roy Rogers was brought in to replace Gene Autry.

So here comes the funny one: Yates called me up and said, "Art, I want you to record Roy Rogers quick and get a nice bunch of numbers in by him. We're going to give it to this guy Autry." I said, "Herb, you're not going to give it to Autry so quick. Number one, I've heard Roy Rogers sing. He's as much country as you are, and you're not! . . . I'll tell you before I record him he's not going to sell." He said, "So you won't record him?" I said, "If it's your wish I'll record him. I'm still your vice-president."[73]

Tuska corroborates the same story from a different point of view.

Sol C. Seigel, associate producer for Westerns at Republic, was rather upset by the fact that Gene Autry, in his demands for more money, had walked off the job. Autry had telephoned Joe Kane, the director assigned to his pictures, and told him he had no intention of being on call to shoot his next film. Gene went on a personal appearance tour through the South, followed by process servers in an effort to restrain him from doing any work other than that specified by Republic. Before departing, Autry had completed *The Old Barn Dance* (Republic, 1938), released in January. He had $50,000 banked in Chicago and would not make any more pictures until his original Levine contract was renegotiated. Siegel button-holed Dick Weston, who had wandered again onto the Republic lot seeking work; he had a singing part in *The Old Barn Dance*. Weston was signed to a contract under the name Roy Rogers . . . [and] made *Under Western Stars* (Republic, 1938), which was the next picture scheduled for Autry, with support from Gene's side-kick, Smiley Burnette. Seeing the results, Republic President Herbert J. Yates capitulated and renegotiated with Autry.

"Gene was so popular below the Mason-Dixon line," Joe Kane recalled, "that people simply surrounded the process server and walked him out of town."

It took Yates three tries before he got Autry to agree to terms. When the 1938–39 season began in fall 1938, Autry was back in the saddle[74] for one of his best films, *Gold Mine in the Sky* (Republic, 1938), while Roy replaced the Johnny Mack Brown series with his first entry, *Billy the Kid Returns* (Republic, 1938).[75]

Autry's own account of these events is not dissimilar, and he cites the block-buying practices as the main cause of his walkout:

I hurried back to Hollywood and confronted Herb Yates. I wanted that practice stopped, and, while I was about it, a fairer share of the profits my pictures were producing. That was the wrong approach to take with Yates. But if there was a better one I didn't know it then, and I don't now. . . .

I had a new movie scheduled to start in two weeks, to be called *Washington Cowboy*. When I walked out of his office, we both knew I wouldn't be there when the cameras rolled. The trade papers made it sound like a range war. . . .

Of course, when I failed to show up for the first day's shooting on *Washington Cowboy*, the studio suspended me. Yates said he would make the film without me and create a new cowboy star. That was when they gave a screen test to Leonard Slye, who had appeared in a couple of my pictures as Dick Weston, and whose name was soon to be Roy Rogers. They changed the title of the movie to *Under Western Skies*.

Yates had threatened to break me—"if you won't work here you won't work anywhere." The studio took out an injunction to prevent me from appearing on stage until my contract had been fulfilled. We hit the road, through Arizona, New Mexico, and Texas, always one step ahead of the process server.

Back in Los Angeles, I was getting help from a powerful lobby. Republic's distributors were holding their annual convention and they climbed all over Herb Yates. It was going on six months since an Autry movie had been released. They made it sound not like a business problem, but a national famine. Many of them had gone along with the block buying, to the extent that they would buy a package of twenty, my eight plus twelve others, and ship back the ones they didn't want without using them. Now they demanded some assurance I would be working for Republic next year. Otherwise, they warned Yates, their theaters would be in trouble.

At that point, Yates called. While our attorneys got together and worked out a compromise, we went off to play golf. In a curious way, there were no hard feelings. All he had done was call me disloyal and threaten to ruin me. In return, I had called him a cheap skate and a tyrant. In those years, in Hollywood, no one took anyone else seriously. So we played golf.

My salary was raised to ten thousand dollars a film (escalating to fifteen and twenty over the next seven years), and the clauses I found objectionable were removed. The package deals continued; they were by then too entrenched to undo.[76]

Rogers himself has a different perspective on the situation, one which remains vivid in his memory:

Talk about being in the right place at the right time. I went out to Glendale—there's a little hat shop out there with an old fellow that cleaned hats. He used to be with Stetson Company. So I went out there to get my hat and there was a guy in the shop all excited. He was about 6'4"–6'6", a big tall guy and his name was Carter. I'd never seen him before, and I've never seen him since, but I got to talkin' to him, and he was goin' to have a screen test the next morning. I found out that it was Republic. He said "Yeah, they're looking for a new singing cowboy out there."

The next morning, I get up and I saddled up my guitar and went out to Republic Studios. I couldn't get in to see Sol Siegel, who was the producer of the pictures at that time. I didn't know how to make an appointment or anything, so I waited around 'till noon came and there was a bunch of extras goin' back to work, so I just walked in with them. And as I got through the door, a hand fell on my shoulder—I thought the security guard got me. And I turned around and it was Mr. Siegel, who knew me as one of the Sons of the Pioneers. And he said, "Roy, we've been testin' for a new cowboy. We tested 17 different guys, and we're lookin' for a musical singing cowboy to start a new series. And you never entered my mind until you walked through that door."

They liked the screen test, and they signed me October the 13th. I was there 14 years.[77]

As noted, Bob Allen was one of those "17 different guys"—as we must assume was the tall fellow named Carter—and apparently several other established stars were contacted. Johnny Bond reports Tex Ritter was approached but turned the deal down. His contract was with his producer Ed Finney, rather than with the company, Grand National, and Republic felt they had enough staff producers, wanting only Ritter and not Finney. Bond also reports in his book *The Tex Ritter Story* that "the man" from Republic was considering not only Slye/Weston/Rogers, but "a singer back east named Red Foley . . . but," he said, according to Bond, "we'd rather have Tex Ritter."[78] Red Foley's candidacy may seem surprising, but it too is corroborated by Arthur Satherley, who claims he himself approached Foley, who eagerly referred him to John Lair, then acting as Red's manager. Satherley recalls being rebuffed by Lair, who claimed:

"That would break up my outfit. Besides, I haven't any time to go to Hollywood!"[79]

Roy Rogers, born Leonard Franklin Slye on November 5, 1911, in Cincinnati, Ohio, grew up as a singer and mandolinist in a musical family near Duck Run, Ohio. The Slye family moved to California in 1930, and after a period of manual labor, Len decided to become a professional singer, Depression or no Depression. He became a featured vocalist with several prominent West Coast cowboy bands before forming in 1933 the original Pioneer Trio, the forerunners of the Sons of the Pioneers. Apparently it was he who was the sparkplug of the group, badgering, cajoling, and begging a reluctant Tim Spencer to leave the security of his job as a manager of a Safeway food store, and a truculent Bob Nolan to bring his considerable talents back into a music business he had already quit in disgust. The Pioneer Trio quickly became the Sons of the Pioneers with the addition of first Hugh, then Karl Farr. The Sons of the Pioneers made their film debut in *The Old Homestead* in 1935, and by 1937 were signed to a series of westerns with Charles Starrett at Columbia, although Len appeared in only the first few before pursuing freelance efforts. Tuska maintains that "there was some friction between Roy and Bob Nolan during this period."[80] But Ken Griffis, the Sons of the Pioneers' foremost biographer, makes no mention of it (he has, however, a way of characteristically glossing over intra-band friction); Ray Whitley, who managed the group at the time, states unequivocally that there was no such conflict.[81]

At any rate, it was Len Slye (Dick Weston/Roy Rogers) who was signed, with this revealing note appearing in the trade press in November of 1937:

ROGERS: GENE AUTRY'S WALKOUT WAS LUCKY BREAK FOR COWBOY SINGER

The row between Gene Autry, the western star, and Republic Pictures is following the familiar course of such feuds in Hollywood. Republic now has named a successor to Autry in Roy Rogers, a 25-year old radio singer who has worked in a couple of pictures. Exactly the same tactics that MGM used in the Freddie Bartholomew dispute. By the way, what has become of Rennie Sinclair since Freddie went back to work? . . .

Some of you movie-goers may wonder why all this bother about a western star. But there are 7500 theaters in the U.S. who play Hollywood "horse operas." Get a few miles out of a city and Autry and his competitors are big shots with the fans.[82]

With the release of Rogers's *Under Western Stars* in 1938, and Autry's return that fall (supported by Pee Wee King and his Golden West Cowboys in *Gold Mine in the Sky*), Republic had two singing cowboys. In one sense they were not competitive, for immediately upon his return, Autry once again got the big budgets, the best films, and the best songs, while Roy Rogers went about making solid films and surprising more than a few people with his genuine acting ability in secondary roles in major features such as *Dark Command* (1940), starring John Wayne. It was not until Autry entered the Army Air Corps in 1942 that Rogers got his real break into big budget films and adopted the inflated—but eventually accurate—title "King of the Cowboys." His career on film, on television, and on record continues to this day despite recent open-heart surgery.[83]

Though primarily a singer, not a cowboy, another singing cowboy to emerge in 1938 was George Houston. Born in 1898 in Hampton, New Jersey, Houston attended the Juilliard Institute of Music and after graduation joined the American Opera Company of New York City, where he had the privilege of presenting *Faust* before President Calvin Coolidge. He had a notable career on Broadway—appearing in *Shooting Star*, *New Moon*, *Thumbs Up*, and *Casanova* among others—before heading west to try films, his first major role coming in *The Melody Lingers On* (1934). Miller succinctly sums up his career:

An opera singer gradually working his way down the scale from a Nelson Eddy-type romantic lead to an adventurous action player in indies. . . . Houston was undoubtedly the best singer among the cowboys,[84] on the basis of pure vocalistics. But he was afflicted with the curse of most opera-type belters, stolidity.[85]

Like many, Houston was tapped for singing cowboy roles for the wrong reasons. After *Frontier Scout* in 1938, co-starring Dorothy Fay, Tex Ritter's bride to be, Houston began a series of Lone Rider singing westerns for Producers Releasing Corporation. Known commonly as PRC, the firm was the brainchild of several "poverty row" producers, and was on shaky financial ground from its inception. Beginning with *The Lone Rider Rides On* in 1941 and ending with *Outlaws of Boulder Pass* in 1942, George Houston made eleven singing cowboy films for the unstable corporation before both parties realized that opera singers do not make singing cowboys. Thoroughly discouraged, George gave up films and died a couple of years later (November 12, 1944) of a heart attack.[86]

A final entry into the singing cowboy sweepstakes of 1938 was Gene Austin, multimillion record seller of the 1920s, with hits like "How Come You Do Me Like You Do?" (1924), "When My Sugar Walks Down the Street" (1924), and, of course, "My Blue Heaven" (1927). "Cruel to contemplate," writes Don Miller, "but Austin could then no longer trade on his own name, but rather the shadow of Gene Autry, for success. . . . *Songs and Bullets* (Harry Fraser, 1938) was a haphazard indie that encouraged no followup and merited none."[87] It was Austin's only attempt at singing cowboy films, though he did record two sides of cowboy material late in his career for the Universal label (on which Dick Foran also cut a couple of sides): "I'm Coming Home" and "Give Me a Home in Oklahoma" (Universal 131). Born in Gainesville, Texas, on July 24, 1900, Gene Austin died in Palm Springs, California, January 24, 1972.[88]

Tex Ritter left Grand National in mid-1938, quickly, if inadvisedly, replaced by George Houston. Grand National was to go through several more singing cowboys and a singing cowgirl—always with the air of grasping at straws—in the ensuing years, bringing two more ill-fated songsters to the screen before the firm's demise. Repeating the miscalculation they had made with Houston, they signed on New York City-born Art Jarrett for a film called *Trigger Pals* in 1939. A big band vocalist, guitarist, and trombonist with Ted Weems who had recorded on his own for Columbia, Victor, and Brunswick, Jarrett had been in films since 1933, when he played opposite Joan Crawford in *Dancing Lady*. *Trigger Pals* was, for good reason, to be his only singing cowboy film.[89] He was replaced by a slightly more authentic country singer who recorded extensively for Decca in the 1930s and on smaller labels thereafter: Jerry Bisceglia, known as Tex Fletcher on record and radio. A left-handed guitar player, he might have had a future in films, but Grand National finally gave up the ghost in 1939, and Tex's *Six Gun Rhythm* was his only—and Grand National's last—singing cowboy film.

Grand National's final efforts may have had an air of desperation, but they proved to be ahead of their time, regardless. In 1938 they cast Dorothy Page as a singing cowgirl in a short-lived series of three westerns—*Ride 'Em Cowgirl*, *The Singing Cowgirl*, and *Water Rustlers*—all of which appeared in 1939. Ms. Page, who had worked her way up from inspired features like *Manhattan Moon*, *King Solomon of Broadway*, and *Mama Runs Wild* in the middle 1930s, was a talented woman who rode, roped, shot, and sang with skill and enthusiasm, but even the force of her personality and the unique premise on which her westerns were built could not overcome the ill effects of a moribund studio. *Variety* reported, "*Water Rustlers* is a western cheapie whose only redeeming feature is Dorothy Page."[90]

Wonder Woman and equal rights aside, the world was apparently not yet ready for an action heroine, and Grand National's bold and visionary step—or desperate last gasp—began no trend, and the concept of the singing movie cowgirl faded into the realm of the obscure. Ms. Page, despite her avant-garde role thirty years ahead of its time, apparently did not return to the screen.[91]

It was also around this time that Bob Nolan began to have bigger and bigger parts in the Charles Starrett westerns. A handsome strapping man whose voice was not pretty but was unique, he seems to have been a natural for leading parts, an observation which has not escaped leading film historians. "[In *Two Fisted Rangers*] Bob Nolan had a speaking role in tune with his abilities. (Nolan was a sure bet to star in his own series, but somebody missed the boat.)"[92] "The most surprising aspect of the film [*The Durango Kid*], in retrospect is, given Bob Nolan's physical resemblance to George O'Brien, why no one ever attempted to capitalize on it and build him into a star in his own right, which had long been Nolan's ambition. Starrett, for his own part, never begrudged Nolan the opportunity, itself rather an unusual posture among Western players."[93]

Whether starring parts had been his ambition is a question still unanswered in the infrequent interviews conducted with the retiring Nolan. Ray Whitley states flatly, "Bob was always reluctant to take any kind of leading role. Aside from his humility, I think he had reservations about his ability to act."[94] Regardless, with the completion of *Outlaws of the Panhandle* with Charles Starrett in 1941, the Sons of the Pioneers' contract with Columbia expired, and they were persuaded to make a fine series of films with Roy Rogers at Republic, beginning with *Red River Valley* in 1941. Nolan's personal roles were reduced, though the Sons of the Pioneers were featured as a group, and his candidacy for singing cowboy stardom slipped into the realm of what might have been.[95]

In 1940 Bob Wills made his first western film. Surely the most popular country bandleader of the era, Wills was cresting with the overwhelming success of "San Antonio Rose." Efforts had been made to get him into films before, but Wills finally accepted an offer from Monogram to provide musical support for Tex Ritter in *Take Me Back to Oklahoma*. Though he was forced to use an uncharacteristically small band, response was good, and Columbia signed him for *Go West Young Lady* in 1941. This led to an eight-film deal with Columbia the following year; the Texas Playboys provided musical support for Russell Hayden, with Bob himself doing a stiff but creditable job as second lead in most of these films. Except for a few shorts, however, this was the extent of Bob Wills's career as a singing cowboy.[96]

Also in 1940, a cowpoke named Dusty King rode into the Range Buster trio—trios were becoming extremely popular at this point in the western film cycle. Born Miller McCloud Everson in Cincinnati on July 11, 1909, King had apprenticed as a big band singer and announcer over WCKY and WKRC in his hometown before breaking into movies—as John King—with romantic leads in *Ace Drummond* (1936), *Charlie Chan in Honolulu*, and many others. King drifted out of films after the Range Busters series ground to a halt in 1943, and went back to singing in a style more befitting his big band training. He currently owns a waffle shop in southern California.[97]

A new crop of hopefuls thundered on screen in 1941, though none were destined for major careers. At last, Red Foley made his debut, singing and playing guitar in support of Tex Ritter in Monogram's *The Pioneers*, released May 10, 1941. Although he would continue to appear in films from time to time, and even have both dramatic and musical television series in years to come, the times were apparently not as ripe for him as they had been in the autumn of 1937, and Red Foley never attained singing cowboy stardom.[98] Yet another full-fledged country singer, Ernest Tubb, made his first film in 1941: *Fightin' Buckaroo*, in support of Charles Starrett. He followed this with *Ridin' West* in 1942, and *Jamboree* in 1943. Tubb was self-conscious and uncomfortable looking before the cameras, and did not pursue a film career after joining the Grand Ole Opry in January 1943. A 1947 musical extravaganza called *Hollywood Barn Dance* was his last Hollywood film; his stage and recording career, for which he was better suited, occupy his energies to this day.[99]

Tubb was not the only one to support Charles Starrett once the Sons of the Pioneers left his films. An obscure singer named Tex Harding played in eight Durango Kid westerns with Starrett in 1945,[100] before being replaced by an ex-vaudevillian named Cliff Edwards (1895–1971). Edwards, commonly known as Ukulele Ike, played the role of Harmony in several Starrett westerns before heading over to RKO and similar roles with Tim Holt. He is best remembered as the voice of Jiminy Cricket in Wait Disney's *Pinnochio*, and made a lasting impression on the national consciousness with his breathy tenor rendition of "When You Wish Upon a Star."[101] Jimmie Davis, a major record seller of the era—"Beautiful Texas" (1934), "Nobody's Darling But Mine" (1935), "It Makes No Difference Now" (1939), "You Are My Sunshine" and "Too Late" (1940), "A Worried Mind" (1941), and "Sweethearts or Strangers" (1941)—and soon to be Governor of Louisiana was another who got a couple of shots as a vocalist in Starrett's westerns. Though his term as Governor interrupted his musical and film career, he was later to star in the story of his own life, *Louisiana*, in 1947.[102]

Western swing fiddler Art Davis, a former member of Bill Boyd's Cowboy Ramblers and Gene Autry's band, also appeared on screen in singing roles. "Everybody said the same thing about Davis," writes Don Miller, "if he'd lose some weight, he'd make a promising Western lead." [103] Davis sang in Tim McCoy's last PRC feature that year, *The Texas Marshall*. He also played a singer in a film about a masked good guy, in which he sang a few songs and rode around with a special guitar-shaped saddlebag fitted for his instrument. Billed in the latter as Larry Mason, he looked trim and fit, though he did grow to unstylishly stout proportions in his later years as a western swing bandleader.

Davis, a native Texan, had fiddled with Bill Boyd's Cowboy Ramblers as far back as their hit Bluebird record of 1934, "Under the Double Eagle." He was reunited with Boyd, his former employer, and actor Lee Powell (who was later killed in World War II) in a series of six PRC cheapies known as the Frontier Marshalls series. All six, beginning with *Texas Manhunt* and ending with *Along the Sundown Trail*, were released in 1942. Art Davis made no more westerns of consequence, nor did Boyd, who returned to Dallas to resume his extremely successful radio, record, and stage career. Born in Fannin County, Texas, April 29, 1910, Bill Boyd recorded for RCA and Bluebird from 1934–1950; he died in December of 1977 in Fort Worth. His main legacy to the western film was adding to the already considerable confusion between William "Stage" Boyd and William "Hopalong Cassidy" Boyd. None of the three were related.[104]

Such trio pictures were becoming popular at the time, in imitation of the Three Mesquiteer series dating from 1936, which featured John Wayne among its many players through the years. One member of such trios was often a singer (sometimes two, in the case of Boyd, Davis, and Powell): Bob Baker, as we have seen, ended up his career this way, and Tex Ritter was featured in more than a few. Comedians Max Terhune and Rufe Davis had both portrayed Lullaby Joslin as one of the Three Mesquiteers; in 1942 a youthful Jimmy Dodd took over the role for a few pictures, beginning with *Shadows on the Sage*.[105] He is far better remembered as the bubbly emcee of television's *Mickey Mouse Club*.[106] Also entering the sweepstakes in 1942 was James Newill, a baritone profundo in the George Houston school of operatic cowboys, with *The Rangers Ride On* in the Texas Rangers series. A singing Mountie (shades of Nelson Eddy) as far back as 1937,[107] with the successful *Renfrew of the Royal Mounted* and subsequent Renfrew adventures, Newill lasted but two years with the Texas Rangers, replaced by Tex Ritter, who was more suitable for the role.[108]

The big news of 1942 was not, however, this crop of newcomers, but the war which had a drastic effect on all American life. Singing cowboys were no less affected, least of all Gene Autry, who enlisted in the Air Force during a "Melody Ranch" broadcast in 1942, and was gone for four years from the screen, four years in which a whole new crew of hopefuls tried to fill his boots, years in which he and his audience changed drastically.

THE WAR YEARS AND AFTER: 1942–1945

▌When he left, Gene Autry was still unquestionably at the top of the heap.[109] Tex Ritter and Roy Rogers had their following, Bob Baker was fading fast, and the operatic types were never even in the same ball park. Autry's last pre-war film was released in September 1942, though several of his earlier films were re-released during his absence; Roy Rogers's films were immediately upgraded with the December release of *Heart of the Golden West,* and over the course of the next four years, he overtook Autry while his mentor was flying supply planes in the Far East.

It is more a matter of taste than anything else, but despite his high budget westerns, his pleasant voice and great yodeling, his acting ability, and the benefit of the Sons of the Pioneers, Rogers's pictures were not as successful as Autry's had been and would be. One reason was the unbearable gaudiness of his clothing, what Don Miller calls the "era of the shreiking Rogers costumery," [110] stretching the willing suspension of disbelief to the breaking point. Roy told Jon Tuska that the heavy indulgence in costumes and production numbers in his wartime movies was a result of a directive from Yates himself: "Mr. Yates had gone to New York and seen the stage show Oklahoma. He came back to the studio and put out a memo that from then on my films were to be made in the mold of *Oklahoma*. He wanted musicals more than westerns from me." [111]

More a problem than this, however, was Rogers's basic inability to put over a country song. Gene Autry and Tex Ritter's huge record selling successes amount to more than a combination of good songs and good productions: both were country singers who took some pains to remain so. Even with a huge orchestra, Autry featured Johnny Bond's guitar runs, Frankie Marvin's distinctive steel guitar, and his own comfortable, relaxed voice. Roy Rogers with Country Washburn's Orchestra was just another good singer walking through a country or countryish tune. It is little wonder that his most successful record, "Blue Shadows on the Trail," featured the Sons of the Pioneers so heavily that it is virtually their performance.

Although it is hard to agree totally with Jon Tuska's Autry Fantasy as the explanation of Autry's success, it is the most lucid and creditable and thoughtful explanation by a film historian to date, and does cast considerable light on the fundamental differences between Gene Autry and Roy Rogers:

Ultimately, because there was no underlying fantasy about Roy's person, as there was about Gene Autry, he remained merely a wholesome, likeable man who sang and performed and had great camaraderie with the Pioneers and who, invariably, embodied the impulse to make beautiful westerns which later filmmakers strove so earnestly to contradict. [112]

In the meantime, Gene Autry changed drastically, turning toward a dedication to the financial. He told Tuska, "I don't think I ever appreciated money until I had been in the service. I learned what it was like to work for almost nothing, and I didn't like it." His current press release tells the same story: "In 1941 I made $600,000 with pictures, radio, records and personal appearances. Suddenly, I found myself in uniform at $115 to $125 a month as a tech sergeant. It started me thinking. If it hadn't been for royalties from things such as sweatshirts, pistols, boots and hats and records, I would have been in a mess. I knew I could make good money as long as I could work. But suppose I was incapacitated? Where would I get my income? I decided I better start investing in some business."[113]

Autry elaborates, with a folksy homily:

I was reminded once by Johnny Bond, who toured and worked with us on radio, of a tradition of the Old West. Whenever a lone cowboy or Indian needed to take a long journey by horseback, it was customary for him to ride one saddled horse while leading another bareback. When his mount began to tire, instead of stopping for a rest, he merely slipped the saddle onto the spare horse and rode on. In just about that way I eased out of my life as a performer and began to devote my full energy to business. I just changed horses.

I had discovered during the war how quickly your security can be threatened by conditions beyond your control. It was a jolt to the nervous system to find myself staring at an Air Force salary of less than two thousand dollars a year, after earning up to ten thousand dollars a week. I thought to myself, well, as long as I can work I know I can make money. But what if something happened to my health? Or my voice went haywire. Times change, too. If you don't part your hair right, they, the public, will find someone who does. I knew the time had come to start looking for an interest that did not depend on my being able to perform.[114]

Because the acquisition of wealth became Autry's principal occupation after his return from war, plus the press's attention to that subject alone, Gene Autry's genuine contributions to country music have been unfairly ignored and overlooked. This is true also of his role in the history of the American film. A typical comment, largely truthful though obviously condescending and unsympathetic, is Fenin and Everson's:

Autry actually was just a shrewd businessman who had no great interest in or respect for the Western as such. He realized that his value as a show business personality (taking in also radio, rodeos, and ultimately television and his own production companies) depended on his almost comic-opera approach to the Western. He also had the happy knack of being able to hide his shrewdness behind the amiable facade of the hillbilly singer; he was both a popular idol of the people, in the manner, if nothing else, of Will Rogers, and at the same time a highly successful businessman.[115]

As stated, there is truth here, hidden among loaded words like "just a shrewd businessman," "happy knack," and "amiable façade." There is no question that Gene Autry returned from World War II a profoundly changed man; he realized he was a commodity to be merchandised to its fullest extent, and doubtless it is at this point that money became his primary concern. However, that this should in no way obscure his genuine contributions is so obvious as to hardly be worth committing to paper, except that the opposite approach has for years been so prevalent. For the moment, suffice it to say that Tuska's axiom "the acquisition of wealth itself has concerned Autry primarily in his career"[116] holds true, especially for the post-World War II phase. Whatever drove and spurred him in his rise to success in the entertainment world before the war—and this is difficult to ascertain—it is certain that with a combination of shrewdness and luck, he pursued the goal of becoming a millionaire with intensity and zeal. Wealth has preoccupied Autry, and the story of his successful pursuit of it has overshadowed his very real contributions to country music and to American entertainment.

At any rate, during his absence the pace of the world of the singing cowboy began to accelerate rapidly, not only for Roy Rogers but for a fresh new crop of hopefuls, singers, in general, who were far more authentic country singers than the George Houstons and Bob Allens and James Newills of the recent past. The singing cowboy genre was by now nearly a decade old, and perhaps by that time the film colony had come to a glimmering of understanding that it was not the operatic projection of the singer's voice that attracted the customers, but the basic virtue of the country singer: believability.

First among the new breed was Jimmy Wakely, often unfairly accused of being an Autry imitator; the main similarity was that both were primarily country singers, and while they were able to hold their own in the action sequences, they were basically vocalists.

James Clarence Wakely was born in Mineola, Arkansas, on February 16, 1914, and raised in eastern Oklahoma. By 1937 Wakely, Johnny Bond,[117] and Dick Rhinehart had formed a western trio based on the Sons of the Pioneers called the Bell Boys, named for Bell Clothing, their sponsor in Oklahoma City.

They blithely headed west in 1940, arriving in Hollywood on June 4, and by November of that year all had recording contracts—Wakely with Decca, Bond and Rhinehart with Columbia. In addition, they had become regulars on "Melody Ranch," and had appeared in their first film, *Saga of Death Valley*, with Roy Rogers.

Wakely left "Melody Ranch" after two years—replaced by Eddie Dean—as his film roles as a singer in Hopalong Cassidy and Charles Starrett movies began to grow. Due to the success of his records—"Too Late," a major hit in 1942, foremost among them—he began his own starring series for Monogram in 1944 with *Song of the Range*. After twenty-eight films for them, *Saddle Serenade* and *Song of the Sierras* among them, Wakely closed out with *Lawless Code* in 1949. He made but one more film, writing the score and playing a singing "buddy" to Sterling Hayden in a big budget A western made in 1954 called *Arrow in the Dust*.

Wakely remarks, "I'm so glad that I was a singer, because if I hadn't been I'd have gone down the tubes."[118] Indeed, by 1949 his singing had become so popular he scarcely had the time or need for films. His Capitol records "I Love You So Much It Hurts Me" and "One Has My Name (The Other Has My Heart)" had been major successes in 1948, and in 1949–50 his duet with Margaret Whiting, "Slipping Around," sold well over a million copies. A whole series of successful Wakely-Whiting duets followed including their Christmas classic "Silver Bells" (1950). Jimmy Wakely has pursued an active musical career ever since, recording for Capitol, Decca, Coral, and his own label, Shasta, and playing the nightclub circuit in Nevada and southern California. More recently he has begun re-releasing many of his older performances on Shasta along with those of Tex Ritter, Merle Travis, Eddie Dean, and others, and has guided the firm into a thriving mail-order concern. Perhaps more than any other singing cowboy, his film career served not as an end in itself, but as a promotional vehicle furthering his career as a successful country singer on radio (he had his own CBS network show for some years), records, and in person. Today he is an active, outspoken, and extremely busy devotee of country music, an individual totally dedicated to the singing cowboy and the preservation of its legacy.[119]

Wakely's dedication is admirable, though at times a bit self-serving, as was Tex Ritter's. There is no question of economic need or ego satisfaction, simply love of a form they themselves helped create, a form with black ink on the bottom line. Perhaps because he was first and foremost a country singer (albeit with a decided pop tinge), Wakely still has much love for the music outside of the trappings of success that tend to overwhelm residents of Hollywood and its environs.

Another singer of similar background was Eddie Dean, born Edgar Dean Glosup in Posey, Texas, on July 9, 1907. Though he has had a long and honorable career as a country singer, Dean has long (and rather unfairly) been scorned by film critics; he has been called "perhaps the most inept western hero of them all,"[120] "not a particularly good actor nor even average in the saddle,"[121] "a poor actor with an unattractive face and singularly inept at action."[122] Miller states that "while Dean could sing, his attributes as a two-fisted strong-willed cowboy hero were dubious. He went through the motions professionally, but there was the look of the bumpkin about him, and that drawback was difficult to overcome."[123] "[His] pictures were even cheaper and more singularly horrible than the Buster Crabbe . . . Westerns of 1940–45 that they replaced,"[124] claims Jon Tuska.

Dean was certainly not the greatest thespian to ever hit the screen; however, on the whole, this kind of poison-penned criticism does considerable injustice to a fine singer and a good singing cowboy. That he has survived with such grace after this stinging round of abuse seems to be in itself a credit to the man.

After an early career as a gospel singer, Eddie Dean moved to Chicago in 1926, intent on pursuing a career. After appearing on stations in Shenandoah, Iowa, and Yankton, South Dakota, he and his older brother Jimmy Dean[125] joined the cast of the National Barn Dance[126] from 1933 through 1936. In 1936 he was chosen for the part of Larry Burton in the radio soap opera "Modern Cinderella," and acted and sang in that series until 1937, when he flipped a coin, heading to Hollywood or New York depending on how it landed. It came up heads, and Dean blew into Hollywood, where he quickly began to land small roles in support of other heroes. In 1942 he and his brother replaced Jimmy Wakely and Johnny Bond as Autry's backup vocal group, as Wakely left to pursue his own career and Bond was upgraded to sidekick. Dean stayed two years before going to a featured spot on Judy Canova's network radio show.

A prolific songwriter, he has at least two country classics ["One Has My Name (The Other Has My Heart)" and "I Dreamed of a Hillbilly Heaven"] and one western classic ("On the Banks of the Sunny San Juan") to his credit, and over the years has recorded a remarkable amount of material for Decca, Capitol, Majestic, Mercury, Crystal, Sage and San, ARC, and Shasta. As for his entry into starring roles, he ascribes it largely to luck:

I met Pete Canova, and by meeting Mr. Bill Crespinell, who had the color [process of his own invention], who'd made all the tests for the color in my back yard. He said to me, "Eddie, why don't you do a series with my color? . . . We have a good color process."

Well, what they had to do, they had to run two films through at the same time . . . so you had one a sort of grey-blue and the other a sort of orange. And through that process they got this beautiful color, called it Cinecolor. So I went to work on it, and I told Pete Canova, and we went to Monogram, and Monogram turned us down. And then we went out to PRC, and PRC took their series. 'Course Monogram tried to buy my contract right after, but I was already on my way. And I think what happened, I got started a little late . . . well, I know I did, as far as what you call the picture cowboy, 'cause I only had three years. But I made the top ten moneymakers their first year! For the three years I was in the top ten moneymakers. That was '46, '47, and '48.[127]

Dean starred in twenty features for PRC and the equally unstable Eagle-Lion firm that rose phoenix-like from the ashes of PRC, although only the first few were in Cinecolor, an attractive, subdued color system which never threatened the Technicolor system because of its complexity.

Today Eddie Dean continues to pursue his singing career; he even managed to obtain Colonel Tom Parker as a personal manager for a time. Parker dressed him up in gold lamé and called him "The Golden Cowboy," presaging Elvis's similar costume by some years. Though now in his early seventies, Eddie Dean's voice is still booming, and he frequently plays engagements in southern California.[128]

Next of the new breed to arrive was Ken Curtis, who had been born Curtis Wayne Gates in Lamar, Colorado, on July 2, 1916. Though he came from a pure country background—his father a fiddler, his brother a banjo player—Curtis developed a smooth, rich voice that so well adapted itself to pop music that he spent some time with Shep Field's Orchestra and replaced Frank Sinatra in Tommy Dorsey's Orchestra, recording "Love Sends a Little Gift of Roses" and "Anniversary Waltz" with them. After a stretch in the service (1942–1945) he returned to Hollywood, and having sung "Tumbling Tumbleweeds" as a guest on Jo Stafford's radio show, he was signed by Columbia Pictures, who were in the process of reactivating their singing cowboy series.

Often supported by Andy Parker and the Plainsmen (and sometimes even the Hoosier Hot Shots), Curtis made twelve films in two years, beginning with *Song of the Prairie* in 1945. Likewise, in 1945, Gene Autry returned from the Army Air Corps. Tuska describes the situation at Republic:

Yates had been preparing himself for this moment and felt well armed . . . with Duke Wayne and now Bill Elliott, he was marching forward into the ranks of the majors. He was able to control Roy Rogers. Gene's first picture after his discharge was *Sioux City Sue* . . . released in November [1946] and produced on a modest budget. . . . Gene's contract was again coming up for renewal, and he had best not be unreasonable in his demands.[129]

However, as we have seen, Gene's focus had drastically changed during his stint as a soldier, and upon his return he opened secret negotiations with Columbia Pictures.

Autry made four Westerns for Republic that were released in 1947. . . . Autry felt that as a Western property he was worth more than any player on the screen. He refused to put up with Yates's attempt to humble him and negotiated himself an excellent package with Columbia. He also signed a lucrative radio contract and was able to quickly regain his preeminence in the field. Of all people, Yates understood the least, apparently, about the magic of the Autry Fantasy.[130]

Autry, with blandness so typical of his public statements, says: "There had been quite a break at that time because—well, my contract was out, and I wanted to have control over my own pictures. By that time Republic had Roy over there, and I just didn't feel that there was enough room for one company to really promote two of the same type. I made five pictures at Republic, and then went over to Columbia to set our own corporation up."[131]

He adds, becoming a bit more specific in *Back in the Saddle Again:*

By the time *Robin Hood of Texas* had reached the movie houses, I had parted ways with Republic. The courts had upheld my suit and I was now free to make my own deals, and pick my own friends. We had offers from several studios. But I wanted to form my own company, frankly, because of the tax angles. If you earned over $100,000 in those days, 85 per cent of it was taxable. The only way to hang on to your money was to form a corporation. So I became the president and executive producer of Gene Autry Productions, and we signed a contract with Columbia to release our pictures. It was as good a deal as anyone in Hollywood had at that time. I had complete say over my films and I could take home half the profits.[132]

Autry's defection to Columbia affected a great many people, among them, of course, Ken Curtis. It was obvious that if Republic, in Autry's view, could not adequately support two singing cowboys, then neither could Columbia. After his 1947 series, therefore, Ken was cast adrift. Although he was to make a couple of independents as a singing cowboy hero, his next step was to join the Sons of the Pioneers, with whom he remained from 1949 to 1953, his lovely voice highlighted on such Victor recordings as "I Still Do" and "Room Full of Roses." Curtis settled in the Los Angeles area, working as an actor and a singer, and recording western material through the years for Mercury, MGM, Capitol, and Dot. For a time, he even had his own television series, *Ripcord,* and came up with a grizzled hillbilly character called Monk in the *Have Gun, Will Travel* series. Ultimately, he brought this character to *Gunsmoke,* where he spent well over a decade portraying Matt Dillon's faithful deputy, Festus. So pervasive has this characterization been that few remember, or can even conceive of, Ken Curtis as a fine pop and western singer or a handsome western movie hero. Yet he was one of the finest.[133]

Monte Hale was another person profoundly affected by Gene Autry's move to Columbia. Born June 8, 1921, in San Angelo, Texas, Hale became a professional singer at the age of twelve. In the early 1940s, he was discovered singing on a USO tour and brought to Hollywood. His first film roles came in 1944 in such productions as *Stepping In Society* and *Big Bonanza.* When Yates moved Roy Rogers into A budget westerns with *My Pal Trigger* in 1946, Monte was promoted from supporting roles in the

Sunset Carson series to his own musical series with *Home on the Range* (1946) and *Out California Way* (1946), where he was usually supported by Foy Willing and the Riders of the Purple Sage. The purpose of this move on Yates's part was not only to fill the void left by Autry's departure and Rogers's move into A westerns, but also to provide the same kind of insurance against Rogers's demands at contract time that Rogers himself had provided against Autry years earlier.

Enough was thought of Hale that eight of his nineteen films were shot in color. After his series ended in 1949, he returned to singing, though his country records on MGM and other smaller labels were not particularly successful financially or artistically. He appeared in only two more films, *Giant* (1956) and *Guns of a Stranger* (1973). A genial man, he is popular on the western film festival circuit held around the country, as are fellow singing cowboys Eddie Dean and Ray Whitley.[134]

An amusing entry into the singing cowboy race in 1945 was Johnny Mack Brown, who had ridden many a trail with Bob Baker, Tex Ritter, Jimmy Wakely, and other singers in the past. An action cowboy from start to finish, Brown looked uncomfortable as a singer (with a dubbed-in voice) in *Drifting Along* (1946), an experiment that was never repeated.[135]

THE FINAL DAYS

■ Time was running out on the singing cowboy, however, as World War II had drastically changed America, physically as well as spiritually. Romantic, dreamy, clearly fantastic films about the old West that never was, or a new West with old West trappings, whether featuring singers or not, were no longer attractive to a public that had experienced five years of real injury and death, and was beginning to cower under the spectre of atomic attack. Then, too, the impact of television was sudden and dramatic, staggering the film industry in general, and virtually eliminating the need for new low budget westerns. In fact, this was especially true since so many of the older westerns were being edited and shown on the small screen.

Though in its waning days, the singing cowboy film showed a bit more life, however, before it finally cashed in its chips. Striving for that special something to catch the fancy of the public, it came up with some unusual solutions. For example, radio singer and modern-day balladeer Red River Dave began a series for Universal in 1948. Miller says he "warbled well but was painfully camera shy," and that the series was, of all things, "filmed on the plains of upper New York state."[136] Red River Dave—born David McEnery in San Antonio, Texas, on December 15, 1914—had appeared in singing roles in *Swing in the Saddle* (1948) with Jimmy Wakely, and returned to his native Texas and elsewhere, after *Hidden Valley Days* and *Echo Ranch* wound up his film career.[137] He was joined in films that year by another country singer, and a more popular one at that, named Elton Britt, who made the first of his three westerns, *Laramie*, in 1948. Britt then returned to the singing and yodeling which had justly made him famous.

The story was virtually unchanged in 1949: popular country singers stuffed uncomfortably into cheap singing cowboy westerns, probably with the hope of attracting country music fans to the theaters in the ever-loyal southern market. However, television was making its inroads into the South as well, and ultimately this latest move on the part of the film industry was a lost cause. Universal moved their Red River Dave series west in 1949 replacing Dave with vocalist-band leader Tex Williams, who made a series of fifteen musical shorts known as "Tales of the West." They were then spliced into four musical, though somewhat incoherent, feature films capitalizing on his recent 1947 hit "Smoke! Smoke! Smoke!" After years of providing musical support for many westerns, western swing band leader Spade Cooley—who had begun his film career as an Indian in one of those little Ray Whitley shorts for RKO, *Redskins and Redheads*—at last took a shot at starring roles in *The Silver Bandit* in 1949 and *Border Outlaws* in 1950. Although Cooley was the snappiest of dressers and a charismatic musician and bandleader, his films left little mark on the genre. At the same time Eddy Arnold made a couple of what might loosely be called westerns, though they were actually more in the "Southeastern" mold, similar to Roy Acuff's Republic features. Arnold was hot as a firecracker with staggering record sales, a fine singer and a handsome man, and his films were produced by a major studio, Columbia. For whatever combination of reasons, however—the lateness of the hour more than likely—no one ever tried to develop him further as a singing cowboy, and *Feudin' Rhythm* (1949) and *Hoedown* (1950) sum up his career in western musicals.

In 1949 Monte Hale's contract was allowed to run out, and he was replaced by the last of the singing cowboys—Rex Allen. Yet another alumnus of the National Barn Dance, Allen had been a rodeo star born in Willcox, Arizona, on December 31, 1924, and had gotten his first radio work at WTTM in Trenton, New Jersey, in 1944. He worked from 1945–1949 in Chicago at the National Barn Dance and recorded for Mercury before heading west, where he ultimately would appear in some thirty-two western films, nineteen of them as star, beginning with *The Arizona Cowboy* in 1950.

Rex Allen was likeable, believable, a powerful singer, and a good actor; but he was also too late. Dwindling budgets had been cut further and further, nowhere more evident than in poor Rex's films: "Key action footage was repeated endlessly, and even songs were doctored—even by just one word—so that an 'old' Roy Rogers song like 'Roll on Texas Moon' would re-emerge as a 'new' Rex Allen song, 'Roll on Border Moon.' "[138]

Allen went from B westerns into a television series called *Frontier Doctor*, and pursued his singing career, with "Crying in the Chapel" becoming his biggest hit in 1953. He has also had a unique career as narrator in a great number of Walt Disney films and television programs.[139]

Thus, the cycle of singing cowboy westerns ground to a sad halt, outmoded by changing American tastes and the advent of an exciting new medium of entertainment. Tex Ritter had made his last film in 1945, Eddie Dean in 1948, Jimmy Wakely in 1949. Roy Rogers's finale—except for a couple of guest appearances—came with *Pals of the Golden West* in 1951, while Gene Autry bowed out, appropriately enough, with *Last of the Pony Riders* in 1953. Rex Allen brought the whole thing to a close in 1954 with *The Phantom Stallion*, just a few months before Wayne Morris made his last film, *Two Guns and a Badge*, not a singing western but still the last B western film. Since *Two Guns and a Badge*, western films have been produced sporadically by independent producers operating on big budgets.

As Autry himself says, with some poignancy:

There were no farewell toasts, no retirement dinner with someone handing out a pocket watch for twenty years of faithful service. Actually, nineteen years, between the release in November of 1934 of [*In*] *Old Santa Fe,* when I made my first appearance with Ken Maynard, for Mascot, until Columbia released my last [*Last of the Pony Riders*] in November of 1953. It just kind of slipped up on us. I don't recall ever saying that I had quit, or that I would never make another motion picture.[140]

The genre seems a natural to have moved to television, which in a way it did, although the musical content was the first thing to go. Gene Autry, in fact, was so discerning about the future of television that he began his own half-hour series in 1951, ending it in 1954 after eighty-five programs. Having formed Flying A Productions out of many of his most capable and favorite people associated with his film productions, he provided early television with a host of western shows: *Annie Oakley, The Range Riders, Buffalo Bill, Jr.,* even a series for his horse, Champion, which luckily lasted but half a season. In the Gene Autry episodes, with Pat Buttram as his sidekick, action was stressed and usually just one song featured.

Roy Rogers likewise became a staple on early television, filming one-hundred episodes between 1952 and 1957. Here the emphasis on music was even less, and most of the attention given to gimmicks like a smart dog and Pat Brady's jeep, Nellybelle. Republic's entry into television was Rex Allen's *Frontier Doctor*. Heavy on stock footage from Republic's files, it was also light on music. The others, like *The Cisco Kid*, *The Lone Ranger*, and *Hopalong Cassidy*, were not musical.

The passing of the B western and the singing cowboy coincides neatly with the coming of rock, the music which made instant anachronisms of a wide number and variety of styles, sounds, singers, and musicians. It can hardly be blamed for the fall of the singing cowboy, of course; the genre had been in a state of gradual decay for nearly a decade, despite the fact that many fine new talents—among them some good country singers—appeared in its waning years. In fact, because of this new crop of country singers, the singing cowboy films probably were given a few years of added life. At last, the studios had figured out that the public wanted to see pleasant cowboy singers, not operatic baritones. Of course, there were no Hank Williams or Roy Acuffs; however, Eddie Dean, Jimmy Wakely, Ken Curtis, Monte Hale and Rex Allen all had good credentials as soft country singers, and made credible singing cowboys.

Rock and the Southeastern sound revival (in the form of Hank Williams, Kitty Wells, Webb Pierce, Carl Smith and the like) did not kill off the singing cowboy; that was already done. Worse, they tarnished its image. The raw energy of rock and the hard-hitting, gut-level realism of early 1950s country music made the dreamlike world of the singing cowboy look foolish. Consequently, the music went into such a decline that few scholars or even popular writers and historians mention it much in overviews of country music history, except to remark on the indignity of grown men wearing those funny clothes, of six-shooters which never needed reloading, or of orchestras swelling from behind cacti and rock formations. The growth of the folk movement at the end of the 1950s and the early 1960s beat the dead horse with a vengeance: nothing seemed more antithetical to their notion of valuable music than made-in-Hollywood, western music sung by guys in gaudy suits, playing $1,000 guitars on top of $5,000 saddles.

The singing cowboy represents in its most innocent manifestation an American dream, albeit a dream which has far more to do with self-image than reality. It has come to a devaluation in recent years, as America turned away first from dreams, then from heroes. It is a dream which did not sour, but staled, no longer new nor suited to its times. Yet it is a powerful dream, one in which we have all shared, for it is the nature of mankind to set his mind free to dream such dreams. The singing cowboy in his prime gave us some of those dreams, those flights of fancy, and gave us much fine music to boot, despite the inherent artificiality of the on-screen situation. The singing cowboy gave much to country music in style, repertoire, and gifted singers, musicians, and writers, and in dignity and glamour in a time when country music was seen by outsiders and critics as possessing neither.

The singing cowboy and his version of the American dream speaks strongly of its era; Autry was in the forefront of his contemporaries in turning from the escapist mentality of the Depression-haunted thirties to the financial growth of the aggressive, victorious, booming late 1940s and 1950s; he simply turned his attentions from one reality to another, as he had so adroitly shifted musical styles early in his career when it was to his advantage to do so. He was the first to outgrow his own mythos—though he continued to milk its financial possibilities for some years—as a profoundly changed America turned away from the glamourous and fantastic towards harsher, realer concerns in film as well as in music.

The glamour of the singing cowboy is today nostalgic, campy; yet some of the music is very, very fine, as pure and real a type of country music as any, and as moving. The indelible legacy of the singing cowboy is a naive innocence that America has always prized in itself, a stirring version of the American dream, and a great deal of the finest music to branch from that magnificent shade tree we call country music.

Author's Postscript: In the interest of completeness, the following is a list of the principals herein who have died during the nearly two decades since this essay was written. Many were friends, some close; all will be missed: Bill Boyd (d. 1977), Andy Parker (1977), Johnny Bond (1978), Dick Foran (1979), Ray Whitley (1979), Bob Nolan (1980), Jimmy Wakely (1982), Smith Ballew (1984), Tex Fletcher (1986), Arthur E. Satherley (1986), Fred Scott (1991), and Ken Curtis (1991).

NOTES

1. Austin E. and Alta S. Fife, eds., *Cowboy and Western Songs: A Comprehensive Anthology* (New York: Clarkson N. Potter, Inc., 1969), p. ix.

2. John I. White, *Git Along, Little Dogies: Songs and Songmakers ot the American West* (Urbana: University of Illinois Press, 1975), p. 196.

3. Nick Tosches, *Country: The Biggest Music in America* (New York: Stein and Day, 1977), p. 112.

4. George F. Fenin and William K. Everson, *The Western: Front Silents to the Seventies*, rev. ed. (1962; rpt. New York: Grossman Publishers, 1973), p. 176.

5. In strict point of fact the first records made by a cowboy film star were two poems, "Lasca" and "Big Ben," recorded by silent film star William S. Hart on Victor's Red Seal label, normally reserved for classical music and other "timeless" performances. As far as we know Bill Hart, the grand old man of the western film, did not include singing among his talents or aspirations.

6. William Henry Koon, "The Songs of Ken Maynard," *John Edwards Memorial Foundation Quarterly*, 9 (1973), 70–77.

7. "CSR's Western Movie Hall of Fame: Ken Maynard," *Country Song Roundup*, June 1978, p. 28.

8. Jon Tuska, *The Filming of the West* (Garden City: Doubleday, 1976), p. 272.

9. White, pp. 139–41.   10. Tuska, p. 159.

11. Tuska, pp. 172–73.

12. Tuska's work is also the most sympathetic to the singing cowboy, a genre which sets the teeth of most film historians on edge.

13. Tuska, p. 292.

14. Tuska reports of Maynard's later film making (1937): "Ken's singing had been off key when he worked for Darmour; in fact, he had exploded when Darmour dubbed him. At Grand National, Maynard's brand of music-making was—to put it charitably—grotesque." (p. 399).

15. White, p. 117.   16. White, pp. 167–75.

17. White, pp. 153–54.   18. White, p. 153.

19. Roger D. Kinkle, *The Complete Encyclopedia of Popular Music and Jazz 1900–1950* (New Rochelle: Arlington House, 1974), II, 1105–6.

20. Much of the information on the careers of the Sons of the Pioneers and its members has been gained from Ken Griffis' invaluable compilation *Hear My Song: The Story of the Celebrated Sons of the Pioneers*, JEMF Special Series, No. 5 (Los Angeles: John Edwards Memorial Foundation, Inc., 1974).

21. Griffis, p. 71.

22. Personal interview with Bob Nolan, 28 April 1976.

23. Bill C. Malone, *Country Music USA: A Fifty Year History* (Austin: University of Texas Press, 1968), p. 197.

24. Douglas B. Green, "Gene Autry," in *Stars of Country Music: Uncle Dave Macon to Johnny Rodriguez*, ed. Bill C. Malone and Judith McCulloh (Urbana: University of Illinois Press, 1975), pp. 142–56.

25. Autry, Gene, with Mickey Herskowitz. *Back In The Saddle Again*. (Garden City, New York: Doubleday & Co., 1978).

26. Autry, p. 6.

27. Personal interview with Frank Marvin, 1 April 1975.

28. Autry, p.13–15.

29. The October, 1928 issue of *Radio Digest* contains a photo and caption of "Tiny Renier, The Singing Cowboy, who rounds up listeners with his western songs at WDAF, Kansas City." Exactly when the term singing cowboy came into usage is uncertain, but Autry was certainly quick to adopt it.

30. Gene Autry, "Three Pals," *Country Song Roundup*, Jan. 1950, p. 15.

31. The first was called *Mountain Ballads and Cowboy Songs*; the second, significantly, was *Cowboy Songs and Mountain Ballads*, both published by M.M. Cole.

32. Malone, p. 154.

33. Gene Autry, Letter to Raymond Hall, 8 Sept. 1933, copy graciously provided to the author by Nolan Porterfield.

34. Personal interview with Arthur E. Satherley, 27 June 1974.

35. Tuska, p. 294.   36. Autry, p. 33.

37. Don Miller, *Hollywood Corral* (New York: Popular Library,1976), p. 68.

38. William K. Everson, *A Pictorial History of the Western Film* (Secaucus, N.J.: The Citadel Press, 1969), p. 147.

39. Tuska, pp. 305–6.   40. Miller, pp. 127–28.

41. Arthur F. McClure and Ken D. Jones, *Heroes, Heavies and Sagebrush: A Pictorial History of tile "B" Western Players* (New York: A.S. Barnes, 1972), p. 46.

42. Kinkle, p. 916.

43. It is difficult to discover exactly who came when, but the following biographical list is presented roughly in accurate chronological order. As with all statements of fact within this essay, the dates, places, people, and events discussed are accurate to the best of the author's knowledge, but correction of any errors found by readers is eagerly welcomed by the author, as is additional information on any singing cowboys mentioned or inadvertently ignored.

44. Griffis, p. 142.

45. Frank Matheny Jr., "An Interview with Fred Scott," *Film Collector's Registry,* Sept. 1976, pp. 3–4.

46. McClure and Jones, p. 95.

47. Kalton C. Lahue, *Riders of the Range: The Sagebrush Heroes the Sound Screen* (New York: Castle Books, 1973), pp. 207–11.

48. McClure and Jones, p. 15.

49. Telephone interview with Ray Whitley, 21 April 1978.

50. Gerald F. Vaughn and Douglas B. Green, "A Singing Cowboy on the Road: A Look at the Performance Career of Ray Whitley," *Journal of Country Music* 5 (1974), 15.

51. Gerald F. Vaughn, *Ray Whitley: Country-Western Musicmaster and Film Star* (Newark, Delaware: privately printed, 1973), n. pag. Though brief, this is the definitive work on Whitley to date.

52. There has been some confusion over Ritter's birth date for years: even his plaque at the Country Music Hall of Fame reads 1907, the commonly given date. Actually the publicity department at Grand National thought that thirty-one was a bit mature for a hot new discovery, and promptly made him twenty-nine—in fact, Johnny Bond quoted Tex as saying, "They made me twenty-nine for a couple of years, and then moved me back to twenty-eight!" At least they didn't have to move his birthplace as they had with Ken Maynard.

53. Edward Finney, "The Making of a Star," *Classic Film Collector* (Fall 1975), p. 11.

54. Miller, p. 131.

55. Johnny Bond, *The Tex Ritter Story* (New York: Chappel Music Co., 1975), n. pag.

56. Johnny Bond, "Gene Autry: Champion, or My Thirty Years with Gene Autry," MS, unpublished.

57. Film historians uniformly comment that the fantastic success of the Autry films was often responsible for keeping Republic in the black, and was sometimes the *only* thing.

58. Kinkle, pp. 541–42.

59. Lahue, p. 44.

60. Actually 1910.

61. Tuska, pp. 419–20.

62. Lahue, p. 45.

63. Tuska, p. 421.

64. Letter received from Gerald F. Vaughn, 21 April 1978.

65. Vaughn's letter.

66. Not necessarily. These authors prove time and time again through their impressive landmark work that they have little sympathy for and less understanding about country music, its inherent greatness, and its strong appeal.

67. Fenin and Everson, p. 217.

68. McClure and Jones, p. 86.

69. Whitley interview.

70. Harry T. Sampson, *Blacks in Black and White: A Source Book on Black Films* (Metuchen, N.J.: Scarecrow Press, 1977), p. 63.

71. Everson, p. 148.

72. Kinkle, p. 1170.

73. Personal interview with Arthur E. Satherley, 27 April 1975.

74. The layoff certainly didn't hurt his record sales—he racked up three major hits that year alone with "Gold Mine in the Sky," "Take Me Back to My Boots and Saddles," and "When it's Springtime in the Rockies."

75. Tuska, p. 420.

76. Autry, p. 61–63.

77. James Morgan, "Conversations with the Cowboy King," *TWA Ambassador,* Oct. 1976, p. 38.

78. Bond, Tex Ritter, p. 56.

79. Satherley interview, 27 April 1975.

80. Tuska, p. 400.

81. Whitley interview.

82. Griffis, p. 25.

83. Everson, pp. 148–52.

84. Again, a highly subjective judgment.

85. Miller, pp. 168–69.

86. Miller, pp. 167–69.

87. Miller, p. 136.

88. Kinkle, pp. 524–25.

89. Kinkle, p. 1166.

90. *Variety,* March 15, 1939, p. 18.

91. Miller, p. 248.

92. Miller, p. 147.

93. Tuska, p. 404.

94. Whitley interview.

95. Tuska, p. 401.

96. Charles R. Townsend, *San Antonio Rose: The Life and Music Bob Wills* (Urbana: University of Illinois Press, 1976), pp. 207–12.

97. David Ragan, *Who's Who in Hollywood 1900–1976* (New Rochelle: Arlington House Publishers, 1976), p. 226.

98. Bond, p. 335.

99. Townsend Miller, "Ernest Tubb," in *Stars of Country Music,* p. 230.

100. D. Miller, pp. 151–53.

101. McClure and Jones, p. 116.

102. Gus Weill, *You Are My Sunshine: The Jimmie Davis Story* (Waco: Word Books, 1977), pp. 59–60.

103. D. Miller, p. 41.

104. Bob Pinson, Jacket Notes, Bill Boyd's *Cowboy Ramblers,* Bluebird, AXM2-5502, 1975.

105. D. Miller, p. 163.

106. Ragan, p. 598.

107. Ragan, p. 321.

108. D. Miller, p. 210.

109. This was as true of his record sales as well, with "Back in the Saddle Again" (1939), "South of the Border" (1940), "You Are My Sunshine" (1941), "It Makes No Difference Now" (1941), the Academy Award-nominated "Be Honest with Me" (1941), and "Tweedle-O-Twill" (1942) having all been major hits. He had also begun his extremely successful "Melody Ranch" radio show in 1939; it was to last until 1956.

110. D. Miller, p. 119.

111. Tuska, p. 461.

112. Tuska, p. 468.

113. Dave Distel, "The Good Guy in the White Hat or The Cowboy with the Midas Touch: A Horatio Alger Story for Our Time," Press release, Golden West Broadcasters, p. 3.

114. Autry, p. 168.

115. Fenin and Everson, p. 216.

116. Tuska, p. 480.

117. Placing Johnny Bond in the context of this narrative is a conundrum. He became a familiar face on screen and a staple of "Melody Ranch" for over a decade, one of country music's most successful record sellers of the 1940s (with a career lasting until 1977 on record), and more recently the author of two valuable studies—his autobiography and Tex Ritter's biography—as well as a massive unpublished study of Gene Autry. Bond was a sidekick of sorts, an occasional singer—nearly always in trios on film—but never played any parts which called for heroics. A frequent singing cowboy player, he was never a singing cowboy star; yet his musicianship, songwriting, and prominence in the field deserve considerable mention. Autry's longtime steel player Frank Marvin is, to a lesser extent, a similar case, as is Merle Travis and most members of the vocal groups that provided musical backing and occasional speaking parts in numerous westerns. There are another whole set of purely country music performers who have likewise made westerns—or in Roy Acuff's case, perhaps southeasterns. *Night Train to Memphis* (1944) opens with a shot of a train rumbling through the California mountains, ostensibly on a Nashville to Memphis run. His other films for

Republic were, similarly, filmed in California but with a southeastern setting. Among Grand Ole Opry stars, Eddy Arnold made a few musical films for Columbia in the late 1940s, and Zeke Clements appeared in a few films, most prominently as the voice of yodeling dwarf Bashful in *Snow White and the Seven Dwarfs*. Cowboy Copas had singing roles in a couple of cheapo westerns like *Square Dance Jubilee* involving little or no acting. Well into the fifties country singers like Johnny Cash, Faron Young, and Marty Robbins all appeared in super cheapies as quasi-cowboys, the emphasis being more on their latest hit than in production values or stories, the films meant to play in that new phenomenon—drive-ins—in areas where these artists were popular. So vile were most of these things they made PRC westerns of a decade earlier look like lavish productions. Country music extravaganza films enjoyed a limited vogue in the 1960s—films with titles like *Second Fiddle to an Old Guitar* and *Country Music Cavalcade*—but were basically thin plots pasted lamely around performances of current stars, the heroes played by then up-and-comers like Del Reeves and LeRoy Van Dyke. The trend is not dead—Waylon Jennings starred in a bit of hokum called *Nashville Rebel* (apt title as things turned out) in the late 1960s, while an R-rated drive-in special with Johnny Rodriguez was cranked out just two years ago: *Nashville Girl*.

118. Personal interview with Jimmy Wakely, 25 June 1974.

119. Dellar, P. 238.   120. Fenin and Everson, p. 216–17.

121. Lahue, p. 256.   122. Fenin and Everson, p. 257.

123. D. Miller, p. 231.   124. Tuska, p. 425.

125. His real name was, of course, James Glosup, and he went on to appear for some time as a singer and musician in southern California, especially noted for his work with Foy Willing and the Riders of the Purple Sage. He is no relation to Seth Ward, another Texan, whose professional name is Jimmy Dean and who is now chiefly noted for his sausage.

126. With Gene Autry, Eddie Dean, Bob Baker, and Rex Allen all having gone from its stages to Hollywood and singing cowboy films, the National Barn Dance proved to be an extraordinarily fertile breeding ground for singing cowboy stars.

127. Personal interview with Eddie Dean, 24 June 1975.

128. Ken Griffis, "The Eddie Dean Story," *John Edwards Memorial Foundation Quarterly*, 8, No. 26 (1972), 66.

129. Tuska, pp. 455-56.

130. Tuska, pp. 455-56.

131. Bob Birchard, "Gene Autry: Back in the Saddle Again," *Westerner*, Sept.-Oct. 1974, p. 46.

132. Autry, p. 97.   133. Kinkle, p. 767.

134. Dellar, p. 105.   135. D. Miller, p. 230.

136. D. Miller, p. 239.   137. Dellar, p. 147.

138. Dellar, p. 149.   139. Kinkle, p. 490.

140. Autry, p. 103.

BIBLIOGRAPHY

Autry, Gene, with Mickey Herskowitz. *Back in the Saddle Again*. Garden City, New York: Doubleday and Co., 1978.

Autry, Gene. Letter to Raymond Hall. 8 Sept. 1933. Provided by Nolan Porterfield.

———. "Three Pals." Country Song Roundup, Jan. 1950, p. 15.

Barbour, Alan G. *The Thrill of It All*. New York: Collier Books, 1971.

Birchard, Bob. "Gene Autry: Back in the Saddle Again." *Westerner*, Sept.–Oct. 1974, p. 46.

Bond, Johnny. "Gene Autry: Champion, or My Thirty Years with Gene Autry," MS, unpublished.

———. *Reflections: The Autobiography of Johnny Bond*. JEMF Special Series, No. 8. Los Angeles: John Edwards Memorial Foundation, Inc., 1976.

———. *The Tex Ritter Story*. New York: Chappell Music Co., 1975.

Bowen, William G. "Movie Memories." *The Pioneer*, 2, No. 1 (1978), 3.

"CSR's Western Movie Hall of Fame: Ken Maynard." *Country Song Roundup*, June 1978, p. 28.

Dean, Eddie. Personal interview. 24 June 1974.

Distel, Dave. "The Good Guy in the White Hat or The Cowboy with the Midas Touch: A Horatio Alger Story for Our Time." Press release. Golden West Broadcasts, n.d.

Everson, William K. *A Pictorial History of the Western Film*. Secaucus, N.J.: The Citadel Press, 1969.

Fenin, George F. and William K. Everson. *The Western: From Silents to the Seventies*. rev. ed. 1930; rpt. New York: Grossman Publishers, 1973.

Fernett, Gene. *Next Time Drive Off the Cliff!* Collectors' ed. Cocoa, Fla.: Cinememories Publishing Co.,1968.

———. *Hollywood's Poverty Row 1930–1950*. Satellite Beach, Fla.: Coral Reef Publications, Inc., 1973.

Fife, Austin E. and Alta S., eds. *Cowboy and Western Songs: A Comprehensive Anthology*. New York: Clarkson N. Potter, Inc., 1969.

Finney, Edward. "The Making of a Star." *Classic Film Collector*, No. 48 (1975), pp. 11, 39.

Green, Douglas B. "Gene Autry." In *Stars of Country Music: Uncle Dave Macon to Johnny Rodriguez*. Ed. Bill C. Malone and Judith McCulloh. Urbana: University of Illinois Press, 1975, pp. 142–56.

Griffis, Ken. "The Eddie Dean Story." *John Edwards Memorial Foundation Quarterly*, 8 (1972), 63–69.

———. *Hear My Song: The Story of the Celebrated Sons of the Pioneers*. JEMF Special Series, No. 5. Los Angeles: John Edwards Memorial Foundation, Inc., 1974.

Horwitz, James. *They Went Thataway*. New York: Dutton, 1976.

Kendall, Pete. "Smith Ballew Remembers Bix and Big Bands." *Texas Music*, June 1976, pp. 36–40.

Kinkle, Roger D. *The Complete Encyclopedia of Popular Music and Jazz 1900–1950*. New Rochelle: Arlington House, 1974. Vol. II.

Koon, William Henry. "The Songs of Ken Maynard." *John Edwards Memorial Foundation Quarterly*, 9 (1973), 70–77.

Lahue, Kalton C. *Riders of the Range: The Sagebrush Heroes of the Sound Screen*. New York: Castle Books, 1973.

Longworth, Mike. *Martin Guitars: A History*. Cedar Knolls, N.J.: Colonial Press, 1975.

McClure, Arthur F. and Ken D. Jones. *Heroes, Heavies and Sagebrush: A Pictorial History of the "B" Western Players*. New York: A.S. Barnes, 1972.

Malone, Bill C. *Country Music U.S.A.: A Fifty Year History*. Austin: University of Texas Press, 1968.

Marvin, Frank. Personal interview. 1 April 1975.

Matheny, Frank Jr. "An Interview with Fred Scott." *Film Collector's Registry*, Sept. 1976, pp. 3–4.

Miller, Don. *Hollywood Corral*. New York: Popular Library, 1976.

Miller, Townsend. "Ernest Tubb." In *Stars of Country Music: Uncle Dave Macon to Johnny Rodriguez*. Ed. Bill C. Malone and Judith McCulloh. Urbana: University of Illinois Press, 1975, pp. 222–36.

Morgan, James. "Conversations with the Cowboy King." *TWA Ambassador*, Oct. 1976, p. 38.

Nolan, Bob. Personal interview by Lee Rector. 28 April 1976.

Osborne, Jerry. *55 Years of Recorded Country/Western Music*. Phoenix: O'Sullivan, Woodside & Company, 1976.

Pinson, Bob. Jacket Notes. Bill Boyd's *Cowboy Ramblers*. Bluebird, AXMZ-5502, 1975.

Ragan, David. *Who's Who in Hollywood 1900–1976*. New Rochelle: Arlington House Publishers, 1976.

Rasky, Frank. *Roy Rogers: King of the Cowboys*. New York: Julian Messner, Inc., 1955.

Russell, William. *Tumbleweed: Best of the Singing Cowboys*. Fairfax, Virginia: Western Revue Publications, 1977.

Sampson, Henry T. *Blacks in Black and White: A Source Book on Black Films*. Montclair, N.J.: Scarecrow Press, 1977.

Satherley, Arthur E. Personal interview. 27 June 1974.

———. Personal interview. 27 April 1975.

Swann, Thomas Burnett. *The Heroine or the Horse: Leading Ladies in Republic's Films*. New York: A.S. Barnes, 1977.

Tosches, Nick. *Country: The Biggest Music in America*. New York: Stein and Day, 1977.

Townsend, Charles R. *San Antonio Rose: The Life and Music of Bob Wills*. Urbana: University of Illinois Press, 1976.

Tuska, Jon. *The Filming of the West*. Garden City: Doubleday, 1976. Variety, 15 March 1939, p. 18.

Vaughn, Gerald F. Letter to Douglas B. Green. 21 April 1978.

———. *Ray Whitley: Country-Western Musicmaster and Film Star*. Newark, Delaware: Privately printed, 1973.

———. and Douglas B. Green. "A Singing Cowboy on the Road: A Look at the Performance Career of Ray Whitley." *Journal of Country Music*, 5, No. 1 (1974), 2–16.

Wakely, Jimmy. "My Early Life." *Country Music People*, Nov. 1976, pp. 28–29.

———. Personal interview. 25 June 1974.

———. Personal interview by Lee Rector. 17 Feb. 1976.

Weill, Gus. *You Are My Sunshine: The Jimmie Davis Story*. Waco: Word Books, 1977.

White, John I. *Git Along Little Dogies: Songs and Songmakers of the American West*. Urbana: University of Illinois Press, 1975.

Whitley, Ray. Telephone interview. 21 April 1978.

Wilmott, Vaun. "Jimmy Wakely: Trailblazing Outlaw Rides with Waylon and Willie." *Country Rambler*, 10 Feb. 1977, pp. 45–46.

Zwisohn, Lawrence J. "The Sons of the Pioneers, Part One—The Early Years." *The Nostalgia Monthly*, March 1978, pp. 13–16.

PATSY MONTANA

PATSY MONTANA AND THE
DEVELOPMENT OF THE COWGIRL IMAGE

ROBERT K. OERMANN AND MARY A. BUFWACK

■ As singing cowboys proliferated during the 1930s, it was only a matter of time before cowgirls would join them on screen and on record. Patsy Montana was the first woman singer to popularize this image and to strike a blow for women's equality in country music. Her groundbreaking career is carefully considered here by Mary A. Bufwack and Robert K. Oermann. When this article was first published in 1981, Oermann was then employed as a Country Music Foundation librarian. He now works as a full-time music journalist for print and television. For her part, Bufwack has become the executive director of United Neighborhood Health Services in Nashville, though she has continued to keep her hand in country music writing and research. In 1993, Oermann and Bufwack's work on women artists in country music culminated in the book *Finding Her Voice: The Saga of Women in Country Music.*—Ed.

■ Summaries and overviews of Patsy Montana's career generally hang on the fact that she was the first woman in country music to have a million-seller. While the astounding popularity of "I Want To Be a Cowboy's Sweetheart"[1] is certainly a milestone in country music history, Patsy Montana's ultimate importance to American popular culture is as the popularizer of the cowgirl image. In her songs and stage presence she rewrote the myth of the American cowboy to include women, providing a new role option for women country singers, and popularizing an innovative independent female image. Until Montana's arrival on the scene, female country musicians were mainly restricted to performing images like mother, sweetheart, and rube comedienne. Her adoption of the cowgirl image is the most striking contribution of Depression-era female country music performers; and this image exerts influence even today.

Like the mother, sweetheart, and rube comedienne stereotypes, the cowgirl image was rooted in nineteenth-century popular culture. Indeed, the cowgirl seems to have been first commercially exploited at the same time as the cowboy. As early as the 1850s Mary Ann Whittaker gave public exhibitions of her western horseback riding abilities. Dime novels of the 1860s told of Hurricane Nell, the queen of the saddle and lasso, Bess the Trapper, and Mountain Kate, all of whom rode and shot as the equals of frontier men in fringed buckskin and leather.

Wild west shows brought such performers as sharpshooter Annie Oakley to prominence. Best known of all was Calamity Jane, whose 1896 autobiography was extremely popular, and whose many personal appearances capitalized on her cowgirl exploits in the West of an earlier era. Lucille Mulhall grew up on an Oklahoma ranch, became a star in her father's wild west shows, astounded audiences with her roping and riding skills, and eventually earned a million dollars from appearances in silent movies.

The popular interest in folk music and in distinctly American music during the early part of the twentieth century encouraged further use of the cowgirl image by performers. Female costume recitalists performed on lecture circuits popularizing folk music; among these personalities were Grace Wood Jess, who sometimes performed southwestern material in costume, and Ina Sires, a Dallas schoolteacher who toured on the Chautauqua circuit as a cowgirl and published *Songs of the Open Range* (1928), one of the earliest cowboy song collections.

In country music, Patsy Montana's predecessors were few. Vernon Dalhart's partner Adelyn Hood had frequently enacted western heroine characters on record in the early 1930s ("Calamity Jane," "Alaska Ann and Yukon Steve," "The Daughter of Calamity Jane"). Cowgirl-garbed Mommie Gray had been quite successful as a singer of sentimental songs in Otto Gray's Oklahoma Cowboy Band. Billie Maxwell, an actual cowgirl, had recorded her fine collection of western songs for Victor in 1929. Buerl Sisney recorded as "The Lonesome Cowgirl," Lois Dexter did duets of western ballads with Pat Patterson, and Kitty Lee sang western material with her husband Jack. Louise Massey dressed as a cowgirl in the late 1920s and early 1930s, but sang little western material.

These were only hints of what was to come in the 1930s. The cowgirl image was to take hold in this decade to a completely unprecedented degree. And, as the leading cowgirl on the nation's leading barn dance show, Patsy Montana was virtually to define the role.

Patsy Montana's tremendous popularity was a signal that women had fully arrived in country music. Using the cowgirl image, she fronted a band that played uptempo swing and dance music, not parlor songs and ballads. This performance style signaled the emergence of country music women from family harmony group members and duet partners to headline status as soloists, bandleaders, songwriters, and stars.

When Patsy Montana arrived at WLS in 1933, all three of the predominant female performing images (mother, sweetheart, rube comedienne) were embodied in the persons of Grace Wilson, Linda Parker, and Lulu Belle. Their antecedents in nineteenth-century show business made their popularity with country music audiences logical and predictable. Although the cowgirl image never completely displaced these, cowgirls such as Patsy, the Girls of the Golden West, Louise Massey, and their followers became the most notable country female performers of the Depression era.

That Montana and her successors achieved fame with this fresh cowgirl image indicates the effect of the Depression on country music audiences. Early female country stars like Moonshine Kate, Elviry Weaver, and Judy Canova had traded on an exaggerated hayseed image, and used humor to turn the unsophisticated qualities of poor people's culture into virtues. During the Depression, however, this image was a grim reality for many, more than ever. It was difficult for any in the working class to retain pride and dignity in the face of economic ruin; and although the rube provided comic relief, there was somehow a negative quality to this portrayal: A comic bumpkin was still a bumpkin.

The cowboy was a reasonable replacement, for like the farmers and workers who listened to country music, he was a manual laborer, but dignified, independent, strong, and romantic. The dime-novel fascination with this attractive image in the nineteenth century had blossomed with the movies of the 1920s and 1930s into a full-blown American craze, and country musicians began to capitalize on this. A 1930s country string band could perform in cowboy regalia and give its music a respectability that performing in hayseed getups never could. The cowboy image gave hillbilly music a measure of esteem during an era when rural culture was widely viewed in "Li'l Abner" and "Tobacco Road" stereotypes. That women, too, became accepted in this role illustrates both the genius of Patsy Montana's contribution and the profound need for this western escapist fantasy among women as well as men of those times.

Unlike many of her contemporaries, Patsy Montana was not just a hillbilly singer in cowgirl garb. Nor was she a girl playing at being a cowboy. Rather, she pioneered an entire image in both looks and song content of a modern cowgirl who would meet the modern cowboy on equal terms. Her lyrics consistently stressed the desire to do all the activities that cowboys do alongside a loving cowboy companion. Thus, the singing cowgirl image as developed by Montana was a fantasy of male-female egalitarianism, as well as an emancipating dream of outdoor living, freedom, and independence. Perhaps her great success came because she represented the kind of woman that women had to be to survive in the Depression. Young working class women needed new models as they put extra work into food processing and providing, as they took on jobs where they could, as they were left by men who took to the roads, and as they had to forsake frills, luxury, and dependence. More than the vote that women had acquired in 1920, the Depression raised fundamental questions about women's relationships to men, caused women to rethink their status with men who could no longer successfully provide in an uncertain world, and made women acutely conscious of their need to be able to do what men could do.

Montana's ascendance was not only a signal that the cowgirl image had fully arrived in the 1930s, it was also a historic event in the arrival of country music as a commercial popular culture form. "I Want To Be a Cowboy's Sweetheart" is reputedly the first record by a woman in country music to sell a million copies. When it was recorded in 1935, million-sellers of any country music recording were still quite rare. That the sale of this disc took place in the midst of the Depression when record sales were down makes it all the more impressive. The record is also a testament to the musicianship and professionalism of its creator.

Although just twenty-two at the time, Patsy Montana was already a show business veteran when she came to Chicago and WLS. While only a teenager she had been a radio headliner in California, Oregon, and Louisiana, and she had also recorded for Victor in New Jersey. Her rough-and-tumble upbringing in a family with ten brothers must have had something to do with her gutsy entrance into show business at such a young age.

Patsy was born Ruby Blevins on October 30, 1912, near Hot Springs, Arkansas, the only daughter of the eleven children born to Augustus and Victoria Blevins. Her father was a schoolteacher, sometime farmer, and postal clerk. Ruby grew up in Hope, Arkansas, scrapping and doing chores alongside her many brothers, and learned to take care of herself from a very early age.

I was the only girl and there were ten boys, and we did a lot of fighting and quarreling, and yet we sang a lot, believe it or not. I think we used to love fighting, but the music sort of lulled our spirits.[2]

Nearly all of her early publicity biographies imply that she was brought up a "tomboy."

The main musical influence seems to have been her mother, who encouraged her musically, played the parlor pump organ for the family, and taught the children many religious songs. The Blevins household also had an old wind-up record player for musical entertainment. The musical and social influences on a child raised in an area where the cultures of Texas, Louisiana, and Arkansas converge were many and varied. She says her main influence, however, was old-time country music; and she heard both local string bands and recorded hillbilly music as a girl.

The family did not own a radio, so the early barn dance shows were not particularly influential in her musical development. At a young age her vocal efforts included yodeling, which she practiced with her brothers on the way to school.

She taught herself to play guitar from an old instruction book, wrote a few ditties, and took violin lessons. Her mother always told her she could yodel better than she could fiddle, so Ruby began emphasizing her singing more and more. She had her first professional music job in 1926 at the age of fourteen; and in 1928 while still in high school she won a talent contest singing "My Mother Was a Lady." These experiences encouraged her to finish school early, as she felt ready for a show business career. Deciding that her first name sounded too homespun, she added an "e" to the end of it. Thus, as Rubye Blevins she moved to California with older brother Ordie and his wife in 1928.

In Los Angeles, Rubye continued her violin studies at the University of the West (now UCLA); but she rapidly fell under the influence of the western music and singing cowboys of Hollywood. This western influence came to the fore shortly after she won a talent contest singing the songs of one idol, Jimmie Rodgers, and dressing like another, Kate Smith. She sang two Rodgers tunes, "Yodeling Cowboy" and "Whisper Your Mother's Name,"[3] strumming her guitar with one leg up on a chair while dressed like a nightclub sophisticate in a lacy, black-beaded gown with a butterfly on the front. Backstage, a woman suggested to her that western garb might be more appropriate, and Rubye took this advice to heart. She won $10 and a spot on KMTR Radio's Breakfast Club show.

Although her father wanted her to call herself "Ruby, The Jewel of Arkansas," she billed herself in these early years as "Rubye Blevins, The Yodeling Cowgirl From San Antone." By late 1930 her transition to the cowgirl image was complete. In this new guise she gained experience rapidly. Her stint on KMTR, where she was not paid, lasted only six months, but she also worked as a duo with her brother Ken on Culver City's KFVD. She soon met Stuart Hamblen, who was to have a profound influence on her early career. The handsome singer and songwriter (later famous for "This Ole House," "Remember Me, I'm the One Who Loves You," and "Open Up Your Heart and Let the Sun Shine In," among others) had his own new radio show on nearby KMIC in Inglewood, and he invited her to join his fledgling troupe.

There she met Ruthy DeMondrum and Lorraine McIntire, the only other women in town performing western material. A tour with world champion roper and cowboy Monty Montana encouraged the naming of the trio the Montana Cowgirls; and Hamblen, sensing the potential confusion between the names Ruthy and Rubye on the air, suggested Patsy as a good Irish name for his new starlet. In the Montana Cowgirls,

Patsy and Lorraine fiddled, and Ruthy played guitar.[4] The only other female member of Hamblen's 1931 radio troupe was singer and guitarist Sue Willie.

The Montana Cowgirls were an immediate hit. They quickly became favorites on the Los Angeles music scene, benefiting from and contributing to the development of cowboy harmony, such as that practiced by the Sons of the Pioneers, who were also emerging at the time. The trio gained further radio experience on KHJ (Los Angeles), Patsy's KMTR alma mater (Hollywood), KGW (Portland, Oregon), and other western stations. They rode as cowgirls in rodeos as far afield as Pendleton, Oregon, and Saugus, California (at movie star Hoot Gibson's ranch); and the girls also appeared in the 1931 feature film *Lightnin' Express*, as well as several movie shorts.

Like many groups of the time, the Montana Cowgirls often dissolved and re-formed. Ruthy and Lorraine sometimes made appearances with the Beverly Hill Billies' young star Elton Britt and his brother Vernon, while Patsy continued to sing with her brother Ken. With Ruthy's marriage to Robert Welch, however, the complexion of the girl trio was changed, and the Montana Cowgirls went their separate ways.

Patsy and Ken returned to Arkansas to visit the family. She was just twenty, but she already had two years of radio and film experience behind her. So that her family could hear her as the radio cowgirl she had become, she got a week's booking as a solo act on nearby Shreveport, Louisiana's KWKH.

It proved to be a fateful decision, for she was heard there by Victor recording artist Jimmie Davis, who invited her to fiddle and sing backup for him at an upcoming Camden recording session. The Depression was at its height and Patsy was in no position to refuse job offers of any kind, much less one to travel East to record for Victor. She accepted. Davis's sessions were scheduled for the third and fourth of November, 1932. At the second day's session, Patsy played fine fiddle and yodeled on four of his numbers ("Gambler's Return," "Bury Me In Old Kentucky," "Home In Caroline," and "Jealous Lover"), but was uncredited on the released discs. She was also given the chance to record by herself.

As "Patsy Montana, Montana's Yodeling Cowgirl" she recorded four titles on this occasion. Of her selections, "Montana Plains" (her reworking of Stuart Hamblen's "Texas Plains") was the most logical choice, since it had been her Los Angeles radio theme song, yet Victor chose not to release it. Instead, another Montana-themed title, "When the Flowers of Montana Were Blooming," was released as her first record. It, "Sailor's Sweetheart," and "I Love My Daddy Too" reveal a strong Rodgers influence, but her own distinctive style clearly emerges on these early discs as well.

Montana returned to California to resume her radio career after this. Her old mentor Hamblen married Suzy Daniels in 1933; later that year Patsy again returned to Hope, Arkansas. Brothers Claude and Ken Blevins had hit upon the idea of taking the "world's biggest watermelon," grown in Arkansas, to the Chicago World's Fair, and Patsy decided to accompany them. Again, this was a fortuitous decision. At WLS a female vocalist was being sought to add to the Kentucky Ramblers string band. Patsy heard of this opening, auditioned, got the job, and never returned home with her brothers. She had become a member of one of the finest bands in the history of country music.

The band had been together since late 1931 and was composed of fellow-Kentuckians Floyd "Salty" Holmes (guitar, tenor vocals), Shelby "Tex" Atchison (fiddle), Jack Taylor (bass), and Charles "Chick" Hurt (mandolin). When Patsy Montana joined in mid-1933 she was accomplished on fiddle, vocals, and guitar, but her main contributions were her sense of showmanship and image. This talent soon lifted the band from being just another National Barn Dance act to being a headline attraction. To accommodate their new member's western image and repertory, the four men renamed themselves the Prairie Ramblers.

Patsy Montana & the Prairie Ramblers were at first primarily a road act. They frequently appeared at western moving picture theaters, performing two matinees and three night shows. The yodeling cowgirl learned to sleep on backstage chairs and travel in one car holding five people plus instruments for the sum of $7.50 a day. It was rough, but the experience taught Patsy how to work an audience, how to choose songs that people would respond to, and how to work her image. She discovered that her yodeling frequently brought her standing ovations, and that uptempo danceable tunes were quite popular with her listeners. The hard work paid off, for Patsy Montana and her Prairie Ramblers remained from 1933 to 1949 one of the most consistently excellent touring and recording groups in country music.

The ensemble recorded together for the first time for Victor in December 1933. Patsy again recorded her old favorite "Montana Plains," as well as "Waltz of the Hills," "Homesick for My Old Cabin," and "Home Corral." Oddly, the discs were released as by Rubye Blevins. But these were to be her last efforts under her old name; and this occasion was to be the last one for some time on which she recorded non-cowgirl material.

The following year Patsy Montana got married. Like many women at WLS, she married into the National Barn Dance "family." In 1934 she wed Paul Rose, the manager of the blind Mac & Bob duet (Mac—Lester MacFarland—was Rose's uncle). Unlike female stars elsewhere, the WLS country music women usually remained active as musicians after marriage since they so often married men in the same business. This was true of Patsy, and it was lucky for the young couple that she did, for when Mac and Bob split up, Rose was left temporarily jobless. With her husband free to travel, Patsy and the band went to New York City to appear regularly on WOR. Daughter Beverly was born there in 1935.

After being replaced on WOR by the Carter Family's program, Patsy and the Prairie Ramblers returned to Chicago and WLS. In a few short years Beverly was performing with her mother, probably as the first mother-daughter singing team on national radio. Patsy's second daughter Judy, born in 1938, continued in this role into the mid-1970s.

By 1935 the market for records was quite low. Few new artists were being recorded, and female country acts, in particular, were not considered good prospects. Nevertheless, the American Record Company's Art Satherley believed in Patsy and the Prairie Ramblers enough to record them. Encouraged by their radio and touring popularity, he entered the studios with them in New York in August 1935, and came out with the biggest records that both she and the band were ever to make. On August 15, the Prairie Ramblers cut their biggest hit, "Nobody's Darling but Mine"; the following day Patsy Montana recorded her self-composed classic "I Want to Be a Cowboy's Sweetheart."

Patsy's own explanation for this record's success is that it was a musical synthesis, and that its timing was right. Gene Autry's films of the cowboy lost in the modern world were huge box-office draws at the time. Bob Wills had begun recording and popularizing the combination of country and swing that the Prairie Ramblers played so well. The lively fiddling and the blue yodel gave the song a western yet contemporary sound. Patsy also notes that the song has a polka rhythm, which made it popular with ethnic groups in northern cities. Certainly, "I Want to Be a Cowboy's Sweetheart" appealed to the dance spirit that was sweeping the country following the 1934 repeal of Prohibition.

She also believes the lyrics were important to the song's success. Despite its title, the song is not about a traditional sweetheart. It is expressive of a woman's desire for independence in the rugged outdoor life of a cowhand. Although she wants the companionship of a man, the "cowboy's sweetheart" mainly sings of wanting to rope and ride on the plains, sleep on the ground beneath the moon, feel the wind in her face, and play guitar and yodel. The song is a story of freedom and companionship which is at once down to earth and independent. This notion of being a cowboy's buddy and lover was repeated over and over in Patsy Montana's subsequent recordings.

The elaboration of the cowgirl image took place over the next five years while recording with the Prairie Ramblers, the period of Montana's greatest popularity. "Sweetheart of the Saddle" (1936) is about being a cowpuncher alongside her "cowboy pal." "I Wanna Be a Western Cow-girl" (1939) expresses dissatisfaction with dull city life to the accompani-ment of the band's hot fiddle and accordion breaks. In "Ridin' Old Paint" (1935) Patsy sings that she loves life on horseback and that she "won't settle down and be a wife." "I Want to Be a Real Cowboy Girl" (1938) takes the theme nearly to androgeny. Most independent-spirited of all are "The She-Buckaroo" (1936) and "A Rip Snortin' Two-Gun Gal" (1939). "The She-Buckaroo" begins as a female version of the male west-ern boasting song, bragging of "tough ridin' " rodeo prowess and declar-ing, "I'm a man-hatin' lassie, a she-buckaroo," before confessing the eventuality of settling down and learning to bake and sew. The cowgirl in "A Rip Snortin' Two-Gun Gal" is "T.N.T.," "dynamite," and "tough as I can be," who warns that she "never knew no fear of fight," and con-cludes, "You better keep your distance, boy, far from my corral."

Patsy also used her status as an independent cowgirl to spoof the drug-store cowboys who were a by-product of the era's craze for all things western. "I'd Love to Be a Cowboy (But I'm Afraid of Cows)" (1939) is one example; while the hilarious Prairie Ramblers ensemble number "I'm a Wild and Reckless Cowboy" (1937) deflates an urban cowboy to whom Patsy sings "all you've ever shot . . . is lots and lots of bull."

Patsy built and sustained the cowgirl image with numerous releases of western songs. Even a partial listing illustrates the extent to which she popularized such material: 1936's "Give Me a Home in Montana," "Lone Star," "Chuck Wagon Blues," "I'm an Old Cowhand," "Blazin' the Trail," and "Montana"; 1937's "There's a Ranch in the Sky," "Out on the Lone Prairie," and "Ridin' the Sunset Trail"; 1938's "Strawberry Roan," "That's Where the West Begins," "An Old Saddle For Sale," and "Give Me a Straight-Shootin' Cowboy"; 1939's "Old Nevada Moon," "My Song of the West," "Singing in the Saddle," and "My Pancho Pony"; and 1940's "Leanin' on the Old Top Rail" all draw on the rich vein of western imagery.

Several of her numbers were written as love songs to women from the male point of view. These included "Cowboy's Honeymoon" (1937), "Lit-tle Sweetheart of the Ozarks" (1938), "Shy Little Ann from Cheyenne" (1940), "Pride of the Prairie" (1937), and "Little Rose of the Prairie" (1938). One other song usually identified with the male voice was used to reprise her independent cowgirl theme in a non-western context. This was "I Only Want a Buddy Not a Sweetheart" (1937), in which she asks to be liked not loved, following her previously developed theme of a woman's desire for egalitarian companionship.

Also scattered in the Montana cowgirl repertory are a few songs cele-brating domesticity and leaning toward more traditional sex roles. These include "I Wanna Be a Cowboy's Dream Girl" (1940), "Rodeo Sweetheart" (1938), and "I Want to Be a Cowboy's Sweetheart No. 2 (I've Found My Cowboy Sweetheart)" (1937).

Patsy Montana was by no means musically one-dimensional. In addition to all the yodeling cowgirl numbers, she recorded several other types of tunes. The pretty "My Baby's Lullaby" (1937) was written and sung by Patsy to her first daughter Beverly. "Cowboy Rhythm" (1938) is a fine swing number as is "Swing Time Cowgirl" (1940) which chronicles a prairie flower who becomes a city jazz baby. They feature hot fiddling by Prairie Ramblers Tex Atchison and Alan Crockett (an ex-Crockett's Mountaineers member who joined the band in 1938 when Atchison went west). "With My Banjo on My Knee" (1937) was performed in pure string band style. An interesting woman's statement is contained in the pop-styled "Your Own Sweet Darling Wife" (1937). This number protests that there are love songs to mother, to silver-haired daddys, and to girlfriends, but that "the one who's been neglected in song and actual life . . . is your own sweet darling wife," "the one who gave up everything."

Patsy Montana's exuberant yodels remained a familiar sound from WLS all during the 1930s and 1940s. She found time to make at least one more film, *Colorado Sunset* with Gene Autry in 1940, but her major activity besides radio work was her tireless touring. She became a solo touring act in 1940, although she continued to sometimes record with the Prairie Ramblers until 1949. The 1946–1947 radio season featured her own national radio show, "Wake Up and Smile," on the ABC network. Her broadcast greeting "Hi Pardner, It's Patsy Montana," accompanied by the stamping of horses' hoofs, was familiar to millions during this phase of her career. In 1948 she again returned to Arkansas to live, inaugurating a daily show of her own over KTHS, Hot Springs, and commuting to Shreveport for KWKH's Louisiana Hayride on Saturday nights. The CBS network carried the latter show nationally, gaining her new fame as Patsy Montana, "The Girl With the Million-Dollar Personality." (A 1939 Montana single had been titled "My Million Dollar Smile.")

During this period, Patsy's recording career became more checkered. She split with the Prairie Ramblers in 1940 because she and the Ramblers were pursuing different musical directions. The band added drums and electric guitar, and recorded many jazz-influenced numbers throughout 1940–1941 without her. Patsy switched labels to Decca and recorded with the Light Crust Doughboys as Patsy Montana & Her Pardners in 1941. The next year she recorded with the Sons of the Pioneers in Los Angeles (again identified as "Her Pardners" on the discs). These sessions produced a version of "Deep in the Heart of Texas" that again built on her cowgirl image: "Gals can do what cowhands do, deep in the Heart of Texas," she sang. "Boogie Woogie Cowboy" was unreleased, but again demonstrated the musical synthesis of country and jazz she had accomplished earlier. "I'll Wait for You" (1942) was the first of several songs relating to the war effort that relegated her cowgirl image to secondary status during World War II. Her 1944 Decca single "Good Night Soldier" also addressed the conflict in which her husband was serving.

She returned to RCA Victor toward the end of the 1940s, but the resulting records were to be the most disappointing ones of her career. She was not allowed to choose her own material as she had always done in the past; and often the songs chosen for her were given to her only one day in advance of recording. She was teamed with studio musicians (billed as the Buckaroos), and the cowgirl image was completely abandoned in such material as the pop-country tunes popularized by Esmeraldy ("The Streamlined Hillbilly"): "Slap 'Er Down Again Paw" and "I Didn't Know the Gun Was Loaded." "Mama Never Said a Word About Love" was a straight pop novelty tune without a hint of the country band sound at which she and the Ramblers had once excelled.

With the coming of television westerns in the 1950s, Patsy's cowgirl image was revived. Once again Patsy's "I Want to Be a Cowboy's Sweetheart" was popularized, this time by Patti Page and Dale Evans. The success of such performers as Evans and Gail Davis (television's "Annie Oakley") with the cowgirl image kept the original singing cowgirl in demand as a touring act throughout most of the decade. Montana's own television appearances in this period included a notable guest spot on the Ozark Jubilee's ABC show *Country Music Jubilee* in 1957, among many others. She also retained her ties with the National Barn Dance in the fifties and was on the show's last broadcast from WLS before it moved to WGN to die.

She retired briefly for a few months in 1952 and moved to California, where she lived in West Covina and Manhattan Beach. The blossoming of women's country music in the 1960s, however, led to renewed interest in her music and she resumed touring. Yodelers Bonnie Owens and Judy Lynn had again revived "I Want to Be a Cowboy's Sweetheart" by featuring it in their stage shows, thus familiarizing Patsy's signature song to a new generation of listeners. She recorded it again herself for Starday in 1966 on a remarkable album called *Cowboy's Sweetheart* that was made in the Matador Room of the Buena Vista Hotel in Safford, Arizona.[5] A young RCA artist named Waylon Jennings played lead guitar for her. The new arrangement of her old hit can only be described as a honky-tonk yodel; and she also demonstrated her versatility on the album by recording everything from Mae Axton's "Headed for a Big Big Heartbreak" to the chestnut "I'll Be All Smiles Tonight" to the second landmark woman's western song, Louise Massey's "My Adobe Hacienda." Ever the voice with the female perspective, she included a parody of "16 Tons" called "16 Pounds" that dealt with everything from dirty laundry to weight gain.

In the 1970s she recorded one gospel and one secular album for Chicago's Birch Records, and later had releases in England on Look and in Holland on Munich. Annual visits to England and Europe in the 1970s have made her a favorite overseas, her fan club is still active, and she continues to delight audiences with her clear voice and yodels. Patsy Montana's personal appearances now number well over 7,000. She's been commissioned a Kentucky Colonel and an Arkansas Traveller, had June 2 declared "Patsy Montana Day" in St. Louis, been voted "Queen of Western Music" by the Colorado Country Music Foundation, and will be honored by the Smithsonian Institution in Washington in 1981 along with Pee Wee King. Hugh Downs has featured her on his television show *Over Easy*. In 1970 she was distinguished by a Pioneer Award from the Academy of Country Music in Los Angeles. Her one-time record producer, Columbia's legendary Uncle Art Satherley, has also praised her:

What I have in mind, and have had for a long time, is why we haven't given more thought and credit to the ladies, who also in not a few instances, have been right in there, singing and playing and trouping. . . . Going over my collections and . . . recordings of many, many years, one artist stands out vividly in my mind. The artist is Patsy Montana. . . . I remember well the many songs she recorded. . . . Her records I am sure sold into the millions and in all parts of the world. . . . So maybe the girls will someday receive some recognition or be in the Hall of Fame.[6]

Patsy Montana, the pioneer singing cowgirl, remains one of the most durable troupers in country music. Her showmanship and continuing popularity with audiences are matched by no other performer of her era. She is simply a wonder. And although she has tried various other performing images over the years, she now wears her singing cowgirl label proudly:

Through the lean country music years when folksongs and rock took over, I sorta felt obsolete with my western costumes. I didn't want to be dated . . . so first I tried taking off my boots. . . . I stumbled all over the stage. Then I tried my hat. . . . I felt undressed. So I finally told myself it was time to practice what I have always believed: be yourself. I have worn my western costumes with pride ever since.[7]

Patsy Montana's importance to the development of country music lies in her introduction of an image that allowed women to fully participate as soloists in performance. Her creation and popularization of this new female stereotype place her in the ranks of the genre's major innovators. Her persona as the strong, good-humored saddle-pal drew both on the mythic West and on contemporary social mores. Thus, the cowgirl image gave female performers an alternative image to the shy country sweet-heart without adopting the lone-woman sexuality of the cabaret singer or Broadway star. By using the concept of egalitarianism between working men and women, Patsy found a respectable way to swing.

Patsy's great success with this independent yet compassionate cowgirl image encouraged its adoption by the generation of women performers who followed her. Many gifted cowgirl yodelers emerged in Patsy's wake, enriching country music immensely: Rosalie Allen, Texas Ruby, Carolina Cotton, Bonnie Lou, Judy Lynn. Other singing cowgirls modified and customized the image: Louise Massey, Dale Evans, the Girls of the Golden West, Jenny Lou Carson. And no western swing unit of the 1940s was complete without at least one cowgirl singer: Laura Lee McBride, the McKinney Sisters, Darla Daret, Ramona Reed. Eventually, in the 1950s, all-cowgirl country bands enjoyed a vogue: Ann Jones's Western Sweethearts, Jean Shepard's Melody Ranch Girls, the Rhythm Roundup Girls, the Westernettes, the Saddle Sweethearts, Abbie Neal's E-Z Time Ranch Gals.

Since the apogee in popularity, the cowgirl stereotype has assumed a less prominent place in country music, but it is by no means dead as a performing image. In their much-publicized role as accomplished horse-women, such performers as Lynn Anderson, Reba McEntire, and Tanya Tucker have kept alive the style if not the appearance of cowgirls. Such contemporary country performers as Mary Kay Place, Marcia Ball, and Mary McCaslin have explicitly drawn on the singing cowgirl tradition. Sissy Spacek's country compositions use cowgirl imagery heavily; and such songs as "Even Cowgirls Get the Blues," "Cattle Kate," and "The Cowgirl and the Dandy" recall the image as well. And that paragon of contemporary country artistry, Emmylou Harris, has also sometimes adopted this guise.

As these examples indicate, many elements of this image have not outlived either their usefulness to women performers or their popularity with audiences. Indeed, in light of current social trends, the image of sexual equality represented by the buddy/lover cowgirl may be more timely than ever.

This image serves the dual function of allowing a female independent spirit to be acted out, and of dignifying working class music with a positive stereotype. Singing cowboys such as Gene Autry and the Sons of the Pioneers may have defined this image, but Patsy Montana translated it into female form, and in so doing made a tremendous stride forward for women performers.

THE COVER OF THE ORIGINAL SHEET MUSIC TO PATSY'S BIGGEST SONG.

NOTES

1. The recording, Okeh 03010, gives "I Wanna Be a Cowboy's Sweetheart" as the title. The spelling used in this article is taken from the sheet music.

2. As quoted by Bob Powell, "Patsy Montana," *Country Music People*, 7 (September 1976), p. 14.

3. Chris Comber, "Patsy Montana The Cowboy's Sweetheart," *Old Time Music*, 4 (Spring 1972), p. 10.

4. Ken Griffis, "I've Got So Many Million Years: The Story of Stuart Hamblen," *John Edwards Memorial Foundation Quarterly*, 14 (Spring 1978), p. 8.

5. This information was taken from the album mentioned above, Starday 376. However, Montana claims that the album was recorded in a recording studio in Phoenix.

6. Arthur Satherley, Letter to Jo Walker, 9 September 1967.

7. Patsy Montana, Letter to the authors, 27 March 1980.

BOB DUNN ON LAP STEEL

STEEL COLOSSUS
The Bob Dunn Story

KEVIN COFFEY

▌Country music's story is not just one of great singing stars. Though they have often gone uncredited, the musicians—or sidemen, as (tellingly) they have long been called—have shaped the music all along. Bob Dunn is a case in point. Though acknowledged by western swing aficionados as one of the great steel guitarists, and probably the first country musician to play an electric instrument, Dunn is largely unknown to most country music fans. Bill Malone in *Country Music U.S.A.* (1968) and Nick Tosches in *Country* (1977) did much to restore Bob Dunn to his rightful place in the annals of country music, but their accounts were necessarily brief and sketchy, set as they were in the context of broader discussions. Dunn still remained a shadowy figure, more footnote than chapter in country's history, until 1994 when Kevin Coffey, one of JCM's regular contributors, offered the following detailed retrospective of this fascinating musician's career.—Ed.

"Bob Dunn was the lord of the steel guitar. . . . He wrought a music full of electric wonders. Great yelling dissonances burst from his bastard tool like glass against a stone wall."

—Nick Tosches, *Country*

▌In the fall of 1950, fresh off a tour with Bob Wills, the husband and wife duo of Laura Lee and Dickie McBride returned to their former base, Houston, Texas, to join forces with McBride's old cohort Dickie Jones. They called the new combination the Ranch Hands and brought in former Texas Playboy Herb Remington to play steel guitar because Jones's steel player, the legendary Bob Dunn, had opened his own music store in the Houston Heights and was ready to quit the nightly grind. Remington's first night with the band, at the Riverview Inn in the Highlands out from Houston, was Dunn's last.

Clyde Brewer, barely twenty that fall but already a seven-year dance band veteran, was onstage that night and recalls it clearly almost a half-century later, even through the haze of a thousand-odd gigs. "One sat on one end of the bandstand and one sat on the other," he recalls, "and I didn't think until years later that, 'Man, here I am on the bandstand with the two greatest steel guitar players in the world—one from the past, in a way, and one a great one of that day. On the same bandstand.'"

The night became in retrospect a highly significant and symbolic one: Dunn—the pioneer of the electric steel guitar and one of the most influential country musicians of any era—in effect turning over the reins to Remington, one of the kingpins of postwar steel guitar. Just a gig, but also a changing of the guard, for Dunn's playing days were mostly behind him, and the days when he was *the* trendsetter on his instrument were even longer past. His influence had waned since his return from a Navy stint in World War II, but in the half-dozen years before the war, it had been monumental. His playing had set the Southwest on fire and changed American music forever.

❚ Bob Dunn's name is likely known only to the staunchest country music fan today, and even to aficionados of western swing—the genre that Dunn helped create—he is, unfortunately, too often only a name, accepted as important without much understanding of his significance or, even less so, his genius.

But Dunn stands at the threshold of modern country music. It could be argued convincingly that the first notes that rang from his amplified steel guitar at Milton Brown's January 1935 Decca recording session signaled, both directly and symbolically, the new direction that commercial country music would take from that moment. Bill Malone, in his *Country Music, U.S.A*—a book that almost, but unfortunately not quite, rescued Dunn from undeserved obscurity—argues precisely that point, that "although no one realized it at the time," Dunn's first recordings were a significant "turning point in country music history." They set off shock waves, first in Texas but eventually spreading far beyond. And while other non-musical technology and societal shifts also changed the music and its audience irrevocably, Dunn's appearance on the scene was a major event in country's shift toward a more sophisticated and urban orientation from which—for better and for worse—the music has never really looked back.

Bob Dunn's significance stems from far more than his being the first known musician to record with an amplified string instrument. Alongside his status as a technical pioneer, he was a hugely important stylist, acutely individual, and his impact on those who heard him during his heyday was powerful. When discussing Dunn, his contemporaries fling the epithet "genius" with startlingly casual confidence. The eyes of former colleagues far into their seventies burn fifty years younger at the mention of his name, at the thought of his amazing sound and technique—not from any nostalgia, but from the still fresh visceral impact of his playing.

Milton Brown's brother Roy Lee, just thirteen when he first heard Dunn in late 1934, recalls clearly his slack-jawed amazement at Dunn's revolutionary approach. "It was unbelievable. It wasn't just that it was something like you hadn't heard before. It was something that you never dreamed could be done. That's the way it was with Bob Dunn."

"It was a dynamic experience to hear him," says fiddler-bandleader Cliff Bruner, who first worked with Dunn in 1935 and probably knew him as well as any man now living. "I think Bob was one of the greatest musicians that this world has ever produced."

▌ Robert Lee Dunn's early musical evolution was similar to a number of important musicians who came of age during the years following World War I. His father, Silas B. Dunn, was a breakdown fiddler, and Bob's earliest musical experiences were as his accompanist, so he was heavily exposed to traditional country music in his formative years. But as with so many others of his generation, the new technology of radio, the expanding and refining of phonograph technology, and the shift in America from a decidedly rural society to a much more urbanized one exposed Dunn to countless other musical styles and approaches. He was, as Charles Townsend described Dunn's contemporary Bob Wills, "a product of the Jazz Age."

Dunn was born at Fort Gibson, Oklahoma, in 1908, the oldest of four children. Although he later taught his younger brother, Silas Jr., some guitar, Bob was the only one of the four to pursue music seriously, an ambition that seized him at a very young age. As a child in the oil boom town of Kusa, Oklahoma, he heard a touring Hawaiian troupe and became obsessed with the steel guitar. He eventually obtained one and began to take lessons through correspondence with Walter Kolomuku. The impact of Hawaiian music—particularly its use of the steel guitar—upon twentieth century American music cannot be overstated. From the early 1900s through the 1930s, the enormously popular Hawaiian sound infiltrated American popular music in general, but transformed American folk music, both black and white.

Dunn fell deeply in love with the sound, and though some who have written about him like to position Dunn's steel guitar as the antithesis of "Hawaiian guitar," his music always bore the imprint of its early impact upon him—especially his lead work on ballads and his ringing, beautiful tone, so sure even when he played his hottest jazz.

But even more than being a golden age for Hawaiian music in America, the late teens and early twenties were the beginning of the Jazz Era. Hot music, as its ardent practitioners and fans liked to call it, caught Dunn's ear as well. Oklahoma, barely a state when Dunn was born and still wide open as he grew up, would produce more than its share of memorable musicians, and the jazz that came out of it—and out of Texas to the south—was tough, usually, and blues-laden. Although Dunn would acquire an extensive and sophisticated musical education and adopt an equally sophisticated approach, his playing retained a hard-edged Southwestern stamp and drive, and he became a profoundly gifted blues player.

All those influences and others were yet to be assimilated as Dunn came of age in Oklahoma in the 1920s. His brother John Dunn recalls that Bob had quit school by the eighth grade and that he was playing professionally while still in his teens; it was neither with a Hawaiian group nor a jazz group that Bob gained his first serious experience but with a western outfit called the Panhandle Cowboys & Indians, followed by a long stint with a similar group, California Curley & His Cowboy Band.

It's interesting to speculate on whether Dunn was chiefly playing steel or standard at this point, for in 1927, the steel was just beginning to be recorded widely by both black and white musicians, with the former tending more often than not to play the instrument in a Spanish position and the latter usually adopting the lap style of the Hawaiians. Both were beginning to build a new tradition—blues musicians like Blind Lemon Jefferson and country musicians like Jimmie Tarlton developing melodically and rhythmically intricate styles that, while far removed from what Dunn would develop, were still breaking the instrument away from its Hawaiian origins. At the same time, Hawaiian musicians like Bennie "King" Nawahi were falling in love with American jazz and attempting to adopt a hot approach on the instrument. Where Dunn was headed stylistically in 1927 is unknown, but Clyde Brewer tells a tantalizing story about Dunn's response, years later, to a *Metronome* magazine article about jazz steel guitar, which not surprisingly ignored him. "Man," Dunn complained, "I've got a good mind to write them. I cut a jazz record of 'Sweet Georgia Brown' on steel guitar in 1927." No evidence exists to support this claim; Dunn did record "Sweet Georgia Brown" with Milton Brown in 1935 and may have gotten the date wrong, but the story provides insight into how Dunn viewed himself stylistically and just how early he may have been improvising jazz on his steel. Dunn told Bill Malone a similar story, that he recorded a single record in Little Rock, Arkansas, in the late twenties.

By 1930, according to John Dunn, Bob was working for the notorious "goat gland" doctor, J.R. Brinkley, in Paul Perkins's band at KFKB in Milford, Kansas—voted the most popular radio station in America in 1929. It was in Kansas that Dunn met his wife, Avis; and when, as John Dunn puts it, "they run [Brinkley] out of Kansas" in 1931, Bob and Avis "went down and worked for him a while in Texas." To avoid the legal hassles that had plagued him in Kansas, Brinkley built the 75,000 watt station XER just across the Mexican border from Del Rio and out of U.S. jurisdiction, the first of the powerful border stations that would prove so crucial in spreading country music.

It's not clear how long Bob Dunn remained with Brinkley, but except for his stint with Milton Brown, which was less than two years, he does not seem to have stayed in one place for too long in his early days, as he was infected with a wanderlust that makes his prewar travels almost impossible to unravel. During the next several years, he would work with numerous bands and make several vaudeville tours, traveling at least as far away as New York. Sometime during those years he added trombone to his repertoire of instruments, a move that would profoundly affect his approach to the steel guitar.

By this time—the early to mid-thirties—both electric amplifiers and the first electric guitars were being marketed, and the burgeoning technology slowly began to revolutionize country music. Although true electric guitars were already on the market, the earliest manifestations in country music were adapted acoustic guitars with electric pickups attached. No one knows who the first country musician to utilize the technology was, but it may have been Bob Dunn.

According to what Dunn later told fiddler Jimmy Thomason, it was a chance encounter that occurred while Dunn was in New York working pickup gigs on Coney Island that first alerted him to the amazing possibilities of electrical amplification of the guitar. Thomason told Cary Ginell that Dunn "ran into this black guy who was playing a steel guitar with a homemade pickup attached to it. He had this thing hooked up through an old radio or something and was playing these blues licks. Well, this just knocked Bob out and he got this guy to show him how he was doing it." The man disappeared before long; but Dunn was obsessed with the musician's concept and sound and, according to Thomason, "followed him all the way to New Orleans" to learn more.

◼ It was probably inevitable that Bob Dunn should seek out Milton Brown & his Musical Brownies when a vaudevillian tour brought him to Ft. Worth in late 1934. Since leaving the Light Crust Doughboys in 1932, Brown had built the most popular string band in the Southwest, a band that was defining, much more than any other aggregation, the "Texas fiddle music" that would eventually come to be called western swing. Brown had added slapped string bass and a jazz piano to his string dance band; the Brownies played jazz, with unparalleled energy, and Milton Brown was a jazzy singer who kept an ear cocked for anything that would compliment the Brownies' music.

In Cary Ginell's *Milton Brown and the Founding of Western Swing*, Dunn's visit to the Brownies' KTAT broadcast from the Texas Hotel is portrayed as a formal tryout, although how this came about is unclear. Brownie bassist Wanna Coffman had, up to that point, played a Hawaiian tune on the steel at each of the Brownies' broadcasts. He told Ginell about coming into the studio to find "this great big guy wearing this ragged old suit" playing Coffman's steel, going over a tune with Derwood Brown. Coffman was irked until Dunn started to play "Over Moonlit Waters": "When Bob took off on that thing, why, my whole body felt like it was going to wilt!"

Dunn's hornlike jazz playing stunned the other Brownies and their radio audience as well, and soon he was a Musical Brownie himself. Crowded, noisy dance halls presented an obstacle, however: Dunn could not be heard over the din. It is unclear whether this problem or Dunn's desire to capture a certain sound was more instrumental in causing Milton Brown to drive to Woodward's music in Mineral Wells to purchase an amplifier, but sheer volume was obviously an important consideration. However, Jimmy Thomason's account leaves little doubt that there was more to it than that; Dunn clearly had the sound he wanted in his head and perhaps he told Brown about the black steel player's set up at Coney Island. At any rate, Brown purchased the amplifier and Dunn attached a pickup to what Cliff Bruner remembers as "a great big old wooden guitar that he bought down in Mexico."

Not content with just being louder, Dunn experimented with ways to capture the brassy resonance of jazz horns. According to surviving contemporaries, Dunn emulated jazz musicians like Texas trombonist Jack Teagarden and the great trumpeter Louis Armstrong, and his approach to the steel was based on their styles, their tone, their phrasing and attack. To replicate that phrasing, recalls Deacon Anderson, a Dunn protégé who still plays in a similar fashion, Dunn dampened his strings with his picking hand rather than his bar hand, allowing him more dexterity and the ability to cut off the notes' duration—like the staccato burst of a trumpet—to go along with the trombonelike qualities produced by the slide of the bar. But to achieve the tone he wanted, Dunn found he needed to magnetize his strings. To do so, says Cliff Bruner, Dunn hit upon a "magnet that came out of the coils of a Model-T Ford" that he would run up and down the strings, repeating the process whenever the brilliance of tone began to dim.

Dunn's addition to the Brownies' front line—heretofore made up of the dexterous and gracefully hot fiddle of Cecil Brower and the rollicking barrelhouse piano of Fred "Papa" Calhoun—solidified the band's position as the first classic western swing lineup, a position strengthened a few months later by the addition of second fiddler Cliff Bruner.

Dunn's new contraption took the region by storm. Musicians and non-musicians alike were astounded at his sound and technique. Word of Dunn spread as the Brownies traversed the state in an endless stream of one-nighters. Almost overnight the entire concept of playing steel guitar in the Southwest changed, a phenomenon that mushroomed after the Dunn's first recording session with the Brownies, for Decca, in Chicago in January 1935.

According to Bruner, the idea of recording daunted Dunn. "He's one that never could—and I'm the same way—never could get up and make a good record. He always played better out on a job. That's when he turned loose. It's never really been known what he could do on a job—when he was really playing."

As Ginell points out, Dunn sounds extremely uncomfortable on the first few sides he recorded with the Brownies. To compound that problem, Decca's engineer seemed to have trouble figuring out how to balance the band's sound with the new instrument and at first he positioned Dunn too far back in the mix. Feeling that the Brownies were a little tense, Decca hillbilly A&R man Dave Kapp eventually brought out a bottle of whiskey to pass around. By the end of the first day of recording, Dunn slipped into a historic groove—listen to "Some of These Days"—that would carry him through the rest of the sessions.

Kapp may have been too perceptive in bringing out the bottle, for Dunn was, by this time in his life, consistently drunk—almost certainly an alcoholic. According to most accounts, however, he was also one of those rare musicians who was probably at his best the second or third day of a drunk. He had a breaking point, beyond which his playing would turn into an incoherent jumble, and he might be likely to slide out of his chair, steel and all. But almost to a man his contemporaries argue that he was at his best after a few drinks.

"Man, I'll tell you," former bandmate Red Greenhaw says, "you give him a drink of that good drink—he'd sure play. . . . I guess it knocked him out [playing music]. He'd look up at you sometimes—man, you'd think he's way off somewhere. But he had his mind on his business. He wasn't a showman."

The second day of recording included classic Dunn solos on "Cheesy Breeze," "You're Tired of Me," as well as "Taking Off, Dunn's signature tune and country music's first steel guitar classic. Discussing Dunn's work with Brown forty years later, Nick Tosches wrote,

He mixed loud, lucid notes with fast, jagged triplets and grabbed at variously toned shreds of melody that complemented the song with bizarre, lizard-eye concision. These solos lunged like drunks, or rushed, graceful like hawks, from here to there to here. He even made "Shine On Harvest Moon" sound dirty.

The recordings spread Dunn's revolutionary sound even further than radio and personal appearances had. Soon amplification, not only of steels, but of standards and mandolins, became *de rigueur* in Southwestern string dance bands. Dunn's hornlike approach was emulated almost universally in the region; younger musicians aped every aspect of his playing. In North Texas were Lefty Perkins (who would later replace Dunn in the Brownies), Billy Briggs of the Hi Flyers, and Leon McAuliffe with the Light Crust Doughboys; in Waco, Doug Bine and Tommy Dunlap; Bash Hofner and Eddie Duncan in San Antonio; in Houston, J.D. Standlee and Harris Dodd; Tommy Treme in Beaumont. The list of disciples is endless.

Deacon Anderson, then a teenager in Baytown, perhaps characterizes Dunn's impact best: "I grew up with his licks in my head. He was my ideal."

Some had no idea what instrument they were hearing when they first heard Dunn on the radio or on record. Ken Lasater, who was introduced to Dunn's steel as a teenager in Vernon, Texas, says, "I didn't know what it was, but I made up my mind that if I found out, I was going to get me one somehow."

Non-steel players were no less enthralled and just as puzzled. "When I first heard Bob Dunn," says guitarist Red Greenhaw, who would later work extensively with Dunn in Houston, "[I thought] it was somebody blowing a comb with a piece of paper over it. . . . That's what it sounded like over the radio." Others thought they were hearing a trombone or saxophone, but the vocal quality that Greenhaw heard was undeniable, a quality that became more noticeable later in the decade as both amplification and recording techniques and reproduction improved. Some of Dunn's disciples came close to replicating many aspects of his style, but his irregular phrasing and amazing tone were only remotely approached.

"Nobody'll ever play the tone Bob Dunn got," says Greenhaw. "There's some pretty fair guitar players now . . . [but] they don't get the tone that Bob got out of a two-dollar amplifier."

Dunn's electric amplification of his steel predated such developments in jazz, too, and it's interesting to speculate about what impact he may have had on Southwestern jazz musicians like electric guitarist Charlie Christian, whose first recordings in 1939 would set the jazz world on its ear. Christian, a Texan reared in Oklahoma, and other early electric jazzmen like Eddie Durham and Floyd Smith—both Southwesterners— must certainly have at least heard Dunn on record or radio.

With the addition of Cliff Bruner in the summer of 1935, the Brownies became an even more exciting and tightly knit group, and the recordings that they made in a hotel room in New Orleans in March 1936 were considerably more assured than those from the year before. Dunn was in excellent form, especially on hokum numbers like "Somebody's Been Using That Thing," blues like "Fan It," and a ballad that Dunn played like he owned it, "An Old Water Mill by a Waterfall." Occasionally Dunn would falter—out on a limb dangling, with no place to go—one of the pitfalls of never being afraid to take chances, of constantly reaching for new heights. As fiddler Preacher Harkness, who knew Dunn later when he worked for the Shelton Brothers in Shreveport, put it, "He played way over a lot of musicians' heads. And sometimes I think he even played over his own head."

Just over a month after the Brownies completed the New Orleans session, Milton Brown was critically injured in an automobile accident and died several days later. Derwood Brown, just twenty and not well-equipped for the task, tried to hold the Brownies together, but the magic was gone and by summer the band had begun to fall apart. Cliff Bruner was the first to leave and he formed his Texas Wanderers in Houston shortly thereafter. Dunn stayed on for a while longer, but he, too, soon gave up.

Dunn traveled first to Abilene, Texas, but before long he joined former Brownie Cecil Brower in Roy Newman's western swing band at WRR in Dallas. Dunn and Brower recorded with Newman's jazz-oriented group in June 1937 for Vocalion, and Dunn played extremely well at these sessions. However, he was not very well recorded; his tone on these, his only sides for Vocalion, lacked the body and brilliance captured so fully by Decca and, later, Bluebird engineers.

Not long after the session with Newman, Dunn left to join Bruner, who had relocated his Texas Wanderers to Beaumont—virgin territory. There had never been anything like them in the area and Bruner was making a killing, broadcasting over KFDM and playing out all over southeast Texas and southwestern Louisiana (where the group had a deep and lasting effect on Cajun music). The band, already recording for Decca, included such future stars as Moon Mullican on piano and vocals and vocalist Dickie McBride, as well as pioneering amplified mandolinist Leo Raley. Dunn and Bruner had been close in their Brownie days and Bruner was excited for both personal and musical reasons to coax Dunn to Beaumont.

"Bob was my seat partner on the thousands and thousands of miles that I rode in the Brownie bus," Bruner says, recalling his friendship with Dunn. "He was my seat partner and my buddy. Great, great guy.

"He was very intelligent; he was a historian, a patriotic sort of fellow. I remember he got so mad at me when he found out that I had been raised around Houston and never gone over to San Jacinto. 'You mean you've lived in Houston all your life and you've never been to the San Jacinto Battlefield?' He couldn't believe that.

"We used to have *fun*. He'd bend over and act like he was an ape," Bruner laughs. "And he looked just like one. He was kind of hairy anyway."

Shenanigans aside, Dunn was a quiet, even gentle man, despite being a sturdy, imposing figure. He was kind, affable, and there are innumerable stories of his showing younger steel players the tricks of his trade. Still, he was not a man to be trifled with. Once, when drunk, he caught his jacket sleeve while trying to get in the rear door of the Texas Wanderers' bus. Unable to pull loose, he literally tore the door from its hinges, then climbed into the back of the bus and went to sleep.

Fiddler Darold Raley told Clyde Brewer of another incident that occurred when Dunn went into a diner after a gig one night during the heyday of boxer Joe Louis. Feeling no pain, Dunn mistakenly thought that a Louis bout scheduled for the next night had been fought earlier that evening and asked another patron about the results.

"What?"

"I asked, who won the fight tonight?"

"There wasn't no damn fight tonight."

Irritated at the man's surliness, Dunn slid his plate down the counter, turned, and lowered his gaze:

"The night's not over yet."

Houston drummer Tommy Sanders recalls a night in Houston after the war—by which time Dunn's steel was on a stand rather than in his lap and he had begun to use a volume pedal—when a drunken patron kept leaning on the steel while Dunn played, ignoring Dunn's pleas to stop. "Finally," Sanders says, "Bob unscrewed his foot pedal, which was pretty heavy, and whacked the guy in the head with it." The man fell back onto the dance floor, unconscious, where he remained until the police hauled him out.

The Texas Wanderers were unfortunately aptly named, for several members, notably Mullican and Bruner himself, were not comfortable in one place for very long back then. Whether there was some disagreement, or whether he was simply restless, Bruner had left—temporarily—by the fall of '37. His replacement was Dickie Jones, a young North Texan who had taken up the fiddle after seeing Bruner fiddle at a contest in Breckenridge several years before. Although banjoist Joe Thames tried to hold the band together, soon Mullican and Dunn were gone, too. Dunn returned to his old haunt Del Rio, where Ft. Worth's Hi Flyers had relocated and were playing over XEPN. He spent the winter of 1937–38 there, playing twin steels with protégé Lefty Perkins.

By the spring of 1938, Dunn was in Houston. Deacon Anderson remembers him working around this time with guitarist Chuck Keeshan on a radio show for Egg-A-Day. That summer the Texas Wanderers—who had traveled as far as Hot Springs, Arkansas, and Lake Charles, Louisiana, to recapture the magic that had departed with Bruner—returned to Houston, to their original home, KXYZ. Sponsored by Regal Beer, the group was patched back together under the management of Roy Thames, Joe's brother, who had previously managed Houston's Modern Mountaineers. By the end of summer, Bruner, Dunn, and Mullican were all back in the fold. Steel guitarist Deacon Evans, who had traveled from Shawnee, Oklahoma, the summer before to replace Dunn, was farmed out to the Blue Ridge Playboys to make room for Dunn.

In September, Cliff Bruner's Texas Wanderers travelled to San Antonio to record one of the most exciting sessions in country music history. Without Dunn or Mullican, the band's most recent session, in December '37, had been mildly disappointing. But this time all cylinders clicked. Bruner, Mullican, and Leo Raley were in top form, but Dunn was unbelievable. Dave Kapp had written Bruner before the session requesting "nothing but hot numbers," but he could not possibly have anticipated the heat the Wanderers would generate in "When You're Smiling," "Old Joe Turner Blues," "Draggin' the Bow," and others. Dunn's playing was manic, searing. He transformed the last chorus of the otherwise tame mid-tempo ballad "I'll Keep on Loving You" into a hot-as-hell jazz tour de force. His tone and phrasing were very trumpetlike and when he sailed into the upper registers he sounded at moments uncannily like Louis Armstrong replicated on steel; at others, he sounded more like a trombonist and, as reissue producer John Breckow once noted, Dunn's phrasing on "Old Joe Turner Blues" echoed that of a clarinet.

It was too good to last. By November, Mullican had left again to form his Night Riders in Lufkin. He was replaced by an Oklahoman from Shawnee, Mancel Tierney, who would become one of best pianists in western swing history. Then, apparently sometime in the winter of 1938–39, Cliff Bruner experienced a religious conversion and for a time quit playing music altogether. Breakdown fiddler Grady Hester replaced him, but the fire was gone again. The Texas Wanderers split into two factions, with Leo Raley, Tierney, and bassist Hezzie Bryant going with Dunn to form the short-lived Bob Dunn's Vagabonds.

With drummer Fritz Kehm added, the Vagabonds took up residence at the El Toro Club in Pearland and recorded for Decca at the Rice Hotel in March 1939. The session, Dunn's only one with a working group of his own—his later sessions were ad-hoc, "pickup" sessions—remains a fascinating one; clearly Dunn saw the Vagabonds as more of a jazz-blues ensemble than a country dance band, and it's amazing that Dave Kapp saw enough commercial potential in this odd, fiddleless electric jazz combo to record eleven sides and release them all. Perhaps the added attraction of Mullican, who came down from Lufkin to sing on the session— Tierney remained at the piano chair—tipped the scales. Certainly the name Bob Dunn meant far more to musicians than to the majority of the hillbilly-record-buying public, but the tunes were all good dance music, catchy jukebox fare. Dunn was again in amazing form, playing classic solos on almost every song—particularly "Blue Skies" and "Mean Mistreater"—and even singing one song, "When Night Falls," in a gentle Oklahoma drawl. Raley and Tierney were in fine form as well, and Kehm's brush work added a nice, very un-hillbilly flavor to the proceedings. Mullican's blues-laced singing was never better, and "Graveyard Blues," with Raley's very black-inflected vocal, sounds more like a race record than a country record, an odd harbinger of postwar electric blues.

Because new and more strict musician's union agreements with the major record companies were now effectively keeping non-union musicians from recording, Dunn (a member of the Beaumont local because Houston's had not yet begun to admit hillbillies) also sat in on sessions with Leon Selph, Buddy Jones, and the Shelton Brothers. (Bruner was playing some again by this time and joined his old seat partner at each of these sessions.)

Dunn apparently disbanded the Vagabonds soon after the Decca sessions, and though his recording activity over the next several years would indicate that he remained in Houston, he traveled extensively in the few years remaining before World War II. He seems to have first gone back to the Dallas–Ft. Worth area, where musicians like Doc Eastwood and Red Varner recall working a few dates with him around this time. According to Eastwood, Dunn even travelled with former Light Crust

Doughboy fiddler Clifford Gross to Kentucky and Tennessee when Gross decided to return to that area after a decade in Texas. But Dunn could not warm to Southeastern country music. "They went to the Grand Ole Opry in Nashville," Eastwood writes, "and Bob said, 'I can't handle this s—. I'm going back to Cowtown.'"

Dunn was back in Houston in September 1939 to record. He gathered Mullican, Raley, and Bryant for another Vagabonds pickup session and also recorded with Bruner—as part of Cliff Bruner and his Boys—as well as with the Sheltons, Floyd Tillman, and Dickie McBride. (Dunn is not, however, the steel guitarist at either of the 1939 Texas Wanderers sessions, as has been claimed; this was the Dunn-struck J.D. Standlee.)

Following the September sessions, Dunn went to Shreveport with the Shelton Brothers for a time before heading to Hot Springs, Arkansas, to work with Pee Wee Roberts & the Skyliners, an unfortunately unrecorded group full of fine Southwestern musicians, including the notorious pianist Smokey Wood, who characteristically got married on one of the Skyliners radio broadcasts (it didn't last). Dunn remained in Hot Springs a few months then headed back to Texas. At some point he played in Austin with Grouchy [Tatsch] & his Texas Pioneers and worked with pal Dickie Jones in the Port Arthur Jubileers. In Houston, he worked with a Mullican-fronted incarnation of the Texas Wanderers, led his own trio with bassist Bill Mounce and guitarist/vocalist Clarence Standlee, and also led a jazz-oriented band with a three-horn front line. He recorded a last, disappointing Vagabonds session for Decca in April 1940—singing most of the sides himself—and another session with a disillusioned Bruner, who had just been unceremoniously booted from a government job by Texas governor W. Lee O'Daniel. In April and October 1941, Dunn traveled to Dallas for recording sessions with Bluebird, waxing twice with Bill Mounce, as well as with Bill Boyd, the Sons of Dixie, and the Modern Mountaineers. The second session with Mounce was particularly notable for pairing Dunn with nineteen-year-old electric guitarist Jimmy Wyble, who within a few years would graduate from West Coast stints with the western swing bands of Bob Wills and Spade Cooley to jazz prominence with Red Norvo and Benny Goodman—and who has cited Dunn as an important formative influence.

The late Sock Underwood, vocalist on the Mounce sides, recalled that Dunn was having some trouble around this time getting steady work. "He was drinking a lot," Underwood said, "and he didn't play commercial enough for them. They didn't understand what he was doing. I'd sit down with his steel, play some simple commercial lick for him and say, 'See, that's what they want.'" It was ironic that those "commercial" licks were basically just streamlined, watered-down Bob Dunn.

Although Dunn was apparently drinking more heavily at this point, he resisted the temptation to ease into drugs like marijuana and benzedrine, which were becoming rather commonplace among Houston western swing musicians.

"I think Smokey Wood got Bob down there in Louisiana," Red Greenhaw laughs. "Smokey got him to take a little drag off that grass. . . . And Bob said, 'I walked a little piece and I heard my Daddy say, "Robert! . . . Robert!" Man, I ain't never tried none of that no more! That broke me from it right then.' He said he never fooled with it again."

■ As America's involvement in World War II neared, Dunn may have found himself with agonizingly little to show for all his work, but he remained his instrument's premier stylist, its originator. Nevertheless, others who had followed in his wake—like Leon McAuliffe, Billy Briggs, and Noel Boggs—were beginning to take the instrument in different directions. It was a process that would accelerate with western swing's postwar proliferation and West Coast orientation, and with the technical advances that would eventually change the steel guitar radically from the instrument Dunn played in 1935.

During the war, Dunn served three years in the Navy and seems to have returned a changed man. He had not stopped drinking yet—although he would within a few years—but he had the problem under considerably more control, and many of the men he worked with after the war don't remember him as a problem drinker at all. He settled in Houston; his roving days were over. He and his wife Avis had never had children, but they were by all accounts a happy couple and remained together until Bob's death.

Dunn decided to take advantage of the G.I. Bill. Always an inquisitive type, he had amassed an impressive education—and not only in music—in the years since he had dropped out of school in Oklahoma, so he breezed through the GED and enrolled in the Southern College of Fine Arts. He eventually gained at least a master's degree in music.

He continued to gig during these years. He worked with Freddie Real's band in Baytown in 1946, and surviving home recordings show Dunn to be in as good form as ever. (Still active in Baytown, Real has been leading bands in that city since 1929!) He occasionally booked his own country gigs and also formed a pop-cum-jazz band—the Blue Serenaders—with some young horn students at the college.

Dunn played a lot of trombone with the Serenaders—usually ensemble work—though he concentrated on the steel in his jazz choruses. His jazz ability astounded the young horn men. "He was amazing," says trumpeter Jimmy Siegeler, who would later teach in Dunn's music store.

"I'd give anything to have a recording of Bob playing 'Body and Soul.' Boy he could play that!"

Dunn usually booked the group, but Siegeler recalls one dance that he booked himself, in his hometown of Giddings, that drew 500 people. "It was a big gig. We had a good time. The next week [a very young] Willie Nelson came here and sold about ten tickets. So for once in our lives, we outsold Willie." The Blue Serenaders recorded once, with Dunn unfortunately restricting himself to ensemble trombone. The sides were never released.

By 1948, Dunn had joined the first incarnation of Benny Leaders's Western Rangers. Leaders (real name: Bennie Lueders) led some of the best postwar country bands in Houston, which even by 1948 was drifting away from jazz-tinged western swing toward less adventuresome, more vocal-oriented honky-tonk, a trend Leaders resisted for longer than most. (Leaders recalls that the Dunns were at this time breeding and raising dachshunds to supplement Bob's income.) After Leaders, Dunn reunited with Dickie Jones, and it was while playing with Jones that he participated in his last known recording sessions. Jones had formed his heavily jazz-minded Skyliners after the war, and for several years before public taste began to turn toward a more simple, rural approach in the wake of Hank Williams and others, the band packed them in at the Auto-Tel Blue Room out on the tough Beaumont Highway. The Skyliners recorded little, but surviving airchecks from their heyday—unfortunately before Dunn's arrival—show them to be one of the most exciting and tight western swing bands of any era—more akin to Benny Goodman's sextets than to any country band. By 1949, when Dunn joined, Jones was calling the Skyliners the "Rhythm Rangers" and was taking a more centrist approach in order to compete against local honky-tonk heroes like Floyd Tillman, Jerry Irby, and Leon Payne.

With Jones, Dunn played on sessions backing unknown hillbilly singer-songwriters like Dub Poston, Tommy Dover, and others. He also sat in on a 1949 Cliff Bruner session for Ayo Records, where his steel chorus on Link Davis's "San Antonio Blues" was an absolutely beautiful, Teagarden-tinged twelve-bar blues. He also played beautifully on a 1950 Dickie Jones-Red Greenhaw coupling, released as by "Jimmy Prince and his All-Stars," probably because Jones wasn't thrilled about having to record "hillbilly" material. Dunn's chorus on the ballad "You've Broken My Heart for the Last Time" is one of his best, lingering in the lower registers, sounding as agile and trombonelike as ever—and thoroughly modern to this day. Dunn even showed up on a 1950 session by Cajun fiddle star Harry Choates, taking a particularly fine solo on "I've Quit My Cattin' Around." Although West Coast guitarists like Joaquin Murphy and

Noel Boggs may have been the rage of the day—even among most Texas Gulf Coast steel players—and other, younger steel stylists were more in demand locally, Dunn's skills were undiminished.

By the fall of 1950, Dunn had opened his music store in the Heights and was ready to cut back on playing. He quit Jones, although he kept a weekly gig for a while backing local vocalist Betty Jo (Mary Catlett) at the Cypress Gun Club, and played occasional gigs with Leon Selph for the next few years. Mostly, he concentrated on his store and on teaching.

Jimmy Siegeler, who taught trumpet at Dunn's for about a year, said Dunn told him he was weary of the nightly compromise that most country gigs demanded—which was also one of the reasons he had formed the Blue Serenaders before. "I think that he was before his time," says Siegeler, echoing a sentiment expressed by all of Dunn's surviving contemporaries. "Are you familiar with the Kenton band [jazz bandleader Stan Kenton, whose sometimes avant garde big band was very popular in the postwar years]? The chord structures of those songs, how dissonant they are? Bob liked that kind of stuff. Well, you don't hear that in country music.

"[Bob] told me all these years he'd worked so hard at that—wearing his little tie and his cowboy hat and cowboy boots. He said he'd like never to put on another cowboy hat, because he was drained. You can only do so much."

And so Dunn faded from the scene, playing rarely, usually with Leon Selph (who claims he and Dunn drank two bottles of scotch on the icy New Years Eve that Dunn decided to give up drinking for good, and that the two ended up crawling across the frozen walkway to Dunn's house the following morning, too drunk to negotiate the path on foot). Dunn explained to Clyde Brewer, "I don't play that much anymore and I don't listen to the new steel guitar players . . . and the new styles. If a guy calls me to go play a one-nighter with him, he knows what I do and what he's getting. And if I want it, I go play it."

Pedals and other technology had made the steel a different instrument and made things possible that Dunn had never dreamed of with his six-string lap steel. He became a largely forgotten man as pedal steel players like Buddy Emmons set new standards in the fifties and sixties. Clyde Brewer recalls that Dunn hadn't even heard Emmons, although he carried his records at the store, until a friend forced him to listen to Emmons's "Four-Wheel Drive."

"He said, 'Clyde, it scared me to death,'" Brewer laughs. "'It just knocked me out. I've never heard a steel guitar played like that before.'"

Dunn's music store had had a successful twenty-year run when he decided to retire about 1970. "He was gonna sell the store and get him a place in Florida," Clyde Brewer recalls, "and just really fish and take it easy the rest of his life. And he didn't get to do that. It wasn't too long that I heard he was in the veterans' hospital."

Within weeks of selling his store, Dunn discovered that he had advanced lung cancer. Old cohorts, like Deacon Anderson and Cliff Bruner, visited him during his last days. Bruner remembers: "I was in to see him the day before he died. I said, 'Bob, you're looking pretty good.'

"He said, 'Cliff, I'm not gonna make it, son. I'm not gonna make it. I'm going on. . . . It's gone into my liver. When it gets in there, it's adios.' And he died—I believe it was the next day."

Sadly, old friend Dickie McBride was dying from lung cancer in the same hospital; he lingered only a week longer than Dunn, who died on May 27, 1971. Bob Dunn was buried in Muskogee, without even a Houston memorial service.

❚ Malone's *Country Music, U.S.A.* helped in some way to rescue Bob Dunn's legacy from growing neglect even while Dunn was still alive—it certainly gave him his historical due—but still, Dunn remained a figure known chiefly to musical peers and to scholars. In the seventies, thanks to Tosches's *Country* and a few small label reissues of his old recordings, Dunn achieved some form of cult status among younger generations fascinated with older styles and with the history of guitar amplification. Sadly, he has received little attention from writers and scholars outside country music. Michael H. Price and James Sallis's *Jazz Guitars* devoted some space to him, but the first recognition Dunn received in a full-scale jazz study, Gunther Schuller's *The Swing Era*, puzzlingly dismissed him as a player who "tended to feature more slidy Hawaiian effects," while elevating Leon McAuliffe, a gifted and important musician but not in Dunn's league, to a much higher status, praising him as a musician who "played primarily in a jazz idiom, highly blues-inflected and invariably in a single-note linear style."

Johnny Gimble's occasional Texas Swing pioneer reunion shows, staged in conjunction with Texas Folklife Resources, have kept Dunn's legacy in the public eye via Dunn-disciple Deacon Anderson, who at seventy-two is playing better than ever. The late electric mandolinist Tiny Moore, who knew Dunn around Port Arthur before the war, recorded a tribute—"Well Dunn"—on his album *Tiny Moore Music*. Dunn has also been belatedly voted into both the Texas Steel Guitar Hall of Fame and the International Steel Guitar Hall of Fame, sincere honors, but perhaps more a perfunctory shelf-cleaning of previously ignored pioneers than a historically well-informed, passionate recognition.

The Country Music Hall of Fame in Nashville also keeps on display the body of an old lap steel supposedly built and played by Dunn back in the thirties and found years later in the attic of Ft. Worth's Crystal Springs Dance Pavilion. But the instrument's actual origin and lineage of ownership remain somewhat mysterious.

It's difficult to tell how time will alter the perception of Dunn's legacy. Ginell's recent Milton Brown biography and a box set reissue of Brown's recordings by the Origin Jazz library may generate further interest.

Despite his historical importance and influence, Bob Dunn remains a somewhat shadowy presence—and a romantic figure to fans, and writers like Tosches, for that very reason. To those who heard him in his prime—bursting from a radio set or a record groove, his tone simultaneously gorgeous and obscene, his attack full of whiskey, piss, and vinegar that belied its source's gentle nature—he was a revelation.

"That Bob Dunn! Man!" laughs veteran steel player Hoyt Skidmore, his voice thickening at the memory of the amazing sound. "He was a *cat* on that steel guitar."

A RARE PHOTO THAT APTLY SUMS UP BOB DUNN'S TECHNIQUE, TAKEN AT HIS HOUSTON MUSIC SHOP, CA. 1951

BILL MONROE
(Photo by Jim McGuire)

FIFTY YEARS AND COUNTING
Bill Monroe Drives On

THOMAS GOLDSMITH

▐ This 1989 article about Bill Monroe came about almost by accident. A colleague had assured me that Tommy Goldsmith was working on a full-length biography of Monroe, widely known as the Father of Bluegrass and then preparing to celebrate his fiftieth anniversary as a member of the Grand Ole Opry cast. I approached Goldsmith, then a music correspondent for Nashville's morning paper, the *Tennessean*, and asked him about this biography and about the possibility of being able to publish early portions of it in the *JCM*. It was then that Goldsmith burst my bubble, telling me that a plan to produce an authorized biography had fallen through. But he was interested in trying to write a good historical profile of Monroe, having done a number of in-depth interviews with Monroe, as well as having recently spent some time observing Monroe recording a new studio album. Goldsmith and I agreed that one of Monroe's most interesting traits is his incredible work ethic, which has pushed him to keep playing the road and performing at the Grand Ole Opry through his eighth decade. Even if Monroe did not singlehandedly invent bluegrass (as he likes to maintain), he certainly shouldered much of its load, as this profile reminds us.—Ed.

▐ From a distance, the upright, three-piece-suited Monroe, seventy-eight, exudes tradition and conservatism. He's the revered "Father of Bluegrass Music," the recipient of honorary degrees and plaques, of tributes to his place in musical history. But in life, as opposed to legend, Monroe's contributions to music are far from over. The truth is, Bill Monroe has always been a restless sort of man.

He was already a star singer, songwriter, and mandolinist in 1939, when he quit the successful Monroe Brothers act and first "put together," as he says, his hard-driving bluegrass music. Monroe had little choice about getting musically stagnant—he was kept in motion by a backwoods work ethic, show-business instincts, and a constant need for something new to play. That relentless spirit of creativity has driven the Country Music Hall of Famer long past the usual retirement age—up to the present day.

Monroe is approaching a much-heralded fiftieth anniversary on the Grand Ole Opry. He is widely regarded as a preserver of country tradition and of the style he pioneered on the Opry in 1939. Thus, there's a temptation to make a graven-in-stone institution of this white-haired, tall-standing figure. It's true that Monroe's strict upbringing in rural Kentucky plays a major role in both his music and his strongly held code of beliefs. On his 288-acre farm just north of Nashville, he still plows with mules and performs back-breaking chores as he's done all his life. His nineteenth-century log house has ancient-looking farm implements hanging from its walls. And yet one sunny morning following a hard day on the farm, he sat down with me on a bench outside his house and vigorously played a mandolin piece so new it doesn't have a title. His approach to music and his repertoire, unlike those of his few surviving contemporaries, has never stood still; it's still developing. "I can't understand that, playing the same thing all the time," he offers by way of explanation.

Friends and members of his Blue Grass Boys band attest to it: Monroe is a wellspring of music who never seems to run dry. New tunes can appear at almost any time or place. "It's a constant stream," says former Blue Grass Boy and long-time Monroe associate Raymond Huffmaster. "You'll see him sitting at the Opry, or sitting anywhere, and he'll get up and get that mandolin, and that's where he's going." And he isn't merely prolific. "He is possibly the finest musician, the man containing the most musicianship in the entire field," Richard Greene, another former Blue Grass Boy, has claimed. Which is perhaps as it should be, since bluegrass music would not exist without Bill Monroe. More than any other form of popular music, bluegrass owes its conception to one person.

Monroe of course is proud to say that—as he wrote in a gospel song— "bluegrass music belongs to America." In fact, it's popular the world over. But the catch is that bluegrass from Monroe's point of view is exactly that—whatever he decides it is. The interesting part is that his conception has changed, grown and gone through marked shifts from decade to decade, from year to year, and sometimes from minute to minute.

"I don't know how I do it, but I can write a number in two or three minutes," Monroe likes to say. A tune that was just a set of phrases in Monroe's head can emerge on stage within the hour it's written. Some of these pieces, perhaps many of them, have been lost forever.

"He'd call me at home at night and say, 'You busy?'" Huffmaster says. "I'd say, 'No, I'm just laying here.' He'd say, 'Well, listen to this.' And he went into a mandolin tune that was a beautiful tune in a minor chord. And he said, 'What do you think of that?'

"There's no telling how many of those tunes he's forgotten."

When one asks where Monroe finds the inspiration for the stream of tunes, sounds, and styles, he answers as if the music is just there for the taking. "I pick 'em up as I go along," he says. "I like to do that."

The Monroe story abounds in paradoxes—he's a reclusive, often suspicious man, but also one with a well-developed sense of fun and humor. He's a great educator of his Blue Grass Boys, but rewards them with low pay and hard work. In personal encounters, Monroe can display everything from an opaque mask that baffles old acquaintances to a grandfatherly fondness for toddlers. He's a laconic, eyes-averted interview subject who can startle you with a direct, blue-eyed gaze and almost mystical theories of life and music. And he's a tradition-based player who loves to come up with a new change for the music.

"I don't have to be playing on a stage," he says. "I could sit right here and play and it would pay me. It would give me a wonderful feeling just to play it."

Monroe's inner vision of bluegrass seems to encompass virtually everything that has affected him strongly throughout his long life, including the often-told musical influences—his fiddling Uncle Pen Vandiver, his black bluesman friend Arnold Schultz, the sound of gospel singing, and the old fiddle styles brought over from Scotland and Ireland. But as Monroe discusses the music, it's clear that bluegrass to him also represents a whole ethos built on open country, farm people, hard work, decency, honesty, and love of family. As he once explained to journalist Alanna Nash, "If you take care of bluegrass music right, and play it right, it will tell you down through a lot of it what you should do and how you should treat people." No wonder, then, that whether at home or playing the 200 shows he still books annually, the music is never far from his mind. For Bill Monroe, bluegrass is truly a way of life.

Many of the forces that have shaped his music can be traced directly to the country around Rosine, Kentucky, where William Smith Monroe was born September 13, 1911. He is low-keyed and soft-spoken as he talks about the strong impact of his early life, both the good times and the lonesome times.

"I was the youngest one of eight children," he says. "The rest of them grew up, you know, and they were out having a good time, going different places and I was stuck there at home. My mother died when I was ten years old and my father when I was sixteen, so it just got sad to be there."

Mother Melissa was a fiddler and singer, while father James "Buck" Monroe was a hard-working farmer and sometime miner. Along with his fond memories of family life and of "baching it" with Uncle Pen after his parents' death, Monroe describes the hard life and frequent boredom of the farm community. "Years and years ago, there wasn't much that would go on," he recalls. "We'd go to school through the end of school.

Then we'd stay home and work and help out all we could. There might be a ball game at night; on Saturday night there might be a dance. Uncle Pen and me used to play the square dances; I tried to back him up on guitar. We'd play for the parties and the dances. Sometimes we'd ride the same horse back on the little country roads."

Those lonesome moonlight rides home from dances, and the Sunday morning wagon rides to church, seem to have affected Monroe deeply—he mentions them often. The slow horsepowered trips seem to place that era in time far from the mechanized present. And each important memory seems linked in some way to music—he credits his early days of playing dances for the sense of time to which he lends so much importance. "He'll sometimes break into a fiddle rhythm on the mandolin, and he says, 'Now can't you see the dancers?'" recalled former Blue Grass Boy Peter Rowan in a 1966 interview. "He talks about fiddle tunes all having a 'time,' and the time is based on the dance."

"I learned how to keep time on mighty near every kind of music when I was a boy, real young," says Monroe, "the schottische, waltzes, two-steps and all that, marches, polkas, the old-time square-dance music. It doesn't matter what kind of music you're playing, it doesn't hurt to know the time of all music."

As he gained his first experience at live performance, Monroe was also absorbing the angular gospel harmonies that would later reemerge in bluegrass. "The first singing that I tried to do, we'd go to church there in Rosine, Kentucky, at the Methodist, or Baptist, then there was a Holiness church that moved in later on," he says. "They sang some fine songs there at Rosine, Kentucky. That played a part in the kind of a sound and the kind of feeling that I wanted in my music, too. Taken right from the gospel song."

Monroe later began performing live and on local radio with brothers Charlie and Birch, playing the mandolin, as legend has it, because all the other instruments were taken by the older members of the large family. Bill devoted himself to mastering the mandolin, but he absorbed the music of all instruments. He's proud to have retained so much of his musical heritage. "I have a lot of old-time fiddle tunes. These fiddlers today never did learn them," he says somewhat testily. "A lot of the old fiddlers that could play them are gone. I play closer to the way they would have than any man alive. I play every note the way they put it in. You can go on back to numbers like 'Cackling Hen,' 'Arkansas Traveler,' 'Soldier's Joy,' 'Tennessee Wagoner,' 'Fire on the Mountain'—I know the way they should be played note-for-note. They shouldn't be jazzed up."

By the late twenties, Birch and Charlie Monroe were living and working in Chicago, where Bill joined them while still in his late teens. "I went to work up there in 19 and 30—up in East Chicago, Indiana," he recalls. "I worked at the Sinclair Refinery Co. I worked for them about four or five years and we were playing music on the side. We were playing a lot of different places and singing and it was giving us some practice. In 19 and 32, me and my brothers, we had a set of square dancers. We were dancing at the WLS National Barn Dance."

During those days of hard physical work and nights picking or dancing, were the Monroes convinced that they could make a career in music? "We didn't know," Monroe says with a glint of remembrance in his eye.

It's a poignant answer and one that rings true. It's a reminder of the tremendous distance he came—from a shy Kentucky farm boy to a working man and musician in what must have seemed the unbelievably large and busy city of Chicago. But Monroe was possessed of a strong drive to succeed and there were many more miles to go. The brothers appeared on radio stations in Hammond and Gary, Indiana, before heading out to the Midwest to broadcast in Shenandoah, Iowa, and Omaha, Nebraska. Before they left the Chicago area, Birch Monroe had decided to remain behind. The remaining Monroe Brothers, soon to be a successful country harmony duo, consisted of guitarist-lead vocalist Charlie and eager-to-travel Bill. "You like to see different states," he mused more than fifty years later. "You'd wonder if you'd ever get to go there and see them and then you did."

With the Texas Crystals Co. as sponsors, the Monroe Brothers moved from the Midwest first to Columbia, South Carolina, and then to Charlotte, North Carolina, where they changed sponsorship to the Crazy Water Crystals Co. In addition to their daily radio appearances, Bill and Charlie Monroe were playing somewhere just about every night. This was a change from their Midwestern days, where personal appearances were "just very few, not very many." As Monroe recalled in a conversation with Charles Wolfe: "We had two programs a day on radio, one in Greenville, South Carolina, and one on WBT-Charlotte really early in the morning. We drove 100 miles from one place to another and then we played schools at night. They kept after us to make these records, but we threw away the first several letters they wrote to us. We finally went up to their studio in Charlotte, but we told 'em we didn't have much time, that we had to get back in time to play a school that night."

The music they were producing was not bluegrass, but its quicker-than normal tempos, high harmony singing, and quicksilver mandolin playing contained clear hints of what was to be. By 1938, the two legendarily argumentative brothers had broken up their lucrative act, leaving brother Bill free to make music his own way. Monroe's drive to emerge finally from his family's shadow must have played a big role. "Me and my brother worked together a long time. But when bluegrass started, mine and his singing was put aside and I went with a different style of tenor singing from what I sang with Charlie. So that helped out in the way of bluegrass music having everything of its own."

By October 1939 Monroe had rehearsed his own Blue Grass Boys out of town and successfully brought them to Nashville and the Opry. With Monroe unleashed from his backup role to sing high tenor and leads and to play driving mandolin, the Blue Grass Boys made an instant hit with Opry executives. "I had it pretty well lined out when I came to the Grand Ole Opry, the way that I wanted it to go. It was built around my mandolin playing, and I wanted the fiddle there—it's the king string instrument. Then later we added the five-string banjo . . . to have that old Southern sound and everything, and he helped keep the time straightened out. But 'Mule Skinner Blues' was the first song I sung on the Grand Ole Opry, and I still do it the same way as I done when I came to the Grand Ole Opry."

As Monroe tells it, that was it: bluegrass emerged in full cry on that Ryman Auditorium stage with that first, hell-for-leather performance of the old Jimmie Rodgers blue yodel number. His belief in the style has an existential quality to it: Bill Monroe is, therefore bluegrass is. Even with all the arguments against it—Monroe himself has constantly changed the music, others have made far-reaching contributions—it's an easy mindset to get caught up in. Time, musical history, and even logic can be suspended as you see this man out of the nineteenth century continue to grow in his music.

At a Monroe recording session for last year's Grammy-winning *Southern Tradition* album, I watched and listened as he and the Blue Grass Boys recorded a wild, skirling tune called "Texas Lone Star" and a more conventional mandolin piece called "Stone Coal." When I talked to him during a break, he noted how different recording was from the days when everybody used to gather around one microphone, but he never mentioned how different his music had sounded then. For him, the mid-forties sound, including Stringbean's clanky two-finger banjo and Sally Ann Forrester's accordion, was just as much bluegrass as the Lester Flatt–Earl Scruggs "classic" band that followed. "Bluegrass was already going when they [Flatt and Scruggs] got in the picture," Monroe says. "They didn't have nothing to do with bluegrass music, getting it going the way it's going. The fast time of the music and everything was already there. They just had a job."

Great lead singers like Flatt, Mac Wiseman, and Jimmy Martin could come and go, and innovators like banjoist Bill Keith and, years later, even the great fiddler Kenny Baker, could join and depart the Blue Grass

Boys, but always Monroe forged on. "All of them have played a part in the music," he says. "Everybody that's worked for me has played a part when they were working for me, when they were coming along with some good ideas. Some of the fiddle players, some of the banjo players, some of the guitar players had different ideas that they would come along with that I would use and put in the music."

Monroe and the music, the music and Monroe, twine together like the red rose and the briar. One hundred and seventy-five Blue Grass Boys, two wives, and numerous friendships have passed through his life, but the music lives on. "I write for the music and the sound," he said during that January day of recording, and as I leaned on the wall in the recording room, I began to see what he meant. The "music" is his songs and tunes—the sometimes difficult, captivating melodies and lyrics that Monroe picks out of the air. And the "sound" is the seductive, gracefully blended mix of instruments as they play the music.

Monroe's band heard unamplified in a room has none of the harsh quality of much recorded or amplified bluegrass. For once, I heard bluegrass the way I believe Monroe hears it, not boosted or distorted by electricity, but breathing strongly, vibrantly, and naturally. It is this intoxicating sound that is at the heart of bluegrass music's attraction to its legions of fans and to Monroe himself. He has bent enough from time to time to allow some Music Row meddling with his recordings, but for the most part has fiercely resisted outside changes to the magic formula—even when rock & roll threatened all country music. "They knew I wouldn't do it," he says. "I think bluegrass came nearer to holding up when rock & roll was going than any other music—much better than country. It really hurt country."

As rock and country battled it out, Monroe occupied his own territory—singing spine-tingling stories from his past ("true songs," he calls them) like "Memories of Mother and Dad" and picking innovative instrumentals like "Scotland" and "Rawhide." Bluegrass was just starting to be known by that name, as Neil Rosenberg has pointed out, and few outside the South and the Midwest had heard it yet, let alone understood Monroe's artistic achievement. "They didn't know what it was, where it came from, or why it was being brought out," he says of bluegrass during that period.

The sixties brought him new peaks in popularity because of the folk music boom, the rise of bluegrass festivals, and an influx of talented "citybilly" sidemen. "I wanted to play for the country people and the farm people, because that's how I was raised," Monroe says. "Instead of stopping there, it went all over the world." In 1970, Monroe won induction into the Country Music Hall of Fame, a music-industry honor that placed his contributions alongside those of Jimmie Rodgers, Hank Williams, Bob Wills, and other towering figures. Perhaps given confidence by renewed industry and fan recognition, Monroe reached back during the seventies to some of the earliest music he'd learned. He dedicated an entire album to the fiddle tunes he'd absorbed decades earlier from his Uncle Pen Vandiver and came up with such striking instrumental material as the haunting "Lonesome Moonlight Waltz" and the difficult, memorable fiddle tune "Jerusalem Ridge." The eighties have seen Monroe remain active and creative despite a series of personal setbacks—poor health, a divorce, and a series of unsolved crimes against him including the vicious smashing of two cherished mandolins. He has seemed sad and weary at times, but music has remained his focus throughout. A good example is the ghostly mandolin tune "My Last Days on Earth," which followed an early eighties bout with cancer. "If you listen close to that, you're gonna tell that that's my last days on earth," a pensive Monroe says of the ominous sounding tune. "I'm really proud of that number; it really touches me."

Monroe has been an active performer for more than sixty years and a composer for more than fifty; *Southern Tradition* again presented strong new material, and a new album will feature Bill and the Blue Grass Boys in live performance on the Opry. Several dozen compositions, including the mandolin–trombone piece "Trombolina," await recording. After more than half a century as a country music innovator, Monroe continues to fascinate bluegrass musicians with the vitality of his work. How long will he keep at it? Asked this question in 1966, Richard Greene said, "I think as long as he's alive. He's the type of individual that is not going to decay by natural processes. He's almost superhuman in a lot of ways, and I think that as long as he breathes, he'll be on top of the field. There won't ever be a lapse. It'll take some great physical catastrophe to stop him."

Far from losing interest in music, Monroe remains intensely involved with many aspects of it—music stays on his mind. "If I see a note that should go in some number, I keep that note and put it in that song where it should be to help that song," he says. "I want it to touch your heart if you love bluegrass music."

Music has brought fame, travel, and a measure of earthly riches to William Smith Monroe. At times, he says, music has literally meant life and health to him. "I can get ready to go on stage and really feel under the weather, way down. I get out on stage and play to the people and all that leaves—the good feeling that comes from the music clears it up. Just a little bit later it's all cleared away—that's the most wonderful thing in my life."

THE BOYS IN THE BAND

Just a Few of the Pickers Who've Passed through Bill Monroe's Blue Grass Boys

FIDDLERS

Kenny Baker (1958, 1962, 1968–83)

Byron Berline (March 1967)

Richard Greene (1965)

Buddy Spicher (1961)

Vassar Clements (1950, 1955, 1961)

Bobby Hicks (1955–56, 1958)

Gordon Terry (Oct. 1951, 1955)

Chubby Wise (1942–48)

Carl Story (1941–42)

BANJO

Bill Keith (1963)

Eddie Adcock (1958)

Sonny Osborne (1952)

Rudy Lyle (1949–50, 1954)

Don Reno (1948–49)

Earl Scruggs (1946–48)

David "Stringbean" Akeman
(1942–45)

BASS

Mark Hembree (1978–83)

Doug Green (1969)

James Monroe (1964–69)

Howard Watts (1945–48)

Bill Wesbrooks (1940–45)

GUITAR

Roland White (May 1967)

Doug Green (April 1967)

Peter Rowan (Nov. 1964, 1965–67)

Carl Butler (1960)

Carter Stanley (1951)

Jimmy Martin (1949–50)

Mac Wiseman (1948–49)

Lester Flatt (1944–48)

Clyde Moody (1943–44)

(compiled with the assistance of
Doug Hutchens)

ELVIS PRESLEY
(Photo by Robert Dye)

ELVIS EMERGING
A Year of Innocence and Experience

PETER GURALNICK

■ In early 1987, I had a fortuitous conversation with Peter Guralnick. As it happened, he had been working on a video documentary but left the project retaining full rights to his script. Would I be interested in publishing it, with some revisions to make it more suitable for print? That's how "Elvis Emerging" came to appear in the *Journal*. Guralnick wrote it well before he started on his monumental, and definitive, two-part biography of Elvis Presley. (Part one, *Last Train to Memphis*, was published by Little, Brown in 1994.) "Elvis Emerging," says Guralnick, "was in fact—along with the liner notes that I did for Gregg Geller for *The Complete Sun Sessions*—one of the principal spurs towards writing the book." The following article is of interest, though, not simply because it contained the seeds of one of the most important works of music history ever produced. "Elvis Emerging" stands up on its own terms as a vivid and sharply focused recounting of Elvis's breakthrough year, 1956. Through an accumulation of telling details, not the least of which are Elvis's own ingenuous words, the following essay brings this towering cultural icon back to human scale, yet also reminds us how profoundly this young man's music affected life in America.—Ed.

■ *Hi, this is Elvis Presley. I guess the first thing people want to know is why I can't stand still when I'm singing. Some people tap their feet, some people snap their fingers, and some people just sway back and forth. I just started doing them all together, I guess. Singing rhythm and blues really knocks it out. I watch my audiences, and I listen to them, and I know that we're all getting something out of our system but none of us knows what it is. The important thing is that we're getting rid of it and nobody's getting hurt.*

In a lot of mail I get, people ask questions about the kind of things I do and that sort of stuff. Well, I don't smoke and I don't drink and I like to go to the movies. Maybe some day I'm gonna have a home and a family of my own and I won't budge from it. I was an only child, but maybe my kids won't be. I suppose this kind of talk raises another question: Am I in love? No. I've thought I've been in love, but I guess I wasn't. It just passed over. I guess I haven't met the girl yet, but I will and I hope it won't be too long, because I get lonesome sometimes. I get lonesome right in the middle of a crowd. I get a feeling that with her, whoever she may be, I won't be lonesome anymore.

Well, thanks for letting me talk to you and sort of get things off my chest. I want to thank all my loyal fans who watch my performances and who in a way have become friends of mine. I sure appreciate your listening to my RCA Victor records and I'd like to thank all the disc jockeys for playing them.

Elvis Presley burst like a thunderbolt upon a startled nation in 1956. Eisenhower was president, the Montgomery bus boycott signaled the start of the civil rights movement, James Dean's *Rebel Without a Cause* had just been posthumously released, a vaccine to prevent polio was being widely disseminated for the first time, the Beat Generation was waiting in the wings.

At first no one knew quite what to make of this latest and least likely in a line of rebel heroes who had sprung up in a land of hula hoops and backyard barbecues. Elvis Presley combined the truculence of Marlon Brando with the vulnerability of James Dean, the sleepy-eyed indifference of Robert Mitchum with the cocky self-assurance of Tony Curtis— but he was not a product of the movies. It seemed instead as if he had emerged from an underground from which the country had all but averted its eyes, an America in which youth, sex, and racial complexities had to be served. Rock & roll was the freight train on which he arrived, a bright new fusion of gospel, rhythm & blues, and hillbilly music which had only announced itself, and the simultaneous arrival of youth culture, within the past twelve months and was still in the process of almost daily evolution. It was a time of cataclysmic change, not least for a singer who in a single year would pass from small-time regional success to a stardom so intense that it would not only change the course of American popular music and the way in which we think of our public heroes—it would eventually consume the star himself. In 1956 it was still possible to see a young artist in the process of development, a musician with a voracious musical intelligence working out his own style—you could still discern the private self behind the public myth, the sensitivity, vulnerability, and fierce joyousness that found expression in the music. 1956 did not mark the end of Elvis Presley's career by any means, it just marked the beginning—but it closed off the world's access to him and his access to the world. After 1956 we would never be able to get close again.

"What is your reaction to the comment that you are just a flash in the pan ?"

"Maybe they're right. Nobody knows. In fact, if I knew, I would . . . I would be a mastermind. I'm not."

"Okay, that's a good answer. . . ."

On January 8, 1956, Elvis Presley turned twenty-one. Two days later he entered a Nashville studio for his first RCA Victor recording session. He had put out five records to date over the course of a year and a half on Memphis's tiny Sun label. The latest, "I Forgot to Remember to Forget," was currently riding the top of the country and western charts, bearing out for the first time in hard sales the pandemonium that his personal appearances had created throughout the South. This was what enabled Sun owner Sam Phillips to sell his contract to RCA for $35,000, the largest sum of money ever paid for a "hillbilly" singer up till that time. For all of his regional impact, though, virtually no one above the Mason-Dixon line had heard of Elvis Presley, and if history had followed its predictable course, his career would most likely have continued to follow the same pattern as country singers like Roy Acuff, Hank Snow, and Eddy Arnold, stars whom Elvis himself idolized, but *country* stars. History didn't follow its predictable course, though. Just before signing with RCA, Elvis had signed a management contract with Colonel Tom Parker, who had himself been involved with both Arnold and Snow but who had far more grandiose plans for his new protégé. Together with RCA A&R chief Steve Sholes, Colonel Parker, a veteran pitchman who had worked the carnival and medicine show circuit, plotted to break out of the regional market. The first RCA Victor single release was an original country blues by Florida schoolteacher Mae Axton. It was called "Heartbreak Hotel" and was released on January 27. The first appearance on national television came just one day later, as Cleveland disc jockey Bill Randie introduced the young man whom he had recently touted to RCA with these words: "We'd like at this time to introduce you to a young fellow who, like many performers—Johnnie Ray among them—come up out of nowhere to be, overnight, very big stars. We think tonight that he's going to make television history for you."

It was the Dorsey Brothers' "Stage Show" that provided Elvis Presley with the vehicle for national exposure. Every Saturday night for a month he appeared on the show, each time with increased confidence, poise, and undiminished enthusiasm. All week it was one-nighters on stages across the Southeast—in Richmond; Greensboro; Spartanburg; Winston-Salem; and Newport News—caught up in a frenetic whirl, three hours sleep if you were lucky, an unremitting pace that prevented the players themselves from having any idea of the dimensions of their own success.

"We were working near every day," said guitarist Scotty Moore. "We'd pull into some town, go to the hotel room and get washed up, or go right to the auditorium or movie house, and after we played our shows, we'd get back in [the car] and start driving to the next town. We never saw any newspapers. We didn't know we were getting big write-ups. And we didn't hear much radio because it was drive all night, sleep all day, and there wasn't much radio at night. There was a lot of crowd reaction, but we'd been seeing that for a year. How were we to know? All we knew was drive drive drive."

Then on Saturday it was a matter of getting back to New York for the Dorsey Brothers television show, flying in from North Carolina while the equipment was being driven on to the next night's gig. As a result, on several of their television appearances Elvis and the band appeared with borrowed instruments. The schedule was not much different than the one they had been following for the past year, but network television provided a very different forum than the Louisiana Hayride, the regional showcase on which he first made his name. And network television saw an increasingly different Elvis Presley, one who visibly matured with each passing week, one who spoke of himself as having "been at it a year but I'm ten years older now."

In all he made six appearances on the show. It would be nice to say that he revived the show's flagging fortunes, but in fact the Nielsen ratings didn't show much difference between his first appearance and his last. Record sales did, though. By mid-March "Heartbreak Hotel" had sold 300,000 copies and showed no sign of slowing down. Meanwhile, RCA had released its first Elvis Presley album, and "Blue Suede Shoes," from his first RCA EP, was already chasing Carl Perkins's original up the charts.

"How do you feel about being asked questions about your personal life? Do you think an entertainer should be asked myriads of questions about marriage and what girls he's going with and so forth? How does that strike you personally?"

"Well, let's face the facts. Any . . . anybody that's in . . . in the public eye is— their life is never private. I mean, everything you do, the public knows about it. And that's where it's always been, that's where it'll always be."

"In your—when you get caught in a mob or something, have you ever been seriously hurt?"

"Yes. I . . . I can. . . . I've been scratched and bitten and everything."

"What do you think about being scratched and bitten?"

"Well . . . I just . . . I just accept it with a broad mind, cause actually they don't intend to hurt you. I mean, it's not that. They just . . . they want pieces of me for souvenirs."

"You don't have much of a private life right now, then, do you?"

"No, sir, I haven't."

"I know you're under terrific strain after a show. How do you taper down? What relaxes your nerves after a big show like tonight?"

"Well, take for instance last night. I didn't . . . I didn't sleep any till about 10 o'clock today. I just . . . I get all keyed up and I . . . and it's tough to relax."

"What do you do before a show to help defer some of the excitement for the tension?"

"I just walk around and swallow and [laughter] clench my fists."

Elvis left for Hollywood immediately following his last Dorsey Brothers appearance on March 24. The exposure had served him well. In two short months he had made the journey from someone desperately wanting something he could not even name to someone who was desperately wanted. By early April "Heartbreak Hotel" was selling 25-30,000 copies a day, his album and EP were selling at the rate of another 8,000, and his combined record sales added up to 50 percent of RCA's pop business. Only the movies were left to conquer.

He had his screen test on April 1 in a scene from *The Rainmaker* with veteran character actor Frank Faylen. He also lipsynched a performance of "Blue Suede Shoes" for the test. On April 6 he signed a three-picture contract with producer Hal Wallis.

I guess . . . I guess actually that's about the biggest thing. Of course it's . . . it's a dream come true, you know and everything. It's something that I'd never think would happen to me of all people. But this shows that you never can tell what's going to happen to you in life. I've had people ask me what was I going to sing in . . . in the movie. And I'm . . . I'm not. I mean, not as . . . as far as I know. Cause . . . I . . . I took . . . strictly an acting test. And I . . . I wouldn't . . . actually I wouldn't care too much about singing in the movie. Because . . . I get enough singing around the country and . . .

Later in April, after almost four months of nonstop touring and the presentation of a gold record for "Heartbreak Hotel" in the midst of a one-day Nashville recording session, Elvis made his Las Vegas debut. He was billed, as per Colonel Parker's instructions, as "The Atomic Powered Singer" and was guaranteed $7500 per week. He opened at the Venus Room of the New Frontier Hotel on the same bill as Freddy Martin & His Orchestra and comedian Shecky Greene. It was the first misstep in an otherwise uninterrupted success story, as critics complained that his presence was like "a jug of corn liquor at a champagne party" and Elvis himself declared that "they weren't my kind of audience." He did play a special teenage matinee, though, and contrary to subsequent legend finished out the two-week engagement stronger than he started. He even met Liberace, a counterpart in showmanship, whose autograph he got for his mother and who joined him backstage in a song.

As part of his West Coast exposure he also made two appearances on "The Milton Berle Show." He had appeared for the first time on April 3 in the wake of his Hollywood screen test with about the same impact as his Dorsey Brothers performances, but when he returned in June it was as a conquering hero. He came back with a song that he had picked up in Las Vegas from a lounge act called Freddie Bell & the Bell Boys. Elvis had undoubtedly heard the original r&b version of "Hound Dog" by Big Mama Thornton, but for some reason Bell's performance captured his imagination and the song immediately became a part of his live act and the high point of his second appearance on Milton Berle.

The reaction to the Berle appearance was instantaneous. The show beat Phil Silvers's top-rated "Sergeant Bilko" in the ratings for the first time all season. And it drew the ire of the critics in a way that none of Elvis's previous appearances had. "Mr. Presley has no discernible singing ability," announced the *New York Times*. In fact, "it is wholly evident that his skill lies in another direction. He is a rock-and-roll variation of one of the most standard acts in show business: the virtuoso of the hootchy-kootchy." "He can't sing a lick," declared the *New York Journal American*. "He makes up for vocal shortcomings with the weirdest and most plainly planned suggestive animation short of an aborigine's mating dance." He was referred to—quite seriously—as "unspeakably untalented" and "morally insane." He was denounced from the pulpit, condemned by city ordinance, banned from the airwaves—became in short a symbol of everything that he himself privately abhorred. Although he did not respond directly to the critics, it was obvious for the first time that their condemnations were getting to him. "Those things they said I did wrong," he said in one interview which stressed his Christian upbringing, "that's the biggest lie ever printed. I asked my mother if I was vulgar. She said I was not." There was a serious point here, about being judged for what he was, not for how he looked. Each of his heroes—Brando, James Dean, the great black r&b singers—had made that point. They chose to be outsiders, each in his own way. In many respects Elvis was reacting not just for himself but for an entire generation.

"Sir, those kids that come here and pay their money to see this show come to have a good time. They're somebody's kids. They're somebody's decent kids probably that was raised in a decent home. If they want to . . . if they want to pay their money and come out and jump around and scream and yell it's their business. They'll grow up some day and grow out of that. I'll . . . I'll say this, and I'd like it

to add to what I just got through saying about . . . as a rule most of the adults are real nice. They're understanding. They . . . they . . . I've had them come around to me by the hundreds and say, 'I don't personally like your kind of music, but my children like it and so on . . . and if they like it, well, I haven't any kick about it because when I was young I liked the Charleston. Or I liked the foxtrot. I liked this and that.' They are . . . adults with a little intelligence. I mean, you know, that they don't run people in the ground for having a nice time."

"Okay, back to the clipping. Where did you get the name Elvis the Pelvis?"

"From somebody just like the character that's writing this article here. . . . Of course I don't like to be called Elvis the Pelvis, but—I mean, it's . . . it's one of the most childish expressions I've ever heard coming from an adult. Elvis the Pelvis. But . . . if they want to call me that, I mean there's nothing I can do about it. So I just have to accept it, just like you've got to accept the good with the bad. The bad with the good."

Elvis Presley was at a crossroads, whether or not he knew it himself at the time. After "Milton Berle" he was booked on "The Steve Allen Show" at an unprecedented $7500 for a single appearance. This was Allen's bid to eclipse Ed Sullivan in his previously unassailable Sunday night spot, but NBC was under increasing pressure to cancel the appearance because of the moral outrage precipitated by the Berle show. NBC announced that Presley would not be permitted to bump and grind on this network, while Allen came up with an ingenious solution of his own, in the irreverent spirit of the show if not of Elvis Presley.

Elvis arrived at the New York studio for rehearsal after an all-night train ride from Charlotte, North Carolina, on Friday, June 29. The band had gone on to Richmond for the next night's gig, and Elvis sat alone at the piano backstage picking out a gospel song while waiting for the stars of the show to arrive. He continued playing even as his manager, Colonel Parker, and representatives of the William Morris Agency discussed business, offering up a spiritual for this unlikely audience when he was finally introduced by the Colonel.

At rehearsals he took his dramatic tasks very seriously, just as he had for each of his television appearances, studying his lines and picking up on technical details with the same intensity that he focused on his music. With Allen and Imogene Coca and Andy Griffith he rehearsed a comedy sketch called "Range Round-Up," written as a kind of takeoff on "hayseed" shows like the Louisiana Hayride. Although the skit did not exactly treat its guest star with deference, Elvis approached the whole business with his usual good humor, delivering his lines, as written, without complaint.

Towards the end of the afternoon Steve Allen announced to Elvis that the tailor had showed up. "Yes, sir," Elvis replied. "What about?" He was to be fitted with tails for his appearance, he was reminded, the gag Allen thought would take some of the heat off of his performance. The Colonel made sure that his boy was fitted properly, and Elvis turned his attention back to the piano while the Colonel gave Elvis's cousin and road companion, Junior Smith, travel instructions for the train ride back to Richmond that night.

He arrived in Richmond the next morning, leaving the train station with a newspaper under his arm and an RCA transistor radio blaring rock & roll. After registering at the Hotel Jefferson and getting a little bit of rest, he had some lunch in the hotel coffee shop, eating chili and proudly showing his script to a Richmond friend. Junior Smith reminded him that there was only a half hour to the five o'clock show at the Mosque Theatre, where there was a reception already awaiting him. Backstage he rehearsed with the band and his back-up singers, the Jordanaires, who had only recently joined the show. The Colonel, for whom no task was too small in the furthering of his boy's career, was out front selling programs and souvenirs, while Elvis and his date amused themselves backstage—but when he hit the stage he was jet-propelled, "the world's first atomic-powered singer" once more.

In between shows he wandered restlessly around backstage, fielding questions from the press about the movies, his new home in Memphis, his love life, all the while combing his hair and trying on different instruments for size. After the second show he departed with the band still playing and took an overnight sleeper to New York for his appearance on "Steve Allen" the next night.

Dress rehearsal on Sunday went fine, and so did an impromptu press conference, with Elvis deflecting any difficult questions that came up in characteristically shy and diffident fashion. It was the show itself that turned out to be anti-climactic.

There was no question that Elvis earned his money, as Steve Allen soundly beat Ed Sullivan in the ratings for the first, and perhaps only, time that season. There was no question that he gave it his all. But fan reaction to his painfully stylized performance (at Allen's direction, he sang to a top-hatted basset hound) mirrored what appeared to be the star's own discomfort with his role. The song he sang was the same one he had debuted on "The Milton Berle Show" just a month earlier and which he had yet to record.

By the next morning Elvis fans were out in front of the theater carrying picket signs that said "We want the real Elvis Presley." Elvis himself had already experienced some acute moments of self-doubt. He had appeared tired and distraught on Hy Gardner's Sunday night television talk show which aired just hours after the "Steve Allen" appearance.

Then he had put in a call to his friend Dewey Phillips, the Memphis DJ who had played his first record, "That's All Right," fourteen times in a row the night it had come out. "Hello, you bastard," Dewey said.

"How'd you know it was me?"

"You better call home and get straight, boy. What you doing in that monkey suit? Where's your guitar?"

As discouraged as he might have been on Sunday night, Elvis was in the studio by noon on Monday, with Scotty and Bill and D.J. his drummer plus the Jordanaires for his third RCA recording session, the last he would ever have in New York.

After starting off the session with some spirituals, a custom he retained all his life, he turned his attention to "Hound Dog," which RCA vice president Steve Sholes, the man who had signed him, desperately wanted him to record. Despite the presence of Sholes and several other RCA executives in the studio, it was clearly twenty-one-year-old Elvis Presley who was in charge of the session. The first few takes were perfunctory enough, with the engineer primarily concerned with getting a proper level and Elvis concerned that the drums and guitar were not coming through loud enough. Everything was live, everything was mono, there were no overdubs, no opportunity to mechanically correct a mistake—to get a finished master you had to get through the entire take without making a mistake, and with the feeling intact. After take 28, Steve Sholes announced over the PA, "Okay, Elvis, I think we got it." Three takes later the singer himself was finally ready to quit. Everyone listened intently to the playback. Take 31 was the choice.

After a late afternoon lunch break it was time to pick out a second side. Most performers in this situation would come in with material prepared—studio time after all costs money—but, even when he had the time to prepare, Elvis always worked intuitively in the studio. On this particular day Steve Sholes had brought in a stack of demos from which Elvis selected a song by a New York songwriter and r&b singer named Otis Blackwell. The song was called "Don't Be Cruel," and because it was aimed specifically at Elvis Presley it was sung by Blackwell in a style approximating Elvis's own. Elvis listened to the playback again and again, carefully studying the lyrics sheet and roughing out an arrangement first on guitar, then on piano. By the time that everyone else had gathered around the piano to learn the song, Elvis already knew the lyrics and sang them softly to himself to get a proper feel while the other musicians noted down the chord changes. In about twenty minutes an arrangement was roughed out, including the Jordanaires' "Bop bops." After twenty-eight more takes this time, they had a finished product.

The session went on well into the evening. One more song was recorded from the stack of demos, a ballad called "Any Way You Want

Me." Around nine o'clock the session broke up, and Elvis went back to his hotel to finally get a good night's sleep before leaving for Memphis in the morning.

Elvis was going home for a benefit concert at Memphis's Russwood Stadium.

It was a twenty-eight-hour train trip, Elvis's fourth in five days, but it gave him a chance to relax, catch up on some sleep, read an Archie comic book, study the acetates from his session the previous day, and just fool around like any other normal twenty-one-year-old momentarily out of the public eye. Because a fan magazine had showed him surrounded by stuffed teddy bears, he had recently been inundated with presents from his fans, a publicity angle the Colonel, his wily manager, was not about to overlook. The Colonel was on the train not so much to keep tabs on his boy as to continue mapping out a grand strategy while soaking up every aspect of the human comedy at the same time. To the Colonel every conversation afforded a gambit from which there was an advantage to be gained.

Breakfast was served in Chattanooga, lunch in Sheffield, Alabama. As the train got closer to home, Elvis, who could never sit still anyway but was constantly drumming his fingers or tapping his foot, got more and more keyed up. "You nervous, son?" the conductor asked as he passed by. "Yes, sir," Elvis said, looking up at him blankly.

"You think a lot of your folks, I heard . . ."

"Well, my mother, especially my mother, she is always worried about a wreck, about me getting sick. So I have to let her know, because she's not in real good health anyway, and if she worries too much it might not be good for her, you know. So I . . . make it a habit of calling every day or so."

"You just got them a new house in Memphis?"

"Yes. They . . . they moved in Tuesday."

"What kind of house is it?"

"It's just the . . . it's a ranch type, seven room house. Three bedrooms, a den, playroom. . . . It's a pretty nice place."

"Yeah, I imagine. You gave them a lot of new furniture, too?"

"Yes, we . . . we had to have it to fill seven rooms. You have to have quite a bit of furniture. . . ."

Elvis got off the train alone at White Station, carrying only his records, cut through a deserted field, and made his way home on foot to the new house he had bought just three months before at 1034 Audubon Drive. It was the first home the Presleys had ever owned.

The fans were already out front waiting. They were gathered, as by custom, under the carport, which also housed two Cadillacs, one pink and one white. Elvis's father, Vernon, who had recently retired from work at age thirty-nine to take care of his son's business, was filling up the just-completed swimming pool with a garden hose. Family and friends were all on hand to greet the returning hero, who decided to go for a ride on his motorcycle almost as soon as he was settled. When the motorcycle wouldn't start, there was lots of advice from the crowd, politely gathered on the other side of the picket fence that divided the carport from the back yard. Finally, his father got the motorcycle going and Elvis roared off under the crowd's approving eye.

Upon his return, he waded into the half-filled pool, splashing around with his cousins before he remembered his wristwatch, which his mother Gladys reassured him would be all right. His mother, he told every interviewer who ever asked, was his best friend, his closest companion, his fiercest protector ever since he was a little boy. To buy a home for his parents had been his often-stated goal in show business, and now he had accomplished it.

Before long it was time to get ready for the concert. With his hair still wet, Elvis proudly played the acetate of "Don't Be Cruel" for his family. To the strains of "Any Way You Want Me" he asked his girlfriend, Barbara Hearn, to dance. When she declined, he picked out his stage wardrobe just before the Colonel arrived with a police car to take Elvis to the stadium.

When he took the stage at 10:30 it was as if a promise was being delivered. In front of family, friends, and fellow Memphians who had watched his rise with approval from the start, after an appropriately rapid-fire introduction from Dewey Phillips he declared, "Those people in New York are not gonna change me none. I'm gonna show you what the real Elvis Presley is like tonight."

He showed them. And he went on showing them. For the rest of that hot summer of 1956 Elvis was on the move, as controversy continued to pursue him. On July 13 Ed Sullivan, who had previously declared that he wouldn't touch Presley with a ten-foot pole, announced that he had signed Elvis to a series of three appearances starting in the fall. The price of $50,000 for the three appearances more than tripled Sullivan's previous high. By the end of July "Hound Dog" was a million seller, only eighteen days after its initial release, and in an unprecedented display of fan loyalty the flip side, "Don't Be Cruel," was not far behind. In August the Colonel licensed all Elvis merchandising—which now included hats, T-shirts, blue jeans, footwear, jewelry, bubblegum cards, food, drink, and assorted knicknacks—to Hank Saperstein, who had previously been associated with Wyatt Earp, The Lone Ranger, and Ding Dong School. By the end of the year this new association would generate nearly 20 million dollars in retail sales.

In August Elvis began a series of one-nighters in Florida. In Jacksonville he was enjoined from objectionable movements after juvenile court Judge Marion Gooding attended his opening matinee. To satisfy the court Elvis moved nothing but his little finger, and that created even more headlines. When he arrived in California for the start of filming on his first movie, a western whose title had been announced as *The Reno Brothers*, he was met by signs at the railroad station declaring "Presley for President."

Filming started on *The Reno Brothers* on August 23. Elvis, who played the youngest Reno brother, was slated for a featured, non-singing role in this western drama of jealousy and revenge. He showed up on the first day of shooting not just prepared but with the entire script memorized, knowing both his own lines and everyone else's, too. Also on the first day of shooting he met producer David Weisbart, who not entirely by coincidence had produced James Dean's *Rebel Without a Cause*. Weisbart was thinking of doing *The James Dean Story*, and, he told a reporter on the set, he was considering Elvis Presley for the role. Nothing could have thrilled the novice actor more. Elvis could summon up whole passages of Dean's dialogue from *Rebel* and *East of Eden* at a moment's notice. As for Weisbart, he saw some of the same qualities in Elvis Presley as he had in Dean—and some differences, too. "So far as teenagers are concerned, Elvis is what I call a safety valve," said Weisbart. "By that I mean, they scream, holler, articulate, and let go of their emotions when they see him perform. When they watched Jimmy perform, they bottled their emotions and were sort of sullen and brooding. Part of Elvis's great charm lies in his immaturity. Acting skill will probably ruin him, because his greatest asset is his natural ability."

"There's nobody that helps you out. They have a director and a producer and . . . as far as the acting and as far as the singing and all, you're . . . you're on your own. Nobody tells you how to do that. You have to learn it yourself."

"How do you rate yourself as an actor?"

"Pretty bad. I mean, I . . . that's something you learn through experience. I . . . I think that, well, maybe I might accomplish something at it through the years."

"Do you think it's just a case of . . . acting natural? Don't you do that?"

"In . . . in some scenes I was pretty natural. In others I was trying to act. And when you start trying to act, you're dead."

On September 9, in the midst of filming, Elvis made the first of his three scheduled appearances on "The Ed Sullivan Show." Sullivan was still incapacitated from an automobile accident in August, so Charles Laughton introduced Elvis from New York. Like "Hound Dog," "Don't Be Cruel" had reached the top of all three charts—pop, country, and rhythm & blues—an unprecedented feat and one that has never been duplicated—and on its own reached sales of over a million copies just that week. All twelve songs from the first album, which had itself gone gold, had recently been released on six singles and were on their way—along with a seventh released at the same time—to selling over 100,000 copies each. Elvis did four songs on the Sullivan Show while over 50 million people, 82.6 percent of the viewing audience, watched. Steve Allen didn't even bother to show up. NBC showed a movie instead.

He shook up the airwaves once again with explosive versions of "Hound Dog," "Don't Be Cruel," and "Ready Teddy," but it was another number, a sentimental ballad based on the Civil War song, "Aura Lee," that caused the real stir.

And now, friends, we'd like to introduce you to a brand new song that's completely different than anything we've ever done. This is the title of our brand-new Twentieth Century movie, and it's also my newest RCA Victor escape—release. And I would like to say right now that the people over at Twentieth Century Fox have really been wonderful, all the great stars in the cast, the director and the producer—this is our first picture, they really helped us along. With the help of the very wonderful Jordanaires, a song called "Love Me Tender."

The reaction to "Love Me Tender" was as immediate, and as dramatic, as the outcry that had greeted his previous television appearances—only this time it expressed approval. This time a forgiving public was ready to welcome the bad boy back into the fold. With shooting on the film more than half complete, it was decided to introduce four Elvis Presley songs into the script and retitle the movie after the song. Even the ending had to be reshot to satisfy Elvis's fans. RCA, too, got the message. In the wake of the television appearance, the label got 856,000 advance orders for the record and—with six singles currently in the Top 100—was forced to rush yet another one into release. At this point it seemed as if Elvis Presley could do no wrong; he was the hero of comic books and movies that he had dreamt of becoming as a boy. When he returned to his birthplace of Tupelo, Mississippi, in September, he was, appropriately, given a hero's welcome.

He had grown up in a little shotgun shack on the wrong side of town, sung with his parents at the First Assembly of God Church from the time he was two, and left with his family for Memphis when he was thirteen because, he told an interviewer, "We were broke, man, broke." No one was interested in dwelling on the bad times today, though; on this occasion he was to be treated like a prodigal son. A parade was organized in his honor; Tupelo mayor James Ballard and Mississippi governor J.P. Coleman were on hand; and, with tickets at seventy-five cents and $1.25, attendance at the evening show was estimated at 22,000—at a time when the entire population of Tupelo was only 20,000. Elvis received a scroll from the governor and a citation from the mayor along with a key to the city. The next year he would return from California to raise money towards the creation of an Elvis Presley Youth Center, to be built on a site just behind the two-room shack that had been his birthplace, but on this day he performed in a bright blue velvet blouse that Natalie Wood had had made for him, with his family and his girlfriend Barbara Hearn sitting proudly in the front row. He was forced to miss the parade, ironically, for security reasons, and when he and another girlfriend went to a Memphis theater to watch newsreel footage of the event several weeks later he came out to find his white Cadillac torn apart by fans who had scratched their names in lipstick on the finish and ripped out whole sections of upholstery.

"It's certainly nice to meet you, Elvis. And I wonder . . . I'd like to ask you just a few questions. I know you're in a terrible hurry. First of all, how does it feel? All this tremendous reception, to be back home after these years and have everybody come out to see you and meet you like this."

"It really feels great. I've been, looking forward to it for a long time. . . . I've met a lot of people I went to school with and a lot of my kinfolks that I haven't seen for a long time. And it's really been a great day."

"Well, we met your parents tonight and they're awfully proud of you and I know you're proud of them and Tupelo is certainly proud of you. I'd like to ask you a couple of questions now before we quit. One is how do you feel about the reaction of the teenagers like the young ladies who jumped on the stage this afternoon and the way they act down in the audience? How do you feel about it?"

"Well, I . . . I really enjoy it. I mean, I think it's real great that they care that much about you. People ask me did I think it was silly? I do not. I think it's wonderful. I'm just glad that they think enough of me . . . "

"Well, they certainly do think enough of you, and I think that's evidenced by the fact that they're out there just chomping at the bit right now for you to come on out. And I wonder if you have anything you'd like to say to all of the people of Tupelo and your friends and relatives here."

"Well, I'd like to say to all the people that brought me down here, the mayor

and the governor and all . . . thanks for giving me the most wonderful time of my life and all the wonderful people who came out to see it."

"What song is your favorite that Elvis has recorded, Mrs. Presley?"

"'Baby Play House.'"

Elvis's father, Vernon: *"That's a good one, that one."*

"And 'Don't Be Cruel.' . . . That's my two favorites."

Humility and rebellion were finally enshrined in a mix no more unlikely than the original package in which they came. When Elvis got his first draft notice, it became a national issue, with congressmen vowing that he would serve his time, fans ready to lay their bodies down in front of the troop train, and the center of all this controversy simply proclaiming his desire to serve his country.

Several times he was challenged by overwrought fans and jealous boyfriends. In Memphis Elvis was brought to court over an incident at a filling station. "I can take ridicule and slander, and I've been called names," he said, "but when somebody hits you a guy has got to defend himself." He emerged unscathed from both the fights and the court cases. "Presley's no slouch," said one patrolman admiringly. "He knows how to handle himself real fine." It was becoming more and more hazardous for him to go out in public, though, not so much because of the "guys who thought they had to prove something," as because of the possessive nature of his fans. "A crowd of people can hurt you and not even realize they're doing it," said Elvis philosophically. "You can't go places like other people. You can't go to ballgames. When I'm traveling around, I don't go anywhere. I just eat in the room."

On October 28, he appeared on Ed Sullivan once again, and while he was in New York he re-shot the ending for *Love Me Tender* at the Junco Studio on East Sixty Ninth Street. Fan pressure had been building ever since it had been announced that he would perish in his first screen role, and whether because of that pressure, or simply to take advantage of a good publicity opportunity, the studio flew in a crew to shoot the scene. It showed the image of a heroic-looking Elvis Presley superimposed over the dying Cliff Reno and singing the title song of the film as the character expires. Because it was primarily a head-and-shoulders shot, there was no need for Elvis even to change his shoes, and he played the scene in the same white bucks he had worn on television the night before.

November 16 was the much-ballyhooed New York premiere of *Love Me Tender*, taking place under a forty-foot-tall statue of the main attraction. By eight in the morning, three thousand teenagers had lined up, many of whom would view it continuously throughout the day and week. Five hundred fifty prints had been prepared for a national saturation booking which would earn back the film's one million dollar investment in less than a month. Although it had been rumored for weeks that Elvis would appear at the premiere and the fans strained to catch a glimpse of him, he was vacationing in Las Vegas at the time.

He was staying at the New Frontier Hotel, where he had appeared in April, and caught the acts of Liberace at the Riviera and rhythm & blues greats Billy Ward & the Dominoes, featuring a young Jackie Wilson doing a medley of Elvis Presley hits.

On his return to Memphis he stopped by the Sun studio where he had made his first records a short two years before and enjoyed an impromptu reunion with former labelmates Carl Perkins, Johnny Cash, and brash newcomer Jerry Lee Lewis. For over three hours they fooled around in the studio, mostly harmonizing on the hymns and old gospel songs on which they had all grown up. Elvis provided the cues at the piano, with the others grouped around The Star Who Had Gotten Away and his new friend, dancer Marilyn Evans from the New Frontier.

Three days later he showed up at the WDIA Goodwill Revue, a charity event which Memphis's leading black radio station, known as "The Mother Station of the Negroes," put on each year. This year the show featured B. B. King, Junior Parker, Bobby Bland, Ray Charles, and gospel's Five Blind Boys, all long-time heroes of Elvis's, each one a stylistic mentor. He watched the show intently from the wings, mesmerized by the performances, but it was his own brief appearance onstage—just a bow and a wiggle when he was introduced—that got the biggest response of the evening from the all-black audience, as a near-riot resulted.

Then on December 15 Elvis Presley made his last appearance on the Louisiana Hayride, which shifted its location to Shreveport's Louisiana Fairgrounds to accommodate the overwhelming popularity of its star.

Christmas was spent at home with Las Vegas showgirl Dottie Harmony as his houseguest, and hometown girlfriend Barbara Hearn giving him the gold vest which he wore on his final Ed Sullivan appearance twelve days later. On January 4 he reported for his pre-induction physical, and on January 6 he appeared on Ed Sullivan with Ed's full endorsement—and singing one of his favorite gospel numbers, "Peace in the Valley." It was almost one year to the day from the time a barely twenty-one-year-old Elvis Presley had first entered the RCA recording studio, and he would never again know the feeling of aching desire that he experienced on that day. He was about to start shooting his second picture, *Loving You*. The future looked bright ahead.

Well, I've tried to be the same all through this thing, you know. Naturally, you learn a lot about people, and we were involved in a lot of different situations—but I've tried to be the same. I mean, the way I was brought up. And I . . . I always

I always considered other people's feelings. I've never . . . in other words, I didn't kick anybody on my way. . . . I don't just sign the autographs and the pictures and so forth to help my popularity or to make them like me. I do it because I know that they're sincere. And they see you, and they want an autograph to take home. And they've got an autograph book, or they've got their little camera and everything. So you have to know that. Regardless of what anybody says about it, my private life is my own—well, it is to a certain extent. I mean, everybody has to have a certain amount of privacy. But once you get involved in this business, you have to consider that, and you have to consider that these people are sincere. They don't know the kind of life you lead. They don't know what kind of person you are. And so . . . I try to remember that. That's all. It's simple, it's no problem. It's no big effort that I put forth. Just the way I feel . . . I haven't made any bad decisions or anything . . . but it's the way I was brought up. My surroundings, my mother and my father and the whole family. We were always considerate of other people's feelings.

GEORGE JONES
(Photo by Slick Lawson)

GEORGE JONES
The Grand Tour
NICK TOSCHES

■ No one has placed more hits on the country music record charts than George Glenn Jones. And no country singer is more admired for the sheer musicality of his influential singing style. Heir to the heart-rending vocal tradition of his hero Hank Williams, Jones has had well-publicized battles with alcohol and ex-wives, and in the process has assumed the status of a ragged-but-right legend. Still, no country singer has presented a tougher challenge for interviewers. What do you ask a virtuoso who will not discuss his work? As one who had attempted to interview Jones on more than one occasion during the past twenty years, Nick Tosches was well qualified for the task. In 1992 Tosches met with Jones once again in an effort to understand how such a taciturn man could be so prodigiously expressive in song. Despite Jones's continued reticence, Tosches found a way to get to the heart of his subject, carefully recounting the whole sprawling, sad saga of Jones's life in this immensely revealing portrait. In the end, Tosches finds the answer to the central question that Jones will not address: Must an artist suffer to produce great work?—Ed.

■ George Jones is sober, and he has been for a long time. "I ain't touched a drink in ten years," he announced to the packed crowd that had paid $40 a head to witness his hour-long performance at Tramps in New York City in November of 1992. Like his comment that he had not "been to the big city since '56," his announcement was not quite true. He had performed at Philharmonic Hall in the spring of 1972 and at the Bottom Line in the summer of 1980, and had accepted a Grammy at Radio City Music Hall in early 1981; and ten years ago, he had been drinking like there was no tomorrow. Still, this Manhattan appearance was a triumph of sorts. He was once again on top of the world. Six weeks before, he had been inducted into the Country Music Hall of Fame. His new MCA album, *Walls Can Fall*, was the best work he had done in years. And, though New York had always somewhat intimidated him, now, in his first show here since sobering up, he demonstrated to the cheering demographic crazy-quilt at Tramps that the powers of his unique voice, in a culture mad with neophilia and ephemeral sensation, seemed ever-compelling and everlasting.

Three weeks later, in his dressing-room suite at Bally's Casino Resort in Las Vegas, he strolled back and forth, chain-smoking Barclay cigarettes and imitating Ernest Tubb: "I'm walkin' the floor over you, . . ." he sang, mimicking the deep, gravelly delivery of Tubb's 1941 hit. Jones is sixty-one years old, short, and paunchy. The high-heeled cowboy boots he wears do not much enhance his size, and the robust midsection of his renewed health, combined with the facial characteristics that long ago inspired the nickname Possum, make him appear more possum-like than ever before. His hair in recent years has turned completely white. Fastidiously styled, with its overhanging forward-swerving eaves and impeccable scimitar sideburns, it is never tousled, always in place, like a sculpted pinnacle of incongruous permanence atop a distinctly mortal shell. Beneath his brown eyes, his cheeks are striated with deep fissures that are not so much the natural carvings of age but the ravages of mortification. When he grins, the furrows are less obvious; when his expression is blank or subtly scowled, as is more often the case, the furrows are like the scars of a recondite clawing.

Last night, he had worn a black glittery suit that had been made for him by Manuel of Nashville, the former protégé of and successor to Nudie Cohen of North Hollywood, the tailor who had embroidered the musical notes on Hank Williams's lapels, designed Elvis's gold-lamé tuxedo, and taught a generation of country singers that lavender and orange were complementary colors. Tonight, as in New York, he wore crisp blue jeans and a Navaho-patterned Western shirt. He slapped his gut, that symbol of his return from the dead, smiled once, and his attitude changed suddenly from one of playfulness to one of tired resignation. "Let's get this over with," he said.

His band, the Jones Boys, had already taken the stage of the Celebrity Showroom. The six young men comprised a basic honky-tonk band: a steel guitarist, Tom Killen; a lead guitarist, Jerry Reid; a fiddler, Andy Burton; a piano player, Kent Godsen; a drummer, Bobby Birkhead; and a bass player, Ron Gaddis, who has been with Jones for almost twelve years and serves as the leader of the group. In instrumentation, the band differs only in its degree of skill and sophistication, and its casual, long-haired appearance, from the bands Jones sang with thirty-odd years ago. Back in those days, a good night's pay was $500–$600 a night, for three or four hours of music. These days, Jones gets anywhere from $20,000 to $50,000 a show. He plays a hundred to a hundred and twenty shows a year. The New York show was a rare exception: most shows last less than forty-five minutes. Last night, he was on and off within an hour. He had opened in New York with "No Show Jones," which he used to perform with Merle Haggard. "Tonight is the last night I'm ever going to do that stupid song," he had said onstage that night. Tonight, in Las Vegas, he opened with "No Show Jones," as usual. "We're gonna have a ball tonight," he declared, as he does every night. "We're gonna have a *good* time." As he did in New York, he warned that "We might be here till four in the morning." ("I'm such a hick that I believed him," said Michael Pietsch of Little, Brown after the Tramps show.) He did a total of seven songs, ending with his new single, "I Don't Need Your Rockin' Chair." Then—"Good night, everybody. Thank you!"—he was off in less than twenty-three minutes.

At a concession stand in the lobby area, there were GJ-monogrammed shot glasses ($3), No Show license plates ($3), George Jones embroidered caps ($12), Rockin' with the Possum T-shirts ($15), and George Jones and the Jones Boys satin tour jackets ($60). In the casino, George, his wife, Nancy, and I sat at a blackjack table, as we did last night, donating among us some several thousand dollars to Satan. Nancy drew two cards totaling twelve. "Should I hit it, honey?" she asked George from across the table. "I would," he said. Nancy drew a ten, and the dealer took her little pile of $50 chips. "It's only money," said George, pushing forward several red-and-black $100 chips and purple-and-black $500 chips. He was happy. He was finished with Las Vegas. Tomorrow his pilot, Don, would be flying him to Tennessee in their Lear jet. "I miss my girls," he said. He was talking about his cows.

It is no exaggeration to say that Jones is far more enamored of his cows than his career. Though he is the foremost of country music's living legends, he has not had a #1 hit since "I Always Get Lucky with You," in the summer of 1983. Since then, country music has become the domain of a new generation of rock-nurtured singers.

"They can play middle-of-the-road and pop and call it country all they want to, but I don't think they'll ever take the real thing out of people's hearts," Jones told me. "Nowadays it's strictly all fame and fortune and glory. In the old days, we did it because we loved to do it. It was a wonderful feeling, of course, knowing that you could make a living that way, doing something you loved to do, but it was never really about money. I think to be successful and stay successful a long period of time, you've got to love what you're doing."

Though he remains immensely popular in concert, and though his recent albums have sold hundreds of thousands of copies, Jones today has difficulty getting radio airplay. He is considered too old for the ever-younger image that country music projects. In early 1993, while Palomi-no Road, one of the new "bands with hair," was about to resurrect "Why, Baby, Why," his earliest hit, from 1955, his own current single, "I Don't Need Your Rockin' Chair," had not even broken into the Top Twenty of the country charts. Though Jones dismissed it as "this stupid thing," it was a good record, a nouveau-rockabilly celebration of old honky-tonk ways. Furthermore, its background chorus featured Garth Brooks, Travis Tritt, and many other of the biggest of country music's new generation of singers, nearly all of whom have named Jones as their idol, echoing the sentiment of Waylon Jennings that, "If we could all sound like we want-ed to, we'd all sound like George Jones." As to the adulation he com-mands among the youngbloods, Jones is nonplussed. "That's the hard part to understand," he said. Maybe "they all pretty much like country music to start with, they just didn't get into it themselves." Nor does he understand why he is idolized by an increasing number of rock stars. "I was really shocked and surprised to hear all these rock stars make quotes about me." Likewise, he was "surprised a little, and happy" at the exu-berant reception at Tramps.

The truth, to Jones, is simple. "Country music is something you love. It's a music you love. I don't know, for some reason, being a star or any-thing like that never did really enter my mind. If they hadn't paid me for singing, I would've still done it, long as I could've got enough to eat somewhere. It don't matter to me that much. I like to sing with my heart. I like to sing soul country songs. And that's the way it'll always be with me. And I've always stuck with that, and it's pretty much, I think, what's the answer for my success."

❚ When I first met him, in Nashville, eighteen years ago, George Jones struck me as a prisoner, both in fact and in fancy. His life was falling apart, and, as he had taken increasingly to missing dates and vanishing without notice or trace, his career was crumbling as well. He was to per-form a goodwill show later that day, April 20, 1976, at the Tennessee State Penitentiary, and, the day after next, was to be reunited in the recording studio with his ex-wife Tammy Wynette. To ensure that he stayed in town, his record company, Epic, and his manager, Shug Bag-gott, were keeping him under their guarded watch in the comfortably appointed basement of the Music Row building where Baggott main-tained an office. But, beyond this droll subterranean captivity, his spirit seemed to be darkened by a greater, and indwelling, thralldom.

Back in March 1962, Jones had recorded a song called "Warm Red Wine." It was an old song, written by Cindy Walker and first recorded, in the spring of 1949, by Jones's Texas elder Bob Wills. But there was something about Jones's version, something about the pure, stark sincerity with which he delivered the lament "I'm a prisoner of drink who will never escape," something about it that evoked horripilations of a rare and disquieting sort. It was more than a testimony to the power of Jones's singing; it seemed a personal testament as well.

In a few days, Jones would announce that he had won his battle against alcoholism. But it was not true; and seeing him that morning in his sunless lair, as he paced and sat and fidgeted and rose and paced, buoyant one moment, despondent and anxious the next, dressed in an immaculate athletic suit of sweatpants and sweatshirt, chain-smoking cigarettes and swigging Heineken from the bottle, as if the vestments of sobriety and cardiovascular well-being might abrogate the reality of the beer and the smoke, I could not help but think of the way he sang that song.

He was then, as he is today, arguably the greatest country singer alive. His was, and is, a voice capable of imbuing the commonplace sorrows and joys of the human universe with poignance and puissance, of crystallizing the simplicities of the mundane and the time-worn into subtle, complex new glintings, of discovering in and mining from the plain phrases, tired metaphors, graceless rhyme, and familiar melodies of songs a hidden, underlying honesty and depth, of transforming those songs from expressions of tailored emotion to vehicles of expressiveness itself. These are gifts that have been shared by Jimmie Rodgers, Hank Williams, Jerry Lee Lewis, and to lesser profundity a few other legendary country singers. But while Jones and his idol Hank Williams have both affected generations with a plaintive veracity of voice that has set them apart, Jones, unlike Williams, has further been gifted with a voice of remarkable range, natural elegance, and lucent tone. As Emmylou Harris has said, "When you hear George Jones sing, you are hearing a man who takes a song and makes it a work of art—always. He has a remarkable voice that flows out of him effortlessly, and quietly, but with an edge that comes from the stormy part of the heart." In that same understated edge, Jon Pareles of the *New York Times* has discerned "a universe of lonely torment." Gliding to high tenor, plunging to deep bass, the magisterial portamento and melisma of his onward-coursing baritone send off white-hot sparks and glissades of blue, investing his poison-love songs with a tragic *commedia-è-finita* gravity, inflaming his celebrations of honky-tonk abandon with the heat of careening, heartfelt delight, and turning songs such as "Warm Red Wine" into harrowing wails from the abyss.

Taciturn, inarticulate, withdrawn, brooding, and self-destructive by nature, George Jones has always seemed to express himself, and to assert and redeem himself, primarily through his singing; and the singing, in turn, has seemed to convey some sense of the power of catharsis it has held for him. In his best performances, the songs have served merely as skeleton keys to loose the vague, rhymeless shades of deeper and more mysterious feelings. Without a song, those feelings—all feeling, it seemed—remained hidden. He was a cipher: in song, a well of emotion and creativity; in life, an erasure of a personality evincing but the barest traces of sentience.

He seemed friendly, shy, and vacant. That he was, and for the last twenty years had been, the most successful singer in the business—second only in country-music history to Eddy Arnold, who had a ten-year lead on him—was something that seemed to be far less important to him than the bottle of beer in his hand. He was wholly unassuming and down-to-earth. One could readily believe the accounts of those who had known him for many years, that he had not changed much at all, that he had been impervious to fame and fortune.

I came away from that meeting liking him but feeling that I had been in the company of a man whose unequivocal soulfulness abided incongruously beneath an inert mind. Surely, I thought, this blankness must be an illusion, a deception, perhaps even of self, like the jogging suit. I was not alone. Others who met and worked with him shared similar feelings; and through the years, he, like Elvis, has evaded any in-depth interview, speaking only briefly to journalists and biographers, and then usually only to utter disjointed platitudes that did little more than convey his skewed and innocent sense of what a show-business personality ought to say. In the years after I met him, though lurid news of his deathward dissolution grew more widespread with his every downward lurch, the man who seemed to be self-destroying remained largely unrevealed and unknown.

George Jones is not given much to talk. He is a man of few words, whose passive silence many have found disarming. As his wife Nancy told a music-business executive who felt uneasy in Jones's presence, "George will make anybody nervous if you pay him any mind." There is a well-known story in Nashville of how Jones, yielding to pressure from his record company, once agreed to an interview, excused himself to go to the restroom a few minutes after the interview began, and was not seen for two weeks. Neither the two biographies of him, Bob Allen's *George Jones: The Saga of an American Singer* and Dolly Carlisle's *Ragged but Right: The Life & Times of George Jones*, both published in 1984, nor the many articles devoted to him offer much in the way of first-person revelation by Jones. In a 1981 *Village Voice* cover story, what little Jones had to say was made to suffice among descriptions such as how he "delicately set the glass of cold water on the white formica table in front of him, not too close but easily within reach." A 1992 cover story in the *New York Times Magazine* relied more on the words of Jones's record producers than on his own. When Elvis Costello conducted a brief chat with Jones for *Interview* magazine several months ago, it was done under the subterfuge of a casual telephone call. "Seemed like he was trying to *interview* me," Jones had said suspiciously after hanging up. Chapters of an authorized biography that were recently circulated among New York publishers by the William Morris Agency were regarded as too insubstantial by most of those who read them. Who was this guy, this seeming actuarial blip of a nonentity who belied his own apparent hollowness by singing as if his soul were on fire? What was it that made him the greatest country singer alive, and what was it that was driving him in a panic to his own waiting grave?

I thought about these things, still wanting to figure them out, when I began spending time with George Jones again recently. Passing time backstage, playing blackjack, or simply hanging out together, Jones was easygoing. But in trying to steer the conversation beyond small talk, he countered with a sort of disappointed resistance. Time and again, he promised me that we would sit down with a tape recorder. Christmas passed, the new year began, and still he proved elusive. I was sitting in a motel room in Brentwood, Tennessee, watching television, when Susan Levy of MCA Records and Nancy Jones worked out a plot by which we could snare George for that long-promised sit-down. On television, Sammy Kershaw, a country-music youngblood who wears a diamond stud in his left ear and idolizes George Jones, is promoting Pheroessence Star Clone, a perfume supposedly distilled from pheromones extracted from his sweat. Just dial 1-800-96-SAMMY. As it turns out, Jones is involved in the marketing of a far homelier product: George Jones Country Gold Dog Food. ("*IF GEORGE SAYS IT'S GOOD . . . THEN IT'S GOOD BY GEORGE!*") The stuff is made in Red Bay, Alabama, by Sunshine Mills, Inc., the producer of several other brands of basically identical dog food. Tomorrow Jones is to meet with Sunshine Mills executives. I will travel to Red Bay with Susan, who, once there, will feign being called back to Nashville on emergency business. This will leave no alternative but for me to make the 185-mile return trip aboard George's custom-made Liberty Coach bus.

The next day, at a company lunch, Jones is presented with a six-week-old Labrador retriever. Later we learn much concerning the various grades and price fluctuations of the rendered-pork-and-beef-fat mixture that arrives in Red Bay by the twenty-four-ton truckload at a rate of a 150 truckloads a year. We also learn the nature of "fish digest," one of the ingredients in George Jones Country Gold Ocean Fish Flavor Cat Food. (They are entrail pressings.) Throughout the day, which is one of intermittent rain and clouds, Jones does not remove his sunglasses. Outside the factory, standing in the drizzling rain, an unemployed carpenter named Billy waits in the hope of meeting Jones. "I want to shake that man's hand," he tells me. As we leave Red Bay at dusk, Jones at first is mad at his wife for her part in the plot. Then, after a fashion, he loosens up.

Long ago, I had encountered a prisoner of drink. Since then, he had been written off for dead, but had denied the doomsayers their satisfaction. I expected him to be somewhat changed; and he was, but not quite as I had anticipated. Now he struck me, oddly, as a prisoner of sobriety.

▍The east Texas town of Saratoga lies near Little Pine Island Bayou, in the heart of the Big Thicket, a once-impenetrable 3.5-million-acre expanse of virgin pine, cypress, and hardwood forest, meadowland, and backwater swamp that until the mid-nineteenth century had been the hunting-ground of the Alabama-Coushatta tribe, who are now relegated to a reservation in the Thicket's northern reaches. Located about thirty miles northwest of the port of Beaumont, Saratoga was one of several Big Thicket sawmill settlements that grew into oil-boom towns following the Lucas Gusher at the Spindletop Hill salt dome south of Beaumont on January 10, 1901. Saratoga, like Spindletop, was a salt-dome oilfield, and it was in Saratoga that the Mellon family's newly formed Gulf Oil Corporation drilled its first producing well.

The population of Saratoga, which at the height of the oil boom numbered in the thousands, has now dwindled to less than six hundred souls, though no one has bothered to replace the sign at the town limits which proclaims its populace to stand at a thousand. Those old-timers who remain agree that Saratoga has been dying since the 1950s. First the wells went dry, and then, as boom-town morality ceded ground to the Baptists, the bars were shut down and the town itself went dry. The Big Thicket itself has dwindled as well, down from its 3.5 million acres to less than 300,000, little more than 28 percent of which are presently authorized for protection under the 1974 designation of the Big Thicket as a national preserve. What is left of Saratoga lies at the edge of one of the biggest parcels of protected preserve, the Lance Rosier Unit.

And what is left is not much. The broken stretch of Texas Farm Road 770 that serves as Saratoga's main thoroughfare passes a few rusted, lumbering oil pumps, the tumbledown remains of an old fireworks stand, a Super Pak grocery, whose dirty, broken plastic sign stands as Saratoga's most prominent and modern feature; the First United Pentecostal Church, Dy's Toning Salon, Brown's Gun Shop and Feed, and Don's Barber Shop. And, hidden back among the trees, there is the privately run Big Thicket Museum. "Tourists from around the Nation and the globe visit the Big Thicket Museum each year," says the little leaflet, which describes the two-room museum as being located at the "biological crossroads of North America." Posted on a gate at the entrance to the road leading to the Big Thicket Museum is a sign: SARATOGA, TEXAS. BIRTHPLACE OF GEORGE JONES.

The singer's father, George Washington Jones, the only child of a short-lived and broken marriage, was born in Lufkin, two counties north of here, and brought in his infancy by his mother, Mary Ferris Jones, to the Big Thicket home of her parents. Before he was two, his mother remarried and left him behind to be raised by his maternal grandparents. In the mid-August heat of 1915, twenty-year-old George Washington Jones married Clara Patterson, the nineteen-year-old daughter of a Big Thicket preacher known as Uncle Litt. Moving from one Big Thicket rent home to another, following work from logging-camp to sawmill to oilfield, George Washington Jones and his growing family settled finally in Saratoga, where, on September 12, 1931, in a small log-and-slapboard cabin, George Glenn Jones, the second son and last-born of George and Clara Jones's eight children, drew his first breath.

George's father was a drinking man. The death of his first-born child, seven-year-old Ethel, in early 1926, had driven him more deeply into drunkenness, and by the time his young namesake was born his reputation in Saratoga was that of a no-good drunkard who did not quite deserve the good and decent woman who was his wife. The drinking had caused a cold, deepening rift between him and his wife, who redirected much of her affection to her youngest child. "My mama," George would say, "loved me more than anybody ever did." It was Clara who raised George, like his elder brother and sisters, in the fold of her father's White Oak Baptist Church. It was there, beside her, that young George learned to sing. But it was George's father who gave him his first guitar, when he was eight.

"Little old Gene Autry guitar," George recalled, the better part of a century later, describing that guitar as if he could still see it: "Had a picture of a cowboy on a horse with a lariat, and Gene Autry's name. My Sunday-school teacher taught me the chords on it. I just fell in love with it, and I spent all my time with the guitar. It never warped. I carried it many times in the rain."

In 1938, about the time George got his guitar, his family also got their first radio. On Saturday nights, live from Nashville, there was the Grand Ole Opry, whose newest star, a thirty-four-year-old Tennessean named Roy Acuff, had joined the show's cast in February of that year, and who by the end of the year had enjoyed two immense hits, a mournful song of strange Pentecostal imagery called "The Great Speckled Bird" and "The Wabash Cannon Ball." George was mesmerized by Acuff's high, piney nasal style, and it became an indelible influence on his own singing.

"My daddy always got my sister and I to sing when I was a kid," George remembered. These were not pleasant performances for George or his sister Doris, who were roused from sleep by their father when he came home drunk in the middle of the night, alone or with his cronies, demanding entertainment and threatening violence if he did not get it. The resentment that George harbored for his father's drunken brutishness grew more intense with every command performance.

Huey P. Meaux, a Cajun born across the Sabine River, in Kaplan, Louisiana, in 1928, was raised in the town of Winnie, south of Beaumont. With a resumé that includes pop, r&b, and country hits as well as a federal-penitentiary stretch (and subsequent presidential pardon), Meaux, known as the Crazy Cajun and the father of swamp-rock, is one of the most colorful and irrepressible characters, and perhaps the most accomplished record producer, in Texas music. A friend of Jones since the late forties, Meaux told me that Saratoga, in the old days, "was a place you didn't go to unless you knew someone." The area had a reputation for lawlessness, violence, and hostility to outsiders. Towns such as Saratoga had given east Texas its notoriety as redneck country, as Klan country. "The Big T'ickets," Huey said, in that fine Cajun accent that still flavors his every word, "you just didn't go there."

Brown's Gun Shop is a cavernous warehouse. Feed sacks and farming tools line the walls, but the shadows in whose musty dimness they lie seem to be the real stock-in-trade. The worn floor-planks do not creak in any quaint sort of way, but rather seem to groan meanly at the intrusive affront of every step that dares to break the sepulchral silence of the place. Behind a sagging wooden counter, from other, gloomier shadows, emerged a middle-aged man as unwelcoming but otherwise as expressionless as the floor. His eyes were close together in their sockets and shone as dully as the dark steel barrels of the rifles gathering dust in their display racks. As he seemed to be the only sign of life in town on this bright Friday afternoon, I asked him, more or less, if he was the sole sentinel here at the biological crossroads of North America.

"Try Don," he said.

Indeed, the sign that hangs, swaying forlornly in the breeze, from a post at the entrance to Don's Barber Shop, advertising Family Kuts & Kurls in a sad, handlettered attempt at fully kappa'd, high-mall modernity, does little to prepare the visitor for the biological flurry within.

The young farmhand who sat in the shop's lone shearing-chair said with a grin that he had a George Jones cassette in the tape deck of his pick-up truck right this very moment.

Don let the comment pass. He was a balding man who appeared to be in his fifties, and as he worked his comb and scissors, his features, cast in aloof and faintly condescending detachment, possessed a vaguely sinister air.

"It's just to now to where he admits bein' from round here. We were just white trash, people thought. We had this reputation of hatin' and killin' niggers." He drew a bit of the young man's hair between his fingers and put the scissors to it. "Of course, it wasn't true."

"Yes it was," the young man grinned.

One of the old-timers sitting against the wall, a jovial heavyset man in his seventies, with white hair and a red face, uttered a sound that fell somewhere between a snort and a chuckle. "He'd set up by the drugstore and play his little old three-string git-tar."

"People round here now wouldn't think no more of George Jones than George Strait," said another, a gray-haired man in his late forties. "All the old-timers are gone now. My mother, who's dead ten years, went to school with him."

"His daddy was just a drunk, too," said Don, as if to dismiss Saratoga's most celebrated son as a common drunkard and nothing more. "He'd line 'em all up and whup 'em if they didn't sing."

Don remembered that his daddy was often visited by George's brother, Herman, whose boyhood habit it was to douse himself freely with the old man's hair tonic. One day, Don's father filled the hair-tonic jar with poke-salad oil, and the unwitting Herman barely knew the difference. "Wore it two, three weeks," said the barber with relish. "Stayed on there real good."

The white-haired man seemed to be transported by this talk of olden days. He looked through the window, peering wistfully across the street to a sign that stood among the weeds declaring the presence of the Saratoga First Assembly of God. "Used to be a beer joint right there," he said, as if trying within his mind to bring this place back to life.

Don piped up again. "They called him Greensleeves round here when he was a kid. See, he'd get dressed up in this white shirt when he went round singin' and playin' that git-tar of his for coins, and he had this way of wipin' his nose on his sleeve in between songs."

In 1941, the Jones family moved to Kountze, the Hardin County seat, some fifteen miles northwest of Saratoga. It was there that ten-year-old George began performing at the Saturday-night revival meetings of Sister Annie Stephens, the Sunday-school teacher who had taught George his first chords, and her husband, Brother Byrle. A year later, as wartime brought prosperity to the shipyards, the Jones family moved again, to Multimax Village, a government-subsidized housing-project in Beaumont, where George's father found work as a pipefitter at the Pennsylvania Shipyard. It was in Beaumont, during the war years, that George Jones, having reached the seventh grade, left school behind him.

And it was in Beaumont that young George became aware of a new sort of country music, something quite different from the old-timey string-band stuff that still represented the sound of the Grand Ole Opry. In Texas, as most everywhere else, the biggest hit of 1943–44 was "Pistol Packin' Mama." Written and recorded by a forty-one-year-old Texan named Al Dexter, "Pistol Packin' Mama" became the first country hit to be performed on "Your Hit Parade," radio's weekly presentation of America's most popular songs. (When the show's troupe performed Dexter's song, the word "beer" was censored from the lyrics.) In addition to being an immense country hit, the song, in the summer of 1943, crossed over to become a #1 hit on the *Billboard* pop charts, and, that autumn, crossed over to the "Harlem Hit Parade," *Billboard*'s early black-music chart. Following Dexter onto the pop charts was a cover version by Bing Crosby with the Andrews sisters. Lusty, capricious, raucous, and reflecting the sophisticated influence of western swing, "Pistol Packin' Mama" was the commercial apotheosis of honky-tonk, a burgeoning genre of country—and, at first, distinctly Texan—music that both celebrated the wild side of life and lamented its wages. Al Dexter himself had done much to set a precedent with his "Honky Tonk Blues" of 1936. By the time of "Pistol Packin' Mama," the dark side of honky-tonk was being explored in songs of fatalism such as "It Makes No Difference Now," written by Floyd Tillman and first recorded, in the fall of 1938, by Cliff Bruner's Texas Wanderers, and Ted Daffan's "Born to Lose," the other great honky-tonk hit of 1943–44, which was every bit as bleak and doomful as "Pistol Packin' Mama" was gay and upbeat. Tillman, Bruner, and Daffan had risen to prominence performing on radio station KTRH in Houston, whose broadcasts were heard clearly seventy miles away in Beaumont. These and other Texans—such as Jerry Irby, the Houston singer whose 1946 "Nails in My Coffin" was a danceable paean to alcoholic suicide, and Ernest Tubb, whose cover version of Irby's song became a nationwide country hit—defined the spirit and sound that overtook country music in the post-war years. But the greatest honky-tonk singer of them all, the greatest voice that George Jones had heard since Roy Acuff's, belonged to a twenty-three-year-old newcomer from Alabama.

It was in April of 1947 that George Jones heard Hank Williams for the first time. The record was "I Don't Care (If Tomorrow Never Comes)." It was followed in May by "Honky Tonkin'," and by midsummer, Hank Williams had his first hit, "Move It On Over," a raw-swinging piece of backwoods jitterbug jive that would stand as one of the seminal emanations of nascent rock & roll.

Hank Williams's music was a mixture of grave dirt, whiskey, and lamb's blood. Self-doomed and self-tormenting, Williams wrote and sang of a world where love danced endlessly with loss, sin with salvation, laughter with despair. It was for him quite natural to drift, as he did in a recording studio one day in April 1947, from "Move It On Over" to "I Saw the Light" to "Six More Miles to the Graveyard." For George Jones, there was something in his songs and the way he sang them that made a dark poem of all those things that he, George himself, did not yet, and in a way never would, understand: the drunken desperation of his father, the washed-in-the-blood Baptist howlings, and the powers of the heart that drove one man to whiskey, another to prayer, another to song, and another to all three. By this time, all the Jones children had set out on their own, save George, the youngest, who was left alone with his war-ring parents in a household of deepening misery. Jailed frequently for his drunkenness, George Washington Jones seemed no longer to be a man, let alone a father; and Clara, recoiling from his wretchedness ever further into herself, seemed to be drained of all love and life. To George, home had become a place where happiness never dwelled, and he stayed away as much as he could, wandering from one night to another among his scattered kin and returning time and again to Brother Byrle and Sister Annie. Hank Williams seemed to express something of the enormous confusion, desperation, and pervasive loneliness that George could feel but not grasp. He seemed, in a way, kindred.

"It was the songs," George would say; "the way he delivered 'em." He would search for a way to describe what he heard in them, but, in the end, "just a lot of heart and soul" was all that he could find.

By the summer of Hank Williams's ascent, fifteen-year-old George had teamed up with another teenage musician, Dalton Henderson, who had his own early-morning radio show on KTXJ in his hometown of Jasper, at the northern edge of the Big Thicket. George stayed nights with the Henderson family in Jasper, and it was on KTXJ, with Dalton, that George made his radio debut. He went on to bigger things in 1948, join-ing Eddie and Pearl, a husband-and-wife act that had something of a devoted following in Beaumont. When George's father lost his job at the shipyard and moved with Clara to nearby Vidor, Eddie and Pearl took him in to live at their trailer home. It was in the spring of 1949, while performing with Eddie and Pearl at radio station KRIC in Beaumont, that George met up with Hank Williams.

"He was appearing in town that night," George recalled. "He was a friend of the program director, Neville Powell; and Neville invited him by to do a song on our afternoon four o'clock show, you know, to promote his dance that night at, I believe it was, the Blue Jean Club, or the Old

Corral. I believe it was the Old Corral. He was quite friendly. He came in, sat on the couch, and talked quite a bit with Pearl and all of us. I guess I was too scared to open my mouth; I just listened."

By the time he was eighteen, Jones, appearing alone and with other musicians, was a familiar figure in the Beaumont-area honky-tonks: the Teacup Inn on Sabine Pass Avenue, Lola and Shorty's down by the waterfront, Miller's Café on College Street, Glenn Vista on the old Houston Highway, Yvonne's out on the Port Arthur Highway, the Redtop Drive-In in Silsbee, the Gulf Inn down in Gilchrist, and a slew of other joints. He stood barely five foot seven. It was as big as he would ever get. His voice was something else: as big as the Texas sky, and growing.

It was during this period that Huey Meaux, who was barbering in Winnie and moonlighting as a drummer, came to know and perform with Jones, who, according to Huey, was "like any other kid. In them days, all you did was went to dancehalls and drank beer and fought all night, 'cause there was no other sports to do in them days. And that was the name of the game: who was the best fighter. If you didn't have a fight that night, the dance wasn't worth a shit. It's that way in them days. George was a pretty good fighter, but he was like me, got his ass whipped all the time. I knew him 'cause we'd hang around the joints and the places where music was at. Me and George, we always liked the joints. The *joint* joints, y'know, that would set maybe thirty people and had a little dancefloor maybe ten-by-ten, a jukebox blarin', that was it."

Though Jones would maintain that "it was probably in '56 or '57" that he began drinking, Dalton Henderson would remember him sneaking drinks when they were playing as kids in Jasper. "It would change his personality so much that it scared me," Henderson would say. And Huey clearly recalled of the old days in Beaumont that Jones "always liked his whiskey."

That liking was an ambivalent one. Jones hated whiskey for the grief it had wrought through his father. Huey recalled an incident at the Jones home in Vidor: "They had a frame house and them old-timey hedges, y'know. And George's daddy would stash his bottles in them hedges. I went out there one day with George, and George set fire to them hedges. Poured gas all the way down to the goddamn street, the highway, and set fire to that motherfucker. And when that sonofabitch went to burn, it went to blowin' up, brother, and the old man come runnin' out the goddamn house, man, and I'm gonna tell you somethin', he wanted to *kill* George." On the other hand, George was heading down that same lost highway.

It was at Playground Park, on the west side of Beaumont, that George had first met and performed with Eddie and Pearl; and it was at Playground Park that George met Dorothy Bonvillon, the daughter of a local banker. To those who knew him, it seemed that eighteen-year-old George rushed into marriage seeking all the security and happiness that family life had never provided him. He married Dorothy, in Port Arthur, on June 1, 1950. Ceding to the wishes of his Cajun father-in-law, George took a regular day-job as an apprentice house-painter with the Sargl Paint Company of Beaumont. Other jobs followed. He drove a 7-Up truck and worked as an ambulance attendant for the Williams Funeral Home. But George's heart was in the joints, and his marriage fell apart in less than a year. On June 23, 1951, Dorothy Jones, who was six months pregnant, filed for divorce, charging that her estranged husband was "a man of violent temper" and "addicted to the drinking of alcoholic beverages." She was awarded $35 a week in support, for the nonpayment of which, on August 24, George was held in contempt of court and spent five days in jail before his kin bailed him out. Barely a month later, thirteen days after his nineteenth birthday, he was jailed again for nonpayment. Dorothy gave birth to their child, a daughter named Susan, on October 28; and on November 16, George was brought to court again. Rather than face jail again, he decided to seek refuge in the armed forces. It was as a last resort that he joined the marines.

"I wasn't about to go in the Marine Corps. I tried everything else first. The air force put me on a waiting-list. The navy wouldn't have me, and I didn't like the army. When I went to the navy, they had a pretty strict test that I couldn't pass, but they said, 'You want to go in bad, don't you?' I said, 'Yes. I'd leave today.' They took me right next-door to the Marine Corps, and they swore me in. It was better than goin' back to jail."

He was shipped to California, where he completed his basic training at the San Diego Marine Corps Recruit Depot and was assigned to duty at the Moffett Field Naval Air Station in San Jose. On New Years Day, Hank Williams, age twenty-nine, was found dead in the backseat of a car en route to a show in Ohio. In April, Bill Haley's recording of "Crazy, Man, Crazy" swept through the air, giving America its first taste of white-man rock & roll. And in June, back home in Beaumont, Jack Starnes Jr., a local entrepreneur, and Harold W. Daily, the operator of a Houston juke-box-and-vending-machine outfit called Southeast Amusement, started a little record company named after an elision of their combined surnames: Starday. At the age of fifty-one, Daily was already known by the name of Pappy.

Starnes and his wife, Neva, had been running a joint called Neva's Dancehall out near their home on Voth Road since before the war.

Through their honky-tonk, George had come to know them as well as their teenage son, Bill, who would later gain notoriety as a bank-robber before getting involved in the undertaking and music rackets. ("Very fast cat," Huey Meaux would say of Bill Starnes. "Too fast for the regular guys. He was about seventeen when he robbed the bank in Saratoga. Ran to Beaumont and threw the moneybags behind the jukebox in Neva's, yelled out to Jack, 'They're right behind me!'") For a year and a half, Starnes had managed Lefty Frizzell, a twenty-five-year-old singer from Corsicana, Texas, whose success, since the autumn of 1950, had rivaled that of Hank Williams. A boozer and a brawler, Frizzell, like Williams, was a honky-tonk singer. But his voice was as pure and pretty and melodic as Williams's was raw; and in it, Jones had found the last of his influences, an influence he had absorbed not only through Frizzell's Columbia recordings, but also in person, as Frizzell in 1951 had been a frequent performer at Neva's. By November 1953, when twenty-two-year-old George Jones returned to civilian life in Beaumont, Lefty Frizzell's star had already begun to fade, but the beauty of his voice had not.

Starday's first release, in June 1953, had been a novelty record by Mary Jo Chelette, an adolescent radio performer from Port Arthur who was managed by Neva Starnes. The company so far had enjoyed one hit, "You All Come," by Arlie Duff, a Big Thicket native who was known as "The Singing School Teacher" and was also managed by Neva Starnes. Released in July, Duff's record had appeared on the Houston territorial c&w charts in early October and by December had risen to the national country charts. The little company seemed to be growing: Don Pierce, a former owner and sales manager of 4-Star Records in California, had, for the sum of $333, joined Starday as a one-third partner, opened a Los Angeles office of Starday, and formed another company, Hollywood Records, which he ran as a black-music affiliate of Starday. The Duff record, Starday's first, fortuitous hit, was still on the national charts when, on the evening of January 19, 1954, Jones was summoned to the Starnes home to try his hand at making a record.

Gordon Baxter, a local singer and broadcaster who had begun his radio career, at KPAC in Port Arthur, in the summer of 1945, was also summoned that day to the house on Voth Road. The Starday recording studio was a room whose walls had been lined with cardboard egg-crating to enhance the acoustics. Fourteen-year-old Bill Starnes served as engineer, operating an old Magnacorder. (According to Gordon Baxter, the bank Bill later robbed was in the Thicket community of Sour Lake, and Bill "tried to make his getaway on the bus. They picked him up and the gym bag full of cash at the bus station.").

"I thought I was gonna be a hillbilly star, and so did George. I didn't know him at the time," Baxter recalled. "So, I went to Neva's. She had a few Magnacorders. I did my thing, and we played it back. I thought there was something wrong with the tape. 'It's dragging,' I said. 'No. That's how you sound.' I discovered then and there that I was tone-deaf, that I'd been gettin' away with it all those years. Then along comes this scrawny-ass kid and, damn, with his range and his volume, he sounded almost like an opera singer. I thought, 'Who is this kid?' Then I saw that his name was on the back of his belt: George Jones."

A few days later, there was an item in *Billboard*: "Starday Records has signed three new artists to recording contracts, with releases by George Jones, of Beaumont, Tex., and Gordon Baxter, assistant manager of KPAC, Port Arthur, Tex., scheduled to be released shortly." Released in February, George's first record was reviewed in *Billboard* in early March. "No Money in This Deal" was described as a "lively country novelty" with "a good catch phrase," while the flipside, "You're in My Heart," was perceived as too imitative of his hero: "Ditty, a country weeper, derives directly from the Hank Williams school." Nevertheless, "George Jones belts it out with fair effectiveness." More than forty years later, Jones himself would say that "No Money in This Deal" was, "Oh, just one of them stupid things you write at the time. Bunch of junk. It didn't seem like junk so much back in those days, but it would be junk today."

Beaumont was a wide-open town in the post-war years. Gambling, prostitution, and after-hours joints thrived. Hank Williams, a fervent collector of guns, was one of several honky-tonk singers who enjoyed a special relationship with the Beaumont Police Department. "Whenever he came to Beaumont," said Don Jacobs of the *Beaumont Enterprise*, "the cops would gather up all the Saturday-night specials they'd confiscated and sell them to Hank." Once, in town to do a police-benefit show, Hank took to shooting out the streetlights from the window of his suite at the King Edward Hotel. "They merely asked him to stop," recalled Ken Ritter, a music-business entrepreneur who became Beaumont's mayor in 1968. In the fifties, under the benison of Charlie Meyers, the Jefferson County Sheriff, and Jimmy Pocono, the mayor of Beaumont, the sway of the rackets remained unvanquished until 1961, when a senate investigating committee led by glory-hunting Congressman Tom James set Beaumont on its way to becoming what it is today: a town defined by sepulchral, dead-modern Methodist and Baptist church buildings, a downtown whose life has been lost to the malls and where the only thing open after sundown is a shabby McRory's on a deserted corner. In the days when George Jones was coming into his own, before it fell to decency, Beaumont was the honky-tonk heaven of the Golden Triangle, as Texans call that mating-ground of sin and salvation whose cornerstones of demarcation are Beaumont, Port Arthur, and Orange.

Beaumont, like Houston, had been a hotbed of western swing, the jazz-inflected music of the thirties and forties that had introduced both drums and the amplified steel-guitar to country music; and the honky-tonk bands that were heard thereabouts built upon that tradition of drums and amplified instruments. On occasion, George made music at the Gulf Inn in Gilchrist and elsewhere with old-timers such as Cliff Bruner, the western swing fiddler who had been one of the great pioneers of east-Texas honky-tonk. Floyd Tillman, the author of the honky-tonk classic "It Makes No Difference Now," was also one of Jones's early supporters, proclaiming one night from the stage of Yvonne's, "This guy's destined to be one of the greatest country singers in the world." But it was among musicians of his own age that he managed eventually to summon the power to free his own voice from the influences of Acuff, Williams, and Frizzell. In 1954, a new sort of sound was blossoming from the common soil of honky-tonk and other Southern music. They would call it rockabilly, and Elvis, who made his first records that summer, would be seen as its avatar. At the Ritz Club, a Beaumont after-hours joint where musicians congregated after work to drink and often play informally together until dawn, George and others breathed new life into the honky-tonk music that they had cut their teeth on; a new life that, through George and a few others, would keep country music alive and compelling through the rock & roll years to come. And, though he would never acknowledge it, the rockabilly impulse affected his sound as much as the lingering voices of Acuff, Williams, and Frizzell.

In early 1954, Starday teamed him with Sonny Burns. Not quite a year older than Jones, Burns was a hard-drinking singer from Nacogdoches who had begun recording for Starday in the fall of 1953 and in the spring of 1954 had a local hit with "A Place for Girls Like You." Like Jones, he was a honky-tonk singer, with somewhat more pronounced leanings toward rockabilly. It was a duet with Burns, "Wrong about You," that resulted in Jones's first appearance on the Houston charts; and the flipside of that record, "Play It Cool, Man, Play It Cool," recorded several months before Elvis's debut, bordered on pure rockabilly. The Burns-and-Jones duo became a familiar presence in Houston, performing at the Plantation Club, Bob's Tavern, the NCO Club at Fort Polk, the Magnolia Gardens east of town, and, most of all, a dive called Amma Dee's that was located on Canal Street, near Sonny's apartment. They became regulars as well on the KNUZ "Houston Jamboree," broadcast every Saturday night from City Auditorium (where, as an added attraction during the show of May 22, 1954, not long before "Wrong about You" hit the local charts, Sonny took the vows of his first, ill-fated marriage). In addition, George began working as a disk-jockey at KTRM in Beaumont, the station where twenty-four-year-old J.P. Richardson of Sabine Pass was developing the rockabilly radio persona that would bring him fame a few years later when he recorded "Chantilly Lace" as the Big Bopper.

Gordon Baxter, who served as the best man at Richardson's wedding, was by then also working at KTRM, and he recalled that it was at KTRM that Jones was nicknamed Possum. "One of the better DJs, Slim Watts, took to calling him George P. Willicker Picklepuss Possum Jones. For one thing, he cut his hair short, like a possum's belly. He had a possum's nose, and had stupid eyes, like a possum."

When asked what his KTRM show was like, Jones laughed openly. "Well," he said, "I can't remember what it was like too much, but it was, like, an hour show in the evening. I was playin' records. Had commercials in-between. The big old long reel-to-reel. I'd get nervous at first, when I first had the job; I'd get real nervous and break a lot of the tapes. That was the sad story back in those days, always breakin' tapes and havin' to splice and put 'em back together." Jones, Baxter said, "had to pull a mike shift to make a living." Jones agreed: "It was just a way to pick up a dollar."

Those were drunken days and drunken nights. Sonny, who would later feel that he was "the one who got George started drinkin' hard," was even more grave-bent in his ways than George. They sang drunk, for drunks. Even Jack Neil, the owner and manager of KTRM, was an alky. Every once in a while, old George Washington Jones himself would stagger reeking into the studio seeking to put the touch on his boy.

Once again, George felt himself drawn to the solace of family life that had eluded him. In late August 1954, in Houston, he met an eighteen-year-old carhop named Shirley Ann Corley, in town for the summer from the small Texas town of Center. On September 14, 1954, after a two-week courtship, he married her, in Houston, and together they set up home in Beaumont.

In the spring of 1955, when Elvis Presley covered Houston ground that was now long familiar to Sonny and George—the KNUZ "Jamboree," Magnolia Gardens, and so on—Jones met up with a childhood neighbor named Darrell Edwards. From the settlement of Depot Town, near Saratoga, Edwards, now in his mid-thirties, had been George's babysitter back in the Big Thicket. He was an aspiring poet and lyricist, and he gave George a copy of a song he had written, an uptempo god-damn-her-eyes honky-tonk ditty called "Why, Baby, Why." By this time, Jack Starnes had sold his interest in Starday to Pappy Daily and Don Pierce, and Starday had a new studio. From 1946 to 1951, Bill Quinn's

Gold Star Records in Houston had issued records by a wide and exciting range of local talent, from Cajun fiddler Harry Choates to bluesman Lightnin' Hopkins. Now Pappy Daily had helped finance the reopening by Quinn of a bigger Gold Star Studio, which was to serve as the new Starday recording-center. It was to Quinn's new studio, on Brock Street, that Jones took "Why, Baby, Why." Pappy wanted to record the song as a duet by George and Sonny, but Sonny got drunk and failed to show up, so George did it alone. Upon its release that summer, it was the flipside of the record, "Seasons of My Heart," a song that Jones and Edwards had written together, that garnered attention, appearing on the Houston charts in late August. But "Why, Baby, Why" eventually overtook it, and, in late October, the month that saw the birth of Jones's second child and first son, Jeffrey Glenn, "Why, Baby, Why" broke into the national country charts.

"Why, Baby, Why" remained on the charts for more than four months, rising to the #4 position and allowing him to perform on the Louisiana Hayride. Broadcast by KWKH from the Municipal Auditorium in Shreveport, and carried by twenty-seven stations in four states, the Saturday-night Hayride was where Hank Williams had made his big-time debut and where Elvis Presley was now being featured. "I didn't get to know him that well," Jones recalled of Elvis in those days when they were both at fame's edge. "He stayed pretty much with his friends around him in the dressing-room. Nobody seemed to get around him much any length of time and talk to him." Except for the dressing-room friends, Jones, a loner even backstage, could have been speaking of himself.

Sonny Burns's popularity and record sales had until now overshadowed Jones's. But while "Why, Baby, Why" was rising on the national charts, Sonny's new record, "A Real Cool Cat," went nowhere. Burns lingered at Starday for another year, then faded. "He was a pretty nice guy," Jones would say many years later, adding, "He's a preacher now, in Lufkin. He's got religion." Setting off on his own, George gathered together four Beaumont musicians to serve as his band: guitarist Luther Nallie, who would go on to join the Sons of the Pioneers; his brother, Ray Nallie, on drums; steel guitarist Charlie Tucker; and fiddler Robert Shivers.

"We were with him, on and off, for several years," recalled Ray Nallie, who now runs Ray Nallie Motors in Kountze. "We all had jobs, and we'd work two, three nights a week. We worked all these little old beer-joints. Beaumont, Port Arthur, various places. Four hours a night. Eight, nine dollars a night. That wasn't low wages back then, but we were gonna quit him one night. This was at the 73 Club, in Winnie. We wanted $10 a night and he was only payin' us eight. So, he said, 'OK,' and we quit.

And he got some coon-ass fiddle-player up there and played the job, man. So much for quittin'." George, he said, "was a good singer from the git-go. There's no one that can sing a song like George. He was just a little shit-headed at times, that's all."

In November 1955, Jones was sent on a tour of the Gulf Coast with Link Davis, Jerry Jericho, and other Starday acts. In December, out in the west-Texas town of Odessa, he opened for Johnny Cash, whose first record, on Sun, had just hit the national country charts. Three days after Christmas, the Sun-Starday troupe, which now also included the new-comer Carl Perkins, reached Texarkana, across the state. It was in the course of this tour that Jones sold the elements of a song called "Rock 'n' Roll Ruby" to Cash, who paid him $40 for it. As recorded by Cash's fellow Sun artist Warren Smith, "Rock 'n' Roll Ruby," Smith's debut, sold more than 70,000 copies. In April 1956, the same month that Smith's record went on sale, Starday released a double-sided hard-core rockabilly record by Jones, "Rock It" coupled with "How Come It," issued under the name of Thumper Jones.

"I don't guess I'm ever gonna live that down," Jones told me in 1976, before sobriety had in the least bit tempered the Jonesian flair for self-nullifying phraseology and shuffled-deck chronology. "I was actually gettin' started in the business about 1954 or so when all this rock & roll really started movin' in, and, of course, you know, you didn't have stations back then that played all that much country to start with. So, especially with rock & roll getting as strong as it was at that time, it seemed like country music was really a losin' battle except for the three or four major artists that had it made at the time, like Lefty Frizzell, Ernest Tubb, Roy Acuff, some of those people. So we decided to try one, sort of rockabilly-like. I was sort of ashamed to even do it at the time 'cause I was so country, so I just used a different name, went under the name of Thumper Jones." As for what he really felt about rock & roll (and here one encounters the true essence of Jonesian exposition): "I liked quite a bit of the things that came out then, because really you didn't have much else to like. You didn't have the radio stations playin' enough of the country music for you to really have a chance to listen to nothin' but country, so it was a lot of it forced upon us really." In 1993, he was more terse: "Hell," he said, "when you're starvin' to death, you'll try anything."

Jones had begun the year, 1956, with another hit, "What Am I Worth," which led to his debut on the Grand Ole Opry. The hits kept coming throughout the year, and, on August 25, he became a full-fledged member of the Opry, with his first long-play album following in October. That autumn, while Jones's alcoholic lament "Just One More" was on the charts, Pappy Daily negotiated a deal whereby Starday became an affiliate of Mercury Records, commencing January 1, 1957. "There was no such thing as production at Starday," Jones said, "We'd go in with the band, we'd go over the song, I'd look over and tell the steel player to take a break or kick it off, and I'd get the fiddle to play a turn-around in the middle. I'd just let them know if we were gonna tag it or not. We'd just go through it. We didn't take the pains of making several takes. Back then, over three or four takes, they'd say, 'My God, this is costing us money.' So we'd just get it down as good as we could. If we went a little flat or sharp in a place or two, they'd say, 'The public ain't gonna notice that, so put it out.' So we did, and it wasn't too successful, so I think maybe the public did notice it."

Beginning in 1957, when Starday moved its headquarters to the Nashville suburb of Madison, Tennessee, and George started recording in Nashville, those conditions were behind him. With each new recording, he sounded less and less like Hank Williams, more and more like George Glenn Jones. In the summer of 1958, when the Starday-Mercury affilia-tion dissolved, Pappy Daily sold out his interest in the company to Don Pierce and negotiated a new deal with Mercury for Jones and himself. That July, when Shirley Jones gave birth to a second son, George named him in Pappy's honor: Bryan Daily Jones. Pappy had taken over George's management from Bill Hall of Beaumont. As his manager, producer, pub-lishing-partner, and friend, Pappy seemed to be the paternal presence that George had never truly known. Huey Meaux, who credits Daily with helping his own career as a producer get underway, said that George would have been lost without Pappy. "Oh, yes! He was George's career. He was George's daddy. He was George's everything. And George gave him a lot of goddamn hell, man. Gettin' drunk, gettin' in trouble, gettin' in fights. Pappy carried the big stick in Houston, and he was the only one that could sit down and talk to George. He was a very laid-back old gentleman, and he could talk to George in a way that George listened to him. Sometimes George would get mad at him, didn't want to work with him. But then he would go out there and would really fuck up. Pappy got George back together so many times it's unreal. He was the only guy in the world who could. Pappy had a heart made of gold, and he loved George's singin' above anything, but he also loved George kind of like a son. George was a son to him. I seen that closeness too many, many times, where if it had been me, I'd have kicked George right in the ass."

In September 1958, at Owen Bradley's basement recording studio in Nashville, George made the record that would take him to the top. Writ-ten by his buddy J. P. Richardson, "White Lightning" was fast, frivolous, and infectious, a song that George's singing redeemed and raised from the level of mere novelty. Richardson, whose recording of "Chantilly Lace" was currently high on both the pop and r&b charts, would not live to see the success of his song "White Lightning." On February 3, 1959, barely a month before Jones's record hit the country charts, the Big Bopper, age twenty-eight, went down in the same plane crash that killed Buddy Holly and Ritchie Valens. "White Lightning" remained on the country charts for nearly six months, rising to #1 in April and crossing over in May to the pop charts.

Years ago, George's parents had relocated to the outlying suburb of Vidor. "Serving Port Arthur, Beaumont, Orange, and bloody Vidor," is what Gordon Baxter, still a broadcaster in Beaumont, announces on the air when he gives the call letters of KOLE, which, off the air, he describes as "a little chickenshit station whose signal barely reaches the city limits." Bloody Vidor, as he puts it, is a town of perhaps 11,000 souls. Its one black resident, Vidor's first since the 1920s, lived under protective guard after moving there under a federal desegregation order in February 1993. During the sixties, there was a sign at the town limits: "NIGGER, DON'T LET THE SUN SET ON YOU IN VIDOR." Indeed, black visitors to the Golden Triangle are still warned against traveling to Vidor after dark, and though the town's Main Street, with its fast-food franchises and its one-story brick City Hall resembling a suburban doctors' office, today presents the bland, plastic, have-a-nice-day smile of mediocrity, it is a place not only where George Jones Country Gold Dog Food is on prominent display at Wood's Supermarket, but also where white-robed Klansmen burn crosses, hand out white-pride literature, and solicit funds to "Keep Vidor White." That bland, plastic, have-a-nice-day smile is the smile of the Klan. "Every Klansperson in Texas is invited," read one perky and politically correct rally-announcement, filed from Vidor, in the "News of the Greater Golden Triangle" section of the *Beaumont Enterprise* back in the feminist late seventies. And back in the late fifties, bloody Vidor was an even far bloodier place. It was to that idyllic suburban cracker-land that George Jones, flush with newfound prosperity, moved his family in 1959.

In early 1960, at home in Vidor, Jones wrote a song called "The Window Up Above." Of all the songs he has written, it remains his favorite. "I wrote it in about twenty minutes," he said. "I just came in off the road, about eight in the morning. While breakfast was being fixed, I just sat down in the den and picked up the guitar, and it was as simple as that. Sometimes it's hard to even figure where the ideas come from." The idea, of a man's delusion of happy home-life shattered by a single, providential glimpse of his wife's infidelity, was invested in the song with the uncanny, dream-like quality of well-being subsumed by dread:

I've been living a new way
Of life that I love so;
But I can see the clouds are gathering
And the storm will wreck our home.

Though, as George said, it sometimes might be difficult to figure out where ideas come from, "The Window Up Above" seemed to issue directly from a life-long insecurity and ambivalence, a deep-rooted, heartfelt fear of the anguish that lurked beneath the dream of hearth and home and happiness. Released in the autumn of 1960, "The Window Up Above" remained on the country charts for more than eight months. George even had Nudie of North Hollywood, the celebrated tailor of egregiously gaudy Western wear, make him a stage-suit illustrative of the song, a chartreuse affair replete with teary faces peering from sequin-stitched windowframes. "The Window Up Above" marked what many purists felt to be an egregious development in George's music itself: the use of background voices to sweeten the effect of his own hard-edged honky-tonk delivery. Through the sixties and into the seventies, background voices and orchestral string sections were to become an increasing presence in country music. Jones's voice, however, with its noble gravity, its capacity to wring from every word its full color and power, and its instinctive poet's sense of rhythm, usually was able to transcend the stultifying effects of the so-called "countrypolitan" trend. Considering that Jones, for much of his career, has been a complaisant victim of minimal or bad production, insipid arrangements, and frequently pedestrian or mawkish material, the surpassing power of that voice as documented in such less-than-optimal recordings is all the more remarkable.

In the summer of 1962, "Tender Years," written by Darrell Edwards became Jones's biggest hit to date, remaining in the #1 position on the country charts for seven weeks and crossing over to the pop charts. While the record was at its height, Pappy Daily struck a lucrative deal for Jones and himself, as a producer and artist-and-repertoire executive, with the newly formed country-music division of United Artists Records. Meanwhile, in Beaumont, Bill Hall and Jack Clement, formerly a producer with Sun Records in Memphis and RCA in Nashville, opened a recording studio, Gulf Coast Sound, downtown on Fourth Street, next to the King Edward Hotel. Visiting Gulf Coast one day, Jones became interested in an old tape-recorder that Hall and Clement had lying around gathering dust, while Hall was intent on selling him on a new song written by Dickie Lee Lipscomb and Steve Duffy, two young writers under contract to Hall-Clement Music. As Ray Nallie remembered it: "Bill was tryin' to get him to do this damn tune, 'She Thinks I Still Care.' But

George wanted this old damn tape-recorder that didn't even work; it was just over there in a corner. Bill wouldn't even talk about it. He said, 'Listen to this damn tune, man." And George listened to it, said, 'I don't like it, man. There's too many damn *just because*'s in it. I don't like the goddamn thing, don't wanna do it.' This went on for hours, seemed like, George wantin' to talk about the tape-recorder, which wasn't worth nothin', and Bill wantin' to talk about that 'just-because' song. Finally, Bill said, 'I tell you what I'll do. If you go 'head and record the goddamn song, I'll *give* you the fuckin' tape-recorder. And that's how he did it."

Jones does not remember it that way. "No," he said, "I sorta flipped over the song when I heard it. I don't know where all those tales get started. There's a lot of hearsay." Jones recorded the song, for United Artists, in January 1962, and by mid-May it was a #1 country hit, a perfect country song of heartache and denial. Looking back, Jones would regard his United Artist years as perhaps his finest period. "We did a lot of the pure country then," he said. This was the time of several lackluster but commercially successful duets with Melba Montgomery, but it was also the time of his reconstituted-rockabilly hit "The Race Is On," and of less-known but magnificent performances such as "Warm Red Wine" and "Open Pit Mine," a chilling little tale of adultery and remorseless murder. It was midway through the United Artists years, the fall of 1963, that sixty-eight-year-old George Washington Jones was committed to the alcoholics' ward of the Rusk State Mental Hospital, north of Nacogdoches.

In January 1965, as "The Race Is On" was crossing over to the pop charts, Pappy Daily negotiated yet another and more lucrative deal for Jones and himself, with Musicor Records, a former United Artists subsidiary that had now been taken over by Art Talmadge, a friend of Pappy's from the Mercury days. The late sixties were a strange time for the singer. As the soul of America was set adrift in a Day-Glo cloud of patchouli-scented ahimsa and sensitivity, it seemed as if Jones, in his crewcut and his Nudie suits, strove, with the aid of an increasingly corny repertoire, to singlehandedly defend the citadel of Vidor, and all it stood for, against the encroaching horde of tie-dyed freethinkers. His role in the 1965 sixteen-millimeter redneck musical comedy *Forty Acre Feud* seemed a diametric response to *A Hard Day's Night*; and in the Summer of Love, as Jim Morrison's cry of "We want the world and we want it now" echoed through the land, George responded with a song called "Take the World but Give Me Jesus." At one point, late in 1967—by which time the singer had begun to let his trademark brushcut grow out a bit—he and Pappy Daily gave folk-rock their best shot with "Unwanted Babies," a garbled protest song written for Jones by Peanut Montgomery. Combining his middle name and his mother's maiden name, the record label bore the pseudonym of Glen Patterson. "We did a certain type of song that we thought might would sell at that time," George said, taken aback at the mention of it, "but it wasn't the type of song that I would've normally cut, and I just didn't want to use my real name." But perhaps his lowest moment was "The Poor Chinee," released in January 1968 and containing the unforgettable lyrics "Me likee bow-wow, very good chow-chow." (Perhaps a karmic connection to his future role as dog-food pitch-man.)

By then, Jones had built a new, bigger home, on Lakeview Road, in Vidor, where he had also, in the summer of 1966, opened an ill-fated and short-lived country-music park. In 1967, the year his father died, Jones committed himself briefly to a neurological hospital in the first of many attempts to seek treatment for alcoholism. His marriage, since 1964, had been coming apart. As his wife saw it, his drinking had caused the rift. Shortly after his release from the hospital, George began accusing Shirley of carrying on an affair with J. C. Arnold, a Vidor businessman and former friend of George's. She, in turn, accused him of having taken up with Melba Montgomery, with whom he still occasionally performed and recorded.

"I remember George goin' one night and shootin' his old lady's boyfriend in the ass," laughed Huey Meaux. Though all involved would later deny this alleged shotgun attack, it would remain a part of Golden Triangle legendry.

George and Shirley separated in the spring of 1968. Upon their divorce, George was ordered to surrender his share of their Vidor homestead and pay $1,000 a month in child support. Shirley later married J. C. Arnold, and George packed up, bade farewell to bloody Vidor, and moved to Nashville.

▌ Two years before, while making a record with Melba Montgomery at Columbia Studio A in Nashville, George had met Tammy Wynette, a twenty-four-year-old former hairdresser from Mississippi who had recently moved to Nashville. By the spring of 1968, she was enjoying her fourth #1 hit, "D-I-V-O-R-C-E." One night not long after he moved to town, Jones interceded in an argument between Wynette and her second husband, the songwriter Don Chapel, who had introduced George to Tammy two years before. The couple had not been married long, nor would they be. George's drunken profession of love for her during the course of that angry night precipitated their break-up. The romance of George Jones and Tammy Wynette, the king and queen of country music, was like a Provençal love story in a land of Nudie-tailored troubadours. As if in public celebration of their romance, Tammy's recording of "Stand by Your Man" became a #1 hit that Thanksgiving week, and George soon responded with "I'll Share My World with You." By January 1969, George and Tammy were living together. With her as a singing partner, George rejoined the Grand Ole Opry, which he had left several years before, and together, consolidating their shows, they took to the road. In February, in Ringgold, Georgia, they married, and, in March, they moved to Lakeland, Florida. Together they appeared in *From Nashville with Music*, another cinematic prodigy in the tradition of *Forty Acre Feud*.

After fifteen years together, Jones had a bitter falling-out with Pappy Daily. "We were fairly close at one time," George would say in the way of explaining that sudden and long-mysterious breach. "Then the truth comes out. These people on the other end of the stick are in it for the money too. He was pitchin' me around to different labels and I kind of got tired of that. Made deals on the side for extra money for hisself, which I never found out till later. It was a good association the first few years, and then it kind of got a little more businesslike and they didn't live up to their part of the agreements." Jones began meeting with Tammy's producer, Billy Sherrill of Epic Records, and he made plans to sign with Epic as soon as his Musicor contract ran out, in the fall of 1971. George became a father again, in October 1970, when Tammy gave birth to a daughter they named Tamala Georgette. Once again, however, hearth and home were not enough, and it seemed that Huey Meaux was right, that George was lost without Pappy. Two weeks after the birth of his new daughter, Jones celebrated the opening of his second ill-starred entertainment park, Old Plantation Music Park, built on the forty-three-acre estate that surrounded their new home, a refurbished nineteenth-century mansion in the countryside outside of Lakeland. In the throes of the long and violent binge that followed, Jones was straitjacketed and committed to a padded cell at the Watson Clinic in Lakeland, where he was kept to detoxify for ten days and released with a prescription for Librium to quell his depressive anxieties. Six years later, he would tell Bob Allen, the author of the book *George Jones: The Saga of An American Singer*, that "a special doctor at the Watson Clinic had typed out three or four pages, in his words, describing this person that was me. He started off saying I was a shy person. I disliked violence but took a lot of abuse, just to keep from havin' problems." He had nothing against psychiatrists, he said, sipping from a glass of Jack Daniel's and 7-Up, "but I still think the best counselor in the world is yourself."

Joan Dew, then a journalist with *Country Music* magazine and the coauthor of Tammy Wynette's autobiography, *Stand by Your Man*, believed that Tammy was not only distraught by George's drinking but bored by the marriage as well. "I think she really got bored with him very quick down there," Dew told fellow country-music journalist Dolly Carlisle. "George is a little fuddy-duddy. He's like a little old lady. He's not exciting. He sits around and watches TV all day and goes fishing. George is only exciting onstage. He's not funny; he doesn't have a good sense of humor. He's smart but not intellectually witty. Apparently, he's a lousy lover. I haven't heard of an alcoholic who wasn't." Sex, Dew said, "was very, very important to Tammy. And I think by then she was bored."

In October 1971, Jones signed with Epic and began work with Billy Sherrill on an album called *Me and the First Lady*. Sherrill's production, influenced by Phil Spector's "wall-of-sound" technique, was adept and sophisticated. Though the lush orchestral arrangements and saccharine background voices that were Sherrill's trademark were regarded by many as softening and diminishing the natural grandeur of Jones's voice, there can be no doubt that Sherrill's production helped keep the singer commercially alive at a time when country music was increasingly beset, and the old guard increasingly endangered, by the winds of a new era. Jones himself was ambivalent about the sound of his recordings. "I went along with the record company against my better judgment," he told me in the days when he was still working with Sherrill. "I didn't wanna do it, but I let them put strings on my sessions just out of curiosity, more or less, just to see what they might do. When you use strings and horns and all these things, you just don't have country music anymore. You abuse it. Billy Sherrill has always done what he thought would be best for me. He always has. And the sound he's given me is great. The strings, the big productions—Billy Sherrill thought this was the best thing. But we've talked about it, and were gonna get back to a more hard-core sound. I've got too much respect for country music to abuse it. I don't want eleven thousand violins and twenty trumpets on my records. If the song's there, that's all I need. That's all anybody needs. I like a good, solid honky-tonk song." His next album, *Alone Again*, released in October 1976, did indeed have a leaner and more visceral sound. But somehow, he would not begin to return fully in his recordings to that "more hard-core sound" for years to come; and in 1993, he repeated to me his intention of long ago: "I'm trying to get back to the pure country." It struck me then that, to him, "pure country" might be the unattainable goal that to some degree kept him moving onward.

The first George-and-Tammy duet, "Take Me," appeared on the country charts on Christmas Day. In 1972, the couple returned to live at Tammy's home on Old Hickory Lake in Nashville. Several months later, on the first day of April 1973, while George was off on another long binge,

Tammy filed for divorce. They reconciled and purchased a luxurious new home on Tyne Boulevard in the Belle Meade section. Tammy's taste was as garish as George's, and they decorated their new home together. There was shag carpeting on the ceiling. In the spring of 1974, shortly after the death of his mother, George had the first of two immense #1 hits, "The Grand Tour," a song about a "lonely house that once was home sweet home." In the fall, there followed "The Door," an even bleaker song of marital dissolution and desertion, a song that invoked the memory of "the sound of my dear old mama crying." He was, at forty-three, at the height of his powers. That his own haunted childhood should now have led not to understanding or resolution but only to the plain, inevitable finality, and ultimate abandonment, of his parents' death seemed to deepen the haunted, and haunting, qualities of his own voice. On December 13, while "The Door" was rising toward the top of the charts, Tammy filed for legal separation; and a few weeks later, on January 8, 1975, she filed once again for divorce. George moved to Florence, Alabama, to be near his drinking buddy Peanut Montgomery and Peanut's sister-in-law, Linda Welborn, with whom George had already taken up. By the time Tammy's divorce was granted, on March 14, Linda and George were living together, and George had begun his long, slow descent to the bottom. In June, his old friend Darrell Edwards, having fallen on hard times, traveled to Nashville in an attempt to see George. Failing to do so, he returned to Beaumont and blew out his brains. By then, according to many who saw him, George might soon enough be meeting up with Darrell after all.

That summer, Jones signed a management deal with one Alcy Benjamin Baggott Jr., a local hustler better known as Shug. Together, they reopened Shug's shut-down Nashville nightclub, renaming it Possum Holler. The nightclub became a center of, and Shug Baggott one of the key figures of, cocaine-dealing in Nashville. Before long, George, who had long indulged in amphetamine and sedatives, was addicted to cocaine as well as whiskey; and although in the spring of 1976 he made a pretense of overcoming his alcoholism and co-wrote with Peanut Montgomery a heartfelt song called "A Drunk Can't Be a Man," his addictions worsened. The news of Tammy Wynette's brief marriage that summer to realtor Michael Tomlin, and her subsequent marriage, the following summer, to songwriter George Richey, seemed to unhinge him. "I still love her, and that ain't gonna change," he told the writer Joan Dew, a friend of Tammy's. During a nine-month period in 1977–78, there would be fifteen break-ins at the Wynette home; once she would discover the words SLUT and PIG scrawled on her mirrors and television screen. On October 4, 1978, Wynette would be the victim of a yet-unsolved kidnapping. Abducted by a masked gunman from the parking-lot of the Green Hills Shopping Center, she would be taken to an isolated spot along Tennessee State Highway 31A in rural Giles County, beaten, nearly strangled with her own pantyhose, and finally thrown from the car, bruised, hysterical, and suffering a fractured jaw.

On the first of September 1977, with $36,000 in overdue child-support payments to Tammy outstanding, an order was issued for Jones's arrest. On the seventh—known by now as No-show Jones, he vanished and failed to appear at the Bottom Line in New York City for a show that had been anticipated as one of the media events of the season. On the thirteenth, the night after he turned forty-six, he shot at, and very nearly struck, Peanut Montgomery, who had recently quit drinking and found religion. "All right, you sonofabitch," Jones had hollered before firing his Smith & Wesson thirty-eight, "see if your God can save you now!" In October, pleading that he was "addicted to alcohol," the singer sought the mercy of the judge who had ordered his arrest for nonpayment. In December, citing more than $1 million in debts, he filed for bankruptcy in Nashville. Later that month, he was arrested in Alabama on charges of having "assaulted and beat" his ex-girlfriend Linda Welborn. In January 1978, after Shug Baggott was dismissed by him and filed his own bankruptcy petition, Jones was arrested again in Florence on charges, relating to the Montgomery shooting and its aftermath, of making harassing telephone calls and assault with a deadly weapon. "I realize that time's gettin' short," he told Bob Claypool of the *Houston Post*. "I don't have much time left to straighten up." By February, Jones was homeless, deranged, and destitute, living in the backseat of his car and barely able to digest the junk food on which he subsisted. The songwriter and singer Marshall Chapman recalled encountering Jones in an elevator at the Spence Manor hotel in Nashville. His weight was now down to ninety-seven pounds, and he held the front of his trousers bunched up in his fist to keep them raised. To Marshall, as he hurkled before her, trying dolefully to flirt, he seemed in his grisly deterioration to be no longer a man, or even human, but a creature not unlike the *ex-hominem* hedgehog of ineffable misery and penance described by Thomas Mann in *The Holy Sinner*.

His condition was such that it took him more than two years to complete *My Very Special Guests*, an album on which various other singers who idolized him, such as Willie Nelson, Linda Ronstadt, Elvis Costello, and Tammy, came to his vocal aid and support. Peanut Montgomery, who had dropped all charges against George, was still a sympathetic friend, and in December 1979, soon after the album was released, it was Montgomery who brought Jones to the Eliza Coffee Memorial Hospital in Florence. In mid-December, he was transferred to Hillcrest, a private psychiatric hospital in Birmingham that specializes in the treatment of drug and alcohol abuse. A month later, upon his release, the first thing he did was stop and pick up a six-pack. At the end of the month, after drinking beer and snorting cocaine, he held a press conference at Tammy Wynette's Franklin Road home, at which he proclaimed his newfound sobriety. "I read the Bible a lot while undergoing treatment," he said. "Now I can see all the way down the highway." Somehow, seven days later, he managed to record one of the great hits of his career. "He Stopped Loving Her Today," a song of a man whose pitiable, pining love is resolved only through his own death, became his first #1 hit in over five years.

"He Stopped Loving Her Today" revived his dying career. In October 1980, he swept the Country Music Association Awards; in January, he received a Grammy. But his resuscitated success did little to stay the course of his madness. Once again making a pretense of sobriety, in May 1981, he discussed his supposed rehabilitation with a writer from the *Washington Post*, but ended up saying, "You can't hide it, I'm going to have a drink. Hell, we're human." The singer Lorrie Morgan, who joined the Jones troupe in the early summer of 1981, recalled that "those were the no-show days, and it was very scary. The band would go on and stall for time, and the audience would get restless and start throwing stuff onstage, and sometimes George would show up and sometimes he wouldn't. If he didn't, nobody got paid." He was, she said, "a very hard person to get close to." In July, when Jones sought refuge from the world in the Golden Triangle, his relatives had him committed in Beaumont to Baptist Hospital, where his alcoholic father had died fourteen summers ago. By now, he had a new girlfriend, a thirty-three-year-old divorcée from Mansfield, Louisiana, named Nancy Sepulveda, whom he had met at a show in Syracuse, New York. On March 29, 1982, in Mississippi, they were arrested together on charges of cocaine possession. The next day, still in Mississippi, Jones lost control of his car and was hauled away by an ambulance to the Aberdeen-Monroe County Hospital. On the first of April, he was transferred to Hillcrest Psychiatric Hospital in Birmingham, where he remained for thirteen days. Upon his release, he once again proclaimed that he had straightened out his life, this time for good. "The world will see a big difference in me," he told a reporter from the Associated Press. A few weeks later, on May 25, he was arrested in a drunken rage near Franklin, Tennessee. Yet again he declared his sobriety. "'DRUNK' SINGER CYCLES OFF WITH GIRLFRIEND, TEQUILA," read the headline of a story in the *San Antonio News* of August 16, reporting an aborted show at which Jones had appeared late, announced to his audience that he was drunk, and had been roundly booed, and after which he left town "on a motorcycle, with his girlfriend and a bottle of tequila in a sidecar."

Nancy, who neither drank nor took drugs, found herself lost and confused in the vortex of George's self-destruction. When she had first met him, in 1981, he had not seemed all that far gone. "He was drinking," she said, "but he was fun to be around. We'd sit up all night talking. It wasn't love at first sight or anything like that. But I saw what a good person he was, deep down, and I couldn't help but caring for him. He needed somebody, something, so bad." But the whiskey by now had ingrained its poisonous control on every cell of the fifty-year-old singer's flesh and blood, and held his mind in the tidal sway of toxic psychosis. Still Nancy stuck by him, as none of the others had, neither threatening nor hectoring, condoning nor condemning. As Lorrie Morgan saw it, "Nancy really loved him. She was very devoted and dedicated to trying to help him. She withstood a lot of things that I never would have withstood. She really went through a living hell." On March 3, 1983, George married Nancy at the Woodville, Texas, home of his sister, Helen Scroggins. They set up home themselves in Woodville, and George, beaming with relative sobriety, went to work building a ninety-five-acre country-music park, Jones Country, in nearby Colmesneil. The park opened on the following Labor Day. He was still drinking only moderately and had taken to opening his shows with a self-mocking song called "No Show Jones," which he had recorded with Merle Haggard the year before.

When George had seen his own son Bryan strung out on cocaine earlier in the year, he had interpreted it as his own failing, or perhaps as divine retribution, and it filled him with self-revulsion. Nancy had been surprised to see that quitting cocaine had given George little trouble. The booze, however, was a different matter. His mind and his body still screamed for it, and when he started drinking heavily again, in the fall of 1983, it seemed as if his recent sobriety had been only one last deep breath before going under for good. Rampaging through Alabama, suffering from malnutrition and beset by madness, in early 1984, he ended up in a straitjacket at Hillcrest Psychiatric Hospital in Birmingham. Physicians told Nancy that he was close to death, that any further drinking would be the end.

Released from the hospital in March 1984, thirty years to the month after *Billboard* had reviewed his first record, George Jones performed his first stone-cold-sober show. "It was terrible," Nancy said of that night in Birmingham. "We were alone in the bus, and he was like a scared puppy. 'I can't do it,' he said, 'I can't go on.' He was begging and breaking down and dying for a drink. And when he got out there on that stage, and after the first song, he looked out to me in the audience, and he seemed like such a poor, lost, wounded soul that I burst into tears." But he made it through that show, and he has not taken a drink since then. "All my life it seems like I've been running from something," he told a reporter from the United Press International in June. "If I knew what it was, maybe I could run in the right direction. But I always seem to end up going the other way."

Nancy, who is now George's manager as well as his wife and best friend, has almost singlehandedly set his career aright and kept it going. Not long ago, in the Chisos Mountains of southwestern Texas, I spoke to a twenty-four-year-old man from San Antonio named Mike Alvarez. A rodeo bull-rider, saddle-bronc-rider, and calf-roper who also worked as a trail-guide in the Chisos Basin of Big Bend National Park, Alvarez was an avowed follower and amateur singer of country music. He knew all the singing youngbloods—liked George Strait and Clint Black, disliked Billy Ray Cyrus—but when I mentioned the name of George Jones, the young cowboy seemed not to recognize it. Today Jones is attracting increasingly younger crowds to his shows, which long had been convocations of the middle-aged. Those in the industry see this turnaround as a result of Nancy's long and tireless promotional campaign on her husband's behalf. Serving as a catalyst, she has summoned the full support of record-company executives for an unusually passive artist, and tending to his affairs, she has helped him to clear up his debts and keep his business as well as his life in order. Since signing with MCA Records, in December 1990, George has achieved the stature due him as a living legend and American master; and by helping to keep the world at bay, Nancy has helped him stay alive amid the shadows of demons that still seem to darken his vision.

One gets the impression that, were it not for Nancy, George would not be performing today. He seems world-weary, more distanced from his own fame and idolators than ever before. From March of 1989 until recently, George and Nancy lived in a quiet, secluded area of Brentwood, Tennessee, in a home nestled among the mansions of Nashville bankers and brokers. In December 1993, they moved into a new home George built high on a hill amid the solitude of a hundred acres of prime, million-dollar farmland in Franklin. (George's forty-three-year-old daughter, Susan, lives nearby with her two children. George is estranged from his two sons and sees twenty-four-year-old Tamala infrequently. When I asked about his children, he fell silent, causing Nancy to revive the air with a laughing cry of "Next!") There George tends his prized herd of Santa Gertrudis cattle. These cows, a large, chocolate-colored Texas crossbreed of Brahman and Shorthorn, seem to elicit a large part of George's worldly enthusiasm. He refers to them lovingly as "my girls," and, when he is not on the road, rises early every morning to tend to them and putter around his farmland, building little footbridges across his streams and squirrel-feeders for his trees, inspecting his holding-pen, barbecue pit, stocked ponds, and pear saplings. Like his routine of driving into Nashville every other day to have his hair trimmed and styled by Ray Gregory, his early-morning rounds at the farm have become one of the rituals of his life.

In Brentwood, I found neither many traces of the public career nor clues to the private man: a framed platinum album commemorating *I Am What I Am*; biographies of Connie Francis and Robert Graves on a sparse second-floor bookshelf; a closetful of neatly pressed, nearly identical blue jeans; a pair of large, ugly plaster "oriental" sculptures, the disposal of which Nancy has not yet been able to effect. Downstairs, in the basement, traces and clues become more visible. Above the door, a sign reads GEORGE'S DOGHOUSE. Within are boxes of old Nudie suits ("Looks like something Tammy Wynette would wear," says Nancy, extracting an especially tacky toreador-style jacket from a crumpled heap of sequined vestments), shelves of record albums, a coffin-like twenty-four-lamp tanning bed, and scattered memorabilia. On one wall, there is a painting of a dark-haired girl peering sadly through a window at a display of candy and sweets. George calls it "a picture from life's other side," after the title of a Hank Williams record. "Back in Texas, when he was trying to quit drinking, George used to sit by that picture all night," Nancy said. Beside the painting is a plaque bearing the words of the Alcoholics Anonymous prayer about changing what one can and accepting what one cannot.

"She's been a very big help in saving my life and career and just about everything," George said of Nancy, staring straight ahead into the rainy Alabama night. "They say when you get that low and in that shape, everybody needs some help, and if I hadn't got that help I probably wouldn't be here today."

We crossed the state line to Tennessee. The tape-recorder had been running for some time. It was the longest interview he had ever given. "Honey, are you awake?" he called out behind him through the darkened bus. "Can I have some ice water?" Beneath the mask of his sunglasses, his face lightened into a grin. "This man's talkin' me to death."

I asked him how it felt now, after nine years of temperance, to sing drinking-songs. The mention of alcohol seemed to disturb him. "I don't know why we're even discussing that," he said defensively. "I just think it was the environment that surrounded you back in those days. If I'd've never played in those places, I probably never would have started drinking."

"You think so, huh?"

"I would imagine. Being around it. Not so much stage fright, but being around people drunk all the time in the bars and the clubs and the taverns. Sort of being around it, you know, the environment. I'm fairly sure. It's just being around it all the time and other people doing it. Like the old saying, birds of a feather flock together." The last nine years, he said, have been "really like living in a different world. All the time you thought you were living, you really weren't." He said that he did not miss the other way. "No," he stated resolutely, "I don't want no more of that."

What was it that had finally brought him around? "Well, it was either quit or die. And I surely didn't want to die, so I made up my mind to quit." There had been no understanding, it seemed; nothing had been resolved. There had been only that plain, ultimate finality, death coiled and poised. He seemed no freer now than he had seemed long ago. In fact, he seemed more tense. The quality of clenched-teeth repression that has long been so powerfully effective in his singing seemed now to imbue his everyday speech as well. The demons had not been vanquished; unsuckled by liquor, they were merely subdued, less violent and more brooding wardens of the soul in a penal system wherein the only choice seems to lie between the death's row of abject drunkenness and the solitary confinement of dysthymic abstinence. In one cell or the other, it seems, he has always found refuge as well as attrition; and it has been from this big house of his own device that his profound voice has always risen in song.

But he was alive, and he felt physically better these days. "Oh, Lord, yeah," he said. Then he sighed. It was a sound lost somewhere between resignation and desolation; and in that same tone, staring straight ahead again into the rainy night, he repeated his affirmation, which no longer sounded at all like one of conviction, but rather simply of forbearance.

JIMMY BOWEN

JIMMY BOWEN
Is the Most (check one):
Reviled ☐ Respected ☐ Man on Music Row
BOB ALLEN

▌ From its commercial beginnings in the early 1920s, country music has been guided and shaped by record producers and talent scouts behind the scenes. One of the most influential country producers and executives of the 1980s and 1990s was Jimmy Bowen, who retired in 1995 after being diagnosed with cancer. In a music business that is increasingly becoming the province of specialists, Bowen was a jack of all trades. At various times, he had been a rockabilly artist, a songwriter, a disc jockey, a record producer, and a record company chief. As producer, he had the distinction of running the control board for artists as widely diverse as Frank Sinatra and Hank Williams Jr. As an executive, he was infamous for jumping from one record label to another—and house-cleaning entire staffs in the process. Invariably, Bowen drew strong reactions from those who worked with him. Hence the off-beat title of this 1990 profile by longtime *JCM* contributor Bob Allen. To my knowledge, it is the most in-depth and accurate piece ever published on Bowen, and it captures Bowen at the peak of his career.—Ed.

"Thanks to Jimmy Bowen for once again reminding us that age and treachery will always overcome youth and talent."
> —Charlie Monk at the 1990 Radio Seminar,
> around the time of Jimmy Bowen's move to Capitol

▌ At mid-afternoon on a spring day in early 1990, Jimmy Bowen is hunched over the console in the dimly lit control room at the Sound Stage Studio on Nashville's Music Row. The studio itself is empty, save for him and two members of his team of engineers who assist him in his various production duties. The two assistants are seated just behind him at the sound board. One of the engineers repeatedly plays the same few bars of "When You're a Man on Your Own," an old Carl Perkins song which, the week before, Bowen and George Strait had recorded during sessions for Strait's *Livin' It Up* album, which Bowen and Strait coproduced.

As the music booms through the speakers, Bowen twists the knobs and keeps his eyes glued to the meters as he adjusts the volume level of the steel guitar and background vocal tracks. One of the engineers punches Bowen's terse instructions for changes in the remix into the keyboard of the digital mixing system. The other engineer, as a back-up, scribbles these same changes into the margins of a lyric sheet of the song.

Outside, in the studio parking lot, a chauffeured car (equipped with cellular phone and state-of-the-art video and audio equipment—a mobile office, no less) waits to shuttle Bowen across Music Row to his next assignment at another studio, where, later that afternoon, he will oversee the recording of lead vocals on a forthcoming Gatlin Brothers album, which he is also co-producing. Still later, Capitol Records' recent-ly-installed chief executive/staff producer will supervise instrumental overdubs on sessions for yet another of the dozen or so Capitol artists he is currently producing or co-producing. It is illustrative of Bowen's cele-brated, and unusual, career that George Strait, whom he is producing on this particular afternoon, is not a Capitol artist. Rather, he is one of the top-selling acts on the MCA label, with which Bowen was formerly asso-ciated.

Like a four-star general or a head of state on the move, Bowen takes his office with him wherever he goes. For the couple of hours that he is at Sound Stage, reviewing and fine-tuning the remixes on *Livin' It Up*, the studio also serves as his makeshift executive headquarters. (He spends relatively little time in his actual office at Capitol's headquarters on 16th Avenue South, preferring to work out of his home, in the studio, or on the run. He even takes business calls over a mobile phone while on the golf course.) A call from one of his vice-presidents at the record label is routed into the control room by the studio receptionist; in the corridor outside the sound room, the manager of a Capitol artist and several other music business functionaries are waiting to have brief meetings with him. "Have him take a seat, I'll be with him in a minute," Bowen instructs his executive assistant with a brusque, vaguely imperial air as he is informed of the arrival of yet another scheduled visitor.

Bowen—who stands over six feet tall and appears to be about twenty or thirty pounds bulkier than he was when he first hit Nashville thirteen years, a half-dozen record labels, and quite a few million dollars ago—is an imposing figure as he sits there at the console, deftly spinning knobs, pulling levers, and juggling the dual responsibilities and tasks of producer and label chief. He is affable with visitors and staff alike, if only in a dis-tant sort of way. Yet there is always a sharp glint in his eyes that makes it clear that, for him, the eleventh commandment is not to waste time on frivolities or social niceties: the business at hand is business. Even with an average work day that begins at eight in the morning (with a half an hour of trainer-supervised physical therapy for his chronic back ailments) and sometimes runs until midnight, it seems that there are never enough hours in a day for Jimmy Bowen.

The obvious question—one which many people up and down Music Row are always asking (sometimes with chagrin, even disgust)—is what in the world, besides the heady allure of power and profit, makes Jimmy Bowen run?

Bowen's own insight to this question is typically blunt, off-the-cuff, irreverent, and unrevealing: "I drank too much whiskey in the sixties, and in the seventies and mid-eighties I smoked too much marijuana. I never did too much cocaine, because I have these allergies." He pauses to sniff and sneeze into a handkerchief. "And I have no place to put it into! So, I'm an addictive personality, and the biggest addiction I've had since 1955 is music. I've kicked whiskey, I've kicked cigarettes, I've kicked marijuana. All I have left now is the music, and I'm not trying to kick that. I hope it don't kick me!"

At age fifty-two, Bowen's beard has now gone almost completely gray. As usual he is dressed more like a Venice Beach landscape artist than a country record mogul. He wears a white "whaling cap" pulled down close to his eyes (he claims it helps prevent migraines during his marathon studio sessions), white golf shoes, and nondescript brown slacks and sweater. "I fuckin' hate dressing up," he grouses good-naturedly. "I can't goddamn breathe in a tie. I'm uncomfortable in one, so I don't do that. And nobody suffers from it—especially me!"

"Since arriving in Nashville from Los Angeles just over a decade ago, producer / music executive Jimmy Bowen has changed labels nearly as often as wives. (The second Dixie Bowen had to hyphenate her name to Dixie Gamble-Bowen to avoid confusion with her predecessor, Dixie Bowen.) As he himself often says, Bowen taught Music City hicks how to make a $40,000 album for $150,000. Bully for him. Speaking of bullies, this is the man who screeched about the conflict of interest exploited by producers-publishers, yet saw no conflict in the fact that while heading MCA Records, a great percentage of the artists on the label (and virtually all the heavy hitters) were produced by . . . Jimmy Bowen. And recorded at the studio in which he enjoys part ownership. Though now heading a label (Universal) that will release no product for nearly two quarters, don't cry for Jimmy, Nashville. He is still producing the same MCA artists. Suggested destination: Back to L.A."

—From the *Nashville Scene*, November 1989, in an essay on the busload of Nashville public figures to whom the editors would most like to award a one-way ticket out of town

▌One would be hard pressed to think of another figure whose influence has, for better or worse, been so ubiquitously felt in Nashville's music industry in the last decade as Jimmy Bowen's. Certainly, no one on the scene has been so persistently extolled and reviled, praised and damned, and so endlessly gossiped, speculated, and conjectured about as Bowen has. In less than a decade and a half, he has managed to head the Nashville divisions of no fewer than a half dozen different major record labels: MCA, Elektra/Asylum, Warner Bros., MCA (for a second time), Universal, and most recently, Capitol.

Along the way, Bowen has built some bridges and burned quite a few more; he has inspired unflagging loyalty in some quarters and unmitigated scorn in others. He has made steadfast friends and bitter enemies, and he has become one of the most controversial and enigmatic figures in the country music industry.

"Working with Jimmy Bowen was the most fun I've ever had with any producer or record executive in my whole life. He's one of the best friends a guy could have, and he's one of the smartest men I've ever met in my life," says Waylon Jennings, who recorded several LPs with Bowen during his relatively brief and largely unsuccessful stint with MCA in the late 1980s.

"Jimmy is very definitely artist-oriented," Jennings continues. "He leans toward the artists from beginning to end. He does everything he can to make the artist comfortable. He also works harder than anybody I ever saw. He's a workaholic; he works all the time. He keeps himself so abreast of everything—all the way from studio technology and the cutting of an album, right through to radio and retail. I've never met a man who was so smart about this business, from one end of it to the other.

"My only regret is that he and I never got anything rocking together, never had any hits, though that sure wasn't his fault," adds Jennings, who is now with Epic. "But after three albums, when I went to him and asked him for a release, he went to bat for me. Even though I owed MCA three more albums, he helped me get loose."

"He's just great, we're good friends," says George Strait, who has co-produced a series of best-selling, gold and platinum albums with Bowen. "I'm in a real comfortable position: if I need help, he gives it to me. If not, he leaves me alone. And that's not taking credit away from him: I'd be lost without him. As far as working with the board, with the sound, all that stuff, he really knows what he's doing. I just couldn't do all that, and really don't have any desire to learn. It also helps that we see eye to eye; we have the same musical tastes."

"Who is Jimmy Bowen, and what is he like," Conway Twitty muses when asked that very same question. "You could ask ten different people in this town and get ten different answers.

"For a guy that's as aggressive as Bowen is, to come into a town like

Nashville, with all its cliques, he's sure gonna ruffle some feathers and make some people mad," adds Twitty, whom Bowen co-produced back in the early 1980s, when they were both affiliated with the Elektra, Warners, and MCA labels. "And he's done exactly that. But he's sure left his shoeprint!

"And that doesn't necessarily make him a bad person," Twitty emphasizes with a thoughtful pause. "But overall, as far as Conway Twitty's concerned, and overlooking all those things [Bowen's done] that people consider bad—forget all that. As far as a music man and a record company executive, I'd have to say that I've enjoyed working with Bowen more than anybody I've ever worked with. And I've worked with some nice folks.

"He's a very aggressive man, but he's an artist's man. He looks out for the artists, not just the company he works for," Twitty explains. "He knows a company is nothing without its artists; he looks at it that way. And I always appreciated that. It's something rare."

"Jimmy's not wimpy, he's not wishy-washy," says MCA artist Reba McEntire. "When he's on your side, he's on your side. If you bring him a song and it stinks, he'll tell you. If you do something he loves, he'll tell you. You always know where you stand with him, and I like that."

Naturally, for every public figure that praises Bowen, there are at least one or two others who would just as soon bury him under a heap of opprobrium. MCA country-rocker Steve Earle, to cite one glaring example, recently told *Tower Pulse*, "I learned a lot from Jimmy Bowen, and I have a lot of respect for him on one level, but I don't think Bowen has any respect for artists." It's probably worth noting that Earle was never produced by Bowen, though his first two albums were released and promoted out of MCA Nashville while Bowen was in charge.

Earle is the daring exception, however. Most of those who might have something less than glowing to say about Bowen—in light of the power that he wields—are naturally hesitant to do so on the record. There are, after all, dozens and dozens in Nashville's music industry—artists, managers, label executives, etc.—who've felt the burn of Bowen's byzantine executive style, and/or felt the sting of his draconian penchant for slicing newly acquired label rosters by half and cleaning house of almost entire record company staffs, as he did at MCA a few years back, and more recently at Capitol. (There are a handful of Music Row veterans who have the unenviable distinction of being fired not once, but twice, by Bowen as he has played musical chairs, jumping from one top label executive job to the next at what sometimes has seemed like a frenetic, irrational pace.)

Like Nashville's version of T. Boone Pickens, Bowen has often seized the reins of power at the various labels he's headed in a manner that could easily be characterized as something less than friendly takeovers. Thus, in the imaginations of those whose careers have been affected by his none too subtle corporate power plays, Bowen has assumed an insidious shark-like image: you're never sure just where or when he'll surface next, but you know from the rumor mill that he's lurking out there in the waters somewhere, waiting to dethrone another label head and take his place. "Just when you thought it was safe to go back on Music Row, you pick up *Billboard* and read that he's taken over another label," quips one industry observer.

Such perceptions—be they accurate or not—have, naturally, earned Bowen epithets like "carpetbagger," "opportunist," "arch-manipulator," and worse. "He's a man who's never met a conflict of interest that he couldn't overlook," says one detractor who prefers to remain anonymous. Adds another: "The only person Jimmy Bowen ever does anything for is Jimmy Bowen."

Some have even gone further in their denunciations, accusing Bowen of operating an elaborate system of kick-backs, double-billings, and other under-the-table dealings, such as exacting payoffs from the studio musicians and engineers he uses on his sessions, and requiring artists to record in studios in which he holds ownership. (As a footnote, it's worth pointing out that such practices have been widespread in Nashville's largely unregulated, laissez-faire recording industry almost from the beginning.)

In keeping with the practice of many of the successful Nashville producers whom he himself has criticized, Bowen has also dabbled quietly in the song publishing business. On at least one occasion, with a recording artist with a weak sales record, he reportedly demanded half the publishing on the artist's original material as a condition for coproducing an album with her. While this is not an unusual arrangement in the Nashville recording industry, it is the sort of potential conflict of interest that Bowen himself has often sounded off about.

Bowen also reportedly has a significant financial interest in a publishing company of his own, the Great Cumberland Music Group, whose offices are in the same building as the Sound Stage Studio, where he often records. Cumberland Music has a number of successful Nashville songwriters on its staff, some of whose songs have ended up on recent albums that Bowen coproduced with Reba McEntire.

"As weird as it might seem, I really don't think there's anything unethical about it," says one music business insider. "If you look at the LPs that Bowen's produced, there seems to be a fairly wide range of songs from outside [publishing] sources. And Cumberland's writers have proven track records with hits. Actually, Bowen is one of the few Nashville producers who sends his artists around to the various publishing houses to listen to material."

Bowen himself is well aware of the accusations, and they tend to make him mildly livid—or at least as livid as he ever gets in public. He strenuously and vehemently denies them and categorically denounces those who make them.

"First of all, musicians and engineers don't make enough to give kickbacks," he insists. Though his voice is calm and controlled and there is a contemptuous grin on his face, he appears to be seething inside. "Secondly, a producer who owns his own studio is a damned fool: there's no profit in it, and when it breaks down and the artist is standing there [waiting to record], who do you holler at? I haven't got time for that kind of shit!

"I always tell my wife, I'd like to find one sonofabitch I could nail one time, for saying those things. I've told a couple of people in this town, 'If I could just sue the shit out of you and make it stick, I'd make you bring your tax records [into court] and I'll bring mine.' Because the only money I've made since I've been in this town is either royalties or salaries from the record companies. And I'd like to have that shown one time. I don't care about the individuals [who make these accusations]. I just think it's wrong that you should give young people the impression that you should do those sort of rip-off things to be successful, because the truth of the matter is, if you get the music right, you don't have to steal a penny. You'll make all the goddamned money you can spend. . . . Ah . . . well . . ." he adds with a self-deprecating laugh, "almost all I can spend, anyway!

"Nashville's a small town," he continues, laughing with gentle condescension as he turns warily back to the question of his somewhat tainted public image. "I was in L.A. for sixteen years, and the L.A. *Times* never called me, the L.A. *Examiner* never called me. Not one TV station ever came out to interview me, or gave a damn what I said. But in this little town, it matters, because it's an important industry. And since I say what I think, it's inevitable that I make enemies as well as friends."

Regardless of public perception, Bowen has, in his time, certainly gotten the music right. This former high school glee club singer, amateur deejay, and short-lived fifties teen idol has dominated the charts in the past decade or so as coproducer of artists like George Strait, Reba McEntire, Hank Williams Jr., the Oak Ridge Boys, Conway Twitty, and Loretta Lynn. According to the tabulations of Nashville journalist/executive and longtime Bowen researcher John Lomax III, Bowen has, in his thirteen years on the Nashville scene, produced or co-produced more than 57 #1 singles, 16 #1 LPs, 150 Top Twenty singles, over 40 Top Ten LPs, and more than a dozen gold and platinum LPs. He has been instrumental in taking the careers of artists like Strait, McEntire, and Williams from the journeyman level to full-fledged superstardom.

Certainly one ingredient of his success is his seemingly boundless energy. Bowen is a gloriously unreconstructed workaholic. An immensely aggressive and resourceful man, he routinely—and seemingly enthusiastically—devotes months of eighteen-hour days and seven-day weeks to his formidable responsibilities as both label head and coproducer of more than a dozen different artists. He is assisted in all this by a streamlined back-up organization of a virtual army of first and second studio engineers, song screeners, and hot and cold running executive assistants to whom he delegates heavily. "If you try to slow the process down, you fall down," he insists.

Thus, for months at a time, Bowen dwells in the self-imposed isolation of the recording studio (where he usually has meals catered in to economize on time), his executive suite, his mobile office, and the spacious Franklin Road home (replete with security fence, electronically activated gate, and a large "Beware of Dog" sign) that he shares with his wife, Ginger (his fourth marriage) and his teenage son, Christian.

Indeed, it seems to give Bowen a sort of perverse glee that within Nashville's music industry, which devotes an almost ridiculous amount of time and expense to self-congratulatory, self-aggrandizing social rituals, his loner stance runs so resolutely against the grain. Certainly, his self-imposed isolation and shadowy style of power-brokering has bred a certain degree of curiosity, suspicion, and paranoia, in and of itself.

"I think [all the gossip] has a lot to do with the way I am," he readily admits. "You know: being kind of crazy, delegating quick and talking quick. I don't waste a lot of time saying hello or goodbye to you. I just say, 'Talk.' And pretty soon, this whole . . . mode takes over, and you can get a whole lot more done by cutting out all the wasted time, the pleasantries, and protocol. I like it that way. I can't waste time. I produced twelve or fifteen albums last year. I run the label. I do play golf on occasion, which is really where my sanity is saved from all the heavy concentration."

In fact, an occasional hour or two on the golf course (where he often plays for stakes as high as several thousand dollars a game) with other well-heeled Music Row executives is about the only respite Bowen allows himself from his grueling schedule. (Though he points out that in the course of two hours on the fairway he is often interrupted by as many as forty business calls on his mobile phone.) His only real rest and recreation comes with his annual or biannual retreats with his wife to his vacation home on the Hawaiian island of Maui. To Music Row in general, he often remains invisible for months at a time.

"I started all that interaction shit years ago, with the NMA," Bowen, the isolationist, says with breezy, dismissive disdain. He is referring to the Nashville Music Association (now the Nashville Entertainment Association), an organization which he helped create back in the late 1970s and early 1980s as the music community's pop-rock alternative to the Country Music Association, whose leadership, policies and voting procedures he has often roundly criticized. "I don't have time for all that now. I don't get anything from it, and they don't get anything from me," he adds. "Leadership Nashville doesn't need me. I think it's an absolute waste of time to be on the CMA board—I think it's a done deal before the board even gets there anyway. I hate to go to nightclubs and receptions. And nobody misses me if I'm not there. I had Bruce Hinton and Jim Ed Norman to do that for me [at MCA and Warner Bros.]. They both had suits and ties, and they love that shit. Now I've got Jerry Crutchfield at Capitol to do that. Nobody misses me if I don't show up," he laughs. "Not really."

"When I was 11 or maybe 12, my mother told me to 'always stick with Jimmy Bowen.' I asked her just a few years back, what she meant by that remark. ''Cause he's just serious enough,' was her reply."
—Don Lanier, childhood friend and longtime business associate of Jimmy Bowen's, in an interview with John Lomax III

▌ Born in Santa Rita, New Mexico, Jimmy Bowen spent his formative years in the panhandle region of Texas. His earliest musical experience was singing in the church choir in Dumas, Texas.

Even as a teenager, he was drawn to the music business. While attending high school in Amarillo, he was a glee club member and worked part-time as a deejay on a local radio station. Later, while attending West Texas State College, in Canyon, Texas, he became friends with classmate and fellow gleeclubber, Buddy Knox, who was destined to become a formative figure in early rock & roll. Bowen ended up playing stand-up bass in Knox's band, the Rhythm Orchids. (Don Lanier was also a bandmember.)

One day, Bowen and Knox got wind that another then-unknown rock & roller named Roy Orbison was going to be recording just across the state line, in Clovis, New Mexico. On a whim, Bowen and Knox, and a third bandmember drove over to Clovis and somehow managed to persuade producer Norman Petty to let them have a shot in the studio, as well. They recorded a song called "Party Doll," with Knox on lead vocals, and another called "Stickin' With You," with Bowen (who also co-wrote the song) singing lead.

Bowen—who today admits that he had far more chutzpah than actual singing talent—was particularly impressed by Petty's patience in the studio. "It took us eight hours to record 'Party Doll,' and at least that long to cut 'I'm Stickin' With You,'" he recalled in an interview several years ago. "I was fascinated by all that."

At first, the records he and Knox made generated no interest with any record label. Bowen, however—who even then, evidently had a particularly pronounced streak of aggressiveness and uncanny resourcefulness—began playing them on his own little radio show back in Amarillo. Soon, other local stations followed suit. Finally, Knox and Bowen were offered contracts by Roulette, a New York-based label. Knox's "Party Doll" became a #1 hit and earned a minor niche in rock & roll history. "I'm Stickin' With You," sung by Bowen, managed to get to #9 before sliding resolutely into obscurity.

Even though Knox's "Hula Love" was a Top Ten hit in 1957, neither Bowen nor Knox sustained any luck in following up on these mercurial hits, though Bowen did go on to record one lackluster LP, *Jimmy Bowen* (Roulette Records, 1957), which has since become a hot item among record collectors. During this time, he also made a trek to the Grand Ole Opry where he and his band briefly performed (sans drummer).

Much to the delight of his associates, Bowen, a few years back, returned briefly to the grandstand for the Nashville music industry's annual W.O.R.S.T ("World's Oldest Rock Stars Together") Show where he sang "Jail House Rock" to a set of new, humorous lyrics that he himself had composed for the occasion. "Well," one acquaintance and business associate commented wryly after witnessing Bowen's performance, "at least Jimmy ain't got no worse. . . . He still makes Ricky Nelson sound like Caruso!"

Bowen himself, even as a youth, was enough of a realist to know that his future was definitely not as a rock & roll singer: "I knew some day they'd stop screaming long enough to listen," he laughs. "And I knew that when they did, my singing career would be short-lived."

1959 found Bowen in Colorado Springs, Colorado, working as a disc jockey. By now, he'd been bitten badly by the music business bug; that same year, he moved to Los Angeles, where he soon landed a position as staff songwriter for a company called American Music. In a matter of time, he was not only writing songs, but managing the company and (along with another fledgling songwriter, Glen Campbell) producing demo records. During the next decade or so on the West Coast, every move that Bowen made seemed to be an upward one. For a couple of years he worked for Chancellor Records, where he oversaw the careers of rock & roll glamor boys Fabian and Frankie Avalon. (Also, around this time, he was married to singer Keely Smith.) He later signed on as A&R

man for Frank Sinatra's Reprise label. In 1963 he produced an instrumental by Jack Nitzsche called "Lonely Surfer," which became a Top Forty hit. And he began producing veteran popster/movie star Dean Martin, whose career, at the time, was on a definite downswing.

The Martin-Bowen alliance proved an effective one: the two of them went on to record twenty-six hit singles, fifteen gold albums, and five platinum albums together. Producing Frank Sinatra, Bowen had similar luck: two of Sinatra's biggest and most enduring hits—"That's Life" and "Strangers in the Night"—bore the Bowen production stamp.

"I was with Reprise when it was $2 million in the hole," says Bowen. "Then it was merged with Warner Bros. and [as head of A&R for Warner/Reprise] I watched it grow. That's where I first learned to run a record company. I learned by doing. Nobody can teach you.

"Then later," Bowen continues, "when I had my own companies [Amos Records] and lost everything I had, I learned even more. So, by the time I came to Nashville I was already a seasoned record person on the national level. It wasn't that I was smarter than anybody else. It was just that I'd been around longer and had been through the right things you need to go through to learn how to do it."

It was in 1968 that Bowen launched Amos Records. ("'Artists, Music, and all the Other Shit,'" he jokes of his company's name today. "Toward the end, it got to be where it was too much of the other shit!") Through Amos, Bowen worked with Kenny Rogers & the First Edition, Mason Williams, Kim Carnes, and Glenn Frey, Don Henley, and J. D. Souther (who were then in various groups—Long Branch Penny Whistle, Shiloh, etc.; Frey and Henley later formed the Eagles).

By this time, he'd already begun making periodic trips to Nashville to scout for material for the various artists he was producing. But by 1970, Amos Records was already history. "Before that, I'd done real well in the 1960s," Bowen recalls. "I'd worked for Sinatra and Reprise. I was producing Sinatra, Dean Martin, Sammy Davis Jr., and Kenny Rogers & the First Edition. But then when I started my own production and publishing company, it just proved to be the wrong time to start a label. We had poor distribution, and we didn't have the kind of track record that it took. Ampex put up a lot of money, Decca put up a lot of money, and I put up a lot of money, and we lost it all. After that, for the next few years, I mostly played golf and produced a few albums. I had money saved from the sixties, and I just kind of cleaned my head out."

In 1974, the seemingly irrepressible producer-executive re-emerged, this time as head of MGM Records. "I hated it," he says, grimacing distastefully at the recollection. "It left me so tired I couldn't even face going into the studio. It's really what brought me to Nashville."

When MGM was swallowed up by another company, Bowen was asked to move to New York. When he refused, the remainder of his contract was bought out by the parent company. "They paid me for three years to not be president," he says. "Which I found to be a very worthwhile way to make a living."

By that time, Bowen had suffered a sort of burn-out in L.A. The "old people's music" (Sinatra, Martin, Sammy Davis Jr.) with which he'd long been associated was rapidly falling out of fashion. And having built his own reputation as a specialist in reviving the sagging careers of these aging Hollywood pop crooners, he had little or no connection with Southern California's flourishing rock scene. However, in 1976, he produced a song called "Home Made Love" by a singer named Tom Bresh, which ended up going to #6 in *Billboard*'s country charts, thus opening up a whole new realm of possibility for him.

Hoping to recharge his batteries before making his initial assault on Nashville, Bowen departed the West Coast in 1976 and moved to the resort town of Eureka Springs, Arkansas, where he spent a year.

"Eureka Springs was a real neat town," he recalls with a tone of soft nostalgia. "About a third of the population was the natives who'd lived there all their lives. A third were these hippies who'd started businesses there, and a third were retired people. It was a great mixture of life. You had this huge religious attraction there as well, which people came by the busloads to see. Then right across the street, you had these hippies growing grass in their backyards. It was a great way for me to get back to the basics of life."

During this period, he also spent a lot of time just driving around the greater southeast and southwest: "Missouri, Oklahoma, Arkansas, Texas, Tennessee, Alabama, Georgia . . . I went to barn dances, I listened to country radio everywhere, and I just talked to people. I didn't know much about country music then—hell, I didn't know anything about it! I wanted to find out why people did or didn't buy certain records, who their favorite artists were. I found out that they didn't even know most of [the artists]. I found out how narrow country really was. It was a real change from my Sinatra-Dean Martin days in California. It was like going to another country, another world unto itself."

Before long, Bowen began commuting to Nashville on a regular basis. His first base of operations in Music City was a small office behind Mel Tillis's gift shop. "At first, I couldn't get any work [as a producer], and it scared me," he admits. "For a while I really thought maybe I'd made a mistake. Nobody wanted to hire a 'Yankee' producer from California."

One of the first jobs he did land was producing Tillis. He also began working with other, more obscure singers, many of whom then had as much presence in the country record industry as Bowen himself did: Tom Bresh, Roy Head, Red Steagall, Sterling Whipple. Bowen also became a regular at the Glaser Brothers Studio, which around the same time was becoming famous as switchboard central of country music's "Outlaw Movement."

"I came here in a 1970 Buick which I'd bought in Arkansas," he recalls, laughing. "I loved it! The muffler was broken, the fenders were falling off, the glass was broken. The cops used to stop me all the time, because it would barely pass inspection. Wherever I parked it, I left the keys in it, because nobody would steal the damn thing! I think I finally sold it to Captain Midnight's cousin."

Bowen insists he came to Nashville with very few material resources, other than the buy-out funds from his MGM contract. "I think because I was in that car, and, you know, I don't dress like a business person," he chuckles with barely concealed glee, "I think they thought I had money, but was eccentric about it."

Bowen spent an intense, nearly three-year-long apprenticeship at the Glasers' studio, undergoing a self-styled and self-imposed "cram session" in country music, country music history, and country record-making.

"I didn't know how one fiddle was supposed to sound on a record," he says, laughing incredulously. "With Sinatra I never used fewer than four. The first time I recorded a fiddle, with Mel Tillis, it sounded awful. A steel guitar almost drove me back to L.A.! Every time the steel player would lay that bar on, they'd play fifths, sevenths, ninths, and elevenths, and just wipe out any possible overdub you might want to make.

"Tompall [Glaser] used to walk in the studio where I'd be working with some artist, and he'd lean over in my ear and say, 'You make the worst-sounding country guitar I ever heard!' Then he'd walk out, and for the next three hours, I'd try to make it sound better.

"I basically spent about twenty hours a day for three years in the Glasers' studio," Bowen adds. "Tompall and some of his friends were the ones who taught me what country music was, and what it had become. He'd play me old Bob Wills and Jimmie Rodgers, everybody. Those three years were the most valuable thing that's happened to me since I've been here."

Almost from the start, Bowen insisted on emphasizing the ideological distance between himself and the Nashville music industry's status quo by going on record with his general contempt for Nashville's system of record producing. No doubt, he also discovered that granting colorful, vitriolic, self-aggrandizing interviews with the often undiscriminating local music business press was an excellent way to raise his own industry profile.

"Bowen is an absolute master of verbal communication, both one-on-one, or to a crowd," observes John Lomax III. "I once saw him go up and give a speech at some gathering, a process which began when he took a sheaf of paper out of his pocket, glanced at it, and then launched into a thirty- or forty-minute talk. I asked him afterward if he'd written out his speech on paper. He said, 'Nah, I just carried that up there in case I said anything worth a shit.' He's one of the best extemporaneous speakers I've ever seen—including politicians. . . . And that's a scary thought!"

"I was a Yankee, and I had a big mouth," Bowen concedes with what seems like quiet pride at his shrewdness in turning his brash, opinionated forthrightness into a political asset. "When I thought [Nashville's] records sounded bad, I said so. When I thought their song selection was mediocre, I said so. When I said that the [music business] power structure in Nashville didn't even like this music they were making, but were just making a living off it, and knew that if they could hold it down and keep it small and keep it from growing, they could control it, it irritated people."

"I sometimes try to imagine what it was like for Bowen when he walked into Nashville back in the late seventies," snickers one long-time ally. "He must'a looked around and saw the people at RCA, Capitol, Mercury, the people who were heading the major labels then, and rubbed his hands and thought, 'Man, this is gonna be eeeaaasy pickin's!'"

As has almost always been the case, in order to ascend the corporate ladder in Nashville, Bowen, the music business Machiavellian, went over the heads of the Music Row power structure and called upon his impressive West Coast connections. It was Mike Maitland, Bowen's old co-worker from his Warner/Reprise days, and by then, head of MCA Records, who hired him for his first full-time Nashville label gig in 1978 as vice-president and general manager of MCA's Nashville operations (Bowen had maintained an office in Nashville back in the mid-1970s, when he worked for MGM).

Bowen had only held this position about four months when Maitland became ill and left MCA. Realizing that his own days with the company were probably numbered, Bowen quit too. He was only back on the street for a few months when, in December 1978, Joe Smith, another old friend and coworker who'd since risen to the top position at Elektra/Asylum, hired him to head Elektra's fledgling Nashville operation.

Until then, Elektra/Asylum's Nashville office had been a sort of neglected stepchild of the company's flourishing West Coast division, and had only one real star, Eddie Rabbitt, on its roster. But Bowen, with a blank checkbook and an open line to the company's top brass, was soon able to leverage it into a bustling operation. He signed Hank Williams Jr.,

Conway Twitty, the Bellamy Brothers, Kieran Kane (now half of the O'Kanes), and numerous other impressive talents. "I told [Elektra] I'd give them a $30 million operation in four years," Bowen later boasted. "We missed it by only $1 million. We took the company's 2 percent market share and raised it to 18 percent."

Bowen signed Hank Jr. to Elektra only a day or two after he himself had joined the company. Together, in 1979, they produced Williams's ground-breaking *Family Tradition* LP. They went on to have an incredible run together—eight gold LPs and numerous hit singles.

Bowen is still terribly proud of his long, illustrious association with Hank Jr. He is particularly fond of citing it when anyone dares point out his penchant for latching on to proven big-sellers like Twitty, Strait, and the Oaks (most of whom have since slipped away from him), rather than working with and developing newer or more modest-selling acts.

"Hank Jr. was selling 25,000 an LP when I went to work for him. He was the best blues singer in this country and they were producing Bee Gees songs on him and using eight-piece vocal groups and strings," he notes with disgust. "But I knew what he was, and I went after him. Now he sells a million, a million-two [units per album release], and he's won Entertainer of the Year. I think I did my job. Later, when I started working with Reba, she was selling 40,000 [per album]. Now she's a household name. George Strait was around a quarter of a million, and we were able to take that to platinum.

"I've never claimed to perform magic," he insists in a somewhat more subdued tone. "My whole thing is to help artists do their music. I don't do it for them. I did that in the sixties, with Dean Martin and Sinatra. I hated it. Now I go to bed and sleep good at night. I let the artist worry. It's their life, their music. I'm just a hired hand to help them get it down right. I'm heavy-handed, I'm opinionated, sure. I study 'em and tell 'em what they should and shouldn't do, in my opinion. But the final decision is always theirs."

Reba McEntire, one of the many artists to whom Bowen has routinely extended the opportunity to coproduce her own records and become more actively involved in the creative studio process, recalled the ordeal of that transition in an interview several years ago:

"I remember the first time Jimmy was mixing one of my albums, and he made me sit through the whole thing," McEntire recalls with an exasperated giggle. "Whooah! I hated it! It was boring! He was up there fiddlin' with knobs and listenin', and I had no idea what he was listenin' for. I just sat there and listened and took notes, like he asked me to. I kept askin' him what he was doing, and I'm sure he got tired of answering after while! Finally, I said, 'Jimmy, I can't handle this.' He just said,

'Okay, we'll let you know when we're ready for you to come in and listen and approve the final mixes.' Boy, that's tedious work! The patience he must have to sit there and listen to it, time after time, overwhelms me."

One of the most momentous pieces of serendipity in Bowen's career occurred in January 1983. That was when Elektra/Asylum merged with Warner Bros. With the help of his old friend Mo Ostin [then head of Warner Bros.] Bowen was victorious in the corporate scramble that ensued. Though Elektra's roster was, by far, the smaller of the two, he nonetheless emerged as head of the formidable new combined Warner/EA roster. Ensconced in this position of power, he quickly began making many of the friends, allies, critics, and outright enemies he still has today.

For starters, he dropped twenty-nine of the fifty-four artists on the merged Warner/EA roster. "I've dropped probably a hundred artists since I've been in town," he acknowledges. "That can cause you some problems—even though it had to be done. It touches a lot of people. I don't enjoy letting an artist go. But if I don't, the other artists on the label suffer. It's just nature: you have to cut out the weak, and I've always just gone and done it."

Yet it's sometimes been the manner in which Bowen has performed this unsavory task that has rubbed some people the wrong way. There is one widely-circulated tale as to how he recently turned down a young Capitol artist's newly-completed LP, then rubbed salt in the wounds by ordering the artist to go home and write a two-page essay on why his newly completed album was so awful.

"Ego out of control," frets one long-time Bowen supporter who begrudgingly admitted this was well beyond the bounds of acceptable music biz protocol. "I'd be glad to help write that essay," he adds. "Only Bowen wouldn't know until he got to the last line that I was writing about some of the lousy albums that he's produced!"

By the time that Elektra and Warner Bros. merged, Bowen had learned to stroke and manipulate Nashville's servile music industry press with the same ease that Chet Atkins strokes and strums an electric guitar. Always good copy and always full of colorful boasts and bombastic broadsides, Bowen doled out interviews with the local papers and music trade magazines like peanuts to hungry pigeons. He unleashed sweeping projections, bold proclamations, and blistering criticisms of his Music Row peers. He seemed always eager to take credit for his growing list of accomplishments—and then some. In interviews from this period, he outlined his brash, innovative, and sometimes cold-blooded vision for country music industry's future—the need to move headlong into the age of technology and put new emphasis on LP sales. Promoting himself relentlessly, he repeatedly drew a bead on reigning music producer-executives like Billy Sherrill, whose methods, tastes, and attitudes he considered hopelessly antiquated and dangerously counterproductive to the future growth of the industry. "There's nobody [in Nashville] paying attention to the general record business," he told John Lomax III a few years ago. "I don't think they've heard of Springsteen, of John Mellencamp, or Bon Jovi. They ain't got those people at their house. They need young wives [to keep them in touch]. . . . How can you be a tit on the hog and not know about the whole hog?"

As brash and illogical as many of his predictions, prognostications, and projections for both himself and the music industry seemed at the time he made them, many—particularly those about the advent of advanced technology in Nashville's recording industry—have since proven surprisingly prophetic.

Today, Bowen looks back on his late seventies-early eighties media blitz as, "a conscious thing. . . . Everything I do is a conscious thing. . . . Something had to be done. I saw what the problems were and what had to be done. I wasn't tied to this [business] community by old friends or old business obligations. I was free to move where I wanted. I looked around town and said, 'Wow, there's a lot here!' I could see, first of all, the shackles had to be thrown off: let these artists get control of their own music and not have business people in charge of it. And let those so-called business people learn how to be good business people.

"I said they needed to spend more money making albums," he goes on, rising to the subject with self-righteous enthusiasm. "And they didn't want to hear that. You see, nobody was really producing records at that time. Chet [Atkins] had quit, Owen [Bradley] had quit. The publishers were making records, which is like the sheep tending to the cattle, or vice versa. Then there was also this attitude like, 'You don't need digital, it's country; you don't need echo, it's country; you don't need delay line, you don't need this, you don't need that. . . .' I'd say, 'Ah, bull . . . shit!!'"

One artist who has pleasant memories of working with Bowen—at two different labels (Warner Bros./Elektra and MCA)—is Conway Twitty. "I learned a lot from Bowen, and I hope he learned a lot from me," Twitty remembers. "The very first session I did for Elektra, Bowen sat in and told Dee [Henry, Twitty's wife and coproducer], 'I'm just gonna sit here and watch this guy. Anybody who's had as many #1 records as Conway's had, I'm not gonna put my hand in it until I see what he does.' I thought that was a wise move.

"One of the first songs we recorded together was 'Slow Hand,'" Twitty continues, referring to the Pointer Sisters' pop hit, which he successfully adapted for the country market. "Well, that blew Jimmy's mind! He told Dee, 'I cannot believe you're doing "Slow Hand" as a single!' He nearly had a heart attack! He said, 'They're gonna accuse me of singlehandedly ruining Conway Twitty's career!'

"Of course," Twitty laughs, "'Slow Hand' turned out to be a really big record for me. Later, Jimmy and I had a lot of skull sessions, and it took him a long time to understand that kind of thing, because back then, Bowen really didn't understand country music. He understands it a whole lot better today, and I hope maybe that I'm part of the reason for it."

After only a year or so at Warner Bros., Bowen jumped ship. In May 1984 he resurfaced—courtesy of his old friend and business associate, Irving Azoff, manager of the Eagles and various other supergroups, and then chairman of MCA Records. Azoff appointed him president of MCA Nashville and executive vice-president of MCA Records.

"[Bowen] makes a change or does something different about every five years," observes Bruce Hinton, current president of MCA Nashville (Bowen originally hired him at MCA), and Bowen's former partner in Amos Records.

It is indicative of the paranoia that Bowen is capable of inducing when he is playing corporate musical chairs and is in the midst of one of his not infrequent label-hopping putsches that Warner chairman Mo Ostin was, at first, reluctant to let him out of his contract with Warner Bros. When Bowen finally did get his release, it had ten pages of riders on it. "I can't talk to any Warners acts for a year," he explained at the time. "And I can't steal any Warners personnel for, I think, two years. . . . It's ridiculous."

Perhaps not so ridiculous, though, considering Bowen's administrative methodology. Incredibly enough, Bowen's contract with MCA did enable him to continue right on producing certain heavyweight Warner Bros. artists, like Hank Williams Jr. (whom he tried unsuccessfully to lure on board at MCA), Eddie Rabbitt, and Crystal Gayle, while heading a rival label. (Although this is an unusual arrangement which seems to stretch the boundaries of ethics and propriety, and smacks of conflict of interest, it is not entirely unheard of: MCA Records executive producer Tony Brown does manage to produce his old friend Rodney Crowell, a best-selling Columbia artist.)

Bowen grows defensive at the oft-repeated accusation that he hops from label to label and jumps from job to job too often for anyone's good but his own. "I know people say, 'He moves around too much,'" he growls. "But who's to say? Who's to say that five years is not enough time? Who's to say? I'm a builder, not a maintainer.

"After five years of building Warners [and Elektra]—which is now a great label, a good crew of people, all still friends of mine, I love 'em—I was tired. I was ready to go, ready to retire. But I didn't quite have enough money to retire. Then, along came Irving Azoff, another old friend of mine, who happened to be head of MCA at the time. . . . I gave Irving Souther, Frey, and Henley back when I shut down my companies in L.A. in 1969. They, of course, became the Eagles. Azoff asked me to fix MCA Records for him. His offer, and the challenge of it, got me over being tired. I meant for [MCA] to be a five-year situation, which it was."

Bowen—in somewhat predictable fashion—cleaned house at MCA. Everyone, with the exception of two or three low-level employees, got the pink slip in order to make way for the new team which he'd assembled. The local press criticized the prolonged takeover as sloppily and unprofessionally handled, since it had been preceded by months of rumors, innuendo, and general uncertainty during which all those whose careers were on the chopping block were left twisting in the wind.

"I don't fire people just because somebody else hired them," insists Bowen, who more recently also more or less cleared the decks at Capitol after seizing the reins of that company in late 1989. "But if they can't deal with the system that I put in, then they have to go."

Even most of Bowen's critics are forced to concede that he has been one of the first label heads in Nashville's traditionally sexist music industry to give women—such as Martha Sharp, Janice Azrak, and Shelia Shipley—the opportunity to rise to high-level executive positions. Says artist Reba McEntire: "Jimmy doesn't believe a woman should sit in the corner. Jimmy wants to teach you, and Jimmy's a good teacher. Jimmy, when he was at MCA, had more women working underneath him than any other label head. He believes in women. He knows they're smart, and that they can achieve."

All in all, his stint with MCA was a relatively distinguished one. He produced artists like George Strait and Reba McEntire and helped usher their careers to new levels. He hired A&R man/staff producer Tony Brown who has since gone on to become one of country music's most influential producers. In fact, it took Brown (who is reportedly on something less than good terms with Bowen these days) little time to actually begin stealing some of Bowen's own thunder. He not only launched the much-heralded MCA Masters series, which featured albums by dozens of country and popular music's most celebrated instrumentalists; he also developed and groomed fledgling left-field artists like Patty Loveless, Lyle Lovett, Steve Earle, and Nanci Griffith into successful recording acts.

Bowen bristles at the suggestion that even though he has managed to take various mid-level artists' careers to the pinnacle of megastardom, he has never actually broken in a new artist, from the ground up.

"When I went with MCA, I hired Tony Brown away from RCA and made him head of A&R. I let him develop new acts, and I worked with existing acts so we could get into a profit quick and they [the L.A. front office] would let us do what we wanted to do. That's corporate business. That's why I work with the Straits, the Rebas, the Oaks, the Steve Wariners. It was never a case of me saying, 'I gotta have my share of new acts so I can correct my image,'" he emphasizes. "I don't give a shit, you know. I do it the way I see it's gotta be done. When you run a label for a corporation, they want one thing: profit. They don't give a shit how you get it as long as it's legal and profitable."

In 1987, under Bowen's stewardship, MCA surpassed RCA in overall chart dominance for the first time ever, winning *Billboard's* "best overall label" award, along with its annual "best singles label" and "best album label" awards. That year, Bowen himself proclaimed that the company had, "made a tremendous improvement over 1986, the biggest gross in history for the [Nashville] division, the biggest net in history . . . the biggest pretax profit year for MCA Nashville in history."

But, just as Bowen's stock in Nashville has always risen on the strength of his formidable West Coast connections, so has it sometimes fallen. In 1989, when Irving Azoff was edged out of MCA, Bowen realized that his own highly politicized tenure with the company was on the ropes as well.

With some high-powered behind-the-scenes wheeling and dealing, however, Bowen turned even this defeat into a victory of sorts. Back in late 1988, he had put together his own label, Universal, with a roster that included Eddie Rabbitt, Lacy J. Dalton, the Nitty Gritty Dirt Band, Carl Perkins, and Eddy Raven, among others. Funded by MCA, Universal had its own producers and its own A&R staff, but shared marketing, art, production, administration and promotion teams with MCA. In typical fashion, Bowen—who just a few years earlier had insisted to the press that his own label was the last thing he wanted—proclaimed that within three years Universal would join the "Big Four" (RCA, MCA, Warner Bros., and CBS) as one of Nashville's powerhouse labels. "I needed something to get me excited again," he explained during the gala reception marking the official announcement of Universal's creation. "I thought I was going to have to get out of the business, go to Hawaii, go golfing."

As it turned out, though Universal did issue a Grammy-winning LP (the Nitty Gritty Dirt Band's *Will the Circle Be Unbroken II*), the label itself lasted only a year. As usual, Bowen managed to exit with his own self-styled golden parachute; he is said to have profited handsomely from contract buy-outs and other sources when MCA more or less pulled the plug on Universal. Though the recording contracts of the Nitty Gritty Dirt Band and the Judds (who were signed to become Universal artists as soon as their RCA contract lapsed) reverted back to MCA, Bowen himself kept control of the rest of the Universal roster, having signed the artists directly to himself, rather than to the label. And more recently, when he resurfaced as head of Capitol Records, he quickly merged the bulk of these with Capitol's roster.

Once again, Bowen considered retiring to Hawaii, but then rumors began flying and reports soon surfaced in the local press that he was poised for yet another takeover bid with MCA. (If successful, it would have been his third stint with the company in a little less than a decade.)

"The last time, they came to me," Bowen insists. "Azoff and [MCA exec] Al Teller said they'd like me to take it back over. I was, at that point, still producing for MCA and running Universal. But then, Al Teller changed his mind about re-combining the Universal and MCA rosters. I think basically what happened was that Tony Brown got to him and said he wanted to be out from under me and on his own. And that's under-standable."

In mid- and late 1989, before Bowen again lunged up from the deep to launch his intensive months-long campaign to commandeer control of Capitol Nashville, he maintained he'd actually made a sincere attempt to retire, but had failed miserably at it.

"All three times I've said I was going to retire to Hawaii I meant it, and each time something came up to change that," he explains. "I have a house on Maui and my wife and I go there a couple of times a year. I have buddies there I play golf with, and I started hanging out with them more and going to dinner with them more. They are all about my age or a few years older. I found out that they were all very unhappy people, and that retirement is not what it's cracked up to be. I started to see this, that it was boring. Last summer [1989], instead of going down there for two weeks, I went for four, just to see what it was like. By the fourth week I was beginning to phone back a lot, to get itchy."

He shrugs and continues: "So, I guess the truth of the matter is, when you work eighteen and twenty hours a day, seven days a week, you tend to set a goal, like, 'Four, five years down the road I'll get the hell out of this.' But then, when the time comes. . . ."

"So," he brightens up, "I went to Capitol this time—with the help of my old friend, Joe Smith [the present head of Capitol Records] again. When I first came on board, Joe sassed me about how long I intended to stay with the company," he chuckles. "Well, I can't [change labels] too many more times, because I'm getting too damned old!" He laughs again and shakes his head: "It's just a crazy thing that happened. . . ."

Even now that he is a year into his new job at Capitol, many still wonder what Bowen has in mind for the label's top-heavy, over-stocked roster. Capitol currently has only one ace in the hole (the double-platinum Garth Brooks), suffers from a dearth of bonafide superstars, has a surfeit of newcomers (Wild Rose, Billy Dean, Verlon Thompson), and seems overly dependent on true but tired veterans (Tanya Tucker, Barbara Mandrell, Glen Campbell, the Gatlin Brothers, Lee Greenwood, and Lacy J. Dalton), most of whom have worn out their welcomes at the radio and retail level a long time ago.

"By combining the Universal and Capitol rosters you have the biggest roster in town—which doesn't mean a thing unless you're selling records," points out Bowen, who himself has coproduced John Anderson, Joe Barnhill, Glen Campbell, Lacy J. Dalton, the Gatlins, Gary Morris, and Joni Harms for the label. "But there is a power roster within those two rosters, which will begin to emerge over the next twelve months.

"You see, a record company operation has to include some new artists who can be developed over three to five years. Then you need some of those artists that other people have given up on, that still sell a hundred to two hundred thousand records. They pay your rent. They keep you going. Then you must have two to five superstars who'll sell a half a million to platinum, and there's your profit.

"Well, obviously, I've got plenty of the brand-new and plenty of the middle. All I'm missing is the superstars. But if I've got that middle, I can break even and keep going while I develop some of the new and move two or three out of the middle and into being superstars."

Perhaps it's too early to say, but amidst the dozens of album releases in recent months, a clear strategy or sense of direction has yet to emerge from the crowded Capitol roster. Some insiders also feel that in working with various Capitol artists Bowen's pipeline approach to producing has faltered and production quality has ebbed. Bowen seems to be betting the label's future on such dubious trump cards as the Pirates of the Mississippi, a competent bar band which, thus far, has given no indication of possessing star quality. Bowen also recently made front-page news in Nashville by signing a Capitol development deal with Traci Peel, a modestly talented nightclub singer who's gained flash-in-the-pan notoriety because of her nuptials with Nashville's soon-to-be ex-mayor, Bill Boner.

Granted, the multi-platinum success of Garth Brooks—who reportedly was accounting for 40 percent of Capitol Nashville's record sales in the fall of 1990—can pay the freight on any number of potential misjudgments. Yet given Bowen's questionable recent A&R moves, it's interesting to consider where he would be without Brooks. And he easily could have been, if he had relied on his own judgment, for when Bowen was last at MCA, Garth Brooks had tried to land a deal with that label and was rejected. It was Lynn Shults, then vice-president of A&R for Capitol, and former Capitol chief Jim Foglesong, who had the perspicacity to sign the young singer-songwriter from Oklahoma. Although Bowen has been quick to use Garth Brooks as a shining example of Capitol's new direction, Brooks was well on his way to a gold record before Bowen even arrived at the label. Ironically, insiders say, Bowen has made noises about taking over the reins as Garth's producer from Allen Reynolds, who produced both of the young star's million-selling albums. Under his present contract, however, Brooks has veto power over who will be his producer, and it's likely he'll stick with Reynolds.

Whatever the long-term results may be, Bowen has injected a new sense of life into Capitol. For the last decade and a half, the label's Nashville office has been a slumbering giant. In mid-June 1990, the label had no fewer than six singles in the country Top Twenty—a feat Capitol had not achieved for many a moon.

"Before Bowen came on board, it was sleepy over there. It was dead; nothing was happening," observes an industry insider who works nearby. "You'd go over there, and the phones weren't ringing, nobody would be in their offices, no music was ever playing, the parking lot was empty. It was dead. Now, it's crazy: the parking lot's jammed full, there's music playing in every office, people are working twelve-hour shifts. On the first day, the telephone rang so much that the receptionist quit!"

And so Jimmy Bowen rolls on into the new decade. To his supporters, he is the face of country music in the 1990s. To his detractors, he's just a user, a manipulator, a carpetbagger who came to Nashville, made lots of enemies and milked the industry for every dollar that he could, who will eventually leave, never to return.

But for now, as Bowen hunkers back down at the studio console to put the final touches on a new George Strait album, his adrenalin is pumping; his eyes are riveted on the task at hand and on the greater challenge of turning a lackluster record label into a Big Four contender. Forging ahead, full-steam, he hardly seems to have time to bother looking back.

"When you're being productive, it's very fulfilling, and you're enjoying whatever the hell it is," he proclaims in typical elliptical fashion. "I mean, I don't have to work these many hours a day, yet I do it. So I must be enjoying it. I don't wanta be idle. That's very boring.

"This past summer, in Hawaii, my wife and I had great soul-searching talks," he continues, lapsing into a somewhat uncharacteristic personal and philosophical mood. "It's so peaceful and beautiful over there, and we were were up on this mountain one day, looking out across the sea, the islands, the boats going by. And it occurred to me what a marvelous thing this is: to have music, to play a part in creating something that yesterday wasn't there at all, and today is there.

"I think the nineties are going to be the most exciting era of country music. So I thought I might as well stick around and enjoy it," he says, smiling. "I thought I might as well ride the wave as long as I can, because it does knock you off at some point.

"There's gonna come a time when I don't fit in anymore, and I won't be able to do this anymore, and somebody else will come along," he concedes. "But as long as I can, I'm addicted to it."

JIMMY BOWEN (FOREGROUND), WEARING HIS USUAL SAILOR'S HAT AND WORKING THE CONSOLE AT A 1980s RECORDING SESSION.

TANYA TUCKER

TANYA TUCKER
Almost Grown
DANIEL COOPER

▌She has been a recording artist for nearly twenty-five years; she has been named the Country Music Association's Female Vocalist of the Year (1991); and she continues to be one of country music's most bankable stars. Yet it still seems that Tanya Tucker cannot get the respect she deserves. Too often her considerable contributions to country music are overlooked merely because her private life has been played out, over and over again, in the tabloids. Thus, even though much ink has been spilled concerning Tanya Tucker's exploits, few writers have managed to distill the essence of what makes her such a fascinating artist. In this 1994 profile, Daniel Cooper zeroes in on the relationship between Tucker's mystique and her talent. As I recall, Cooper first proposed this article over beers at Brown's Diner, a favorite musicians' watering hole in Nashville. No doubt, Tucker would see the humor in that.—Ed.

▌The Opryland guy sat down next to me on the couch backstage at the Chevrolet/GEO Theater. Speaking sotto voce, he warned me that Tanya had strained her back and wasn't feeling too well. He was trying to be helpful, the Opryland guy, but he said there was only so much he could do, considering no one had told him I'd be there.

When I first arrived, with neither Tanya nor her people anywhere in sight, he had walked me through the theater complex and showed me where I could find things, like the telephone, in case I needed to call out. "This is Miss Tucker's dressing room," he had said, pointing at an empty room. "And this is where [her road manager] usually sets up an office." Another bare space.

Meanwhile I was invited to help myself to the food laid out near the stage door. No one else was around except for a friendly woman in charge of the spread and a couple of tech guys shooting the bull. "Hey, who won the World Cup?" one asked nobody in particular. "Brazil," I said, but it didn't really lead to a conversation.

Later I went outside and walked around the parking lot. Then I came back in. Eventually there was a small commotion beyond the stage door. A roadie poked his head in and said, "She's here." The Opryland guy and someone from Tanya's camp disappeared to put in a reminder on my behalf. When the Opryland guy returned, he warned me about Tanya and her bad back.

After a few more minutes of waiting, Miss Tucker's personal assistant appeared and introduced herself. She said to follow her. We passed through the stage door and she said, "Wait here." Tanya's bus was pulled up close to the right of the stage.

Looking out over the empty seats—Tanya's concert was still an hour away—the Opryland guy and I talked about "Nashville On Stage," the summer concert series bringing superstar performances to Opryland on a nightly basis for the first time in the theme park's history. Tucker's appearance tonight was to be the last of a week-long run. The Opryland guy assured me that all of her friends and family would likely show up, knowing she was about to pull out of town. Backstage, he said, could be pretty manic by the end of the night.

One of the musicians in Tanya's band then appeared at my elbow and said to come with him. I trailed him to the bus, stepped up through the door, and again was met by Tanya's personal assistant. It was her turn to warn me about Miss Tucker's back.

"She almost didn't do her show last night," the woman said. "That's how bad it is. So if you could just ask your questions, get what you need . . . you know. . . ."

She gave me a piercing look and I got the message. Forget the in-depth, forty-five-minute interview it had taken more than a year to schedule; I was to make it quick.

The assistant took me inside the main body of the bus. Tanya was seated at a side table, halfway back. Nobody else was around—no band members; no partying friends; no children; no daddy—just Tanya and the deathly quiet.

The assistant asked if we'd like anything to drink. Tanya—or "T," as she's otherwise known—said, "Lemme have one of those DP's." Her assistant poured her a Dr. Pepper, then tactfully disappeared.

I sat down at the table, across from Tanya, and made some quick, fatuous introductory speech about how I knew what a forward-looking person she is, but that I wanted to ask her a few questions about her early years and I hoped that would be all right. Tanya, knowing bullshit when she hears it, looked blankly out the window and said in the flattest voice imaginable, "Okay."

We then proceeded to talk about "Delta Dawn," Billy Sherrill, Jerry

Crutchfield, the cover of *Rolling Stone,* and about two decades' worth of image makeovers so complete and constant they have often rendered Tanya Tucker unrecognizable from one album cover to the next. As to the latter changes, she did not much agree they occurred. "I don't really remember too many distinctive ones," she said. "It just really kind of evolved."

She was probably right. For what I remember best from our brief encounter had nothing to do with anything she said. What sunk in deepest was simply the picture of Tanya herself. Dressed down in a white pants suit, with her stage makeup unapplied and her sandy blonde hair hanging straight to her neck, she was, without question, the spitting image of the angelic thirteen year old strolling through a field on the back cover of her first album. A grown up and profoundly fatigued version of that child, but otherwise identical. "The last two days I've been really, really, really feeling bad," she confided sadly, with disarming candor. "Pulled this back muscle and I'm just not wanting to go onstage."

And yet, seeing Tanya tired and alone on her bus, surrounded by none of the goodtime hysteria that legend would have you believe is her element, was not at all like seeing a faded rose from days gone by. It was more like admiring a remarkable rose that's refused to fade a single shade, no matter the drain of twenty-two years in the relentless, withering sun.

▌I don't know when I first knew I wanted to meet Tanya Tucker, but I think it may go back to January 7, 1988, the night the Country Music Association celebrated its thirtieth anniversary with a star-studded TV taping at the Opry House. The party was announced a week in advance, with tickets offered to the general public at ten bucks a pop. For that modest sum, fans would have the opportunity to clap on cue for thirty-plus big name country acts—everyone from Eddy Arnold to Willie Nelson to Reba McEntire. The evening's top draw (this was, after all, 1988) was the reigning CMA Male Vocalist of the Year, Randy Travis. There were also a few choice surprises, not the least of which was Buck Owens joining Dwight Yoakam onstage for a then-unfamiliar honky-tonk number called "Streets of Bakersfield."

But of the evening's highlights, Tanya Tucker provided the funniest. A seasoned TV pro, comfortable taking video direction, she was given the task of choreographing a stage entry more complicated than it looked. She had to time her entrance to coincide precisely with the departure of the Gatlin Brothers before her. Through the first couple of takes, she and the Gatlins were perhaps a half-step away from perfection. But on the next try, Tanya left her position way too soon, or else the brothers retreated too quickly. In any case, Tanya plowed straight into the tall, thin Gatlin (would that be Steve or Rudy?) knocking him flat on the Opry stage. The audience—by now more bored than it wanted to admit—howled appreciatively from the balcony to the orchestra pit. The unfortunate Gatlin, revealing a heretofore unknown reservoir of improvisational wit, scrambled to his feet, pointed at a hole torn in the knee of his pants, and cried, "Look! I'm Dwight Yoakam!"

Tanya ran off stage, laughing and blushing in equal measure. It was then I think I realized I'd like to meet her someday. Not only because she has always impressed me as one of the few singers in Nashville capable of greatness exceeding the bounds of country stardom, but because her potential for greatness has always been colored by an air of being out of control somehow, of being constitutionally resistant to the grooming methods by which Nashville likes to prepare its product for parade. Whatever the real woman might be like, the public Tanya Tucker has always been this vivid personality forever plowing into people—and doing so in such a fashion that they get up laughing and joking.

Her various transgressions against Sunday school morality are, of course, common knowledge. A well-known all-around party girl, she did a stint in rehab in 1988, and, as even the most indifferent country listener is likely aware, she is the unwed mother of two children. The makeup of the Tucker family unit caused no small number of eyebrows to rise when she was tapped to perform at the 1992 Republican convention. Viewing Tanya as some sort of hillbilly Murphy Brown, the press went wild conjuring a possible confrontation between her and Dan Quayle. "I was just there to sing for the President," Tanya says now, dismissing the issue. "And they made a real big deal out of all that, like I was chasing him around somewhere. And it wasn't like that. He's got his version of what a perfect world is, and I have my version."

Certainly her after-hours escapades have done little to harm Tanya's reputation among country fans. On the contrary, to many she represents what a real girl's night out is often like—or what some of the more timid wish it were like, or what they enjoy vicariously seeing it be like. Rumor and gossip, most of it pretty benign, continues to swirl around her in Music City. Her company and whereabouts on any given night are nearly always reported by someone to some other interested fan. What raises the ceaseless gossip about her above the level of mere tabloid titillation is the way Tanya's music plays off her persona, and vice versa. To put it bluntly, the more directly she sings about sex, the better that famous husky voice sounds. From "Delta Dawn" in 1972, through "Soon" in 1994, much of her most memorable music has been about people emotionally unhinged by the strength of their carnal passions. And even when Tucker portrays her characters as in command of their thwarted desires, as in the scintillating "Down to My Last Teardrop," their control seems like that of a pressure cooker ready to pop. Other country singers have had entire successful careers without matching the sizzling effect Tanya gets with one word—*Honey*—in the latter song.

But to this day, what always throws people is Tanya Tucker's age. She is only thirty-six years old, and yet she's been a star long enough to have shared the charts with George Morgan, Lorrie's late father. The day Tanya cut "Delta Dawn," Loretta Lynn's "One's on the Way" was just on its way down the charts. Dolly Parton was still singing duets with Porter Wagoner and her "Coat of Many Colors" was only six months old. Yet look at the numbers and you'll find that Tanya Tucker is younger than Suzy Bogguss, Mary Chapin Carpenter, Vince Gill, Sammy Kershaw, Patty Loveless, and Pam Tillis, to name but a few of the more surprising. George Strait and Reba McEntire? Not even close.

Really, the only current hitmaker with experience at all similar to Tanya's is Marty Stuart, who took to the road with Lester Flatt at the tender age of thirteen. "Marty and I talk about it a lot," Tanya says. "We're the same age, we've been in the business the same amount of years, and we talk about it a lot: that we're still standing is amazing."

After so much time, it should be no surprise that in the pantheon of Nashville mythology, Tanya is viewed as something like the wild offspring of Bacchus and Juno. Road musicians trade Tucker band war stories (usually involving the labyrinthian politics of working for both Tanya and her manager-father) as evidence of some sort of tribal initiation. But the stories are always told through appreciative grins, rarely with any trace of bitterness. What the pickers and fans understand is that Nashville, and the wide world of country music, would be a whole lot duller without Tanya Tucker around.

She first came around—at least so far as anybody noticed—in March 1972. A thirteen-year-old waif-like thing, her precociousness slew everyone who met her—including her producer, the usually unflappable Billy Sherrill, who had brought her into his office to listen to some potential songs to cut. Among the tunes Sherrill and publisher Al Gallico pitched to young Tanya was "The Happiest Girl in the Whole U.S.A." The writer, Donna Fargo, had not yet cut her own single but was about to. All well and good, except that Tanya listened to "The Happiest Girl in the Whole U.S.A." and calmly refused it as too immature for her taste. She had no intention of introducing herself to the world while crowing about her "skippity-doo-da day." She has always respected Sherrill for not forcing her to do so. "Anybody else'd probably made me record it," Tanya says. "But he didn't."

The willful girl in the office that day was the third child born to Beau and Juanita Tucker. (An older sister, La Costa, had her own brief run at country stardom in the 1970s, while big brother Don worked for many years as Tanya's road manager.) Beau and Juanita had known each other since elementary school in Denver City, Texas, and had married at the age of fifteen. Beau worked a variety of blue-collar gigs as the couple made a go of life in and around the oil-rich Texas-New Mexico border district centered on Hobbs, New Mexico. Tanya was born October 10, 1958, thirty miles from Hobbs in Seminole, Texas. Beau, it seems, was something of a dreamer, for rather than content himself with life on the oil rigs, or down in the copper mines, he went out looking for his own oil and copper. His prospecting, apparently pretty fruitless, brought the family to Willcox, Arizona, shortly after Tanya was born. There she spent her early wonder years, dreaming her own sort of dreams and listening to hillbilly music past and present.

"Loretta Lynn, Tammy Wynette, George and Merle, Sonny James, David Houston—God, there was just so many that I listened to," she says. "I listened to a lot of Elvis, too. Connie Smith. I listened to Jimmie Rodgers. Hank Williams was a big favorite of mine."

Beau always claimed to have a good musical ear (though not much of a voice, his skills being limited to a pretty fair Ernest Tubb imitation), and he found out about his youngest daughter's talent when she was just six years old. In a rather famous cover story for *Rolling Stone,* he told Chet Flippo, "I never even thought about her singing till one day she walked up and said, 'Daddy, you wanta hear me sing a song?' I said, 'Sweetheart, you couldn't sing your way out of a paper sack.' She backed up about ten foot and showed me she could sing. She let me have it."

Three years later, with her daddy's blessing, Tanya had taken the leap from singing for him to singing for strangers. "I just remember performing at a lot of the bars at night," she says. "Like especially the VFW Hall in Willcox, Arizona. Different entertainers would come on, come to town, and I'd sing with them. Ernest Tubb and Little Jimmy Dickens being the first two that I remember."

The itinerant Tucker family moved to Phoenix in 1967. There, Tanya started entering talent contests, and while she never managed to take home a blue ribbon, she did wind up a regular on the "Lew King Show," a children's program broadcast locally. Her job was to look cute and belt out "How Much Is That Doggie in the Window" and "Here Comes Peter Cottontail." Tanya, who preferred to cover the likes of Loretta Lynn's "Your Squaw Is on the Warpath" and Connie Smith's "Nobody But a Fool (Would Love You)," thought her role undignified. She quit the show after eighteen weeks.

Meanwhile, the audacious Beau had made home recordings of his daughter singing and had taken her and the tapes to Nashville. As he later told *Country Music*'s J. R. Young, he played the tapes for "a prominent Nashville record store owner" and asked for his opinion. "The owner listened a few minutes and then looked over at his secretary and said, 'If you just got $50,000 in the mail today, would you put one penny in this girl's singing career?'

"'Nope,' the secretary announced coolly.

"'Does that answer your question?'"

In August 1970, the Tuckers moved to St. George, Utah, where Beau had a $9-an-hour construction job waiting. While living in St. George, word reached Beau and Tanya that glitzy country beauty queen Judy Lynn—the former Miss Idaho who had recorded for United Artists—was to play the Arizona State Fair back in Phoenix. Father and daughter drove three hundred miles to see if Tanya could sing her way onto Lynn's program. Tanya's backstage audition was a success and she got to sing two songs on the state fair stage. And when word reached Tanya that a Hollywood team was on location near St. George shooting the Robert Redford movie *Jeremiah Johnson*, she talked her mother into letting her answer the casting call. As it turned out, the producer was less interested in hiring Tanya than he was in using her horse. Tanya turned him down. "I'm real particular about who rides my horses," she reportedly said. The producer found her a spot. Tanya shows up in a startling close-up as part of a scared settler's family hiding from Injuns in a corn crib.

A year after the move to St. George, Beau quit his good construction job and the Tuckers moved yet again—this time to Henderson, Nevada, a small town south of Las Vegas. Beau made the risky decision explicitly to further his daughter's career—to give Tanya proximity to the starmaking machinery burning neon on the Strip. The family settled into a bonafide double-wide trailer home while Tanya proceeded to make her mark on the local nightlife. It wasn't long before the boys at the Henderson Vets hall were calling her the "Little Cheating Heart Girl" in honor of her fondness for singing Hank's famous tune.

Figuring the next step in his daughter's career was to get her voice on tape in a real studio, Beau raised eleven hundred dollars to pay for cutting some demos. Legend has it he made the money with a forty-eight hour run at a Las Vegas casino. "We had six demo tapes," Tanya says. "We made 'em in Las Vegas. Had just stock musicians, and went in and did some little songs. 'For the Good Times' was one. 'Proud Mary,' and, um, 'Put Your Hand in the Hand.' He just sent 'em to everybody."

One of the people for whom Beau graciously provided a tape was none other than Dolores Fuller, famed companion of cross-dressing B-movie legend Ed Wood (subject of the Tim Burton film) and co-star of his *Glen or Glenda* and *Jailbait*. Fuller, who was promoting musical shows at the Flamingo Hotel at the time she met Beau, had made a name for herself in the music industry after leaving Wood to her angora. While studying stage acting in New York, she had started writing songs and eventually had them cut by the likes of Nat King Cole and Peggy Lee. She had also managed Johnny Rivers and brought him to Nashville for his first recording session, for which she hired Ricky Nelson's band to back him. But Fuller's real bread and butter—a gig she had landed almost by accident—was writing songs for Elvis movies. (Among her credits are "Rock-a-Hula Baby," "Do the Clam," and "Spinout.") Hence, one night the Tuckers were at home in their trailer, watching an Elvis flick on TV, when they noticed Fuller's name in the credits. Beau knew she was based in Las Vegas. Figuring that anyone who could get the King to sing her songs must have some serious juice, he looked her up in the phone book and called to see if he could arrange a meeting.

"He heard I was as good as Colonel Tom Parker, which is a damn lie," Fuller says, "but I mean it was the bull that he gave me." She listened to Tanya, however, and told Beau his daughter belonged in Nashville. "He says, 'Well, we've already been there and we've tried all the record companies there.' So he didn't think I had any doors I could open that he couldn't."

What Beau didn't know was that Fuller was friends with Billy Sherrill and had done some writing with him. "I sent the tapes on to Billy Sherrill with letters," she says, "and I wrote so many letters to Billy to keep him excited. Then he promised me—because we were good friends—he promised me that the next time he came in to Las Vegas . . . that he would meet with her."

When that next time arrived, Sherrill checked into the Riviera Hotel "with Charlene, his beautiful wife, and with Al Gallico." Having set up an appointment in advance, Fuller, to locate Sherrill, paged him on the casino floor. "And Charlene came to the phone," Fuller says, "and she said, 'Billy can't come to the phone now, he's on a million dollar roll.' I said, 'Well Charlene, I've got a million dollar baby here waiting for him, and she's only thirteen, so you don't need to worry.'" Fuller headed straight to the hotel. Sherrill and Gallico saw her coming from across the casino floor. "They both waved to me, 'Oh Dolores, wait, stick around, we're on a big roll.' So sure enough they had chips stacked up real high. And I stood there and waited and watched those chips go down, down, down."

At Fuller's suggestion, Sherrill quit while he was ahead. He and Gallico then went over to Fuller's house and she played them Tanya's demos. Sherrill said to meet him that night back at the Riviera. "We sat in a booth at the little coffee shop with Bobby Vinton and Billy, and he met with Tanya and her dad . . . and when he got through, he promised me he would draw up some recording contracts . . . and he said, 'I'll tell you when I can work her into the session.' So, oh, about three weeks later I guess is all it was, we were on our way to Nashville with a new wardrobe for Tanya—which I bought her—and airplane tickets for her and her dad."

(In Tanya's own version, which otherwise lines up pretty well with Fuller's, the session didn't happen so soon after she met Sherrill in Vegas. "We waited awhile, till we went to Nashville," Tanya says. "That was in like October, November, and we didn't get to Nashville till March.")

Precocious though she was, Tanya could not have known too much about Nashville industry politics circa March 1972. She could not have known, for instance, that Sherrill was the hottest producer on Music Row—that his success with the likes of Tammy Wynette (whose "Stand By Your Man" he had co-written), David Houston (ditto Houston's "Almost Persuaded"), and a commercially resuscitated Johnny Paycheck was about to earn him a Columbia Records vice-presidency courtesy of label honcho Clive Davis. Nor could she—or Sherrill, for that matter—know that in a year's time Sherrill's sponsorship would have pushed Charlie Rich to #1 on both the pop and country charts and that his new prize signee, Wynette's husband George Jones, would prove to be the most famous ongoing project of his brilliant career. As she headed to Nashville for her first non-demo recording session, Tanya did not know that in Music City, U.S.A., Billy Sherrill was The Man. But she was soon to find out.

"Everybody kept telling me," she says. "I knew before it was all over for sure, because that's the first thing everyone would say to me. And I was just really glad to be there—anywhere. But of course, as I worked with him more and more, I realized how very special he was, how wonderful it was that I got him as my first producer. 'Cause I have a feeling that if I had gotten anyone else, they'd have tried to control me too much, you know?"

Sherrill, the Tuckers, and Fuller spent a week—perhaps two—in Nashville preparing for the session. (During their stay, Fuller managed to get Tanya a three A.M. slot on an Earl Owen telethon, the results of which were two encores for Tanya's one scheduled song.) Besides the Fargo tune, Sherrill had suggested four or five other songs which he put on a tape for the Tucker camp to listen to. One of them was "Delta Dawn," a Southern Gothic tale of a forty-one-year-old madwoman whose father "still calls her baby." It was co-written by Alex Harvey and Larry Collins, the ex-Collins Kid, and apparently Sherrill had taken a shine to it after hearing some other little-known vocalist's version. (A story that Sherrill picked up on "Delta Dawn" after hearing Bette Midler sing it on the "Tonight Show" is, according to Fuller, pure fiction.) Harvey, a native of Brownsville, Tennessee, had already shown a knack for writing songs with hit potential on both the pop and country charts. His "Ruben James" had assailed both formats in Kenny Rogers's 1969 version, and separate takes on his cutesy "Rings"—country by the Glaser Brothers, pop by Cymarron—had seen action on the two charts respectively in 1971.

After spending a night with the song—playing it in her hotel room, running it by her daddy—Tanya decided that "Delta Dawn" was it, the single she wanted to cut. Following one night of rehearsal, Sherrill brought her into Columbia's famous 16th Avenue studio for a ten a.m. session on March 17, 1972. Tanya, as she later told a reporter, walked into the studio and looked around—at the Coke stains; the tipped over music stands; the general wreckage of a Music Row landmark gone to seed—and thought to herself, "This is my piece of heaven?"

Yes it was. For Billy Sherrill meant business. The pickers he had hired were all A-team Nashville players: Pete Drake, Billy Sanford, Ray Edenton, Pete Wade, Hargus "Pig" Robbins, Jerry Carrigan, Tommy Allsup, Charlie McCoy, and Henry Strzelecki. "I remember the session well," says McCoy, who doubled on harmonica and vibes, "because, I mean, she was thirteen. And when somebody calls you and says, 'Oh, we're gonna record a thirteen year old,' usually you'd think, 'Oh, what's this.' But then, you know that if it's Billy Sherrill doing it, then there must be something to it. So your curiosity gets piqued because you know Billy Sherrill's not gonna fool with anything that isn't good."

The two songs Tanya sang were "Delta Dawn" (curiously mistitled "Dream Dawn" on the session sheets) and "Take Care of You for Me," a song Fuller had co-written. Apparently, the session almost didn't get off the ground, for according to Fuller, Beau's overprotectiveness towards Tanya cramped Sherrill's producing style bigtime.

"We were very excited about the session," Fuller says, "but Beau would stand there and hold her hand while she was recording. And Billy had to take me aside and say, 'You know, I have to try to communicate with Tanya. And I can't do it with him holding her hand like that.'" Sherrill was so uptight about the situation, Fuller says, that he asked her to take Beau outside. "Well, you know that a manager never has to do those things. And that was awfully hard on me," she says. "I wanted to be in that record session more than anything in the world."

Despite the awkwardness, Sherrill remained patient enough to draw from Tanya one of the most melodramatically exciting country performances of the era—and this from a thirteen-year-old child. "When she sang," says McCoy, "she was right on the money there. No problem with that." From the production standpoint, Sherrill's deliberately heavy touch on "Delta Dawn" accentuated the cutting rawness of Tanya's quavering vocal by blanketing it with other voices. The record's effect was like watching a shard from a broken mirror slicing through layers of silk. Afterwards, there was nothing for the Tuckers to do but go home to their double-wide trailer in Henderson, Nevada, and wait for heaven to break loose.

Two months later, on May 13, 1972, "Delta Dawn" entered *Billboard*'s country singles chart at #64 with a bullet. From there it rose slowly and steadily through the sweltering summer months, eventually peaking at #6 in August. (It didn't take long for that #6 position to inflate to #1 in her followers' recollections—an assessment true only if one were familiar with the *Record World* charts.) It did not take till August, though, for the industry sharks to close in on Tanya. By early June, she was already said to be in line for a couple of Walt Disney and Hal Wallis movie roles. (The offers from Wallis, who produced the Elvis flicks, were probably Fuller's doing.) That same month, she was snatched up by Nashville's powerful Buddy Lee Attractions booking agency, and she made her Grand Ole Opry debut in July. Much as the Opry date meant to her, it was perhaps less memorable than a show three months earlier—Tanya Tucker's first paying gig—in which she joined Judy Lynn and the ghost of Mark Twain at the annual "Jumping Frog Jubilee" in Calaveras County, California.

"It was a big deal," Tanya says. "Thirty thousand bikers come in; it's really wild. Got paid two hundred bucks for that gig."

▌Cut to the year-long chase. Prior to the summer of 1993, the management team for a by-then grown-up Tanya Tucker worked out a two-year corporate sponsorship deal with Black Velvet Canadian Whisky. Billboards reading "Smooth Duet: Tanya Tucker and Black Velvet" sprang up along several strategic Nashville thoroughfares while Tanya herself hit the road for 250 tour dates as the Black Velvet Lady. She wasn't in bad star company. Previous Black Velvet Ladies included Christie Brinkley, Cybill Shepard, and Cheryl Tiegs.

In August that year, Tanya rode her sweet deal back into Nashville. The finals of the Black Velvet Smooth Steppin' Showdown, a national two-step dance competition, were to be held before a Tanya Tucker concert—again at Opryland's Chevrolet/GEO Theater. In an effort to hype the event, the Black Velvet people announced that Tanya would hold a press conference prior to the Opryland shindig. As instructed, myself and a few other writers and photographers showed up an hour early. We were given our passes and told to hang loose till the press conference. Some time later, after making the rounds of "Chubby's Drive-In," the "Shake, Rattle 'n' Win," "Bob B. Sox's T-Shirt Shop," and various other Opryland outposts, I found my way to the front of the GEO stage, where a couple other reporters were standing around looking glum. Tanya was running late, they said. The conference had been canceled.

About that time, Demetria Kalodimos, the much-loved anchor of Nashville's Channel 4 news, breezed into the open-air theater with a full camera crew in tow. Surprise! Tanya wasn't running so late after all; the press conference was back on.

All of us were led backstage and pointed toward the waiting area. The bola-tied and yoke-shirted contestants were lined up against the wall. A couple of cameras were stationed in the center of the room, a director's chair facing them. Off to the side, a closed door read "Production Office." A photocopy of Clint Eastwood's face had been tacked to the door with the caption: "Go Ahead . . . Make One More Change."

Suddenly, with zero fanfare, Tanya emerged from her dressing room, crossed the floor, and sat in the director's chair. She was dressed in two-tone cowboy boots—black and aqua-blue—and a fringed black dress. She posed for the cameras while a nervous young production man was given the dicey task of affixing her microphone to the front of her lowcut threads. He fumbled with the setup while Tanya cracked a mildly amused smile. Reading from cue cards, she then launched straight into a video plug for Black Velvet—an in-house commercial that seemed destined for the Emerald Isle. "I'd like to say a big country hello to all of you there in Ireland. . . ," she enthused.

When the commercial ended, it was Kalodimos's turn. Famous for her casual, easy-going rapport with the Nashville glitterati, the anchorwoman asked Tanya a couple of questions about her brand new CMA nomination for single of the year, to which Tanya gave properly sound-bite-able responses. "It's been awhile since I've been up for that award," she said.

Demetria thanked her and Tanya returned to her dressing room. The camera crews packed their equipment. The lowly print journalists stood in dismayed silence while the smooth-steppin' dance couples fidgeted, preened, and filed into the spotlight outside.

Later that night, in the middle of Tanya's concert, one of the male dance contestants approached the stage and handed her a bouquet. She leaned over and accepted the flowers with a canned smile. Stepping back, Tanya said an automatic "thank you," then stopped, turned back around, gave the dancer a closer head-to-toe once-over, and in the sultry voice that has wrecked men for over twenty years, added, "—*cowboy*!"

▎I won't let her have a hair dresser because she can fix her own hair. I won't let her have a clothes designer because she can make her own clothes. And Tanya has taken all this pretty well. She's got a pretty level head on her shoulders. All her money goes into a trust fund, so she hasn't been affected by that. She still has to ask me for a quarter to go to the soda fountain.

That was Beau Tucker describing his management style in 1972. To say that the indefatigable ex-prospector has had a hand in shaping his daughter's career is like saying that Col. Tom Parker was known to give Elvis advice. From the moment she first stepped back and blew him away with her six-year-old pipes, Tanya's big daddy has been her most tireless and effective advocate. It's no pushy stage-father scenario, for the two have had coequal ambition from the start. Far from resenting her father's intrusions, Tanya has been content—nay, very proud—to let him conduct her affairs. There have, of course, been other managers, other advisers, but none that really lasted. By the end of Tanya's first year in the business, three different names—Dolores Fuller, Judy Lynn, and Lynn's husband, John Kelley—had all been mentioned in the trade press as acting the role of Tanya's manager.

Fuller, who had worked so hard to arrange Tanya's all-important career breakthrough, says she was abruptly given her walking papers while "Delta Dawn" was still on the rise. After the historic first session, she had made the deejay rounds with Tanya, had put her up in her Beverly Hills home for a week, and had even, Fuller says, paid for Liz Taylor's dentist to fill a gap in Tanya's front teeth. Looking back, she thinks it was simply too much outside input for Beau to accept. "The first chance he got," Fuller says, "he had an attorney send me a letter saying, 'We don't need you anymore.'"

Sure enough, one week after Tanya's Opry debut, *Billboard* pointedly noted that Tanya Tucker was "now under management contract to John Kelley."

The episode so upset Fuller it gave her ulcers. But it never affected the way she felt about Tanya herself. "No, no, I loved her," she says. "I really just adored her." The last time Fuller saw Tanya was several years ago, when she chanced to be eating downstairs at a Nashville restaurant while Tanya was throwing a birthday party upstairs. "She put her arm around me and took me all around and introduced me to everybody and said, 'This is the woman that got me started, that gave me my break.' And she was just sweet as could be."

Given the near-Svengalian dimensions of Beau's role in Tanya's life, the only people who have had more fun at her expense than the tabloid paparazzi and Music Row gossips have been amateur pop psychologists. One quick look at Tanya's trail of broken romances with older men, and they feel like they've got her and her music pegged. Well, there has to be some way of nailing the essence of that unsettling woman-child paradox. For right from the get-go, the phenomenon that was Tanya Tucker was that of a child not only singing, but *delivering* lines the meaning of which no one could fathom a thirteen-year-old girl understanding. When Tanya sang about love, she sang about it in its adult form—about kissing her man goodbye in the morning to bring him home at night. That was from "Love's the Answer," her second single and second Top Ten hit. Cut in July of 1972, while "Delta Dawn" was still red hot, it emerged from Tanya's first album session, a typical three-day rush job. Perfectionist that he was, Sherrill had never cared for Nashville's insta-LP syndrome but had learned to deal with it. On average, the albums he supervised under those circumstances would produce two or three gems and a bunch of quickie filler. With Tanya he fared even better. The July sessions (collected on the *Delta Dawn* album) included "Loving You Could Never Be Better," a genuinely moving Tanya performance of a song about a sexual tryst (and on which, by God, she held her own against the George Jones version just then climbing the charts); "New York City Song," in which Tanya convinces us that she's a poor Southern girl lost and alone in the city; and the version of "The Happiest Girl in the Whole U.S.A." that Sherrill had been looking for all along. Damn if it wasn't worth the wait.

The album session also produced "The Jamestown Ferry," Tanya's lamentation for the loss of her high-toned lover. "He had a soothing Southern drawl/Made me feel like a lady through it all." Released as the B-side of "Love's the Answer," it strengthened her innocent-girl-telling-grown-up-stories image and turned her second single into a double-sided hit. (According to Fuller, the first single also enjoyed two-sided action until Sherrill, not wanting to have his new act's airtime split in two, called the deejays and asked them to stick with "Delta Dawn.")

"Love's the Answer" and "The Jamestown Ferry" were positively bland, however, compared to Tanya's third release, "What's Your Mama's Name." Written by Dallas Frazier and Peanut Montgomery (both of whom wrote the kind of splintered-soul material that brought out the best in George Jones) and cut the first week of January 1973, it was the first of Tanya's records to self-consciously exploit the unnerving fact of her age. The structure of the performance was that of a little girl singing about an old man searching for a little girl. Frazier and Montgomery gave the lyrics the Gothic tragedy treatment through allusions to pedophilia, out-of-wedlock children, a pauper's grave, and—oh, the perdition of it all!—"*a place called New Orleans.*" Tanya's raspy, straining voice heightened the Southern pulp fiction mood of the song—a mood that Sherrill likewise worked to the hilt, bringing up Pete Drake's swirling steel guitar to where it seemed to be following the doomed seeker straight to his inner hell. It's an awesome record and was, deservedly, Tanya Tucker's first #1 hit.

"What's Your Mama's Name" broke out in March 1973, a time when Southern Gothic was much on America's mind. Vicki Lawrence's "The Night the Lights Went Out in Georgia" was simultaneously ascending the pop charts, while the movie version of James Dickey's *Deliverance* was, at that very moment, successfully reinforcing every paranoid vision of the South the nation at large had ever entertained. Tucker could have played innocent narrator to either of those stories, as was driven home with a vengeance when later that summer Helen Reddy's deltaless cover of "Delta Dawn" shot to the top of the Hot 100. Tanya always felt her version could have done the same had she been given the promo push an established artist like Reddy rated. She may have been right, for even without such help the sheer force of Tucker's "Delta Dawn" had broken it through to the lower reaches of the pop charts.

Taking a dangerously formulaic approach, Sherrill followed "What's Your Mama's Name" with "Blood Red and Goin' Down," a child-narrated story-song probably deemed commercial not only for the wealth of off-color inferences one could read into the title, but, more importantly, because the story takes place in Georgia. The formula worked; it gave Tanya her second #1 in a row. Again, the latter single was pulled from a quickie album session—this one held March 21–22, 1973—and again the album itself transcended its knee-jerk impetus. Even better than her first LP, *What's Your Mama's Name* included stellar versions of "California Cotton Fields" (another killer tune from the team of Dallas Frazier and the criminally underappreciated Peanut Montgomery); Harlan Howard's "The Chokin' Kind"; and "Teddy Bear Song," a smash hit for Barbara Fairchild which everyone had the good sense not to release as a single for Tanya. Having the fourteen-year-old star purveyor of lust and murder ballads sing "I wish I was a teddy bear . . ." on prime-time radio might have knocked her career back to the "Lew King Show."

No, Tanya had quite something else in mind. Maintaining a pace worthy of George Jones, she and Sherrill returned to the studio in late August. There they cut six more songs over a two-day span. One was Kris Kristofferson's "Why Me, Lord," while another was "Would You Lay With Me (In a Field of Stone)," a tender love ballad written by, of all people, David Allan Coe. The latter was picked as Tanya's next single. It was the most adult material she had sung to date—too adult for a number of programmers. Some would have thought long and hard before airing Conway Twitty singing: "If my needs were strong would you lay with me?" No way were they going to take it from a fifteen-year-old girl.

Then again, for every isolated station that banned the song, ten others jumped all over it, making "Would You Lay With Me" Tanya's third consecutive #1 hit. The record sold a reported 300,000 copies and came six points shy of cracking the pop Top Forty. Beau started thinking about that expiring Columbia contract while the editors of America's #1 music magazine likewise laid some bets.

The cover photo of Tanya Tucker was taken by Doug Metzler, an ex-fashion photographer who now does "rock & roll and surrealism." "I tried to make her look very foxy and sexy," says Doug. "The photos were taken in a New York fashion photographer's studio, in glamorous gowns rented from Saks Fifth Avenue and Bonwit Teller, some of them sheer, some clinging satin. But she insisted on wearing her bra under them—a cheap wire bra, it looked ridiculous. Her father was there as chaperone the whole time, and she said something about sex ruining the country, but for one shot I asked her to look as if she were waking up after a wonderful night, and she did it just great, very languorous."

Rolling Stone
September 26, 1974

It's important to understand that to be on the cover of *Rolling Stone* was probably never more important than in the early 1970s. By that point Jann Wenner's upstart music rag had been around long enough to consolidate its reputation as the ultimate arbiter of rock & roll taste, without yet having made the questionable corporate maneuvers that have cut into its reputation ever since. While "What's Your Mama's Name" was climbing the country charts, the most infectious sing-along hit on pop radio was Dr. Hook and the Medicine Show's "The Cover of Rolling Stone," a song that affirmed through satirization the magazine's marketplace power. So when the editors slapped Tanya's visage on the front cover with the headline—"Hi, I'm Tanya Tucker, I'm Fifteen, You're Gonna Hear From Me"—one would have thought it a moment the singer would treasure. Not so.

"I didn't really take it that seriously," Tanya says. "You know, now looking back on it I see where it was a pretty historical moment. But I didn't think too much of it at the time."

For one thing Tanya and her family were deep in the throes of a tortured label change—a far more serious business than any kind of press coverage, as it was going to make the Tuckers very rich, but at the expense of Tanya's golden relationship with Billy Sherrill.

"My contract was up, and my dad wanted a certain amount of money, and Columbia turned it down," Tanya says. "So MCA, I guess, came through. It was a hard thing for me to go through, but I got through it. It was hard to leave Billy. It wasn't hard to leave the label so much as it was hard to leave him."

But she did. On October 10, 1974, two weeks after the *Rolling Stone* article appeared, Tanya celebrated her sixteenth birthday at a party thrown by MCA Records in honor of her having signed with them that very day. The deal, cut by Beau, was rumored to be for a cool seven figures. Tanya confirmed that figure many years later when she corrected an interviewer who wondered if it was true she was a millionaire before her sixteenth birthday. "The day I turned sixteen I was a millionaire," Tanya said.

Then MCA did a curious thing—they sent Tanya to Los Angeles for her first session on the label, as if their million dollar investment could not be entrusted to the perceived yahoos manning the boards on Music Row. West Coast producer Snuff Garrett—noted at the time for his work with Sonny & Cher, Jim Nabors, and Telly Sevalas—was hired to supervise the album-length session.

"It was really a high-pressure album because I had to leave Columbia," Tanya says. "And I didn't really have a lot of fun making that album. 'Cause it was right out of Nashville, thrown right into L.A. where all the musicians read the music. Sometimes [Garrett] didn't want me showing up for the band tracks. I just didn't understand that. 'Cause we do it so— just so comfortable. Comfortable and natural in Nashville. It was just like having culture shock, you know?

"Of course, that album produced two #1 records," she adds. "So definitely my career was not over."

Hardly. The first of those two chart-toppers, "Lizzie and the Rainman," also became Tucker's first—and to date, only—Top Forty pop hit. And an odd one, at that. Cast in the by then near-obligatory story-song mode, its the somewhat indecipherable tale of a mystic promising some parched West Texas folks he can make it rain for a hundred dollars. The story doesn't really go anywhere, and the title of the song is nowhere sung within the lyrics.

Far more arresting was "San Antonio Stroll"—the second #1 off Tanya's MCA debut. Probably the most infectious tune she has ever sung on record, and still a concert favorite, it's another one of the productions designed to play off her youth. Tanya narrates from the perspective of the youngest daughter left home on Saturday night while the rest of the family heads to the square dance. It's precisely the sort of nostalgic family number that commercial country can promote till you want to puke— except that this one has no suffocating moral in mind, and it has Tanya

Tucker singing it. In the end, "San Antonio Stroll" is about nothing more than enjoying romance on a Saturday night, and bless you all for taking romance to mean whatever you want it to.

But despite the short-term success of her first MCA session, Tanya knew that for the long-run she would have to be more at ease with the recording set-up. For her next project, in 1975, she looked back to comfortable Music City. Brought in to produce the second album was Jerry Crutchfield, the head of MCA Music publishing in Nashville, who seemed to be the right man for the record. In fact he was much more than that. For as it turned out, other than Beau Tucker himself, no one else has played as longterm and pivotal a role in Tanya's career as producer Jerry Crutchfield.

A soft-spoken Music Row veteran, Crutchfield, though relatively young at the time, already had considerable songwriting, plugging, and session work experience before hooking up with Tanya. Besides directing MCA's Nashville publishing arm, he'd had his own material cut by Elvis Presley, Rick Nelson, and Tammy Wynette, among many others. (His brother, Jan Crutchfield, is author of the stately "Statue of a Fool.") As Sherrill had been in 1972, Jerry Crutchfield in '75 was a powerful player still on the rise. He had really turned heads in town as the man behind the boards for Dave Loggins's lugubrious pop smash "Please Come to Boston," which was impressing the hell out of kids like Garth Brooks at the same time Tanya was posing for *Rolling Stone*. Ironically, Crutchfield had also discovered Barbara Fairchild and produced her "Teddy Bear Song," though it's safe to assume that that had nothing to do with his getting the call for Tanya's second MCA project. On the contrary, Crutchfield, whose contact with Tanya to that point had amounted to little more than a song-plugging session or two, felt it was time she grew out of the music that defined the star she had been at thirteen.

"When we first started recording, the very first album I did with her I really felt that we had to make a move from where she had been," he says. "She had this tremendous success, and tremendous impact with a particular type song: a 'Delta Dawn' and 'What's Your Mama's Name' and 'Blood Red and Goin' Down'—all these very hot, sultry kinds of songs. So when she left CBS and went to MCA, another producer did her first album. And I felt that what they did was really their version of what Tanya had done previous. I felt very strongly that we needed to tweak Tanya's musical focus, and we had to get her into a little bit of a younger musical arena, so to speak, and really try things that Tanya had wanted to try for a long time."

The resultant album, *Lovin' and Learnin'*, was indeed a switch in mood for Tanya. By "younger arena" Crutchfield didn't mean kiddie regression, he meant letting Tanya tap into her natural audience—the under-twenty-five fans in small town America who maybe didn't buy all that Gothic jive about lust and murder in Georgia. The direction of the album was much more mainstream contemporary, the sex angle much less overt. It produced a couple of decent-sized hits, but not one that became a Tucker classic. It did, however, mark Tanya's first attempt to present herself as a woman of her time—no more or less—and as such prefigured the direction her career has taken in this, her latter-day stardom. It also just so happened to have Tanya's rendition of "After the Thrill Is Gone," giving her bragging rights on being one of the first kids in town to cover an Eagles tune.

With Beau in command of her business and Crutchfield in command of her sessions, Tanya settled into what may have been the only moment in her life when her country career looked in any way typical. The Tuckers by then had moved out of the trailer in Henderson and bought their Tuckahoe Farm outside Nashville, providing for many a photo-op with the cutting horses and stray dogs and cats that Tanya loved to raise. With her and Crutchfield churning out the hits ("Here's Some Love" being the biggest) Tanya took her show on the state fair circuit road, playing such hardcore hillbilly gigs as the Carowinds Amusement Park in Charlotte, North Carolina; the Eastern States Explosion in West Springfield, Massachusetts; the Arizona National Livestock Show in Phoenix; and the grand opening of the Wal-Mart store on Highway 63 in Rolla, Missouri. In April 1976, she made a three-day run from Savannah, Georgia, to Miami and Tampa, Florida, "with Merle Haggard, known as 'the Hag'," as one report happily noted. "Tanya rode with Haggard in his bus from Miami to Tampa. They sang and wrote a few songs. The Hag is planning on writing some songs for Tanya to use and she is understandably excited about this prospect." (So far as we know, the Hag never did write those songs.)

Reviews from this period were generally kind, usually focusing less on Tanya's child-star status than on her emerging country-rock crossover sound—which to some ears sounded radical. She often opened her shows with "Burning Love," and it was in those days that, with straight faces, people started calling her "the female Elvis." Also of note to some observers was a clever medley Tanya had worked up of "Mr. Bojangles," "Desperado," and Guy Clark's "Desperadoes Waiting for a Train," the last of which she probably knew from Jerry Jeff Walker's classic version.

Still, though she was no longer freakishly young, Tanya was young enough to make her child-woman public image look ever more schizophrenic. She was quickly growing into the adult themes of which she had always sung, yet her publicists—probably with Beau looking over their shoulders—were having trouble keeping up. Photos of Tanya in the mid-seventies would show her one minute in hip-hugger leather onstage, the next with her arm around Mickey Mouse. In May 1975, she and LaCosta were trotted out in tutus and pigtails for the "Hoyt Axton Country Western Boogie Woogie Gospel Rock and Roll Show." As with any old-school country star, the best evidence of Tanya's public identity could be found in the pages of her fan club newsletters. In her case, they included Q & A sections reminiscent of teen heartthrob fanzines.

Q: What is your favorite flower?

A: I like them all, however, I do prefer flowers that keep their beauty longest.

Q: Is it true that Tanya is going steady with Anson Williams, of "Happy Days?"

A: No, we are just good friends!

On the other hand, one could also find in the newsletters such hard Tanya news as a nasty car wreck she was in when she was just seventeen.

"At approximately 1:00 a.m. on Wednesday, November 5, Tanya was driving home after a late night rehearsal in Nashville. She was within a mile of her farm where the sports car she was operating left the road on a curving section of Highway 49, struck a culvert, and overturned." Tanya crawled out of the wreckage and was found by two men who took her to the emergency room. She suffered "cuts and bruises and a possible concussion" but was released from the hospital later that morning. The 1973 Mercedes Benz she was driving was totaled. The accident's cause was unknown, though a state trooper mentioned some "loose gravel on the road which may have contributed to the accident."

By her eighteenth birthday, Tanya was facing identity questions usually reserved for veteran stars twice her age. People were already wondering about her image, about the changes she'd gone through from the narrator of "Delta Dawn" to "female Elvis" to a mature young woman who "looked more like she'd stepped out of the pages of *Vogue* than *Seventeen*," as *Country Music*'s Mary Ellen Moore put it.

Tanya herself seemed bewildered by it all, but at the same time tuned to the subtle frequency of the issue: the unasked questions about her artistic mortality. She told Moore about the time she finally met Elvis, about sitting with him and LaCosta backstage at the Hilton in Las Vegas. "It was perfect, man. Nobody else was in the room, no girls, nothing. We sat there and talked about jewelry. Somebody said, 'Hey, man, she does you in her act.' I said, 'Well, no, not anymore, I got kind of bored with it.' And he laughed, he *cracked up*. He was talking about his jewelry and how he had to put bandaids on his hands to keep girls from pulling off his rings. . . .

"If I was Elvis, I'd quit, I'd retire," Tanya added, "get out of it, let everybody remember the way he was. You have to get old. I'm growing old, everybody's growing old."

Tanya's comments appeared in July 1977. She was eighteen years "old." Elvis had a month to live.

▌A couple months after attending the Black Velvet gig at Opryland, I got a cold call from the editor of a Nashville music industry newsletter who wanted to know if I would write an article for them about Charlie Lico, the special projects wizard at Liberty Records who had masterminded the Garth Brooks Super Bowl halftime show of 1993. Despite the fact that some rich, powerful Nashville suits are on the board of the organization behind the newsletter, the piece, I was regretfully informed, would be for free. Strictly a "make some contacts" deal. I was just on the verge of declining—not because I cared so much about getting paid, but because I care about who's unwilling to pay—when the editor mentioned that Lico was also the man behind the Tanya Tucker workout video about to hit the streets. A week or so later, I was in Lico's office.

As it turned out, Lico was a good guy to talk to—a sharp, easy-mannered West Coast expatriate who had once managed jazz guitarist Larry Carlton, among others. He and I talked about his industry background; about the Garth extravaganza; about interactive media; and about Chris LeDoux. But mostly we talked about *Tanya Tucker Country Workout.*

"The exercise video was something that Tanya wanted to do for a long time," he said. "She always wanted to do it. And I had three offers across my desk for Tanya—not using her music, just her." Lico explained how he and Beau got together to consider the offers, then picked the company they felt had the most credibility—the Maier Group, who brought you *Buns of Steel.*

"Then it was in Tanya's lap. Yes, she wanted to do it. But no, she's not a Jane Fonda, and she never wants to be a Jane Fonda. She does this stuff on her bus, to stay in shape, to get her heart rate up. She does it to her music, because she likes her music.

"It was about helping to make Tanya a household name, even though she's very well known," he added. "It was helping to define her direction and focus and image—as a mother, as someone who cares about her health, as much as her past will give her not so much that credibility. So it's important for us to focus on who she is now, and who she wants to be."

Before I left, Lico gave me a copy of the video. At home that afternoon I stuck it in the VCR. The program opens with a front-view shot of Tanya riding a motorcycle without a helmet. The soundtrack pulsates with her singing, "It's a little too late to do the right thing now."

■ By 1978, the talk around Nashville was that Tanya had reached some sort of career ceiling, that to break through to some grander stardom, à la Dolly Parton, she would have to first break free of Beau. His steadfast belief in her natural talents, his refusal to let her be corrupted by professional training of any sort, had a definite unorthodox charm, but was viewed in that glitzy Mandrell era as the epitome of backwards thinking. Dolores Fuller had learned of Beau's attitude as early as "Delta Dawn," when she enrolled Tanya in a dance class to better prepare her for TV spots.

"She went to a couple of classes," Fuller says, "and then Beau just took her arm and dragged her right out of the class. I said, 'Beau! Why did you do that? She needs that training so badly.' And he said, 'Nobody's gonna teach her anything but me.'"

Six years later he had not budged from that position. Whatever the town thought of it, the point was that Tanya was not about to break away from her father—not because he wouldn't let her, but because she didn't want to. The man had made her a millionaire. Beau at least admitted that his daughter had been through a rebellious phase—as in past tense—but it was no more than one would expect from any young woman her age. Crutchfield had likewise endured his share of headaches thanks to teenage Tanya, but none that he felt wasn't worth the joy of capturing her voice on tape.

"She'd entered that mid-to-late teenage period where she had a little more freedom, and was enjoying herself more, was a little more mature," he says. "So consequently she was less disciplined and, you know, she'd show up late for rehearsals, or not at all, or she would always be late getting to the studio. And the thing that I noticed in view of all this— because . . . for my own sanity and comfort level I would have been much happier for her to be there on time—but the thing I was always aware of [was] once the recording process started, once the red light came on, I've never seen an artist, a singer, who was more in control of their artistry than Tanya. Because once she knows that she has been signaled to give her best and perform, she's absolutely incredible."

"God has really blessed me with someone wonderful," Tanya says of Crutchfield in return. "Because he's got such a wonderful temperament. He's not egotistical, he's just very easy to work with. I mean, there's probably times he'd like to have screamed at me, but he didn't. I think he saw some of the agony, maybe, or torment that I was going through as a kid . . . and kind of looked at the picture from the outside."

But Tanya and Beau had proven with Sherrill that if her career requirements dictated a change in producers, they would not let sentiment interfere. Hence in 1978, having decided it was time for a career overhaul, Tanya opted for a second look at the city of lost angels. She and Beau hired the services of Far Out Productions, a fancy L.A. promo firm that had dazzled them with bright lights talk and big city crossover promises. "They were exactly what I was looking for," she told Dolly Carlisle a year later.

A West Coast session was put together with Jerry Goldstein to take the helm. Goldstein was probably best known for producing every War hit that ever mattered—"Cisco Kid," "The World Is a Ghetto," the works—though he was also behind the McCoys' golden oldie "Hang On Sloopy" and would later take on the L.A. punks the Circle Jerks. Picking him to produce Tanya Tucker was either inspired creative casting or Hollywood sunstroke lunacy.

Judging from the final product, it sounds like he was flatout intimidated. Goldstein's Far Out-orchestrated mandate was clearly to let Tanya rock, but the album she cut with him, called *T.N.T.*, was about as explosive as a glow worm. Surrounded by lame seventies pop/rock production, she sounded like Pat Benatar on Thorazine. Just in case the record still showed signs of life, Goldstein brought in Seals & Crofts to sing backup.

Perhaps Far Out knew the record was DOA; perhaps they would have done this anyway. But whatever their thinking, they oversold the near-empty package with cheesecake cellophane wrapping. The now-famous front cover of *T.N.T.* showed Tanya in paint-on-by-numbers black leather pants with a mike-cord stretched between her thighs. The inside foldout was even sillier raunch—Tanya in a red spandex body suit, barebacked, high-heeled, holding a fistful of dynamite and licking her lips suggestively. She looked like a cheap, non-union stand-in for Olivia Newton-John in the finale of the movie *Grease*.

"I didn't necessarily have a real good time making that album," Tanya says now, rather dryly. "So, it really wasn't a real memorable one for me. But, sometimes you make an album and have a good time and not sell a one."

Indeed, *T.N.T.* was reportedly a gold record five weeks after its release. Ironically, the one Top Ten hit off it was the only throwback country cut, "Texas When I Die." Never mind the music, though, the media went nuts. They followed Tanya's tour as she played the Bottom Line and the Roxy instead of Wal-Marts and stock shows. *Playboy* called her "Nashville's little Levied Lolita." All of that was taken in stride until Tanya showed up in *Hustler*—in a paid ad. "This album will make your ears hard," the copy boasted. Beau got wind of the plug and fired everyone in sight. "I never did find out who placed that ad," he groused to Dolly Carlisle.

But by then Tanya was well-esconced in Los Angeles. With Far Out

out of the picture, the Scotti Brothers took over her management. Mike Chapman, who really did produce Pat Benatar—as well as Blondie and the Knack—signed on for Tanya's next album, *Tear Me Apart*, which was cut late summer 1979. Given Chapman's success with female leads, the combination of him and the Levied Lolita had definite possibilities. And to their credit, *Tear Me Apart* is not a bad effort by the power pop standards of *Get the Knack* or Blondie's *Parallel Lines*. In fact, Tanya's revisionist take on the faux-hippie chestnut "San Francisco (Be Sure to Wear Flowers in Your Hair)" would have had skinny-tied cool jerks going berserk had Debbie Harry sung it. But *selling* new wave Tanya was another matter. *Tear Me Apart* was cutout city all the way. Tanya Tucker turned twenty-one years old with no record anywhere on the charts.

▌ Winter passed and I lost track of Tanya for reasons entirely my own. But early last spring, out of the blue, her new publicist called and said she was ready to talk about scheduling an interview. This, of course, was news I'd been waiting a year to hear. The publicist and I kicked around potential time-frames—when Tanya would be in town, when my deadline would fall, so-on and so-forth—then settled on a mid-April window of opportunity. She said to sit tight and she would get back to me with a specific date.

Not too many days later, the publicist called to ask if it would be okay if we made that mid-April date more like early May. Tanya was in the studio; her schedule was pretty overwhelming; it would work better later on. No problem. Of course, early May became mid-May, and mid-May became month's end. I knew this was no one's fault and was happy to work things out—was happy, in fact, just to have the dialogue continue. Finally, it was agreed that four o'clock, May 30th—Memorial Day— would be the optimum time slot. An in-person interview could not be arranged, but I could have forty-five minutes with Tanya on the telephone. I said that that would be great.

I spent most of Memorial Day puttering around my apartment, thinking about the interview just enough to be clear about the questions I thought might be important. Two o'clock turned to three o'clock, three o'clock to three-thirty, then four o'clock rolled around. At 4:05 the telephone still hadn't rung. I looked at my wife and said, "She's going to stand me up."

As if on cue, the telephone rang that very instant. Suddenly I was talking to Tanya's assistant. Tanya was really tired, she said, she had just come in off the road and wanted to spend time with her family. Would it be okay to reschedule. I said it would be okay. I really had been wondering how the Tucker family typically spends Memorial Day.

❚ Here's the good news: Tanya Tucker did not appear anywhere in the credits or on the soundtrack for *Urban Cowboy*. The bad news is she did contribute "Pecos Promenade," her first Top Ten hit in almost two years, to *Smokey and the Bandit 2*. And a year before that, in 1979, she had taken a starring role with Don Johnson in a made-for-TV movie called *Amateur Night at the Dixie Bar and Grill*. The gossips said there was something between Tanya and Johnson. If so, it didn't last. Tanya was after a man with true grit.

Personally I've never met anyone who really cares what went on between Tanya Tucker and Glen Campbell. It's not a love story that repays contemplation. The only interesting question is what Tanya saw in a man twice her age who had taken a switch to Kim Darby on film. The Campbell/Tucker affair made for good tabloid copy but lousy music (their duet revival of Bobby Darin's "Dream Lover" is as unmemorable a record as either one ever made) and has since given Campbell one more shot at publicity by allowing him to trash an ex-lover now more famous than he. For in his recent autobiography, Campbell talks about Tanya as if she were Satan's minion armed with a coke spoon and sent on a personal mission to destroy him. He never acknowledges her side of the story. He doesn't mention, for instance, the lawsuit she later filed against him alleging physical abuse.

But more important than details of the affair is that the Campbell episode was Tanya's entry into the world of high-stakes gossip. The Rhinestone Cowboy says she loved tabloid publicity, and he may have been speaking the truth. After the couple's breakup, Tanya couldn't resist mentioning her *Enquirer* headlines to her concert audiences. Introducing "I Don't Believe My Heart Could Stand Another You" she'd say, "This is my favorite song to dedicate to cowboys. But you got to remember to watch those ones who wear rhinestones, though, if you know what I mean." Meanwhile, she seemed much happier mugging for the cameras than ducking them. The press corps spied her at a country music club in New York City; at Bjorn Borg's anniversary party at a Big Apple disco; at Studio 54 with Cindy Gibb ("one of the stars of 'Search For Tomorrow'"); and reported her attendance at parties with Andy Gibb and the not-so-great-white-hope boxer Gerry Cooney.

Tanya's last album for MCA, *Should I Do It*, outdid *T.N.T* in terms of selling terrible music by means of sex on the cover. Released in 1981, the album jacket showed her in frilly lace-up lingerie, her two hands holding the ends of the laces. One quick tug, the message was, and we'd all see what Campbell saw. On the other hand, the record that followed *Should I Do It* was among the most interesting of Tucker's career—one of the few, in fact, that Tanya herself admits was a real departure. She cut it for

Arista Records, a label now known in Nashville for breaking the careers of Alan Jackson, Brooks & Dunn, and Pam Tillis, among others, but which in 1982, when Tanya signed on, had seen no more of Music City than what was visible from Barry Manilow's "Copacabana." Tanya joined the Arista stable at about the same time as Aretha Franklin. "I was the first one on the label—country, that is," she says.

The Arista record was called *Changes* and was produced by David Malloy, who knew how to make a commercial record, as he had done a lot of work with Eddie Rabbitt. He clearly put a lot of thought into his project with Tanya, surrounding her vocals with a moody, low-grade glossy sound pitched halfway between Crutchfield's radio-ready mainstream style and Sherrill's aural melodrama. Tanya's song choice was the most interesting it had been in years. Among the more noteworthy cuts on the album were a cover of Barbara Lewis's r&b chestnut "Baby I'm Yours," and an almost biting version of Rodney Crowell's "Shame On the Moon" that was forgotten the minute Bob Seger's single hit the streets.

But the real big surprise on *Changes* was the title cut, which listed as co-writer one Tanya Tucker. Rebounding from the Campbell affair, she had started hanging out with honky-tonk anti-heroes Dean Dillon and Gary Stewart. It was fast company, but creative company; their examples inspired her late-waking muse. (Tanya had written her own songs as early as the mid-1970s, but had not recorded them as they weren't, she said at the time, "as good as I'd like them to be.") A lush ballad pushed towards the Sherrill end of the production spectrum, the song "Changes" was easy to hear as Tanya's comment on the Campbell relationship, as her decidedly more tasteful way of settling old accounts. "You took the part of me that I was proudest of/Now you're sayin' that's the part that you can't love." It wasn't exactly poetry, but Tanya sang it as if it were. It was her most sincere, believable effort in ages.

"I thought it was a really good album," Tanya says of *Changes*. "I was going through a lot of changes at that time, so it just seemed to go with what was happening in my life."

What was happening in her life, however, was not commercial success. Four songs from *Changes* made the country charts, but only one rose higher than #20. The most disappointing showing was that of Tanya's self-penned title cut. It never cracked the Top Forty. Her contract with Arista was clearly no million-dollar, multi-LP deal, either. There would be no follow-up album on the label. There would be no follow-up album at all. *Changes* stiffed (go ahead, try to find a copy) and left Tanya without a record deal for the first time since she was in the eighth grade. From 1983 to 1985 she had no career worth mentioning. That didn't stop people from mentioning her name—particularly people who had seen her roaring the night before at this or that nightlife outpost in Nashville. But after ten good years in the spotlight, there was every reason to assume that Tanya's life had gone the sordidly tragic way of so many entertainers who peaked too young and destroyed their careers on a white line fever route to oblivion. Not yet thirty years old, Tanya was already dangerously close to being no more than a footnote on seventies country music trends, the answer to a "Jeopardy" question about child stars in America.

And so it might have ended had not Beau Tucker gone to Jerry Crutchfield, the quiet man left behind when Tanya first stepped into spandex.

It wasn't like Crutchfield and Tanya had had no contact in between. As a matter of fact, it was Crutchfield who produced Tanya's *Dream Lover* album in the midst of the Glen Campbell fiasco. But he'd played no visioning role in her life as he had when they first hooked up. Now it was precisely that role that Beau and Tanya needed someone to take. Who better, Beau lucidly surmised, than the ultra-professional Crutchfield.

"Basically," Crutchfield says, "it was a conversation of: 'You know Tanya's here, and you're here, why can't the two of you get together and do what you've done before?' And we started talking about it a little bit. And so I proceeded to take Tanya over to Capitol Records, and communicated to Capitol what I really believed then and still believe—and that is that Tanya was the most refreshing, energetic person in country music."

The sales pitch took. Capitol signed Tanya and released her first album for the label, produced by her old friend and advocate Crutchfield, in early 1986. "The first album I thought was an outstanding album," he says. "And again, I really put a lot of thought to it, and I knew that, once again, we had to develop a little bit of a new focus for Tanya, that we had to come out of the chute really pumping and running.

"First of all," he elaborates, "we had to really send the message to radio that Tanya Tucker is a premier, blue ribbon country artist. Without question. And anything that had gone on—let the music speak for itself, and then make a decision on that. And if the music's not right, we can accept it. But if the music was right, then it would give us a real opportunity and a real chance. And I must say that radio was extremely receptive. It was like they were thirsting for a new Tanya Tucker record to play."

The first song to slake that thirst was "One Love at a Time." It reached #3, spent twenty-five weeks on the charts, and started for Tanya an eight-year run of Top Ten hits less remarkable for their consistency than for their consistent radio-friendliness. As a producer, Crutchfield has done a masterful job of making Tanya Tucker a "blue ribbon" country artist again. She sells more records than ever before, and in 1991, on the very day her second child was born, she was voted the CMA Female Vocalist of the Year. Eight years after her comeback, she is probably a bigger star now than she has ever been. As guide and shepherd of her second career, Crutchfield has not only earned her undying loyalty, he has added immeasurably to the respect with which other people speak of him on Music Row. But he has done it all with mainstream country programming in mind, and as a result, many of Tanya's post-comeback hits have had a shelf-life no longer than their stay on the charts. They'll get you through the morning commute, but few will remind you that Tanya Tucker, at age thirty-six, can already make a pretty strong claim on a future spot in the Country Music Hall of Fame.

Then again, the few that do convince—the defiant "Down to My Last Teardrop," for instance; and the dolorous "Silence Is King" from *Soon*—rank with the best of her teenage years. By no means coincidentally, what may be the most effective cut from her Crutchfield-produced catalogue—the song in which Tanya seems most deeply immersed in the meaning of the lyrics—is not one of the "woman's songs" she talks about doing these days but her 1989 remake of Jimmie Rodgers's "Daddy and Home." "I've grown so weary of roaming around/and I'm going home to my dad." Released at a time when every singer in Nashville was recording some kind of song about daddy, Tanya's prodigal girl's lament was one of the few that sounded in any way personal, like something more than a calculated lesson in abstract family values.

Those few standout cuts notwithstanding, Tanya Tucker continues to represent, in some frustrating, essential way, the most fully unrealized potential in Music City. "I don't think I've accomplished everything I want to accomplish in my music," she acknowledges. "There's so many things. I mean, I haven't had a triple-platinum album yet, so that'd be nice. Maybe I'd retire after that, who knows. I don't know, I'm just gonna take it where it leads me. It always has led me. And someone has always led me. So, I feel like there's some sort of guardian angel that is making sure that I make the right decisions. And if I make the wrong ones, that I learn from them. And I just wanna be the best I can be, and I just don't think I've been able to do that yet."

What it all comes down to is the sense that Tanya Tucker's career-defining record—her "Coal Miner's Daughter" or "He Stopped Loving Her Today"—is still ahead of her. When I suggested as much to Tanya herself, her tired, distant-looking eyes suddenly flamed, revealing in an instant's glint the intensity of the woman and her misunderstood artistic drive.

"Right! Exactly!" Tanya said, almost pounding the table. "That's what I'm saying. That's exactly what I feel. I feel like there's another 'Delta Dawn' around the bend, you know?"

▌The backstage crowd of friends and family members never did materialize. Maybe five or six people—most of them connected to Tanya's band, not her—stood in the wings and watched her work at the Chevrolet/ GEO Theater. By the time she hit the stage her hair had been teased and curled and her makeup well-applied. She came out in a black leather skirt, a silver-trimmed jacket, black boots, and some kind of bodice-type garment the real word for which most women probably know while most men never will.

If Tanya's back was in pain, she hid it admirably well. Her only visible discomfort was due to a poorly-attached wireless transmitter hanging from her belt. She ran through what seemed like an hour-long set without once letting on to the audience the way she was truly feeling, and without ever failing their expectations. Even up close, one could not tell if Tanya's smiles—most often flashed to the boys in the band—were put on for effect or sincerely felt. It was Tanya at work with the red light on. A class, professional job all the way.

As she closed out her program to the cheers and hollers of the audience, Tanya disappeared behind the stage curtain, then emerged from a dark, narrow walkway in back. She hit stage-right heading straight for her bus. A crew member held out a cigarette, already lit. Tanya took it between her lips without breaking stride. The look on her face was of utter desolation—of Delta Dawn returning to the intolerable still of a room where silence is king. *That* Tanya Tucker, I thought to myself, is the one I would wait all my life to hear sing.

ALAN JACKSON
(Photo by Jim McGuire)

ALAN JACKSON
Who He Is
MICHAEL McCALL

▊ In the mid-1990s, at a time when country music seems to be moving closer and closer to rock, Alan Jackson stands out as a stubborn anomaly. He is determined to make music squarely in the tradition of George Jones or Hank Williams rather than compete with the platinum flash of Garth Brooks or Tim McGraw. In the following 1995 essay, journalist Michael McCall (who has interviewed Jackson several times and even, on one occasion, hit the road with the singer) comes to grips with what makes Alan Jackson worthy of special attention. Among other things, McCall finds that Jackson's unwavering sense of who he is and his ability to convey evocative everyday details in his songwriting have done much to separate him from the pack and bode well for his staying power.—Ed.

▊ At 6'4" superstar Alan Jackson always stood a bit above the hat act crowd. But with country gone pop, and pop gone country, we're starting to see how far he stands apart from his peers as well.

Alan Jackson is more than the other male superstar of the 1990s. He's also the lone multi-million-seller to cling to the music's traditions and roots without wavering into crossover territory. His fiddle-and-steel allegiance supports the sincerity of such statements as "I don't think I'll ever venture too far from what I do." His refusal to follow others into big drum beats, Southern rock, or dramatic power ballads backs up a statement by Zack Turner, who has co-written and toured with Jackson: "He's real headstrong about keeping his stuff country, true to his roots."

Many of Jackson's peers pay lip service to country's past, but the music underscores a devotion to a twangy compound of pop sounds from the past four decades. That's fine, of course. It's become a cliché to say that part of country music's renewed strength comes from its diversity, but there's truth in those words. Country music has become as broad and as disparate, as contradictory and as indefinable as the nation from which it emerges. And, as with America, country music yearns to conform, to ignore its wild, lusty edges and dismiss its primitive, sometimes malevolent heritage to present a poised, smilingly eager suburban face that is earnest, homogeneous, and puritanical.

In its zeal to be all things, country music can become as facile and artificial as a politician or a mall. The rush toward progress and the future sometimes bulldozes the past; Jackson is the primary preservationist of current times, the chivalrous voice who honors the past by resurrecting it in a way that makes it useful and relevant to modern times.

Jackson succeeds partly because he's palatable, even charming in his unassuming, shy way. Unlike rawboned honky-tonkers like Billy Joe Shaver, Jackson's manner is smooth, pleasant, and conventional. But, along with George Strait and Mark Chesnutt, he's among the few modern stars who steadfastly maintains his ties to the sounds and themes of country music's past. His heart has never been with the Rolling Stones—or with the Eagles (despite his fine version of "Tequila Sunrise" on *A Common Thread*), Lynyrd Skynyrd, James Taylor, Journey, or the Beatles. He'd quicker cite the Kendalls as an influence before mentioning anyone who gained fame in Southern California. Of recent country music, he said, "There's some good stuff out there, but it seems like everything now is slide guitars and Hammond organs. It's like the old country sound is kind of disappearing. I hate to see that. Not everybody needs to sound like a George Jones record. But that's what I've always done, and I'm going to keep it that way—or try to."

A couple of years ago, I arrived at the home of George and Nancy Jones for an interview, only to find Jackson, his wife Denise, and daughter Mattie had dropped in unannounced to surprise the couple. When Jackson realized an interview was scheduled, he immediately excused himself—despite Jones's protests and invitation to stay. The two couples worked out a compromise, with Jackson promising to return with his family that night for dinner. As they said goodbye, Mattie picked up a telephone and squeakily sang into the receiver, "I want to hear some Jones." The room erupted in laughter, and Denise lifted her child, cradled her, and turned her toward the homeowner to point out that the man in her father's song was standing right next to her. Mattie bit her finger and giggled; her father beamed. Outside, Jackson's jacked-up, polished red pickup featured a Jones sticker in the back window. Garth Brooks may have sincerely wept when George Jones walked onto a Fan Fair stage to present him with a platinum record, but I'm guessing daughter Taylor Mayne—named for Sweet Baby James—isn't home reciting lyrics that George would recognize.

But it's not Jackson's old-fashioned tastes that set him apart from other country stars. Garth may fly on a trapeze with a look of unease and smash guitars to sawdust on network TV; Billy Ray may awkwardly quote Ralph Waldo Emerson, then go out and bare his chest and shake his rump. Heck, even a Texas club mammal like Tracy Byrd brags about how he's loosened up and learned to twist his tailfeather instead of just standing onstage concentrating on delivering a good song.

But Jackson, like Acuff and Tubb and Jones and Haggard and Strait before him, prefers to let his songs and his voice provide the evening's entertainment thrills. He'd sooner sell his prized Center Hill vacation home than take stage cues from Neal McCoy. It just isn't in him to draw attention to himself in that fashion. Nonetheless, with Brooks beating his chest from Ireland to Australia in 1994, Jackson stayed home and headed the top-grossing country tour in America—while adorning his music with nothing more than an awkward smile, a few modest waves, and the occasional "yee-hah." For the previous two years, the same man and his non-showy show led everyone in country concert earnings except the genre's all-time biggest seller.

Of course, Jackson is not the only singer on Music Row to pledge allegiance to the province of Haggard and Jones. It seems as if every fellow who passes through the mill must learn those names in order to pass go and collect his first development deal. But Jackson arrived in town in pre-Travis times, back before Music Row began reeling in young, attractive male vocalists with furious frequency. When Jackson arrived, the odds of a tradition-minded singer getting a record deal were about as likely as an Appalachian yodeler opening for Kenny Rogers. A couple of years before Jackson's arrival, a record producer told George Strait he should ditch the hat and rodeo belt buckle because that look was out-of-fashion in modern times. The same guy urged Strait to sweeten his songs with pop sounds; fortunately, the Texan eventually convinced his record label to let him work with someone else.

Meanwhile, Jackson met Randy Travis by walking into the Nashville Palace to perform. Travis, then still the fry cook in the Palace's kitchen, apparently recognized a kinship in the musical tastes and unpretentious manner of the young Georgian, and the two struck a lasting friendship. At the time, they, too, were getting told by Music Row that they sounded too old-fashioned to fit into the dwindling country marketplace of the mid-1980s. But one would lead the charge toward rejuvenating country's album sales and heading the Nashville industry in a new direction; the other would be there to carry the torch into the next decade.

Travis's success also led to another important step in Jackson's career when the blond Georgian, who by then was learning the ways of Music Row, noticed that Keith Stegall had coproduced Travis's initial hits. So he called him up and introduced himself, and the two met and stayed in touch over the years. Stegall, who had his own short-lived recording contract in the late 1980s, loaned Jackson his bus for a trip to Mississippi to open a concert for Ronnie Milsap back in Jackson's pre-Arista Records days. Stegall later recalled that Jackson "came back with peanut shells all over my bus." Jackson, sitting next to him as he told the story, said, "Yeah, but I helped you wash the dang thing." Stegall eventually took Jackson into the studio to record several of his songs, including "Blue Blooded Woman," a song the two co-wrote with Roger Murrah that turned out to be Jackson's introductory single.

Jackson earned his record contract the old-fashioned way, by arriving in Nashville as an extreme longshot and persevering through the frustrations and heartbreak of being turned down by nearly everyone he met. For many, the process has become a little easier. Nowadays, an ambitious show-biz wannabe with sharp features and a decent voice figures he's got a good chance of getting pulled out of the water and into the big-time just by making himself visible in Nashville. Post Garth, everyone who travels to Nashville arrives knowing the country music industry orders up young talent with the unquenchable desire of a drunk.

In 1995, a traditional flavor once again has returned to the bar: Wesley Dennis, Woody Lee, and Daryle Singletary all present hardcore honky-tonk promise. But would they have been as devoted to the cause, or as foolhardy as to think they could make it in country music, if the situation was the same as when Jackson hauled his family into Nashville in the mid-1980s? The question will loom as long as country is as successful as it is. It wasn't a part of the equation when Jackson originally arrived, but he came anyway, and he struggled for years with little encouragement before getting his break.

At the time, Nashville was further north than Jackson, a son of a Ford factory worker, had ever traveled. A late (but fast) bloomer, he didn't start singing publicly until after high school, and he didn't write his first song until age twenty-three. He may never have gambled on a move to Nashville if his wife hadn't accidentally encountered Glen Campbell in an Atlanta airport. Denise Jackson boldly approached Campbell and asked for advice for her singing, songwriting husband. Campbell's answer was to the point: If he wants to make it as a country singer, he has to move to Nashville.

When he arrived in Nashville, Jackson didn't know what a music publisher or a record producer was. "Maybe that's why he moved here," Denise Jackson said when accepting her husband's award as 1993 Songwriter of the Year from the Nashville Songwriters Association International. "He didn't realize how hard it was really going to be."

He learned quickly enough. Jackson and his wife struggled to keep their old pickup truck on the road while the future star worked for low wages as an Opryland mailroom clerk. But the Campbell connection would prove momentous once again. Thanks to a monthly stipend earned after signing a songwriting contract with Campbell's KayTeeKay Music, Jackson quit his job to concentrate on music. He also formed a honky-tonk band that performed three-to-five sets a night, five-to-six nights a week. When someone in the crowd called out a rock tune, another band member had to step up to the mike. Jackson only knew country songs. He lost work because of it, but he had no desire to expand his repertoire in order to earn more money or make bookings easier.

Tim DuBois seemed like an unlikely catalyst for Jackson and for traditional country music in the late 1980s. His primary success had come with shaping the sound of Restless Heart, a quintet he produced that devoutly pursued pop careers from a Nashville country base. Several band members went as far as to openly scorn traditional country music in interviews. But DuBois must have felt differently, or he never would have detected Jackson's talents. By picking Jackson to be the artist who introduced Arista Records' new Nashville division in 1989, DuBois proved his acumen as a talent scout—and he's repeated the trick with amazing proficiency in the following years, leading Arista to the top of the country heap through shrewd artistic decisions.

"Blue Blooded Woman," Jackson's first single, was far from the best song on his debut, *Here in the Real World*. But it did feature a jumping fiddle as lead instrument, with steel guitar providing most of the jaunty accents. Written with Roger Murrah and coproducer Keith Stegall, Jackson had come up with the primary lyric of the chorus, "she loves the violin, I love the fiddle," as well as the song's most distinctive line, "I live my life in Wal-Mart fashion, and I like my sushi Southern-fried." Jackson had remembered uttering the latter sentence to his band. "They were harassing me about going out and eating sushi with them," he recalled in a promotional CD sent out with his first single by Arista in 1989. "I said no, I like my sushi Southern fried."

Scott Hendricks coproduced Jackson's debut. He was brought in at the suggestion of DuBois, who had worked with Hendricks on the Restless Heart albums. Now head of Capitol Nashville, Hendricks dropped out after the second album at Jackson's request. "I liked Scott, and I respect him too," Jackson said. "But it's hard to have two guys in there directing things. [Producers] are like artists. They're creative people too. It's like two egos in there fighting over it. We worked around it at first. It wasn't like they were in there screaming at each other. It's just easier to work with one person. Keith and I have been working together for a long time, and we're friends. Keith had cut the demos that got me the record deal, and I'd been talking and working with him for years before I got involved with anybody in Nashville. I became friends with Scott, too, but I made the switch because there was some friction. It's gone a lot better just working with Keith. I really respect him a lot."

DuBois originally was drawn to Jackson because of the strength of his songs. Labeling himself a "songwriter junkie" and saying, "In general, I'm just turned on by that side of the business, it's what keeps me going," he remembered being struck by the depth of Jackson's writing abilities. "One of the most absolutely wonderful problems I've ever faced in my life was that we had so many good songs to choose from when sitting down to do [*Here in the Real World*]," DuBois said. "We had sixteen or seventeen good songs to choose from. Having worked on many projects where the opposite is true, it's just a real luxury to have just really, really high quality songs."

Stegall agreed, recalling the early days when he first got together to write songs with Jackson. "In Nashville, there's a tendency to want to sit down with somebody and rewrite a song and tell them what's wrong with it," the producer said. "Alan had a way of doing things that was not really orthodox, but it worked. That's what gave the songs a different turn on them. . . . I was talking to Roger Murrah about it one day. He said, 'You know what? It's not like we do it, but it's right. Man, that's what's going to separate him from the pack.'"

Murrah was right, and the distinctiveness of Jackson's work was evident on the first album. Jackson masters a blend of catchy choruses and traditional instrumentation, and he fills the songs with images extracted from real-life scenes anyone who has spent time in rural America will recognize. His subtly different style gives him originality, while his ability to draw on places and emotions that matter gives his songs heart.

On *Here in the Real World*, "Home" features well-placed, telling details drawn directly from the relationship of his mother and father, as well as his feelings about the strength of their love and the value they found through working to build a life together despite a lack of wealth or privilege. "I'd Love You All Over Again" was written as an anniversary gift to his wife, Denise; its heartfelt honesty is obvious and moving." Dog River Blues," like "Chattahoochee," draws on a location Jackson visited often as a teen and young adult.

Jim McBride, who co-wrote "Chasin' That Neon Rainbow" as well as such subsequent hits as "Chattahoochee" and "Who Says You Can't Have It All," remembers coming up with the title chorus of "Neon Rainbow" while riding in a car with his wife. McBride had never earned a living traveling through the Southern honky-tonk circuit. Jackson had, and when McBride suggested the title, Jackson provided the details. Just as the song says, his father really did win a radio when Jackson was young; his mother really did sing to him as he grew up; he did travel to gigs with his five-piece backing band in a beat-up Dodge van; he did play many nights for free while struggling to meet his overhead and pay his band members; and, yes, he did make it up to Music Row, and, yes, the wheels did turn slow, at least back then. When writing the song, however, Jackson couldn't have known exactly how well he was going to live out that honky-tonk dream.

Since his debut, Jackson has managed to maintain a sense of reality and truth while craftily expanding his rendering of the traditional sound he loves. With "Don't Rock the Jukebox," the title song and massive hit from his second album, some accused him of applying rock dynamics to a song celebrating country music. But that view exposed the critics' lack of familiarity with country's past more than it revealed any attempt by Jackson to deceive. Unlike Travis Tritt's "Put Some Drive in Your Country" or Little Texas's "Kick a Little," Jackson's song does draw on the most solid bedrock of country's foundations. "Don't Rock the Jukebox" is a direct descendant of Hank Williams's "Move It On Over" and George Jones's "The Race Is On" rather than anything by Lynyrd Skynyrd, ZZ Top, or Aerosmith. It swings, it doesn't thunder.

"Don't Rock the Jukebox" provides more evidence of how Jackson draws on real-life experience for his material. The phrase reportedly came out of the mouth of bassist Roger Wills of Jackson's Strayhorns band. One night while relaxing after a concert, the singer leaned his six-foot, four-inch frame against an old Wurlitzer, making the needle jump on the 45 spinning below him. When Wills shouted "don't rock the jukebox," a song idea was born.

But it was "Chattahoochee," the third single from *A Lot about Livin' (And a Little 'bout Love),* that shot Jackson past such peers as Clint Black, Vince Gill, and Tritt in terms of sales, radio play, and audience response. Ostensibly a simple tune that combines Cajun bounce with honky-tonk swing, the song's secret strength, besides its inherent catchiness and snappy wordplay, is how Jackson works in specific, true-to-life details that caught the fancy of listeners all over the world. Who can't identify with the joys of innocent, unassuming summer fun? Country music has flooded radio with silly novelty songs that try to capture the same spirit, but most of them sound contrived. "Chattahoochee" turned into a timeless classic because of the honesty of Jackson's hot Georgia scenarios: stacking cans in the moonlight, laying rubber on the asphalt, talkin' about cars and dreamin' about women, fogging up backseat windows and settling for a burger and sno-cone when she says she's not ready. It's ripe with the kind of experience that's as difficult to counterfeit as a computerized voice print.

Jackson performed "Chattahoochee" on the Academy of Country Music awards and the TNN Music City News awards within the span of a few weeks in 1993, and the award-winning video of the song was released during the same period. The sales for *A Lot about Livin'* shot from an average of 9,000 a week to 40,000 a week—and stayed in that range throughout the summer. The album stretched out his string of consecutive #1 hits (he's had more than any other country artist in the 1990s) and kicked in his habit of regularly being the top nominee for the various country awards programs. Interestingly, when it comes time to hand out the awards, the only night Jackson dominates is the one voted on by fans. He may not put on the kind of flashy concerts or take part in the kind of politically correct events that tend to draw votes from industry insiders; instead, he usually wins the awards that honor the art and craft of music (albums, singles, videos) while the showier honors for entertainer and top vocalist go elsewhere.

As his star shot higher, Jackson began to assert more of his authority. In the early days, he seemed so humble as to be almost compliant; all of a sudden, the same fellow who had sometimes reticently moaned about the demands of his career began speaking out with more confidence about gaining control of that career and of his schedule. He still worked to make sure he didn't come across as cocky or arrogant; at the same time, his mild complaints turned to forceful statements about changes in store. "If you have people telling you how great you are all the time, it's hard not to get that way," he once told me. "I hate the star part of the business. I like the singing and writing and all that goes with it. But I wish when I got off the bus I could be more normal and go down to K-Mart and buy me a fishing lure. Not that I mind talking to people or signing autographs. I just don't like for people to treat me so special. I'd rather be a guy people treat like they normally would anybody else."

He started mentioning George Strait more. He admired how Strait had cut his concert schedule back to around 100 dates a years, he would say. He envied Strait for how rarely he appeared on television and how he tightly controlled his appearances in the media without seeming to damage his career. And how he cleared out time to spend at his ranch with his family, without business intrusions. "He's my hero," Jackson said. "He's been doing it for a long time now, and he seems to enjoy his life. Man, that's the way to do it."

Before the release of *Who I Am*, Jackson shocked the music industry by firing his longtime manager, Barry Coburn, and hiring a longtime friend, Gary Overton, a music industry journeyman who had worked in music publishing, A&R, and management. It appeared to most to be a signal that Jackson wanted more autonomy. Coburn is a hands-on manager who had sometimes butted heads with his client over direction, duties, and how business was to be handled. With Overton, it's clear that Jackson is in charge and won't face the same decision-making showdowns as he did with Coburn.

Jackson talked around questions about his decision, praising Coburn while refusing to pinpoint why he'd made the move. "Barry is a really nice man, honest as they come," he told me within weeks of the firing. His nervousness about discussing the subject was obvious, as his words stumbled over each other:

I think he's a really good manager, was for me for years. I think we accomplished a lot of things together. That relationship was really weird. It's a lot like a marriage almost. Just like in a marriage, sometimes people change, and I'm sure I have to some degree. I think we just sort of were growing apart. Personally, although we were friends, we didn't really have a lot in common. We're from different backgrounds and philosophies (Coburn is a New Zealand native). That didn't really affect the decision. I don't really know how to answer it. I don't want to get into the details of it, but it wasn't one terrible thing. He wasn't stealing money from me. It was just . . . we just kind of grew apart, the personalities. We were having a hard time seeing eye-to-eye on where things were going and how I wanted to be represented. It was just a real personal thing.

A few weeks later, Jackson appeared as cohost of the Academy of Country Music awards. His discomfort was conspicuous, although he handled the job with low-key charm. By mid-show, however, he was coming out sporting a Hank Williams T-shirt under his Western-cut jacket, instead of the usual tux, shirt and tie, which seemed more in line with the outlaw days of Willie and Kris as hosts rather than the prim-and-proper nineties.

That night, in front of a Tinseltown audience packed with TV stars and California music executives, Jackson peeled off his dress jacket, rolled up the sleeves of his black Williams T, and introduced "Gone Country" to the music industry and the world. On a night that featured several theatrically over-the-top productions—including the usual hokey numbers that stick new artists nominees on the tourist-park movie sets of the sponsoring Universal Studios—Jackson spoofed the boundless commercialization and homogenization of the music he loved. In the background, Strayhorn drummer Bruce Rutherford mocked the track-synching performance by acting out his part without sticks in hand. Some, like Travis Tritt, howled with laughter and clapped wildly. But the overall response was restrained, at best.

Backstage, producer Dick Clark blasted the drummer and Jackson's staff; later, an on-air, backstage interview between Clark and Jackson displayed the tension between the two.

Jackson underscored his newfound defiance with *Who I Am*. He fought to put thirteen songs on the record, instead of the customary ten, which meant he took a cut in his publishing income. Besides "Gone Country," the album featured such revelatory tunes as "Job Description," "Let's Get Back to Me and You," and "All American Country Boy"—all of which staked out personal ground in a deeper, more self-exposing way than anything on the previous three albums. "Hole in the Wall" cheekily exhibited a man psychotically tearing into a living room wall with a hammer to let out his anger over a departed spouse. If "Summertime Blues" was a bit too obvious in its attempt to follow the success of "Chattahoochee," it was balanced by the choice of Rodney Crowell's "Song for the Life" as a late single. It's not a song that would have fit on any other Jackson album; amid the intimate disclosures of *Who I Am*, it not only fit, but further exposed Jackson's feelings that he had reached an apex where he felt like devoting more time to inner peace and less to worldly fame.

"I'm probably more at ease with life now than I've ever been," he said in 1994. "I guess you reach a level where you've accomplished more than you ever thought you would. I've been lucky enough; it's all gravy now. It gives you a chance to enjoy things more, and not be worried about a song and whether you want to do it, if it's going to be commercial enough. I don't worry so much about failing."

Artistically, *Who I Am* was a bold stretch for a performer who could have played it much safer. By pushing to reveal more of himself, he actually contradicted the mold set by George Strait. Jackson may have followed Strait's actions behind the scenes—cutting back concerts, making fewer media appearances, spending more time with his family. But he didn't settle into an easy formula of ballads, shuffles, and swing tunes. Instead, he made a turn toward the rarely traveled Haggard path: Maintaining an allegiance to the music he loves while pushing to explore his life and expose his emotions in his lyrics. It'll be interesting to see where he goes from here.

THE JCM GALLERY

▌ Country music has always been photogenic. Its singers and musicians are often as expressive physically as they are musically, and distinctive costuming has long played a major role in country music presentation. One might say that there is more to country music than meets the ear. For this reason, a separate section featuring country music photography, called the Gallery, has been a regular part of the *Journal of Country Music* since 1978. When the Gallery first appeared, it was rare for country music publications (or music publications of any kind) to showcase photography in this way. But the Gallery was a natural for the *Journal*, since we could easily draw on both the rich archival collections of the CMF and the talents of the many interested photographers who crossed our path. To represent the dozens of Galleries published over the past twenty-five years, we have chosen some of our favorite images from ten memorable Gallery collections, presented chronologically in the order in which they were originally published. The ten Galleries sampled here include the work of five active commercial photographers: Gerald Holly, Slick Lawson, Jim McGuire, Ed Rode, and Raeanne Rubenstein. The remaining Galleries consist of historical collections: portraits of 1926 fiddle contestants taken by Louisville's Caufield & Shook Studio, portraits from the 1930s of performers from the WLS National Barn Dance, portraits by Nashville photographer Walden Fabry, candid photography from the 1950s by retired Nashville photographer Elmer Williams, and bluegrass festival snapshots originally published in the *Muleskinner News* magazine between 1965 and 1974. We settled on these particular photo collections primarily because the images themselves pleased us, not because any of the subjects seemed more important than others. Though we have not attempted any kind of all-inclusiveness, these photos, taken together, represent a kind of family album of country music. Like a family album, the images collected here remind us of lines of ancestry, changing fashions, and favorite moments. And every one is precious.

DOC WATSON

THE DILLARDS

WILMA LEE AND STONY COOPER

JOHN HARTFORD

VASSAR CLEMENTS

LESTER FLATT

JOHNNY CASH, 1979

CHARLIE RICH, 1972

EARL SCRUGGS, 1973

RAY STEVENS, 1979

DOLLY PARTON, 1975

LORETTA LYNN AND SISSY SPACEK, 1979

PORTRAITS FROM "THE MOST POPULAR COUNTRY SHOW ON THE AIR," 1924–1939, BY THE THEATRICAL CHICAGO STUDIO

THE HOOSIER HOT SHOTS, WLS CHICAGO, 1930s

BRADLEY KINCAID, WLS CHICAGO, 1930s

EXHIBITION SQUARE DANCERS AND THE CUMBERLAND RIDGE RUNNERS BAND, WLS
CHICAGO, 1930s

LULU BELLE WISEMAN AND RED FOLEY, WLS CHICAGO, 1930s

GEORGIE GOEBEL (THE LITTLEST COWBOY), WLS CHICAGO, 1930s

GENE AUTRY, WLS CHICAGO, 1930s

MINIE PEARL, NASHVILLE, 1950s

HANK SNOW, NASHVILLE, ca. 1962

MEL TILLIS, NASHVILLE, ca. 1957

LORETTA LYNN, ca. 1962

WILLIE NELSON, NASHVILLE, ca. 1962

MOTHER MAYBELLE AND THE CARTER SISTERS, NASHVILLE, ca. 1954

FIDDLES AND FORDS

Photographs from Louisville's Caufield & Shook Studio

UNCLE JIMMY THOMPSON WITH MODEL T FORD, JANUARY 21, 1926
(Photo courtesy of University of Louisville Photographic Archives)

HOMER RYAN OF HIGHLAND PARK, KENTUCKY, JANUARY 16, 1926
(Photo courtesy of University of Louisville Photographic Archives)

MARSHALL CLAIBORNE OF WESTMORELAND, TENNESSEE, JANUARY 20, 1926 *(Photo courtesy of University of Louisville Photographic Archives)*

JOHN L. "UNCLE BUNT" STEPHENS OF TULLAHOMA, TENNESSEE, JANUARY 20, 1926
(Photo courtesy of University of Louisville Photographic Archives)

J. T. STALLINGS OF SAMUELS, KENTUCKY, JANUARY 20, 1926
(Photo courtesy of University of Louisville Photographic Archives)

W. H. ELMORE OF EAST BADEN, INDIANA, JANUARY 20, 1926
(Photo courtesy of University of Louisville Photographic Archives)

HANK WILLIAMS JR. AT HOME, AGE SEVEN, 1956

RIGHT TO LEFT: GENE VINCENT, PRODUCER KEN NELSON, CLIFF GALLUP, AND JACK NEAL, BRADLEY STUDIOS, NASHVILLE, OCTOBER 1956

LITTLE JIMMY DICKENS BACKSTAGE AT THE GRAND OLE OPRY, DECEMBER 30, 1956

AUDREY WILLIAMS, HER SON HANK, JR., AND HER DAUGHTER LYCRETIA AT THE GRAVE OF HANK
WILLIAMS, MONTGOMERY, ALABAMA, 1957

MITCH MILLER WITH THE MADDOX BROTHERS & ROSE AT THE GRAND OLE OPRY, LATE 1950s

FERLIN HUSKY ON HIS FARM IN ROBERTSON COUNTY, TENNESSEE, 1950s

A DECADE OF BLUEGRASS FESTIVALS

The Muleskinner News Photographs, 1965–1974

RICKY SKAGGS AND KEITH WHITLEY, ca. 1971

MARTY STUART AND ROLAND WHITE, LAWTEY, FLORIDA, 1972

MOTHER MAYBELLE CARTER, CALLOWAY, MARYLAND, 1973

BILL MONROE IN PROFILE

BLUEGRASS FESTIVAL, VIEW FROM THE HILLSIDE

THE BLUE SKY BOYS, GETTYSBURG, PENNSYLVANIA, 1974

MINNIE PEARL AT OPRYLAND, NBC-TV SPECIAL, 1972

WEBB PIERCE AT HOME, EARLY 1970s

PAT BOONE AND BRENDA LEE AT THE RYMAN AUDITORIUM, ca. 1956

EMMYLOU HARRIS, DOLLY PARTON, AND LINDA RONSTADT TAPING THE SYNDICATED TV SERIES "DOLLY," ca. 1976

ROGER MILLER SURVEYS THE WRECKAGE WHERE PATSY CLINE, COWBOY COPAS, AND HAWKSHAW HAWKINS DIED, MARCH 6, 1963

HANK WILLIAMS WITH CHET ATKINS AND ERNIE NEWTON, EARLY 1950s

KENNY GREENBERG AND WALLY WILSON

GRETCHEN PETERS

BILLY JOE SHAVER

BOBBY BRADDOCK

GUY CLARK

JIM MCBRIDE

ROGER MILLER, LAKE TAHOE, NEVADA, 1975

WILLIE NELSON AND LEON RUSSELL, AT THE WILLIE NELSON PICNIC, BRYAN, TEXAS, 1974

CONWAY TWITTY, OKLAHOMA CITY, 1975

TAMMY WYNETTE AT HOME, NASHVILLE, 1975

JOHNNY CASH, NASHVILLE, 1975

BARBARA MANDRELL, BEFORE A "HEE HAW" TAPING, NASHVILLE, 1975

PART THREE
REVIEWS

JCM REVIEWS

■ Book reviews have been an integral part of the *Journal of Country Music* since 1978. Not only have these reviews allowed the *JCM*'s readers to keep up with the steady growth of country music literature, they have also regularly offered some of the liveliest and most incisive writing in the magazine. Readers of the *JCM* count on these reviews, usually written by acknowledged experts, to provide a fresh and compelling perspective, if not the last word, on a country music book. Although book reviews are generally regarded as ephemeral, the six presented here are exceptional. In each case, the subject being addressed is central to an understanding of the evolution of country music, and the review itself is a thought-provoking piece of work well worth considering on its own merits.—Ed.

COUNTRY MUSIC, U.S.A.

By Bill C. Malone

(Austin: University of Texas Press, 1985)

Review by Bill Ivey

■ Bill C. Malone's *Country Music, U.S.A.* had a dramatic impact on the world of popular music scholarship when it was first published in 1968. Here, from the pen of a historian, came a work that described the fifty-year development of country music—a work which defined the terms and staked the territory that had been explored piecemeal by two generations of researchers. Though Malone's somewhat-revised doctoral dissertation was footnote-laden and occasionally exhibited the weighty style associated with academic writing, the need for the book, combined with Malone's meticulous research, elevated it to the status of instant classic. Now, nearly twenty years after its first printing, *Country Music, U.S.A.* is available in a revised edition.

The revision is timely, for country music entered a period of expansion and change just as Malone's work first appeared. Between 1968 and 1985, country music finally became part of America's national music vocabulary. By the early 1980s superstars like Kenny Rogers, Dolly Parton, and Willie Nelson not only achieved landmark success as crossover artists, but were featured on network television and in major motion pictures. From a contemporary perspective it is clear that *Country Music, U.S.A.* appeared just as country music was entering its period of greatest popularity, overcoming the remaining cultural and regional prejudices which had prevented mass-culture acceptance.

The organization of the new edition is substantially like the original. Footnotes have been eliminated, however, and a first-rate bibliographic essay has been added in their place. Relevant photographs have been included; the chapter dealing with bluegrass has been extensively revised. Country music since the work was first published is mostly treated in a forty-six page chapter entitled "Country Music, 1972–1984."

In his revision Malone has taken us some distance from the excessive focus on the role of singers and ensembles exhibited throughout the first volume. The revision incorporates a notable new emphasis on songwriters, which shows at least an effort to credit the many individuals who contribute to the final recorded product. Still, other creative individuals—session musicians, producers, engineers, and executives—are almost never singled out for the biographical validation accorded the most obscure singer, and the book reveals only the slightest indication of how records actually reach the public. While the importance of radio, promotion, and marketing are undeniable today, they have doubtless been critical factors in the visibility or obscurity of singers and performances throughout the history of country music. (These oversights are symptomatic of a serious shortcoming in Malone's book, and I will have more to say about this below.)

Though the changes incorporated into this new edition are substantial, a look at the new work inevitably draws one into thoughts of the original. Because *Country Music, U.S.A.* has been a touchstone of country music scholarship for so long, some evaluation of the original work and its impact on our thinking seems in order.

Malone's work—then and now—appears deceptively untheoretical. Certainly much of the continuing value of the work lies in its thoroughly researched biographical sketches of hundreds of performers and ensembles; in fact, well over half the volume is just descriptive stuff. On the other hand, the book is highly theoretical in its organization, in its use of terminology, and in the presentation of key assumptions about the origin of country music and about the underlying dynamics which have caused it to change or to maintain its identity.

It is *Country Music, U.S.A.* that established "country music" as the term describing an entire musical tradition (as opposed to, for example, "country and western"), and it is Malone's work which clearly placed bluegrass, western swing, and cowboy music as subsets within that large tradition—relationships that were by no means accepted in the late 1960s. He makes explicit the notion that country music is a recorded art form. By beginning with the folk roots of the music and moving toward the commercial present, Malone gives the reader a sense of continuity and change within the larger tradition. One feels country music as a living thing, containing many substyles, energized by individual artists, jarred by technology, and altered by the vicissitudes of the business world and the American economy. Malone's ability to weave the various strands at work in country music and to support his narrative with factual detail has given *Country Music, U.S.A.* its staying power. But there are pitfalls in Malone's method.

At times, for example, *Country Music, U.S.A.* is nearly too much a reference work to read at a single sitting. Locate a favorite performer through the index, and the reader is treated to at least a concise biography or, in the case of artists like Jimmie Rodgers and Hank Williams, to sensitive, rounded portraits which capture the special qualities that earned those singers legendary stature. Read a chapter through, however, and the names and faces blur, taxing the powers of recall of even knowledgeable country music observers.

In some chapters Malone seems determined to construct relationships simply by controlling proximity. "The Cowboy Image and the Growth of Western Music" begins with a discussion of cowboys recorded in the 1920s, moves to a treatment of the impact of Jimmie Rodgers, then to Texas singers, to movie cowboys, to honky-tonks, to Ernest Tubb, to a discussion of amplified guitars, and to western swing. Though much of this is in some sense "western," significant connections are not established.

In viewing country music as an essentially free-standing artistic tradition subject to occasional interference from an insensitive business community, Malone overlooks forces of change within country music which overshadow any artistic impulse. It is conventional wisdom in Nashville that it "is easy to make a record"—that is, easy to make a high-quality, intellectually-honest, creative recording. The hard part is to sell it, get it on the radio, into the warehouse of a distributor, and into a store. The real interpretive story of country music during the past two decades (and, perhaps, during its entire seventy-year span) lies in these very business activities which define country music as "commercial."

Malone's emphasis on star performers and musical styles ignores the possibility that other forces—industrial, psychological, etc.—may be central to an understanding of country music and even to an understanding of individual performing careers. For example, it is more than reasonable to assume that country music may be best described, from its inception, as a business, with the mouthings of vocalists the mere commodity battered about in the marketplace. The fact that a product is an art form does not place it outside the world of commerce. Malone sees the impact of business on country music most clearly in the recent past, but even then business interests are described as merely an occasional intrusion into what is essentially an artistic process.

Certain large assumptions of the work can be challenged as well. It is clear from Malone's bibliographic essay that his book draws upon three intellectual wellsprings: a social history of the South, the hard data assembled by fans and disc collectors, and the interpretive writings of folklorists interested in country music as a popular-culture extension of a community-based oral tradition. These intellectual resources are mixed and modified by Malone's obvious enthusiasm and affection for the music he studies.

Each resource can, to some extent, be questioned. Malone concentrates on performers, and his historical methodology demands that the work of these artists should reflect regional experience. Yet virtually every biography of a country entertainer (both in this book and elsewhere) presents quite the opposite view by emphasizing the highly individualistic personality traits which separate these unique individuals from their communities and families. Country singers (and of course, stars in any tradition) have so distanced themselves from the commonplace that their work may do nothing more than reveal the depth of their need to stand before an adoring multitude.

Record collectors, discographers, and fans, because of their special loyalties to artists or specific musical styles, overemphasized a sense of country music as a discrete tradition. Connections between black and white musicians in the South and ready access to national and international musics provided by radio and records may make a discussion of country music as an isolated tradition misleading. Malone, in other writings, is clearly sympathetic to a cross-cultural view. But reliance on the work of collectors and fans in *Country Music, U.S.A.* tends to diminish the sense of country music as a connected part of a popular music whole.

Of the various underpinnings of *Country Music, U.S.A.*, Malone's largely unacknowledged debt to folklore research is both the most unstated and the most unsettling. Folklorists have always given great emphasis to the individual artist. The artist is seen as both individually creative and representative of group or community values. The singer as the focus of creativity may make conceptual sense in the analysis of oral musics in a community setting, but it is a concept much less applicable in a multi-faceted popular culture context. Malone accepts this folkloric assumption rather uncritically, and thus *Country Music, U.S.A.* is, from beginning to end, the story of singers and instrumentalists. Businessmen, songwriters, and other players in the country music game have walk-on parts or a quick scene here and there, but the roles of law, institutions, and commercial alliances are virtually ignored.

Since 1940 the following developments have truly shaped country music: first, the creation of BMI and a resulting dramatic increase in payments to writers and music publishers working in such indigenous American traditions as rock, blues, and country; second, the growth of a slavishly dependent relationship between major record companies and radio—a relationship which makes significant record sales impossible without radio airplay; third, the adoption of certain marketing techniques—generally borrowed from book publishing—which gradually made it virtually impossible to distribute a record unless it is likely to sell hundreds of thousands of copies. Each of these developments is part of a fascinating story. None is adequately explored in *Country Music, U.S.A.*

An even larger conceptual difficulty with *Country Music, U.S.A.* arises from another twist of folkloric thinking which underlies the work. Though folklorists are notoriously unwilling to apply conventional critical standards to folk performance (cultural relativism demands that anything the folk do is "good"), they will readily pass judgment as to the performance's traditionality or authenticity. Though Malone criticizes this folkloric view, the feeling that country music has, under commercial influences, "devolved" from some more traditional stage of development pervades the book. A sense of artistic gloom rises like a mist whenever country music stumbles on good times, and that sense is accompanied by nostalgic longing for another era, one in which country music held a truer course.

Malone, in fact, describes a "Golden Age" of country music (the years immediately following WWII) and then proceeds to employ that standard of traditionality to evaluate more recent performances. Artists who carry on those postwar traditions are praised, others are criticized. Those singers associated with the Nashville Sound era or those who have pop success are particularly susceptible.

Malone's enthusiasm for those artists who steer a traditional course is so great that it forces him to play favorites and occasionally to skew evidence. George Jones (a Malone favorite) and Nashville producer Billy Sherrill, according to this book, "produced some of modern country music's biggest hits and some of Jones's finest performances." This artistic success occurred despite "the elaborate lush vocal and instrumental arrangements."

Kenny Rogers, on the other hand, apparently falls victim to production: "While his songs are often country in theme and mood,

the production behind them . . . is thoroughly Las Vegas in tone." An objective listening
comparison of Jones's "The Grand Tour" or
"He Stopped Loving Her Today" and Rogers's
"Lucille" or "The Gambler" reveals clearly
that the Rogers recordings present a more
basic, mainstream country instrumentation
than do Jones's "finest performances." It
appears, then, that Jones's vocal style and
lifelong proximity to the honky-tonk, country tradition validates any performance,
while Rogers's pop identification and varied
career pattern undermine the authenticity of
his country-sounding recordings.

A definition of country music which relies
so completely upon text, tune, and musical
style may be of little help in either describing
or analyzing country music. The inevitable
division of music reality into "authentic" and
"inauthentic" is counterproductive to an
understanding of the commercial dynamic
which energizes popular art. For three
decades the country-music industry has
explicitly defined country records as "records
that country radio will play and that country
fans will buy." Only such a definition can
comfortably commingle Ricky Skaggs,
George Jones, Kenny Rogers, and Crystal
Gayle. No doubt a similar definition was
implicitly applied by an earlier indus-try
which mixed Vernon Dalhart, Jimmie
Rodgers, and the Carter Family.

It is equally clear that a commercial definition of country applies to all the players in
the game. Critics and scholars should not be
dismayed if a favorite artist attempts a pop
record or employs a sophisticated instrumental arrangement. The star or aspiring star has
made a decision in favor of fame, in favor of a
certain mass acclaim which seems to replace
contact with family and community. The pursuit of fame absolutely requires a willingness
to adapt one's basic talents to the demands of
radio and consumers. Notions of traditionality and authenticity can be applied in analysis
of the commercial music world, but they will
not ultimately yield the insights of a hard
look toward the real business at hand.

To the extent that country music is a discrete musical tradition defined by the combined performing talents of its most visible
practitioners, *Country Music, U.S.A.* has given
scholars and fans the final word on a seventy-year history. As country music is a business, the commodity of a complex of commercial endeavors directed toward the promotion and sale of the creative result of
artistic ambition, the story is not written at
all. It is in business history, legislative record,
and in the innovation of key executive talents that the dynamic within country music
can actually be explained.

COUNTRY, THE BIGGEST MUSIC IN AMERICA

By Nick Tosches

(New York: Stein and Day, 1977)

Review by Roy Blount Jr.

▌ Any book whose language ranges from
"Panta rei, indeed," to "the Nashville steel
sound . . . : those dark swoonings fluid as
seaweed in a bay, and often as turgid," to
"Christ, lemme out of here," and whose content ranges from bursts of near-pedantic dis-

cology, to a reproduction of the disk label from Troy Hess's "Please Don't Go Topless Mother," to an impressionistic blind-item sketch in which a singer gets his brains shot out and covered up with a paper bag—any such book should interest students of that rich gumbo of strains and counterstrains known as country music.

Especially if that book actually captures!, briefly, Jerry Lee Lewis, and reveals that Roy Acuff once recorded a song whose verses included:

> *I wish I was a diamond ring*
> *upon Lulu's hand.*
> *Every time she'd take her bath,*
> *I'd be a lucky man—*
> *Oh, lordy, bang away my Lulu,*
> *bang away good and strong:*
> *What're ya gonna do for bangin'*
> *when Lulu's gone?*

The book of which I speak is *Country, The Biggest Music in America*, by Nick Tosches. It could be said against this funny, surprising, brief, vagrant, well-indexed and drolly illustrated treatise that it fails to cover all the ground, since such obscure figures as Emmett Miller (whom Tosches calls the gutsier precursor of both Jimmie Rodgers and Bob Wills) and Bob Dunn (whom Tosches calls the first and greatest maestro of the steel guitar—"great yelling dissonances burst from his bastard tool like glass against a stone wall") get considerably more attention than Rodgers or Wills or the Carter Family or Hank Williams or Willie Nelson, and Loretta Lynn and Merle Travis are mentioned only once briefly, and Roger Miller and Billy Sherrill and Dolly Parton and Tammy Wynette not at all. But those famous figures have been covered before. I don't think anybody has dramatized country's connections with rock & roll or delved into country's black, blues, folk-ballad and racist roots with

as much élan and bite as Tosches does here.

Born in Newark and a contributor to *Rolling Stone*, the *Village Voice*, and *Creem*, Tosches would seem to have come to country music by way of rockabilly, because the music of Jerry Lee and Carl Perkins and the Elvis of Sun is what stirs his greatest enthusiasm. Tosches likes music that he can call "ghostly, drunken," "Macabre, funereal," "crazy, and great." So does any lover of country, whether he wants to say so explicitly or not, but I think Tosches neglects some of the quieter, homier, more pietistic glories of the music.

My friend Ann Lewis, who grew up in South Carolina and is no relation to Jerry Lee, says, "While I was going to school, I worked several nights a week at the telephone office, Central. There was a woman named Mrs. Fields who had just gotten a telephone and liked it. She would call up whoever was working at night and ask if they wanted to hear something pretty. And then she would play and her little girl Neecie would sing, 'I wish I had never met Sunshine and Sunshine had never met me,' or 'Seven years with the wrong woman is more than any man can stand,' or, great favorite, 'Wreck on the Highway.'

"One time the Briarhoppers, a singing group from Charlotte, had a flat tire in front of our house, and they came in and sang for Nannie, our great aunt who had broken her hip and was in bed for ten years. There was a Baptist preacher's wife named Mrs. Cave who used to come in wearing a black cape and flap around the room and tell Nannie she could get up and walk if she wanted to. But the Briarhoppers did her a lot more good."

I doubt that Jerry Lee Lewis would have done Nannie any good, and he might have tried to marry Neecie away from Mrs. Fields. Don't get me wrong, I'm not saying anything against the Killer, especially after reading Tosches's account, which approaches sublimity, of a Lewis recording session during which Jerry Lee's father seemed to be "speaking in Hittite" and "a woman with bleached hair was referred to by all as 'the curse of the family,' a distinction of awesome implication." But country's craziness is all the more delicious for the real if highly reappraisable proprieties that frame it. Tosches seems to have no patience for religiosity.

That's like a baseball writer with no patience for ritual. But Tosches knows music and writes with edge and zest, and he has done a lot of original research, and he turns his highly developed taste for the lowdown-orneryandmean to good account. I wish somebody today were making country music that revived the essential hairiness of the tradition as well as this book does.

BLUEGRASS BREAKDOWN
The Making of the Old Southern Sound
By Robert Cantwell

(Urbana and Chicago: University of Illinois Press, 1984)

Review by Joe Wilson

▌ In his preface Robert Cantwell calls bluegrass a representation of traditional Appalachian music in its social form, one drawn from Afro-American and European sources that are largely Celtic. This familiar theory follows the scenario created by folksong revival writers who have been defining bluegrass in print for thirty-five years. Cantwell's subtitle, "The Making of the Old Southern Sound," has two sources. Bill Monroe, "the acknowledged 'Father of Bluegrass,'" believes his music is "the old southern sound," and Cantwell finds in it links to the minstrel stages of the nineteenth century and believes it is a continuation of Celtic folklife handed through the generations and best preserved in Appalachia.

Much of this book is about Monroe and his creations. The social context of his youth is discussed along with the milieu of country music during his career, the rise of bluegrass to popularity, African and Appalachian antecedents of his music, other notable bluegrass creators, folk revivalism, the imagery and rituals of his music, and its evocative powers. Cantwell demonstrates an analytical grasp of musicology in his descriptions of bluegrass and in comparisons with other forms. He includes a bibliography and excellent notes.

Cantwell is a literary critic who writes with verve and eloquence, addressing a dizzying range of matters he feels have impinged upon bluegrass at one time or another. He hopes some bluegrass musicians will read it, but says his book is addressed, "with great assiduousness and constancy," to a former academic colleague who told him that he should not write about bluegrass if he wished to advance in academia. The hoped-for bluegrass reader will be able to understand Cantwell's concepts but may have difficulty with his examples. For instance, Cantwell mentions Shakespeare's Falstaff when reference to Junior Samples would suffice. Unfortunately Cantwell does not subject his former colleague to the strain of reaching that far outside the classics.

Cantwell also comes from that school of literary criticism where it is commonplace to assume that the critic's every thought and emotion is of interest to the reader. This— coupled with a tendency to overexplain the trivial—gives the book a mind-clogging intensity. Let the reader beware: this is a book to be taken in very small doses; a chapter per sitting is plenty.

He has a keen sense of humor, though. Jeannie Seeley's band members "surround her with a sort of proprietary zeal, as if they had just won her from a gumball machine." There's no point in trying to talk to Monroe when he is resting on his bus before a show: "one might as well address a gardenia." Monroe and Seeley have a conversation and "the Bluegrass Boys, like pastured cows, look on impassively."

There are a few errors of fact. For example, Jimmie Rodgers did not introduce the Hawaiian guitar to country music. Tom Ashley lived in Tennessee, not North Carolina. There are some incomprehensible generalizations. For example, few students of older country music would agree that old-time string bands had "a mechanical quality."

In concept this work is an intellectually agile and highly detailed restatement of the folkie history of bluegrass, the accepted one that has been gathering steam since Alan Lomax wrote his "folk music in overdrive" piece for *Esquire* in 1959. It is a far more erudite statement than most, but it follows the familiar folkie pattern of simplified sociology and romanticized history to support building the pedestal upon which the hero will perch. The initial folkie hero was Earl Scruggs, but during the 1960s Ralph Rinzler supplied a course correction and since then Bill Monroe has been the Christopher Columbus of bluegrass. And he deserves enormous credit, of course.

Cantwell offers no evidence to support his thesis that bluegrass is primarily a social form of Appalachian art. No one ever has. Bluegrass was assigned to Appalachia at its moment of creation. No member of Monroe's original band was a native of the southern mountains; all were flatlanders. But their new creation sounded old when compared to other modern country musics, so it was assigned to Appalachia. It was from the first as technologically dependent as any other form of modern country music; the taking of breaks on various acoustic instruments from stage was impossible before the advent of microphone technology. But the instruments were not plugged directly into electricity, so an illusion of purity was preserved. And bluegrass soon became popular in the mountains, as it did everywhere in the Southeast.

Cantwell's favorite sociologist seems to be Claudia Lewis, a daring Manhattan schoolmarm who came to the wilds of Tennessee during the 1940s and found the natives speaking—surprise, surprise—what was almost a dialect of Elizabethan English. Cantwell guesses that Monroe's childhood in Kentucky a generation earlier was similarly rustic. The romanticized isolation theory of Appalachian history that the antiquarian folkies borrowed from the late nineteenth-century local color writers recurs in quotes: Peter Kennedy's silly supposition that fiddles and banjos were hidden when the word went up the hollow that Professor Sharp was coming; the Lomax comment that mountain singing is more "British" than British singing. Cantwell buys even the common fiction that mountain people are largely Scotch-Irish in ancestry, because he went to Scotland, and he detected in bluegrass "the imprint of the Celtic imagination." He finds bluegrass "restrained and severe" and its Nashville cousin "irrepressibly ostentatious and vulgar" and between them "a yawning moral gulf."

That he is repelled by the audience and performers of Nashville music and, to a lesser extent, the performers and indigenous audience of bluegrass is also clear in repeated gibes about dress and physiognomy. The distance that the romantic and scholarly vision allows is preferred. Up close he realizes that even Monroe "is only a hayseed after all"; yet he retains the power to fascinate, this strong and handsome father figure who says so little in words and so much with his music.

There's nothing new about the fictional attribution of musical innovation to specific regions or to people viewed as having greater authenticity. A nineteenth-century example is minstrel music, largely a popular Yankee creation but attributed to Southern plantation slaves. Thus the "Old Southern Sound" in Cantwell's title is really an old Yankee sound. But Cantwell believes the hoary claims made by the burnt cork performers about Southern fieldwork: "the minstrel show extracted the comedic elements of black folk music, subjecting it to theatrical laws." From this you'd think Emmett, Rice, and Christie were the nineteenth-century counterparts of the New Lost City Ramblers, socially acceptable performers of the music of socially unacceptable people.

Those who build pedestals for heroes seldom make room for more than one. Given the quality of his early associates, Monroe's perch seems especially lonely. In 1948 he reacted to the departure of Earl Scruggs and the magic banjo that had been mesmerizing the crowds by hiring Sally Forrester, an accordionist. A few days later, after a Grand Ole Opry show without a banjo in the band, Don Reno came seeking work, certain that Monroe needed a banjoist. The bold young Reno walked uninvited onto stage during a Monroe concert in North Carolina, banjo in hand, and it is thus clear that at that time Reno understood at least as well as Monroe what this sound should be.

HANK WILLIAMS
The Complete Lyrics

Edited by Don Cusic

(New York: St. Martin's Press, 1993)

Review by Lee Smith

▌ Never mind that he's been dead for over forty years, or that his career didn't even span a decade. Hank Williams's songs are still the pure heart of country music, just as Hank himself remains the prototype of the "country artist as tortured genius . . . a light and a darkness, a dream and a nightmare, a shining example and a shame," in the eloquent words of country music scholar Don Cusic, who has gathered and assembled this first (and definitive) collection of all the Williams lyrics known to exist—more than 130 of them, starting with a fragment from "W. P. A. Blues," which Hank composed and sang at amateur night at the Montgomery Empire Theater in Montgomery, Alabama, when he was only thirteen years old, winning first prize. Though Cusic gives us a short introductory essay that puts Williams's work in the context of his life, the concentration here is upon the songs themselves—or the words to the songs themselves—and this sharp focus brings us some surprises.

It is Cusic's contention that Hank Williams really was the "hillbilly Shakespeare," which he was often called; Cusic reminds us that "Shakespeare reached the masses with his words, his plays, and especially his sonnets, articulating the emotion of every man and woman. Hank Williams achieved the same thing." It's true that as poetry has become a little-known and increasingly academic art, songwriters have become our popular poets. We have relied on Bob Dylan, Bruce Springsteen, Merle Haggard, Woody Guthrie, Kris Kristofferson, Loretta Lynn, the Beatles, Paul Simon, Joni Mitchell, Willie Nelson, and others to tell us who we are and how we feel and what we hope for. We have relied on Hank Williams. And surely there is nobody better at capturing those essential moments of the human spirit: the anguish of lost love, the frustrations of love gone wrong, the hell of loneliness, the complexity of our feelings, the fragility of our relationships, our fear of death and belief in a life hereafter. Hank Williams was especially effective when he wrote about the joy of high spirits and feeling good—stepping out and cutting up.

But—poetry? I can't agree with Cusic here. To insist upon poetry seems to limit the scope of song. For me, listening to Hank Williams's songs is a lot better than reading their lyrics. I think Hank Williams was a great songwriter, but I don't think he was a great poet. A set of rhymes is not a poem. Poetry depends upon metaphor. The poet must connect the unconnected, see relationships to which most of us are blind—find a fresh image for a familiar feeling.

"I'm So Lonesome I Could Cry" (1949) is, for instance, a very fine poem. Here Williams gives us a whole set of indelible images for being lonesome: a whippoorwill "too blue to fly," the low whine of the "midnight train," time "crawling" by, the personified moon who has disappeared "behind a cloud to hide its face and cry," the weeping robin who has "lost the will to live," the "silence of a falling star" as it "lights up a purple sky." These wonderful images speak to all our senses—we can hear, see, and feel loneliness in many new ways. This poem is both specific and universal.

But look at the lyrics of "I Can't Help It (If I'm Still In Love With You)," written about the same time (1951). And (key point) pretend you don't know the tune.

> Today I passed you on the street
> And my heart fell at your feet
> I can't help it if I'm still in love with you
> Somebody else stood by your side
> And he looked so satisfied
> I can't help it if I'm still in love with you.

Do the same thing with the first verse of "Your Cheatin' Heart," surely one of the greatest songs ever written.

> Your cheatin' heart
> Will make you weep
> You'll cry and cry
> And try to sleep
> But sleep won't come
> The whole night through
> Your cheatin' heart
> Will tell on you.

Here we have no metaphor at all, just bald statement of raw emotional fact, given to us in sing-song doggerel verse. So let's face it: a great song is not necessarily a great poem. For a great song brings us also the gift of music, the tune, which renders its words and its images (no matter how trite they may be) totally unique, totally memorable. We listen to it again and again. We connect its words to events and situations and emotions in our own lives. Even later when we are stuck in traffic or shopping in the supermarket or having a fight with our spouse, we hear that song running through our minds. It thus becomes ours, totally personal, though its language may be trite and its theme is usually universal.

With all the lyrics collected before us, it's interesting to look at Williams's themes. Out of the legacy of the more than 130 songs he left us, over half deal with love lost or love gone wrong. That's a lot. And many of them are his best songs ("You Win Again," "Cold, Cold Heart," "There'll Be No More Teardrops Tonight," for example), the very songs we know him by.

Some of these sad songs are awfully deep and dark indeed, crossing over into that kind of existential loneliness that lies at the heart of the human condition. "I'm So Lonesome I Could Cry" fits this category; so does "Somebody's Lonesome," "I'm So Tired of It All," and "A Stranger in the Night," which includes this verse

> Like a lonely dove that flies from pine to pine
> My heart can't be gay and light
> Like sightless eyes that will never see the sun
> I'm lost like a stranger in the night.

Pretty good poem, pretty sad stuff.

Twenty or so songs present—in strikingly realistic fashion—the torments of a tortured relationship:

> I just don't like this kind of livin'
> I'm tired of doin' all the givin'
> I give my all and sit and yearn
> And get no lovin' in return
> And I just don't like this kind of livin.'

> Why do we stay together
> We always fuss and fight
> You ain't never known to be wrong
> And I ain't never been right.

> (from "I Just Don't Like
> This Kind of Livin'")

Though these songs obviously derive from Hank's unhappy marriage to Audrey, they are universal in their depiction of a couple who can't live with each other and can't live without each other. It is in his deft handling of this kind of ambivalence that Williams seems so modern, so contemporary. Often he does this by combining a sad lyric with a catchy upbeat tune, as in "Wearin' Out Your Walkin' Shoes," "Long Gone Daddy," and my particular favorite, "Why Don't You Love Me," which contains the tragicomic lines "My hair's still curly and my eyes are still blue, Why don't you love me like you used to do?"

Williams's irony and humor often leavened his essentially dark view of life. He captured for all time the sheer goofy exuberance of falling in love with songs like "Hey Good Lookin'," "Baby We're Really in Love," "Howlin' at the Moon," or "There's Nothing as Sweet as My Baby":

> I like candy, I like cake
> I like jam but goodness sake
> There's nothing as sweet as my baby.

—or the joys of going out on the town in his honky-tonking tunes. Seeing the lyrics on the page makes us appreciate the intricate rhythm and witty wordplay in a lot of these light-hearted songs, such as the famous "Jambalaya":

> Goodbye Joe, me gotta go, me oh my oh
> Me gotta go pole the pirogue down the bayou
> My Yvonne, the sweetest one, me oh my oh
> Son of a gun, we'll have big fun on the bayou.

Cusic reminds us that those who knew Williams well remembered him as a fun-loving, witty person—which belies the tragic image we have of him now.

Another surprise for me, reading these lyrics as a whole, lay in the large number of religious songs. Of course I know and love the great hymn "I Saw the Light," but I didn't expect to see nineteen others, most of them "calling songs," which ask the essential question "When the angel of death comes down after you, Can you smile and say that you have been true?" He recorded some of these as "Luke the Drifter," also the pseudonym for a number of dark, maudlin story-songs with sentimental messages, such as "A Picture from Life's Other Side," "Mother Is Gone," "The Funeral," about a baby's death; or "Help Me Understand," about divorce. The classic "Ramblin' Man"—which establishes Hank Williams firmly as the first Outlaw in country music—was also recorded by "Luke the Drifter."

What we will never know about these songs is exactly how much Fred Rose is responsible for them. According to Roger Williams, who wrote the fine biography *Sing a Sad Song*, "Hank's lyrics reached Rose in all sorts of stages, from complete lyrics and melody to half verses and a rough outline to chorus and no melody to nothing but a theme or an idea. Rose, who was one of the slickest, most professional songwriters in the history of American popular music, took each song or germ of a song and did what had to be done." About forty of the songs are

actually credited with co-writers, Fred Rose and others. About a dozen are credited as Hank Williams / Hank Williams Jr. songs. These are the "poems" Hank left in a shoebox after his death, to which Hank Jr. added more words and melodies. Still other songs were found in old Acuff-Rose files or have surfaced through modern digital technology.

All in all, it is an amazing body of work, a "national treasure," as Cusic rightly proclaims. My only quibble comes from my own greed to know more than I am given in these pages, where the lyrics are simply presented as poems, arranged in alphabetical order. I'd love to know (without flipping constantly to the back of the book) the date of each song and the co-author, if any. I'd also like to know everything else that's known about each song—where he wrote it, and under what circumstances, and where he sang it, and when, and who else recorded it, because these aren't poems, they're songs; and I can't really separate them in my mind from the doomed and valiant man who wrote and sang them, who added the magic of music and voice to these simple words which tell again and again the truth of the human heart.

ELVIS

By Albert Goldman

(New York: McGraw-Hill, 1981)

Review by Greil Marcus

1: MONEY

▌ When Lamar Fike, for many years a member of the Memphis Mafia, Elvis Presley's stable of paid friends, gofers, and hangers-on, decided to sell his story, he spawned a small industry. Packager Kevin Eggers brought Fike together with

McGraw-Hill, and with Albert Goldman, a fifty-four-year-old former college professor and pop culture critic. The word went out that Fike had the goods, and Goldman was to give the goods some intellectual substance: to turn what might have been just another Elvis scandal-book into "the definitive biography." Serious money was put behind the project, and it paid off; before publication, Goldman's *Elvis* generated well over two million dollars in subsidiary rights (a one million dollar U.S. paperback sale, a $400,000 U.K. paperback sale, a movie deal—Eggers, who shares the *Elvis* copyright with Goldman and Fike, has coproducer status—high-priced excerpts in *Rolling Stone* and *Ladies Home Journal*, newspaper syndication through the *New York Times* service, etc.). This has allowed Goldman to demand, and receive, an advance of one million dollars for a biography of John Lennon.

Because of the money involved, and because of Goldman's reputation as a New York intellectual, Goldman's *Elvis* has been reviewed widely and prominently; as no book about Elvis Presley before it, it has been taken seriously. Despite some partially negative or carping notices, the mainstream reviewing media have accepted the book as it presents itself: as the last book we will need about Elvis Presley.

2: SCANDAL

The promised scandal is there in plenty, and because of the saintliness in which Elvis was wrapped throughout his lifetime, it still has punch. There is, first of all, dope, Herculean quantities of it; then sex, with orgies and homemade pornographic videos piled upon fetishes, phobias, and neurotic dysfunction; then violence, a much thinner theme, but including accounts of cruelty, gunfever, and gunplay; then fat; then waste—all of it testimony to a schizophrenia that was as out of control as it was cossetted. But the significance of Goldman's book is not to be found in its collection of scandals—in Lamar Fike's memories, in rumors, in Janet Cooke-style composite scenes, in old stories pumped up or simply repeated. No matter how many details might be added, this is by now familiar territory. An exile from the real world almost from the day he first made himself known to the nation, Elvis Presley built his own world, and within it—where the promise was that every fear, every pain,

every doubt, and every wish could be washed away with money, sex, drugs, and the bought approval of yes-men—Elvis Presley rotted. It was a fantasy of freedom with the reality of slavery, and the ultimate validation of D. H. Lawrence's dictum on what he took to be the American's primitive idea of freedom: "Men are not free when they are doing just what they like. The moment you can do just what you like, there is nothing you care about doing." The real significance of Goldman's book is in its attempt at cultural genocide.

3: HOW TO DO IT

It is Goldman's purpose to entirely discredit Elvis Presley, the culture that produced him, and the culture he helped create—to altogether dismiss and condemn, in other words, not just Elvis Presley, but the white working-class South from which Presley came, and the pop world which emerged in Presley's wake. For such a task, revelations about the moral weakness and ill-spent life of a single individual are useful—anyone's work can be dissolved in the details of his or her life—but no matter how numerous or squalid those revelations might be, they are not sufficient. It is necessary to utterly destroy that individual's claim on our attention by leading us to feel in every way superior to him; to sever him from the social context that might make sense of his life and work, or allow us to feel kinship with him; to bury what might remain of that social context in bigotry and stereotyping; to selectively omit important sections of the story being told, and to falsify others; and to surround the entire enterprise with calumnies and lies.

4: SO WHAT

Were it not for the money behind the book and the consciousness of the book that money has produced, Goldman's *Elvis* would be little more than a 598-page attempt to prove that Albert Goldman is better than Elvis Presley, just as Goldman's earlier *Ladies and Gentlemen, LENNY BRUCE!!* was a 565-page attempt to prove that Albert Goldman was hipper than Lenny Bruce. How else to explain Goldman's bizarre aside that because Elvis was uncircumcised, "he saw his beauty disfigured by an ugly hillbilly pecker," unless one assumes Goldman is inordinately proud of his own lack of a foreskin, and wants everyone to know about it? But because the book is having its impact, and because Elvis Presley is so large and mysterious a figure, intertwined with the lives of millions of people in ways that have hardly begun to be examined, a good deal is at stake. What is at stake is this: any book that means to separate a people from the sources of its history and its identity, that means to make the past meaningless and the present incomprehensible, is destructive of that people's ability to know itself as a people, to determine the things it might do as a people, and to discover how and why those things might be done. This is precisely the weight of Goldman's book, and it is precisely the weight of the cultural genocide he wishes to enact.

5: SCUM

It is hard to know where to begin: the torrents of hate, distaste, and ethnic slurs that drive this book are unrelieved. On Elvis's background: "The Presleys were not an ordinary family . . . they were hillbillies. . . . A more deracinated and restless race could not be imagined. . . . Just as hillbillies had no real awareness of the present, they had no grasp on the past. . . . [Vernon and Gladys Presley were] the original Beverly Hillbillies. . . . [Vernon Presley was] a dullard and a donkey . . . his deadened dick. . . . Like most Southern men, Vernon had a knack for slippin' away . . . 'I jes' can't see mahself over theah in a fereign country' [Goldman "quoting" Gladys Presley]." On the South: "rickets, a

disease produced by not having enough money or enough brains to eat right . . . a [gospel] sing is one of those parochial institutions endemic to the South. . . . [Pentecostal Christianity is] a set of superstitions . . . the corny old saws of hillbilly faith healers . . . a classic white trash bluegrass song. . . . No matter how much of the black style these white boys take, it always comes out sounding as Caucasian as the Klan. . . . Of all the dumb activities in this dumb working-class school, about the dumbest was shop: Elvis Presley's major." On Presley: "Little cracker boy . . . silly little country boy . . . yokel . . . sang like a nigger . . . his fat tongue . . . his mush-mouthed accent . . . pig junkie . . . his country bumpkin cousins . . . smug, stupid, embarrassingly self-conscious screen rooster . . . [his] dumb jocko-shlocko Memphis-in-Bel-Air milieu . . . the face of a young George Wallace." On there being nothing lower than a male hillbilly like Elvis except any kind of woman: "His middle-aged woman's passion for knickknacks, curios and chatzkahs . . . throwing things like a hysterical woman . . . like an obese go-go girl . . . he would always go inside a stall, like a woman . . . propped up like a big fat woman recovering from some operation on her reproductive organs." And on, and on, and on. Right here, you have the essence of the book.

6: THE MYTH BEHIND THE TRUTH BEHIND THE LEGEND

"Myth," Goldman writes, "is what we believe naturally. History is what we must painfully learn and struggle to remember." Within this remarkably philistine formulation, Goldman makes much of his puncturing of Myths (his capitalization), all of which were punctured long ago, which exist to be punctured because Goldman has labored to inflate them, which are punctured only by fiat and mystification, or which are not myths at all. Goldman notes, for example, that it is a prime Presley Myth that Elvis took much of his inspiration from freewheeling Pentecostal preachers. One Goldman phone call, to the man who has headed the Presleys' Tupelo church since 1944, confirms that services there were invariably reserved and genteel. Another Myth destroyed!

There remain only a few problems. First, the minister in question arrived in Tupelo when Elvis was nine, and says nothing about services during Elvis's formative years. Second (as Goldman himself will claim when he needs to find roots for Elvis's later interest in spiritualism), the Presleys attended tent-meetings and traveling revivals, where the preaching was often far wilder than in a settled church. Third, there are Elvis's own words. "The preachers cut up all over the place, jumping on the piano, moving every which way," Elvis told an interviewer in the mid-1950s. "I guess I learned from them." Why would Elvis lie? Goldman has no need to explain, because he refrains from quoting Elvis on the point.

The real myths a reader confronts in Goldman's book are those of his own invention. By far the worst of these concerns Sam Phillips, the founder of Sun Records.

7: NIGGER

Perhaps the most famous statement in the history of rock & roll music is that attributed to Sam Phillips by Marion Keisker, his co-manager at Sun during the early and mid-1950s, and in fact the woman who truly "discovered" Elvis—noting his name, vocal style, and a number where he could be reached after the eighteen-year-old showed up at the Sun studio in 1953 to make a "hear-your-own-voice" record so that he could hear his own voice. The statement is simple and elegant. "If I could find a white man who had the Negro sound and the Negro feel," Keisker remembers Sam Phillips saying, "I could make a billion dollars."

[From an interview with Jerry Hopkins, cited from Hopkins's *Elvis* (New York: Simon and Schuster, 1971). Marion Keisker recalls saying "a million"; Phillips denies making the statement, feeling (according to Keisker) that it implies he was interested only in money, when his ambition was equally to bring two races and their music together. [Tapes of the Hopkins interview are on file, and available, at Memphis State University.]

In Goldman's book what we are offered is radically different. "If I could find a white boy who sang like a nigger," Goldman has Sam Phillips say, "I could make a billion dollars."

Goldman presents himself as a hipster (in reality he is a hippie, in the fifties meaning of the word—one whose only concern is to be hipper than anyone else in the room), and perhaps to a hipster, who alone understands the genius of the black man, all non-hipster ofays are racists—but Sam Phillips was one of the great pioneers of racial decency in this century. He worked with black people, and in the world of Memphis's small businessmen in the fifties, he was ostracized for it. "Hey, Sam you smell okay today—must not have been with those niggers!" Sam Phillips ran the only permanent recording facility in Memphis, and he had opened it in order to record black musicians.

Inspired by Goldman's example, I picked up the phone and called Marion Keisker in Memphis. (Though Goldman claims to have based his book on more than 600 interviews, he never interviewed either Keisker or Phillips.) I read her Goldman's version of Phillips's statement. This is what she said:

"UNDER NO CIRCUMSTANCES! What? I *never* heard Sam use the word 'nigger'— nothing could be more out of character." She paused, and came back. "Never. Never—*never*. I don't believe Sam ever used that word in his life, and he certainly never used it to me. Sam's respect for black people is overwhelming—his sense of indebtedness to black people who contributed to his life, his philosophy, is real."

Thus we have the myth behind the truth behind the legend.

The effect of Goldman's lie will be twofold. First, because his book will be the most widely read and widely consulted book on Elvis Presley, his perversion of Sam Phillips's statement will replace the statement itself: it will be quoted in articles, reviews, among fans, and in other books, and it will defame the reputation of Sam Phillips. Second, because Goldman has placed a racist slur at the very founding point of rock & roll, and because (here and elsewhere) he makes racism seem ordinary, matter-of-fact, and obvious, he will contribute to the acceptance of racism among Presley fans, who might learn a different lesson from an honest version of their history, and he will contribute to the growing acceptance of racism among Americans of all sorts.

8: DEGENERATE

If not racism, then eugenics. Having established "hillbillies" as a "deracinated race," Goldman sets out to prove that Elvis's line was the most degraded of all—resurrecting the discredited theories of Henry H. Goddard, who in 1912 published a study of the "Kallikak" families (from *kallos*, the Greek for beauty, and *kakos*, for bad). According to Goddard, a "Martin Kallikak" had a one-night stand with a bar woman of low morals, and later married a Quaker. The first liaison produced generations of criminals, drunkards, and morons, while the second produced only "the highest types of human beings." The findings thus proved that poverty and anti-social behavior (and, conversely, wealth and good character) were entirely a matter of inheritance—of genetics. The purpose of the study was to affirm that the poor were poor because they were inferior, that social programs (for, say, the eradication of

pellegra—or rickets) were a waste of money, and that certain sectors of the American population had no place in society. Goddard bolstered his research—he could ascertain a person's level of imbecility by a glance or by hearsay—with faked photographs. "Goddard's Kallikak family functioned as a primal myth of the eugenics movement for several decades," writes Stephen Jay Gould in *The Mismeasure of Man*. Longer than that: as late as 1961, many years after Goddard had repudiated the import of his work, his falsifications were presented as fact in a major American psychology textbook.

Finding "strong reason to believe" that Bob Lee Smith, Elvis's maternal grandfather, may have married a first cousin, Goldman gravely informs his readers that "genetics may explain why the children of Bob Lee's brothers and sisters turned out well, whereas Bob and Doll produced children who exhibited an abnormally high incidence of addiction to drugs and alcohol, emotional disorders and premature death." Goldman turns his tricks well. While most of *Elvis* is written in the voice of the hipster ("they's many a crazy, likah drinkin', pill-poppin' countrah boy that kin get hisser jes' as racked-up 'n' ragged as the craziest coon they ever treed on Beale Street"), in the addled syntax of one who dictates rather than writes ("envying what is beyond one"), or in the tones of a man who simply can't be bothered with decent language when the subject of that language is so obviously contemptible ("What really bugged Elvis was that they could never find one of those trick cars, like they have in the circus"), here Goldman slips easily into the simultaneously vague and definitive cadences of the social scientist. Thus he offers the litany, familiar to any student of eugenics, of "violence," "convulsions," drink, birth defects, and "homicidal madness," until "Finally we come to Elvis Presley, whom we see now as possibly the victim of a fatal hereditary disposition."

Whatever that means—and of course outside of Goldman's intentions it means nothing at all. There is no such thing as a "fatal hereditary disposition." But the claim does have its purpose. Is it possible that the rot, the schizophrenia, that took over Elvis was in some way connected to the fact that, as a working-class hero who (no matter how great his fortune) never left the working class, Elvis could not integrate the worship and derision which were his fate from his twenty-first year? That Elvis's life represented a real American dilemma? By no means. It was all in the genes of the "bad side" of the Presleys, and the Presleys were part of a "deracinated race" from the start. As Goldman says, "there is absolutely no poignance in this history."

9: MIMIC

In order to destroy Elvis as an American original, who might tell us something worth knowing about America, Goldman moves to destroy Elvis as an American ("The Presleys were not an ordinary family . . . they were hillbillies"), as a person ("Elvis was a pervert," we are later told, because, Goldman says, he was fixated on "the vision of black pubic hairs protruding around the edges of white panties"—a pervert, presumably, like James Joyce, who was fixated on the vision of white panties with little brown spots on their rear sides), and as an artist. Goldman has some positive things to say about a few of the early Sun recordings, though they were, he reminds us, nothing new (Elvis's "notion of what was hip was almost quaint"), little more than brilliant "parodies," and essentially fake: Sam Phillips "attached to his new star's raw and untrained voice the electronic prosthesis [Goldman means the slap-back echo Phillips had earlier used on many blues records and used later on many rockabilly records] that masked his vocal faults while it transformed—or shall we say transfigured?—his

vocal quality into the legendary Presley sound." After a justifiable dismissal of "Heartbreak Hotel," which was less an Elvis record than an RCA attempt to bring him into the pop mainstream, Goldman mostly ignores the rest of the early RCA work, and, when Elvis gets out of the Army, jumps straight to a condemnation of such bloated (and still exciting) discs as "It's Now or Never," omitting any mention of *Elvis Is Back!*, the powerful blues and r&b album with which he in fact announced his return to his fans. When it comes to the live, unrehearsed, small-combo rockabilly blues of the 1968 comeback TV special—certainly the most mature and passionate music Elvis ever made, and very likely the best music he ever made—Goldman writes it off as not even worth consideration as "a document," reserving his praise for the shlocky Broadway arrangements that made the rest of the special so conventional. He must do this because the small-combo music can be credited to no one but Elvis himself, who not only sang but played lead guitar—and Goldman grants approval to Elvis's music only when it can be credited to someone else.

To make a rejection of Elvis's music credible, though, Goldman must discredit both the response that greeted it (easily done: "broad, coarse effects . . . appropriate to all the broad, coarse sensibilities in his audience") and the possibility that it had authentic roots. Having already disposed of the Myth that Elvis absorbed, and transformed—integrated into his personal culture—the spirit of unfettered Pentecostalism, Goldman turns to the great question: "How did Elvis learn to sing black?"

Forget that Elvis's first records were rejected by white disc jockeys as too bluesy and by black disc jockeys as too country—forget that to people who knew Southern music, Elvis's version sounded new. To Goldman, Elvis was simply a queerly inspired "mimic": he learned what he knew off the radio. His music had no roots, which was why it was not real music—it was just another commodity, and it was learned as a commodity.

Which leaves one more Myth to be taken care of: the Myth that Elvis spent time on Memphis's Beale Street, drawn by the blues. Goldman wastes little space on this problem: "all one has to do to test that idea is imagine how Gladys would react to such a pastime. Why, every weekend people got killed down on Beale." (People were killed on Beale every weekend—in 1900, not in 1954.) "No, it is unthinkable that the boy who spent his weekends with a little high school girl going to the movies and listening to records at Charlie's would slip into the darkest and most dangerous part of town to hear somebody sing the blues."

Robert Henry and Nat D. Williams are two more Memphians who somehow missed being interviewed by Goldman. Henry was a Beale Street promoter, and he told Margaret McKee and Fred Chisenall, authors of *Beale Black & Blue* (Baton Rouge: LSU, 1981): "I taken him to the Hotel Improvement Club with me, and he would watch the colored singers, understand me, and then he got to doing it the same way as them. He got that shaking, that wiggle, from Charlie Burse, Ukulele Ike we called him, right there at the Gray Mule on Beale. Elvis, he wasn't doing nothing but what the colored people had been doing for the last hundred years. But people . . . people went wild over him."

Nat D. Williams was, variously, a history teacher, a newspaper columnist, a disc jockey, and emcee at the Palace Amateur Nights on Beale. He told McKee and Chisenall of Elvis's performances on those occasions: "We had a lot of fun with him. Elvis Presley on Beale Street when he first started out was a favorite man. When they saw him coming out, the audience always gave him as much recognition as they gave any musician—

black. He had a way of singing the blues that was distinctive. He could sing 'em not necessarily like a Negro, but he didn't sing 'em altogether like a typical white musician. He had something in between that made the blues sort of different. . . . Always he had that certain humanness that Negroes like to put into their music. So when he had a show down there at the Palace, everybody got ready for something good. Yeah. They were crazy about Presley.

"We had a boast that if you made it on Beale Street, you could make it anywhere. And Elvis Presley made it on Beale Street."

Henry and Williams are describing events that took place when Elvis was in high school—well before he showed his face at Sun Records, and well before an electronic prosthesis was grafted onto his voice. Black people, apparently, did not notice its absence. And while *Beale Black & Blue* appeared only last fall, the information it contains has been available for years in Memphis to anyone willing to ask for it—as has the information that Elvis, no matter what Gladys might have thought, spent time as a teenager in Memphis's black neighborhoods, making love with black girls. Such information is missing from Goldman's book not because it is dubious, but because it conflicts with Goldman's portrait of Elvis as "an unregenerate Southern redneck who stopped just short of the Klan."

10: IN HIS PLACE

And that, I think, is enough. I have little stomach for any more: for an accounting of Goldman's endless factual errors (Hank Williams laid to rest in the wrong year; civil rights activist James Meredith, who has surely suffered enough, being killed at the Altamont rock festival rather than Meredith Hunter), misspelled names, songs in the wrong movies, or of his dismissal of Roy Brown, the inspirational voice behind not just Elvis but such blues and r&b greats as B. B. King, Bobby "Blue" Bland, Clyde McPhatter, and Jackie Wilson, as a "mediocre bluesman." I can pause and say that Goldman has done useful work in ferreting out the truth about Col. Parker (a Dutchman, as it turns out, not the West Virginia carny he has always claimed to be), and about Parker's longtime mismanagement of Elvis's career; that the opening chapters of the book, which set Elvis late in his life behind the walls of Graceland and inside the Hilton International in Las Vegas, while clearly journalistic composites, are effectively creepy. And I could detail the exaggerations, undocumentable assertions and conversations, and ethnic slurs that mar even those sections of the book. But there is no point.

"The fascination," Linda Ray Pratt has written of Elvis, "was the reality showing through the illusion—the illusion of wealth and the psyche of poverty; the illusion of success and the pinch of ridicule; the illusion of invincibility and the tragedy of frailty; the illusion of complete control and the reality of inner chaos. . . . Elvis had all the freedom the world can offer and could escape nothing." It is that pinch of ridicule—the ridicule in which a great part of America has always held Elvis Presley—that is the exploitative basis of Goldman's book. Even the book's errors, its disregard for the most easily confirmed facts, its degraded style, and its refusal of documentation (except in the case of Col. Parker) or, most of the time, even attribution, is part of this: it emphasizes that a figure such as Elvis Presley does not deserve a serious biography.

But while Goldman's *Elvis* is not a serious biography, it is a very serious book, if only for what it seeks to accomplish: to exclude Elvis Presley, and the culture of the white working-class South, and the people of that culture, and the culture of rock & roll, and the people of that culture, from any serious consideration of American culture. And the bait has been taken: in the *New York Times* review that was syndicated all over the country, Christopher Lehmann-Haupt wrote that after reading Goldman's book, "one feels revolted at American culture for permitting itself to be exemplified by the career of Elvis Presley."

There is no need to feel revolted: American culture has never permitted itself to be exemplified by Elvis Presley, and it never will. But certain Americans (and of course people from all parts of the world) have recognized themselves, and selves they would not have otherwise known, in Elvis Presley: Americans whose culture had taken shape long before Elvis Presley appeared, and those whose culture would have had no shape, would have been in no way theirs, had Elvis Presley been willing to keep to the place allotted to him.

He wasn't willing to keep to his place, and now he is being returned to it. It is altogether fitting and proper that this be so, because as a hillbilly, as a redneck, as a white boy who sang like a nigger, Elvis Presley was never permitted to join that American culture that has never permitted itself to be exemplified by what he made of it.

WHAT HATH TOM CARTER WROUGHT?

Reba: My Story

By Reba McEntire with Tom Carter

(New York: Bantam Books, 1994)

Rhinestone Cowboy: An Autobiography

By Glen Campbell with Tom Carter

(New York: Villard, 1994)

Pride: The Charley Pride Story

By Charley Pride with Jim Henderson

(New York: Morrow, 1994)

Review by Bob Allen

▌ Perhaps you've seen them lately in your local bookstore—or perhaps you've seen a whole shelf of them: books about country stars. "As told to" autobiographies by Music City's biggest names are definitely one of the hottest items in the literary market-place. Reba McEntire, Naomi Judd, Travis Tritt, Charley Pride, Roy Clark, Glen Campbell, and Skeeter Davis are among the latest wave of artists to bare their souls (or at least selected highlights) for inquiring minds. Dolly Parton, George Jones, Waylon Jennings, k. d. lang, and Nashville Network talk show hosts Crook & Chase are just a few others said to have similar projects in the pipeline.

Looking back, Loretta Lynn seems to be the one who kicked off this whole country autobiography craze. Her 1976 *Coal Miner's Daughter* (written with—well, let's be frank here—written by *New York Times* veteran George Vecsey) was not only a vividly told tale and a valuable piece of country music history, but also a slice of true-to-life Americana that even verged on being folk literature. It of course spawned a hit movie of the same name.

Numerous other country artists followed suit by putting their as-told-to life stories on the block; yet none has really come close to matching the unbridled, almost giddy candor of Lynn's book—simply because few other artists possess Lynn's almost guileless forthrightness or utter lack of premeditation. Tammy Wynette perhaps came close when she let it all hang out with the somewhat less artful but brutally candid *Stand By Your Man* (as told to Joan Dew). Yet even her lusty confessionals and gilded despair ultimately seemed, at least in comparison to *Coal Miner's Daughter*, to be somewhat superficial, self-serving, bitter, and lacking in redeeming insight. The same can be pretty much said for other as-told-to's that followed in the late seventies and early eighties (only a few of which stood out): Hank Williams Jr.'s *Living Proof* (with Michael Bane), Merle Haggard's *Sing Me Back Home* (with Peggy Russell), Mel Tillis's *Stutterin' Boy* (with Walter Wager), Bill Anderson's *Whisperin' Bill* (which Anderson actually wrote himself, doing a credible job, at that), and Willie Nelson's *Willie* (with Bud Shrake).

But for the past few years, the confessional floodgates have opened in country music as never before. Even Garth Brooks has had conversations with various publishers, all eager to squeeze his callow young life into a mass-market epic (soon to be followed, no doubt, by the epic rags-to-riches bio pic).

This gold rush (or perhaps from the reader's standpoint, bum's rush) of over-priced hardcover confessionals can, I think, be traced back to two specific and not necessarily related phenomena. First of all, right around the turn of the decade there were two country as-told-to's which caught a lot of people by surprise by hitting the best-seller lists—one by a recording artist who was virtually dead in the record charts, and the other by a veteran country star who'd only ever had one hit record. Of course, I'm talking about Barbara Mandrell, who gave us *Get to the Heart: My Story* (written with George Vecsey in 1990), and Ralph Emery, who, along with collaborator Tom Carter, served up *Memories* in 1991 (the first of two such books Emery and Carter would collaborate on).

Then, of course, along came Garth, and ever since it's been sort of like the Urban Cowboy era all over again: virtually anything you can hang a tag on and market as country is hot-hot-hot. And meanwhile, the major leagues of the New York publishing world have finally gotten the message that, despite previous assumptions, people who buy country records will buy books . . . at least certain kinds of books.

Thus while the overall quality of these books has not taken any sort of quantum leap (except perhaps downward) since Loretta Lynn's heyday, the advances have. Back in the early eighties, a middling country star might get lucky and squeeze a hundred grand out of a major publishing house (which he would have to share, at least in some degree with his collaborator). But these days, top drawer stars and even some a little past their prime are getting hefty six-figures, and even in a few instances, seven-figure advances for spilling their guts. (And, of course, the more they agree to tell, the higher the price will go.)

"Even though some of these artists tend to be very private with their personal lives and maybe aren't initially inclined to do a book, to be that public with their offstage lives, they end up changing their minds," says one veteran biographer of the stars. "Often it's just a case of somebody coming to them with more money than they can stand to turn down."

"Country music has crossed over," adds Diane Reverand, an editor at Villard Books who is responsible for bringing in both Naomi Judd's and Glen Campbell's recent as-told-to's and who has a similar George Jones opus in the works. "There are many people out there who never used to listen to country—myself included—who do now. I think the market's there and hungry.

"The converts," Reverand adds, "seem to be older people who used to listen to rock & roll and don't anymore. And there's just something real about the music and the lives of these people [country artists] and what they went through to get where they are."

The country as-told-to boom, unlike a lot of similar industry trends, can more or less be traced back to one man: Tom Carter, a former Oklahoma newspaperman who now has a half-dozen of these books to his credit, including the best-sellers he wrote for Ralph Emery and Reba McEntire. He's parlayed his patience (and he's often needed every bit of it), persistence, and journeyman's knack for laying out a good anecdote on paper (the as-told-to's are, above all else, anecdotal) into a string of healthy six-figure advances that have made him the undisputed king of the country as-told-to autobio.

"I think he's very good at capturing a person's voice and listening well and telling stories in the way the artist tells them," says

Diane Reverand, who worked with Carter on both Reba's *My Story* and Glen Campbell's *Rhinestone Cowboy* (both published earlier this year), and will be his editor once more on the forthcoming George Jones book. "Any kind of memoir or autobiography must capture that voice," she adds. "People want to feel they're speaking with the celebrity they adore."

Says Carter: "I am not the author of these books; I'm merely the writer. And I struggle to put them into the vernacular of the subjects. Rewriting is the key. I write these for a celebrity; he or she reads it. If they like it, it stays. If they don't I rewrite it. Sometimes I'll rewrite my rewrites." With a dry chuckle, Carter adds: "At times I feel like a glorified stenographer. And a few literary critics around the country would agree."

Another obvious reason that Carter is so well suited to his work is his demeanor. He is blessed with a sort of slow-talking, dignified yet down-home earnestness and forthrightness which would behoove a small-town minister, and which seems to naturally inspire trust. It's easy to see why a country celebrity, especially when confronted with a contract from a major publisher guaranteeing a pile of money for a book to be delivered on a year's turn-around, would feel comfortable with Carter—even to the point of revealing his or her innermost secrets in a lengthy series to taped interviews, usually done after hours, in tour buses and hotel rooms.

Yet despite his polite disclaimers ("I just happened to be at the right place and the right time when country music went uptown," he insists), Carter also has a couple of other traits that have served him well and which his laid-back demeanor tends to conceal: the unflagging tenacity of a door-to-door Bible salesman and the perspicacity to foresee that a Ralph Emery autobiography would sell like hotcakes long before anyone else thought so.

Like so many down-home success stories, Carter's rise from obscure entertainment journalist (most of the stars he's since written books on he first met while reviewing their concerts back in Tulsa) to the best-seller lists started off small, and with no great expectations. His first book, *Almost Like a Song*, Ronnie Milsap's 1990 autobiography, was a thankless task which netted him so little money that he claims he almost went broke doing it.

"What was intended to be a one-year project stretched into two and a half years, and many times during the project Milsap expressed strong reservations about ever having gotten into it. Milsap's bus driver was making more money than I was. His janitor was making more money!" Carter laughs. "The advance was minimal—the advance I got on the second Ralph Emery book (*More Memories*) was twenty times greater. It was very hard, but I had nothing else going, and I was determined the bring the thing in."

During the couple of years he spent on the road with Milsap, Carter naturally spoke with a lot of fans and had occasion to visit a lot of senior citizens' homes and convalescent facilities. "I noticed that Ralph Emery was always on TV, and I found I was always getting more inquiries about him than I was about George Strait or Randy Travis, whose careers were hot at the time."

Carter's next challenge was convincing Emery, whom he'd never met, that he should do a book. For a while, he practically stalked the radio and TV talk show host. He would wait for him day after day at his parking space outside The Nashville Network's headquarters in the Opryland complex. "I found out where he parked his car and I watched him," Carter chuckles. "When he would leave his dressing room, it would take him about sixty seconds to walk to the car, unlock the door, hang up his stage clothes, and drive away. Six times I waited at his car and got half a minute each time. I don't know how effective I was at being a salesman, but I was effective in being obnoxious! He finally gave me an appointment just to get rid of me."

It actually took several sit-down meetings before Emery finally acquiesced, with the proviso that Carter find a publisher. Despite Emery's reservations, *Memories* became the surprise bestseller of 1992.

Yet Carter, to this day, politely insists that Macmillan, the publisher, seriously fumbled the ball, that *Memories* could have sold many many more copies. "We had a literary dark horse on our hands," he recalls. "The publisher was not prepared for the success of that book. Their initial printing was 25,000 copies. Well, at one point it was selling 50,000 copies a week. They sold out entirely fourteen days before Christmas in 1991. There was not a Ralph Emery book for sale anywhere on the North American continent. They were all sold out. So they printed a bunch more, thinking they'd missed the Christmas rush, which they had. But the thing stayed on the New York Times list for twenty-six weeks—only Shirley MacLaine's book [*Dance While You Can*] kept it from #1. It just wouldn't die."

At that point, Carter's future was assured. Four more books have followed—the second Emery book, publisher Buddy Killen's autobiography, and the recently published Reba McEntire and Glen Campbell tomes.

"I frequently have two books going at once, and at one point I was working on four books simultaneously," says Carter, who cranks out these projects, usually on a year's deadline, with the sole assistance of a researcher. ("Her name's Jane Halley—please print it; she's been integral to the success of these books.")

"My schedule was outrageous," he adds. "But in this business you take the work when it comes."

Carter readily concedes that his greatest asset as a writer is his ability—and willingness—to completely submerge his own personality and literary voice in the writing process. "I want the reader to think that he or she is privy to these celebrities' innermost thoughts, as if the celebrity is actually confiding in them," he explains. "It's an informal conversational style. It's intimate. I try to capture the artist's voice, which often involves a lot of rewriting.

"I've had artists say to me, 'Make me sound more intelligent than I am,'" he adds. "Then I've had artists, like Reba, who insist on using their own natural voice. She did not want to sound pretentious or phony in any way." He laughs. "I had one artist who scarcely even wanted to read the manuscript. He told me, 'Just make me sound smart.'

"I'm getting ready to start my seventh [autobiography with George Jones], and I don't think I've ever had a client that did these books for financial reasons. Many do it because they want to set the record straight. We're talking about people, after all, about whom thousands of stories have been written, many of which were written inaccurately. Many write these books as they're approaching the golden days of their careers, and they feel that they have a debt to their fans to tell their story, and to tell it accurately, once and for all. Many see it as a cleansing experience; many see it as an obligation to a public that has been so good to them."

Carter adds, though, almost in the same breath: "[A book] opens a lot of commercial doors too. The artists get many endorsement opportunities they otherwise wouldn't get. If the book is a hit, it sometimes has a positive impact on their nightly performance fee. They become more visible to new audiences. There are people, for instance, who would not buy a George Jones record but would buy his life story. So it expands the market."

Carter's success ultimately depends on the strength of the revelations, confessions, and insights he's given as raw material. ("I'll go wherever the artist is, whenever they want me to be there," he says of the interview process, which, as each project progresses, tends to take on an increasingly more informal and candid quality.) At times, he admits, "there are disappointments. Many times we've come up with something I felt was pivotal to the artist's life story, but they wouldn't leave it in, even though I argued—I argue a lot. Many times [that's happened], and it hurts."

Carter also depends on a particular artist's personal agenda—his or her philosophies, prejudices, and whatever old axes there may be left to grind. (Inevitably, ex-spouses and lovers usually fare rather shabbily in these things—as evidenced by Reba's portrayal of her former husband Charlie Battles and Glen Campbell's scathing recollections of his former fiancée, Tanya Tucker.)

While Emery's first book is an example of Carter doing what he does best, Glen Campbell's *Rhinestone Cowboy* is a case in point of how such books can go awry. Assuming that the purpose of these as-told-to opuses is to win new friends and fans, enhance one's public image, take the opportunity to settle old scores, and have the last laugh on the press that has perhaps been beating up on the artist for years, then Campbell's book is, in many respects, a failure. (Ironically, Campbell too was a very reluctant subject; it took every bit of Carter's salesmanship and stealth to rope him in. At one point, after already being rebuffed several times, Carter even showed up unannounced and uninvited at a Campbell family reunion in Arkansas: "Just me and two hundred Campbells, and every one of 'em wondering, 'Who is this guy?'")

For one thing, Campbell's narrative voice, despite Carter's best efforts, does not sound natural; too often the former pop/country star sounds pompous, thin-skinned, and self-righteous. It's been said that "born again"

acolytes are the most insufferable kind, and Campbell, in *Rhinestone Cowboy*, more or less proves it's so. Though he professes his new-found Christianity at great length (he's been a frequent guest on Pat Robertson's "700 Club"), he's anything but forgiving towards Tanya Tucker. Realizing its tabloid potential, he and Carter disingenuously serve up lurid accounts of Campbell's and Tucker's drug-addled, dysfunctional romance (which actually comes off sounding like a near-fatal collision between two spoiled children). Admittedly, Campbell serves up dollops of remorse for his own years of bad behavior (which, ironically, in the book business and in rock & roll, often pay off big dividends later in life). Yet in his dour condemnations of this sordid romantic epoch he neatly sidesteps the fact that he, as the proverbial older man, should have known better, and was in fact a 50-50 co-enabler in their high-rolling, coked-out daze.

But now that he's kicked the drugs and booze and found middle-aged solace in the good life that revolves around God, golf, and Branson, Campbell has become holier-than-thou. (He reverentially recalls the time he upbraided Ronnie Milsap—bland, lovable, middle-of-the-road Ronnie Milsap, of all people!—for doing a comic imitation of a TV evangelist during a show the two of them did together at Branson.)

I suppose one can give Campbell credit for honesty—even when he is busy proving himself a horse's ass. But if such misplaced moral smugness is the end result of being clean and sober, then, please, bring on the booze and drugs.

The portrait of Reba McEntire that Carter has cobbled together in *Reba: My Story*, though somewhat artless and disjointed at times (see-sawing wildly between the profound and the trivial), is far more sympathetic—even though McEntire's "voice," despite all her accomplishments, lacks the color, unfettered vivacity, and startling insight that made Loretta Lynn so endearing in *Coal Miner's Daughter*. Don't look for any startling revelations about life at the top, sweeping perceptions about the social responsibility of entertainers, or even worthwhile insights into her own dramatic musical evolution in McEntire's memoir. Alas, everything about Reba (at least *Reba*, the book) is far more mundane and prosaic, like the steady stream of semi-private revelations you might hear at a beauty salon on a slow afternoon.

But what would a good country as-told-to be without some hearty ex-spouse bashing? Though McEntire uses an understated velvet hammer approach (as opposed the bitter gusto Campbell seems to summon when invoking the ghost of Tanya), Charlie Battles, her former husband, ultimately comes off as a pig-headed chauvinistic lout— sort of your worst nightmare about what cowboys are really like. When the couple splits, he even makes a scene over keeping a bag full of the little shampoos and bars of soap that Reba routinely scavenges from hotels. ("I don't ever wanna have to buy another bar of soap," he proclaims.)

Still, the Reba that we encounter in these pages is, ultimately, a very sympathetic figure—which considering the motivations for writing these things—makes her book a success, in and of itself. If in recent years, her unbridled ambition has seemed to take precedence over every other consideration (including her music), her over-compensation and over-achievement suddenly become understandable when we read just what, besides the oafish Battles, she was up against in her early years: fair weather friends eager to hitch a ride on her rising star, managers and record executives who controlled her career and specialized in thinking small. (Even Jimmy Bowen, who later became her coproducer and good friend, was set to drop her from MCA back when he first assumed control of the label.) Then, too, we can feel her brokenheartedness not just over the devastating loss of her band in a plane wreck, but in the trail of broken friendships she's left in her wake as she's gradually outgrown so many of those who were involved in her career at the outset and who simply weren't bright enough to visualize the big picture she saw.

Most interesting of all the latest crop of as-told-to's is one that Tom Carter didn't write: *Pride: The Charley Pride Story* (with Jim Henderson). For one thing, it proves that these books can manage to be heartwarming and a vivid read, yet (like *Coal Miner's Daughter*) can at the same time stand as a worthy document of popular music history.

Not only does Pride have far more history to draw on, in terms of his years at the top of the charts; he's also a far more fascinating, a times even enigmatic character—a towering presence, actually: country music's equivalent to baseball's immortal and heroic Jackie Robinson. And the voice that Jim Henderson has captured, and with which Pride speaks to the reader, is filled with quiet dignity, compassion, and self-effacing humor.

Much of Pride's story takes place in the sixties and seventies, a decidedly more colorful and less corporate era in country music than the one in which we're now living. Pride's candor—about his life-long battle with manic-depression, and about the many business failures he endured before finally hitting a home run as the majority owner of a thriving Texas bank—is admirable. His recollections of his early Nashville years, when he struggled the break the "color barrier," are equally moving. (His description of how Faron Young, Nashville's hell-raising arch-redneck, gradually became one of his best friends and allies is especially touching, as are his remembrances of Waylon Jennings's early and unqualified friendship.)

There is no one more aware of the strengths (and deficiencies) of the genre that he's more or less made his own than Tom Carter himself. He claims he doesn't read reviews; yet one gets the strong impression that he at least takes a peak at them now and then. If he feels any rancor on the occasional critical hits he himself has taken, he certainly doesn't show it. For that matter, he's probably doing a lot of laughing on the way to the bank these past few years—since these books have either made him a millionaire or something very close to one. When the suggestion is politely offered that if one of these as-told-to's was written to satisfy the critics it might very well miss its intended audience, he readily agrees: "These books are not aimed at the literati. They're aimed at Mrs. and Mrs. Joe Everyman. They're aimed at a grassroots audience that buys country music and really doesn't buy a lot of books. [But] they buy books about their favorite country stars."

Once again, Carter is right, and has the last laugh, with the powerful voice of the cash register on his side: as of this writing, Reba's *My Story* is parked at #10 on the national best-seller lists.

NOTES ON CONTRIBUTORS

■ Bob Allen, longtime editor at large for *Country Music* magazine, has also contributed to numerous other publications, including the *Washington Post, Esquire, Billboard,* and *Rolling Stone.* He is the author of *George Jones: Saga of an American Singer* and the editor of *The Blackwell Guide to Recorded Country Music.*

■ Roy Blount Jr., former reporter for the *Atlanta Journal* and *Sports Illustrated,* is currently a contributing editor of *The Atlantic* and *Men's Journal.* His work has also appeared in *Esquire,* the *New York Times,* and the *New Yorker,* among many other publications. The author of twelve books (including *Crackers, Roy Blount's Book of Southern Humor,* and the novel *First Hubby*), he has also written for television and the movies, and has appeared on the "Tonight Show," and "Politically Incorrect," and a "Prairie Home Companion."

■ Mary A. Bufwack is a cultural anthropologist who specializes in women's studies. Her social work in the interest of women includes directing the Nashville YWCA Women's Shelter. She is executive director of United Neighborhood Health Services, a non-profit "family doctor" in Nashville's inner-city neighborhoods. She is coauthor (with Robert K. Oermann) of *Finding Her Voice: The Saga of Women in Country Music.*

■ Kevin Coffey is a freelance writer living in Fort Worth, Texas. He is a regular contibutor to the *Journal of Country Music* and the *Journal of the American Academy for the Preservation of Old-Time Country Music,* and has published music-related articles in the *Fort Worth Star-Telegram.* In addition, he has written liner notes for several country-music reissues on Bear Family Records.

■ Daniel Cooper is associate editor of CMF Press and the author of *Lefty Frizzell: The Honky-Tonk Life of Country Music's Greatest Singer.* He has written for the *Nashville Banner,* the *Nashville Scene,* and *New Country,* among other publications.

■ Walden S. Fabry was one of the few Nashville studio photographers who concentrated on country music celebrities in the 1950s and 1960s. Although he passed away in 1976, his work lives on at Fabry Studios and at the Country Music Foundation, where his photographs are preserved.

❚ Chet Flippo is the Nashville editor for *Billboard* magazine and a former senior editor of *Rolling Stone*. He is the author of several books, including *Your Cheatin' Heart: A Biography of Hank Williams, Yesterday: The Unauthorized Biography of Paul McCartney,* and *Everybody Was Kung Fu Dancing.*

❚ Musician and journalist Thomas Goldsmith has worked for Nashville's morning newspaper, the *Tennessean,* since 1983. As a freelance writer, he has published articles in a wide variety of publications, and he has contributed chapters to several books on guitar playing and country music. His songs have been recorded by Riders in the Sky, the Nashville Bluegrass Band, and David Olney, and he has produced records by Olney, Tracy Nelson, and the Nashville Jug Band.

❚ Douglas B. Green, also known as Ranger Doug of Riders in the Sky, is the author of *Country Roots,* and has written for a number of magazines. He is a former editor of the Country Music Foundation's *Journal of Country Music.*

❚ Peter Guralnick is the author of *Feel Like Going Home, Lost Highway, Sweet Soul Music,* and *Searching for Robert Johnson,* as well as the novel *Nighthawk Blue,* and *Last Train to Memphis: The Rise of Elvis Presley,* the first volume of a two-part biography.

❚ Gerald Holly began his career as a newspaper photographer in 1954 at the *Tennessean,* where his photos landed on the cover of more than two hundred Sunday magazines. His work has also appeared in *National Geographic, Life, Forbes, People,* and *US.* In 1983 Holly joined Vanderbilt University as a publications photographer, where he has won several awards for his work.

❚ Bill Ivey has been the director of the Country Music Foundation since 1971. He has written numerous articles about country and popular music for a wide variety of publications and has contributed scripts for several television specials.

❚ Paul Kingsbury has been editor for the Country Music Foundation and its *Journal of Country Music* since 1985. He is the author of *The Grand Ole Opry History of Country Music* and the editor of *Country on Compact Disc* and *Country: The Music and the Musicians,* which won a Ralph J. Gleason Music Book Award. His writing has also appeared in *Entertainment Weekly, US,* and *Country America.*

❚ Slick Lawson's photographs have appeared in a wide variety of publications, including *Time, People, Newsweek,* and the *New York Times;* and his national advertising accounts have included Jack Daniels, Monsanto, Gulf & Western, IBM, and DuPont. He is currently putting together two major retrospective shows, both of which will be the basis for books.

❚ Michael McCall writes a weekly music column for the *Nashville Scene* and contributes regularly to *Country Music, Country America, The Los Angeles Times,* and *Tower Pulse.* His books include *The Superstars of Country Music* and *Garth Brooks: A Biography.*

❚ Jim McGuire, resident Nashvillian but Trenton, New Jersey, native, first began taking pictures in Vietnam in 1964 and 1965. After his service, he was the corporate staff photographer for United Air Lines, as well as a country music columnist for the *Village Voice* in New York City. He moved to Nashville in 1972 to work on his ongoing project, the Nashville Portraits. His work has appeared in numerous magazines and has been featured on dozens of album covers.

▌ Greil Marcus is the author of *The Dustbin of History, Dead Elvis, Mystery Train: Images of America in Rock 'n' Roll Music*, and *Lipstick Traces: A Secret History of the Twentieth Century*, as well as the editor of *Psychotic Reactions and Carburetor Dung* by Lester Bangs. He lives in Berkeley, California.

▌ Robert K. Oermann is a multimedia music journalist whose work appears regularly in *The Tennessean*, on radio, and on The Nashville Network cable channel. He has won the Media Achievement Award from the Country Music Association. He is the author of *America's Music: The Roots of Country* and the coauthor (with Mary A. Bufwack) of *Finding Her Voice: The Saga of Women in Country Music*. His television writing credits include the special *Women of Country* and the documentary series *Roots of Country*.

▌ Edward Rode, a native of Kansas City, Missouri, moved to Nashville in 1990 to join the photography staff of the *Nashville Banner*. He previously worked for the *Kansas City Star*, the *Knoxville News-Sentinel*, and the *Grand Rapids* (Michigan) *Press*.

▌ Raeanne Rubenstein, born and raised on Staten Island, first began photographing country music stars in 1969 while still a college student at the University of Pennsylvania. Since then she has photographed a wide range of entertainers and her work has appeared in numerous publications, including *Rolling Stone, People*, and *Life*. Her early country music photographs are collected in the 1975 book *Honkytonk Heroes*.

▌ Lee Smith has written nine novels, including *The Devil's Dream, Oral History, Family Linen*, and *Fair and Tender Ladies*, and two collections of short stories. A recipient of the 1991 Robert Penn Warren Prize for Fiction and the John Dos Passos Award, among other honors, she lives in Chapel Hill, North Carolina.

▌ Nick Tosches is the author of several books, including *Country, Hellfire: The Jerry Lee Lewis Story, Dino: Living High in the Dirty Business of Dreams*, and the novels *Cut Numbers* and *Trinities*. His work has appeared in a wide variety of publications, including *Rolling Stone, Vanity Fair*, and the *Village Voice*.

▌ Elmer Williams estimates that he took well over 4,000 photographs during his freelance days in Nashville in the 1950s. He left the business in 1960 to fulfill a lifelong dream of becoming a police officer, from which he retired in 1970. His photographs are preserved in the archives of the Country Music Foundation.

▌ Joe Wilson is the executive director of the National Council for the Traditional Arts in Washington, D.C., a position he has held for twenty years. He has produced forty-seven recordings by bluegrass, country, old-time, blues, and world music artists; thirty-one national and international performing arts tours; and thirty-four large-scale music festivals. He is a consultant in musical history to the Smithsonian Institution and Carnegie Hall.

Charles Wolfe, professor of English at Middle Tennessee State University, is author of more than a dozen books on American music, including *The Life and Legend of Leadbelly* (with Kip Lornell), *The Grand Ole Opry: The Early Years, 1925–1935*, *Kentucky Country*, and *Tennessee Strings*. He has annotated over one hundred albums and has been nominated three times for Grammy awards.

SUBJECT INDEX TO THE
JOURNAL OF COUNTRY MUSIC
1971–1996

Acuff, Roy: "Acuff on Exhibit," by Bob Allen, 10:1

African-Americans in Country: "Charley Pride: Alone in the Spotlight," by Bob Millard, 14:2; "DeFord Bailey: They Turned Me Loose to Root Hot or Die," by Charles K. Wolfe and David C. Morton, 14:2; "O. B. McClinton: Country Music, That's My Thing," by Rob Bowman, 14:2; "Color Me Country: Tales From the Frontlines," by Jeff Woods, 14:2; "Roots of Rock & Roll: Henry Glover at King Records," by John W. Rumble, 14:2

Alabama: "Alabama's Luck and Legacy," by Edward Morris, 11:2

Alexander, Arthur: "Rainbow Road," by Daniel Cooper, 15;3

Allen, Deborah: "After the Flood: Billy Joe Shaver, Deborah Allen, Moe Bandy, and Others," by Bob Allen, 15:1

Alley, Shelly Lee: "Shelly Lee Alley: Reluctant Hillbilly," by Kevin Coffey, 17:1

Anderson, Bill: "City Lights," by Bill Anderson, 12:3

Anderson, John: "John Anderson: When Hard Country Comes Too Easily," by James Hunter, 11:3

Appalachia: Gallery: "*Life* Goes to Appalachia," photography by Eric Schaal, introduction by Charles Hirshberg, 14:3; "The Story of the Blankenship Family of North Carolina," by Robert Coltman, 7:3; "WOPI—The Pioneer Voice of the Appalachians," by Richard Blaustein, 6:3

Arnold, Jimmy: "Jimmy Arnold: Lost Soul," by Eddie Dean, 16:1

Atcher, Bob: "Bob Atcher: Kentucky's Singing Cowboy," by Wayne W. Daniel, 17:3

Atkins, Chet: "The Prime of Chet Atkins," by Bob Allen, 10:3

Atomic Bomb Songs: "Nuclear Country: The Atomic Bomb in Country Music," by Charles K. Wolfe, 7:1

Australian c&w: "Cowboys and Hillbillies Down Under: The First Wave of Australian Country Music," by Andrew Smith, 13:2; "John Edwards: Collector Extraordinaire," by Steven Hirsch, 13:2

Autry, Gene: "The Singing Cowboy: An American Dream," by Douglas B. Green, 7:2

Bailey, DeFord: "DeFord Bailey: They Turned Me Loose to Root Hot or Die," by David C. Morton and Charles K. Wolfe, 14:2

Baltzell, John: "John Baltzell, A Country Fiddler from the Heartland," by Howard L. Sacks, 10:1

Band Names: "What's in a Country Music Band Name," by Marcus V. Gowan and Richard A. Peterson, 2:4

Bandy, Moe: "After the Flood: Billy Joe Shaver, Deborah Allen, Moe Bandy, and Others," by Bob Allen, 15:1

Banjo: "A Musical Analysis of the Banjo Style of Earl Scruggs: An Examination of 'Country Music,'" by James D. Green Jr., 5:1

Banjo Styles: "Manual Formulaic Composition: Innovation in Bluegrass Banjo Styles," by Thomas Adler, 5:2

Barn dance: "Belle of the Barn Dance: Reminiscing with Lulu Belle," by William E. Lightfoot, 12:1; "Gallery: Nights at the Old Dominion," photography and text by Jan Edwards, 15:2;

Barn Dance (*continued*)
"Hillbilly Music Among the Flatlanders: Early Midwestern Radio and Barn Dances," by Timothy A. Patterson, 6:1; "Gallery: Portraits from the Most Popular Country Show on the Air, 1924–1939," introduction by Patsy Montana, 10:3; "Take Me Back to Renfro Valley," by Charles K. Wolfe, 9:3; "The National Barn Dance on Network Radio: The 1930s," by Wayne W. Daniel, 9:3

Beck, Jim: "Honky-Tonk Starts Here: The Jim Beck Dallas Studio," by Charles K. Wolfe, 11:1

Blackburn, Rick: "Conversations with Nash-ville Label Heads," by Paul Kingsbury, 11:1

Blankenship Family: "The Story of the Blankenship Family of North Carolina," by Robert Coltman, 7:3

Blue Ridge Ramblers: "Up North with the Blue Ridge Ramblers: Jennie Bowman's 1931 Tour Diary," by Charles K. Wolfe, 6:2

Blue Sky Boys: "The Blue Sky Boys on Radio, 1939–1940: A Newly Discovered Log of Their Daily Program," by Douglas B. Green and Ruth Walker, 4:4

Bluebird Cafe: "Ten Commandments (Bluebird Cafe's Rules for Songwriters' Night)," 15:2; "The New Place for Songwriters," by Paul Kingsbury, 13:3

Bluefield, West Virginia: "Gordon Jennings: Country Music in Bluefield," by Roy Burke III and Douglas Kirk Gordon, 9:1; "WOPI—The Pioneer Voice of the Appalachians," by Richard Blaustein, 6:3

Bluegrass: "50 Years and Counting: Bill Monroe Drives On," by Thomas J. Goldsmith, 13:1; "Gallery: A Decade of Bluegrass Festivals: *The Muleskinner News* Photographs, 1965–1974," introduction by Fred Bartenstein, 13:2; "Bluegrass to Newgrass," by Bill C. Malone, 10:2; "Cultural Dimensions of the Bluegrass Boom, 1970–75," by John W. Rumble, 6:3; "'I Feel It Down Through Music': World View in the Titles of Bill Monroe's Recordings," by Tom Ayers, 6:3; "Jimmy Arnold: Lost Soul," by Eddie Dean, 16:1; "Manual Formulaic Composition: Innovation in Bluegrass Banjo Styles," by Thomas Adler, 5:2; "The Audience for Bluegrass *Muleskinner News* Reader Survey," by Fred Bartenstein, 4:3; "They Started Calling It Bluegrass," by Neil V. Rosenberg, 10:3

Bowen, Jimmy: "Conversations with Nashville Label Heads," by Paul Kingsbury, 11:1; "Jimmy Bowen Is the Most Respected/Reviled Man on Music Row," by Bob Allen, 13:3

Bowman, Jennie: "Up North with the Blue Ridge Ramblers: Jennie Bowman's 1931 Tour Diary," by Charles K. Wolfe, 6:2

BR5-49: "Nashville's Lower Broadway: A True Story," by Daniel Cooper, 17:3

Bristol Sessions: "The Legend that Peer Built: Reappraising the Bristol Sessions," by Charles K. Wolfe, 12:2

Brooks, Garth: "For Garth's Scrapbook," 14:3; "High Concepts in Low Places," by Chris Dickinson, 17:3; "How Garth Conquered America," by Robert K. Oermann, 14:3

Brown, Fleming: "The Conduit," by Stephen Wade, 17:3

Brown, Junior: "Guit Rhythm," by Daniel Cooper, 16:2

Brown, Tony: "JCM Interview: Tony Brown," by Paul Kingsbury, 12:2

Bryan, Pearl: "Pearl Bryan: Two Ballads in One Tradition," by John M. Vlach, 3:2

Bryant, Felice and Boudleaux: "How Felice and Boudleaux Got Started," interview by John Rumble, 13:1

Bryant, Slim: "A Conversation with Jack Dunigan," by Nolan Porterfield, 7:2

Buchanan Brothers: "'We Was Just Kids Out of the Hill Country': The Case of the Buchanan Brothers," by Howard Wright Marshall, 5:2

Bug Music: "A Bug in the System," by Daniel Cooper, 15:3

Bullet Records: "Bullet Records: A Shot in the Dark," by Martin Hawkins, 8:3

Burlison, Paul: "Train Started Rollin': A Conversation with Paul Burlison of the Rock 'n' Roll Trio (Part 1)," by Rob Bowman and Ross Johnson, 11:2; "Train Kept A-Rollin': A Conversation with Paul Burlison of the Rock 'n' Roll Trio (Part 2)," by Rob Bowman and Ross Johnson, 11:3

Byrd, Billy: "Billy Byrd; The Jazzman Wore Cowboy Boots," by Debbie Holley, 12:1

Byrds, The: "So You Wanna Be a Rock 'n' Roll Star? Goin' Back with Chris Hillman," by Mark Humphrey, 14:1

Canadian c&w: "'Folk' and 'Country' Music in the Canadian Maritimes: A Regional Model," by Neil V. Rosenberg, 5:2

Camel Caravan: Gallery: "A Camel Caravan Scrapbook," introduction by Pee Wee King, 10:1

Captain Stubby: "King of the Gizmo: Captain Stubby," by Wayne W. Daniel, 15:3

Carlson, Paulette: "Leaving the Nest," by Michael McCall, 14:3

Carson, John: "Fiddlin' John Carson: On the Road and in the Studio (1924–34)," by Gene Wiggins, 11:2; "John Carson: Early Road, Radio, and Records," by Gene Wiggins, 8:1

Carter Family: "The Legend that Peer Built: Reappraising the Bristol Sessions," by Charles K. Wolfe, 12:2

Discographies (*continued*)
berg, 13:2; "The Flatt & Scruggs Discography: The Columbia Recordings, 1965–69," by Neil V. Rosenberg, 13:3; "The Flatt & Scruggs Discography: Releases, 1949–1969," by Neil V. Rosenberg, 14:1; "The Patsy Cline Discography," by Don Roy, 9:2; "The Recording Career of Ernest Tubb," includes 1936–1957 discography, by Ronnie Pugh, 9:1; "The Strange and Hermetical Case of Emmett Miller," includes complete discography, by Nick Tosches, 17:1; "'I Ain't No Ordinary Dude'—A Bio-Discography of Waylon Jennings," includes 1964–1975 discography, by John L. Smith, 6:2; "Waylon Jennings: A Discographical Update," includes 1975–1979 discography, by John L. Smith, 8:2

Domino, Fats: "Jimmy Donley and Fats Domino," by Johnnie Allan and Bernice Larson Webb, 15:3

Donley, Jimmy: "Jimmy Donley and Fats Domino," by Johnnie Allan and Bernice Larson Webb, 15:3

Dunigan, Jack: "A Conversation with Jack Dunigan," by Nolan Porterfield, 7:2

Dunn, Bob: "Steel Colossus: The Bob Dunn Story," by Kevin Reed Coffey, 17:2

Dylan, Bob: "Bob Dylan in Nashville," by Neil V. Rosenberg, 7:3

Edison Records: "Old-Time Tunes on Edison Records," by Simon J. Bronner, 8:1

Edwards, John: "John Edwards: Collector Extraordinaire," by Steven Hirsch, 13:2

Eshliman, Billie Jean: "Stand By Your Men," by Colin Escott, 14:3

Event Albums: "On the Record: Event Albums," by Chet Flippo, 16:2

Everly Brothers: "Teenage Idyll: An Everly Brother Looks Back," by Colin Escott, 15:2

Fan Fair: "A Fan Fair Scrapbook," photography by David Kingsbury, includes 1972 & 1992 statistics, 15:1

Fiddle: "Gallery: Fiddles & Fords, Photographs from Louisville's Caufield & Shook Studio," introduction by Guthrie T. Meade, 12:3; "John Baltzell, A Country Fiddler from the Heartland," by Howard L. Sacks, 10:1; "Riley Puckett and Me: A Georgia Fiddler Remembers," by Roger Bellow, 15:2

Flatt & Scruggs: "The Flatt & Scruggs Discography: The Mercury Sessions, 1948–50," by Neil V. Rosenberg, 12:3; "The Flatt & Scruggs Discography: The Columbia Recordings, 1950–59," by Neil V. Rosenberg, 13:1; "The Flatt & Scruggs Discography: The Columbia Recordings, 1960–64," by Neil V. Rosenberg, 13:2; "The Flatt & Scruggs Discography: The Columbia Recordings,

1965–69," by Neil V. Rosenberg, 13:3; "The Flatt & Scruggs Discography: Releases, 1949–1969," by Neil V. Rosenberg, 14:1

Flores, Rosie: "In the High Country: Rosie Flores and Friends in Aspen," by Bob Bradley, 17:2

Folk Music: "Folk and Popular Elements in Modern Country Music," by Patricia Averill, 5:2; "Some Connections Between Anglo-American Balladry and Country Music," by Philip Nusbaum, 5:1

Foster & Lloyd: "Foster & Lloyd's Do-It-Yourself Debut Album," interview by Paul Kingsbury, 12:2

Fowler, Wally: "Wally Fowler's Big Idea: The Origins of the Oak Ridge Boys," by Walter Carter, 12:1

Galante, Joe: "Conversations With Nashville Label Heads," by Paul Kingsbury, 11:1

Gallery: "1937 Opry: A Fan's Cartoons," introduction by Charles K. Wolfe, 7:3; "A Camel Caravan Scrapbook," introduction by Pee Wee King, 10:1; "A Decade of Bluegrass Festivals: The *Muleskinner News* Photographs, 1965–1974," introduction by Fred Bartenstein, 13:2; "A Different Light," photography by Raeanne Rubenstein, 17:2; "At Work on the Portrait," photography by Clark Thomas, 7:2; "Backstage Pass, 1955–1956," photography by Robert Dye, 12:1; "Cowboy Song Stars," cartoons by Mario A. DeMarco, 14:2; "Down to Earth People and Down to Earth Photographs," photography by Marty Stuart, 9:3; "Early WSM Photographs," introduction by Les Leverett, 9:1; "Empire Studio," photography by Ron Keith and Scott Bonner, 11:2; "Fiddles & Fords, Photographs from Louisville's Caufield & Shook Studio," introduction by Guthrie T. Meade, 12:3; "He Made Us Look Glamorous," photography by Walden S. Fabry, introduction by Minnie Pearl, 11:1; "Les Leverett on Assignment," photography by Les Leverett, 8:2; "*Life* Goes to Appalachia," photography by Eric Schaal, introduction by Charles Hirshberg, 14:3; "Nashville," photography by Peter Nash, 12:2; "Nashville," photography by J. D. Sloan, 8:1; "Nashville's Songwriters," photography by Edward Rode, 16:2; "Nights at the Old Dominion," photographs and text by Jan Edwards, 15:2; photography by Butch Hancock, 11:3; photography by Gerald Holly, 13:3; photography by Alan Messer, introduction by William Lee Golden, 10:2; photography by Slick Lawson, introduction by Roy Blount Jr., 9:2; "Portraits from the Most Popular Coun-

O'Kanes, The: "After the Flood: Billy Joe Shaver, Deborah Allen, Moe Bandy, and Others," by Bob Allen, 15:1

Oak Ridge Boys: "Wally Fowler's Big Idea: The Origins of the Oak Ridge Boys," by Walter Carter, 12:1

Obituaries: "Country Music Death Notices, 1977–78," compiled by Robert K. Oermann and Ronnie Pugh, 7:3; "Country Music Death Notices, 1979–1980," compiled by Robert K. Oermann and Ronnie Pugh, 8:3; "Country Music Death Notices, 1981–1982," compiled by Ronnie Pugh and Becky Bell, 9:3; "Country Music Obituaries, 1983–1985," compiled by Ronnie Pugh, 11:1; "Country Music Obituaries, 1986–1988," compiled by Ronnie Pugh, 12:2; "Country Music Obituaries 1989," compiled by Ronnie Pugh, 13:2 ; "1990–91 Country Music Obituaries," compiled by Ronnie Pugh, 14:2 ; "1992 Country Music Obituaries," compiled by Ronnie Pugh, 15:2; "1993 Country Music Obituaries," compiled by Ronnie Pugh, 16:1; "1994 Country Music Obituaries," compiled by Ronnie Pugh, 17:2

Old Dominion Barn Dance: "Gallery: Nights at the Old Dominion," photographs and Text by Jan Edwards, 15:2

Old-Time Music: "Toward a Contextual Approach to Old-Time Music," by Charles K. Wolfe, 5:2

Owens, Buck: "The Buck Owens Discography: Capitol Recordings, 1957–1964," by Patrick Milligan, 16:1; "The Buck Owens Discography: Capitol Recordings, 1965–66," by Patrick Milligan, 16:2; "The Buck Owens Discography: Capitol Recordings, 1967–70," by Patrick Milligan, 16:3; "Under His Spell: How Buck Owens Took Care of Business," by Mark Fenster, 12:3

Parton, Dolly: "Hello, Dolly," by Glenn Hunter and Porter Wagoner, 10:1

Paycheck, Johnny: "Johnny Paycheck: Up From Low Places," by Daniel Cooper, 15:1

Pearl, Minnie: "In the Good Ole Days (When Times Were Bad)," by Susan Quick, 13:3

Peer, Ralph: "Mr. Victor and Mr. Peer," by Nolan Porterfield, 7:3; "The Legend that Peer Built: Reappraising the Bristol Sessions," by Charles K. Wolfe, 12:2

Pennington, Ray: "One Step From the Majors," by Daniel Cooper, 15:1

Penny, Hank: "The Checkered Career of Hank Penny," by Rich Kienzle, 8:2

Phagan, Mary: "'Little Mary Phagan': A Native American Ballad in Context," by Saundra Keyes, 3:1; "'Little Mary Phagan': Further Notes on a Native American Ballad in Context," by Nathan Hurvitz and D. K. Wilgus, 4:1

Pierce, Don: "Don Pierce: Inside Starday Records," by Colin Escott, 17:1

Pierce, Webb: "A Honky-Tonker for All Seasons," by James Hunter, 14:1

Poole, Charlie: "Leaving Home: Charlie Poole's Early Years," by Kinney Rorrer, 9:1

Presley, Elvis: "Elvis Emerging: A Year of Innocence and Experience," by Peter Guralnick, 12:2; "Elvis the TV Show: Nothing But a Hound Dog?," 13:2

Price, Ray: "Being Ray Price Means Never Having to Say You're Sorry," by Daniel Cooper, 14:3

Pride, Charley: "Charley Pride: Alone in the Spotlight," by Bob Millard, 14:2

Producers: "Allen Reynolds: The Zen of Producing," by Michael McCall, 17:3; "Changing Sounds, Changing Methods," by John Morthland, 12:2; "How Producers Shape the Country Sound: A JCM Special Report," by various authors, 12:2; "Jim Rooney: The Cowboy's Apprentice Makes Good," by Michael McCall, 14:1; "Jimmy Bowen Is the Most Respected/Reviled Man on Music Row," by Bob Allen, 13:3; "Stan Kesler: The Flip Side of Sun (Part 1)," by Rob Bowman and Ross Johnson, 12:3; "Stan Kesler: The Flip Side of Sun, Part 2," by Rob Bowman and Ross Johnson, 13:1

Publishers: "Muscle Behind the Music: The Life and Times of Jim Denny (Part 1)," by Albert Cunniff, 11:1; "Muscle Behind the Music: The Life and Times of Jim Denny (Part 2)," by Albert Cunniff, 11:2; "Muscle Behind the Music: The Life and Times of Jim Denny (Part 3)," by Albert Cunniff, 11:3

Puckett, Riley: "Riley Puckett and Me: A Georgia Fiddler Remembers," by Roger Bellow, 15:2

Pure Prairie League: "Vince Gill: The Missing Years," by Bob Allen, 17:2

Radio: "The Blue Sky Boys on Radio, 1939–1940: A Newly Discovered Log of Their Daily Program," by Douglas B. Green and Ruth Walker, 4:4; "Gordon Jennings: Country Music in Bluefield," by Roy Burke III and Douglas Kirk Gordon, 9:1; "Dick Spottswood's Musical Melting Pot," by Jay Orr, 13:3

Record Companies: "Bullet Records: A Shot in the Dark," by Martin Hawkins, 8:3; "Mr. Victor and Mr. Peer," by Nolan Porterfield, 7:3; "One Step From the Majors," by Daniel Cooper, 15:1; "Roland Janes: Behind the Scenes at Sun," by Rob Bowman and Ross Johnson, 10:3; "Stan Kesler: The Flip Side of Sun (Part 1)," by Rob Bowman and Ross Johnson, 12:3; "Stan Kesler: The

AUTHOR INDEX TO THE
JOURNAL OF COUNTRY MUSIC
1971–1996

Adler, Thomas: "Manual Formulaic Composition: Innovation in Bluegrass Banjo
Styles," 5:2; "The Unplotted Narratives
of Tom T. Hall," 4:2

Allan, Johnnie and Bernice Larson Webb:
"Jimmy Donley and Fats Domino," 15:3

Allen, Bob: "Acuff on Exhibit," 10:1; "After
the Flood: Billy Joe Shaver, Deborah
Allen, Moe Bandy, and Others," 15:1;
"Interview: Willie Nelson," 8:2; "Jimmy
Bowen Is the Most Respected/Reviled
Man on Music Row," 13:3; "Rosanne
Cash & Rodney Crowell: Both Sides
Now," 10:2; "Stuck in the Can: Five
Country Albums You'll Probably Never
Hear," 14:1; "The Prime of Chet Atkins,"
10:3; "The View from the La-Z-Boy: I've
Seen It All Before," 16:2; "Tom T. Hall's
Struggle for Balance," 9:3; "Vince Gill:
The Missing Years," 17:2

Anderson, Bill: "City Lights," 12:3

Averill, Patricia: "Esoteric-Exoteric Expectations of Redneck Behavior and Country Music," 4:2; "Folk and Popular Elements in Modern Country Music," 5:2

Ayers, Tom: "'I Feel It Down Through
Music': World View in the Titles of Bill
Monroe's Recordings," 6:3

Bane, Michael: "Behold the Works of Boce-
phus," 15:2;

Bane, Michael and Hank Williams Jr.:
"(Hank Jr. Is) Living Proof," 9:1

Bartenstein, Fred (introduction): "Gallery:
A Decade of Bluegrass Festivals: The
Muleskinner News Photographs,
1965–1974," 13:2; "The Audience for
Bluegrass: *Muleskinner News* Reader Sur-
vey," 4:3

Bellow, Roger: "Riley Puckett and Me: A
Georgia Fiddler Remembers," 15:2

Bernhardt, Jack: "'Like Paris in the Twenties': Notes on a Nashville Scene
1971–74," 13:3

Betts, Stephen L.: "Regardless of the Tide:
Iris DeMent Sails Outside of the Mainstream," 17:1

Blaustein, Richard: "WOPI—The Pioneer
Voice of the Appalachians," 6:3

Blount, Roy, Jr.: "Whiskey and Blood," 8:2;
(introduction): "Gallery (photography
by Slick Lawson)," 9:2

Bonner, Scott and Ron Keith (photography): "Gallery: Empire Studio," 11:2

Bowman, Rob: "O.B. McClinton: Country
Music, That's My Thing," 14:2

Bowman, Rob and Ross Johnson: "Roland
Janes: Behind the Scenes at Sun," 10:3;
"Stan Kesler: The Flip Side of Sun (Part
1)," 12:3; "Stan Kesler: The Flip Side of
Sun (Part 2)," 13:1; "Train Started
Rollin': A Conversation with Paul Burlison of the Rock 'n' Roll Trio (Part 1),"
11:2; "Train Kept A-Rollin': A Conversation with Paul Burlison of the Rock
'n' Roll Trio (Part 2)," 11:3

Bradley, Bob: "In the High Country: Rosie
Flores and Friends in Aspen," 17:2; "Vic
Chesnutt: Tradition and the Individual
Talent," 16:1

Bronner, Simon J.: "Old-Time Tunes on
Edison Records," 8:1; "The Country
Music Tradition in Western New York
State," 7:1

Bufwack, Mary A. and Robert K. Oermann:
"Patsy Montana and the Development
of the Cowgirl Image," 8:3; "Reba
McEntire Walks On," 16:1; "Rockabilly
Women," 8:1

Burke III, Roy and Douglas Kirk Gordon:
"Gordon Jennings: Country Music in
Bluefield," 9:1

Messer, Alan (photography): "Gallery (introduction by Wlliam Lee Golden)," 10:2

Mikelbank, Peter: "Places in the Sun: The Many Splendored Careers of Jimmie Davis," 10:3

Millard, Bob: "Charley Pride: Alone in the Spotlight," 14:2

Milligan, Patrick: "The Buck Owens Discography: Capitol Recordings, 1957–1964," 16:1; "The Buck Owens Discography: Capitol Recordings, 1965–66," 16:2; "The Buck Owens Discography: Capitol Recordings, 1967–70," 16:3

Montana, Patsy (introduction): "Gallery: Portraits from the Most Popular Country Show on the Air, 1924–1939," 10:3

Morley, Steve: "Exploring the End of the World," 17:3

Morris, Edward: "Alabama's Luck and Legacy," 11:2; "Uprooted: The Short, Unhappy Life of Mel Street," 11:1; "Country Music Clones: Dittos, Duplicates, & Deja Vu," 13:3

Morthland, John: "Changing Sounds, Changing Methods," 12:2; "Sizing up the New Hats," 13:1

Morton, David C. and Charles K. Wolfe: "DeFord Bailey: They Turned Me Loose to Root Hot or Die," 14:2

Nash, Peter (photography): "Gallery: Nashville," 12:2

Nassour, Ellis: "Patsy Cline: In the Beginning," 8:3

Naváez, Peter: "Juxtaposition and Syncretism in the Popular Music of Newfoundland," 7:2

Nusbaum, Philip: "Some Connictions Between Anglo-American Balladry and Country Music," 5:1

Oermann, Robert K.: "How Garth Conquered America," 14:3; "Just How Big Is the Nashville Industry?," 13:3

Oermann, Robert K. and Mary A. Bufwack: "Patsy Montana and the Development of the Cowgirl Image," 8:3; "Reba McEntire Walks On," 16:1; "Rockabilly Women," 8:1

Olson, Ted: "Steve Young: Country Music's Original Outlaw," 17:2

Orr, Jay: "Are These Guys Just Too Cool for Country Radio?," 14:2; "Dick Spottswood's Musical Melting Pot," 13:3; "HighTone's Country Roots," 13:1

Parsons, Clark: "Chasin' That Neon Rainbow," 16:2

Patterson, Timothy A.: "Hillbilly Music Among the Flatlanders: Early Midwestern Radio and Barn Dances," 6:1

Pearl, Minnie, (introduction): "Gallery: He Made Us Look Glamorous (photography by Walden S. Fabry)," 11:1

Peterson, Richard A. and Marcus V.

Gowan: "What's in a Country Music Band Name," 2:4

Peterson, Richard A. and Paul DiMaggio: "The Early Opry: Its Hillbilly Image in Fact and Fancy," 4:2

Peterson, Richard A. and Roger Kern: "Hard-Core and Soft-Shell Country Fans," 17:3

Peterson, Richard A. and Russell Davis Jr.: "The Fertile Crescent of Country Music," 6:1

Porterfield, Nolan: "A Conversation with Jack Dunigan," 7:2; "Mr. Victor and Mr. Peer," 7:3

Powell, Larry: "Hank Williams: Loneliness and Psychological Alienation," 6:2

Pugh, Ronnie: "Country Music Death Notices, 1977–78," 7:3; "Country Music Death Notices, 1979–1980," 8:3; "Country Music Death Notices, 1981–1982," 9:3; "Country Music Obituaries, 1983–1985," 11:1; "Country Music Obituaries, 1986–1988," 12:2; "Country Music Obituaries 1989," 13:2 ; "1990–91 Country Music Obituaries," 14:2 ; "1992 Country Music Obituaries," 15:2; "1993 Country Music Obituaries," 16:1; "1994 Country Music Obituaries," 17:2; "Ernest Tubb's Performing Career: Broadcast, Stage, and Screen," 7:3; "The Recording Career of Ernest Tubb," 9:1; "The Ernest Tubb Discography, Part 2, 1958–82," 11:1

Pugh, Ronnie and Paul Kingsbury: "Songs They Gave Away," 13:1

Quick, Susan: "In the Good Ole Days (When Times Were Bad)," 13:3

Renardson, Wayne: "Edgar Meyer: Amazing Bass," 16:3

Roberts, Roderick J.: "An Introduction to the Study of Northern Country Music," 7:1

Rode, Edward (photography): "Gallery: Nashville's Songwriters," 16:2

Rorrer, Kinney: "Leaving Home: Charlie Poole's Early Years," 9:1

Rosenberg, Neil V.: "Bob Dylan in Nashville," 7:3; " 'Folk' and 'Country' Music in the Canadian Maritimes: A Regional Model," 5:2; "They Started Calling It Bluegrass," 10:3; "The Flatt & Scruggs Discography: The Mercury Sessions, 1948–50," 12:3; "The Flatt & Scruggs Discography: The Columbia Recordings, 1950–1959," 13:1; "The Flatt & Scruggs Discography: The Columbia Recordings, 1960–64," 13:2; "The Flatt & Scruggs Discography: The Columbia Recordings, 1965–69," 13:3; "The Flatt & Scruggs Discography: Releases, 1949–1969," 14:1

Roy, Don: "The Patsy Cline Discography," 9:2

Rubenstein, Raeanne (photography): "Gallery: A Different Light," 17:2

THE COUNTRY READER

was composed electronically using Meridien types, with display types in Stone Sans. The book was printed on acid-free, 60-pound Joy White Offset Recycled paper and perfect bound by Thomson-Shore, Inc. Book design is by Kachergis Book Design, Inc., with composition by Vanderbilt University Press. The design of the cover is by Jim Sherraden at Hatch Show Print. Copublished by The Country Music Foundation Press and Vanderbilt University Press, Nashville, Tennessee 37235.